Myths of Coeducation

FLORENCE HOWE

Myths of Coeducation

Selected Essays, 1964–1983

INDIANA UNIVERSITY PRESS
BLOOMINGTON

Library of Congress Cataloging in Publication Data

Howe, Florence.
   Myths of coeducation.

   (Everywoman : studies in history, literature, and
culture)
   1. Women—Education—United States—Addresses,
essays, lectures. 2. Women's studies—United States—
Addresses, essays, lectures. 3. Feminism—United States
—Addresses, essays, lectures. 4. Sex discrimination in
education—United States—Addresses, essays, lectures.
5. Afro-Americans—Education—United States—Addresses,
essays, lectures.   I. Title.   II. Series: Everywoman.
LC1752.H69   1984   376   84-47702
ISBN 0-253-33966-9 (Cl.)
ISBN 0-253-20339-2 (Pbk.)

1 2 3 4 5   88 87 86 85 84

To my students, including Carol Ahlum, Ellen Bass, Alice Jackson-Wright, and Deborah Rosenfelt, from whom I have continued to learn; to the audiences who have been my graduate students, and who have also continued to teach me; and in memory of my own beloved teachers, especially Ann Anthony, Adelaide Bartlett, Hoxie Neale Fairchild, George Schuster, and Marion Witt of Hunter College/CUNY, and Esther Cloudman Dunn and Howard Patch of Smith College.

And most of all to my mother, without whose dedication to a dream I could not have become a teacher at all.

Contents

PREFACE

All my adult life I have been a teacher. During the last twenty years, I have become a writer and a scholar. As the essays included here illustrate, however, I have never ceased being a teacher.

As a relatively young teacher in 1964, I went to Mississippi to teach in a Freedom School. That experience challenged me to continue learning, and in dramatically different ways from those I had been taught in graduate school. As a teacher, therefore, I was prepared for the women's movement: I had learned to open the classroom to experience, to a sharing of ideas, even untested ones. I had learned the importance of asking questions, even unanswerable ones. The women's movement called that process "consciousness-raising" and soon added the new scholarship known now as "women's studies."

The essays that follow chart the development of my consciousness and knowledge as a literary scholar, historian, and feminist teacher. As the introductory notes indicate, many of the essays respond to particular demands of a women's movement that touched the campus in the late sixties and that, by 1970, had begun to effect a quiet revolution in hundreds of classrooms and on the agendas of hundreds of scholars. As I researched, wrote, and then spoke the words of each of these lectures, I learned as much as I taught. Audiences were argumentative through the seventies. Often, the hour's lecture was followed by at least one hour of questions, often debate-provoking, sometimes with tempers unleashed. I remember one occasion at Cornell when a young woman got the floor to rage at me about my willingness to take questions from men in the audience, to answer their ignorance, and to respond to their ignorance with patience. Even if the curriculum on campuses was changing, how could we reach the schools? What about all the elementary school teachers who had learned nothing about women when they were in college? How could they be taught now? What could parents do? And again and again, from women about the men in their lives, or about their male students, other questions: How are we going to reach them? What if they won't listen? How can we interest them?

And so, the essays also chart the development of nearly two decades of the educational stream of the women's movement, a stream generally neglected by the mass media (and healthier, therefore) and even ignored by the educational media. The seventies have been seen as a quiet time on American campuses, and male activists ordinarily assume that "the movement" concluded at the end of the sixties. The seventies were not quiet for women engaged in developing 452 women's studies programs, 40 centers for research on women, 30,000 women's studies courses, more than 500 women's centers, hundreds of centers for reentry women, programs of continuing education for women, rape-crisis centers, committees on sexual harassment, committees on the status of women, not to mention the conferences, literary and arts festivals, special theatre and film programs, and musical celebrations. Thousands of new institutions and varieties of feminist programming now exist that were unknown only a decade ago, involving students, faculty, administrators, staff, and members of the community, mainly women, and women of color as well as white women.

Early in the seventies, one of those new institutions, The Feminist Press, had assumed as one of its central missions the restoration of the history and culture of black women. For me, the first fruits of that commitment, the publication of Alice Walker's anthology of Zora Neale Hurston's works, was still another response to the Mississippi Freedom School experience. By then the young woman I had taught in Mississippi had become my daughter, had graduated from Lake Forest College, and was on her way to law school after a stint in the U.S. Navy, marriage, and motherhood. All the essays in this volume owe a special debt to the quality of that experience, learning to live as a "black" person in the southern city of Baltimore, where to have a black child was to be black. The experience sharpened my understanding of American society and allowed me to reflect as well about what it meant to be female in a male-centered world and Jewish in a Christian one. My conclusion, reflected in many of the essays in the volume, suggests the continued need to hone our differentness—our special histories of race, class, and gender—not to hide them or disguise them. For they are realities that we must individually learn to live with, and sometimes *for*, if we are to change some of the oppressive features of those realities. Only if we can assess our pasts can we accept or reject portions of them, and learn to live with others different from us. And if we want to live with others different from us, or if we *need* to—as in a pluralist society, an international world—only then will we be able to with pleasure and ease.

Why call this book *Myths of Coeducation*? Obviously, the title does not cover all the themes addressed by the volume. And yet, one of the central ideas of coeducation provides a central myth: that if women are admitted to men's education and treated exactly as men are, then all problems of sexual equity will be solved. The myth assumes that the major problem for women is "access" to what men have, and it continues to ignore the *content* and *quality* of what it is women may gain access to. Education that teaches girls and women to accept their subordinate position in a male-centered world does not offer educational equity to them—whether the host institution is a women's college or a coeducational one.

Myths, of course, die hard, if at all. It is not surprising, therefore, that it should have taken more than a hundred years of higher education for women to see that the education they acquired sitting beside men in co-educational classrooms prepared them for domesticity, even as it prepared their future husbands for paid employment or professional training. And even as the penultimate decade of the twentieth century opens, relatively few leaders in academe have named as priority the re-visioning of the myths of coeducation. Those with the knowledge do not have the power to do more than teach—or publish their findings. And while I would not demean teaching—for learning is, after all, the ultimate human power—the process of change that depends on teaching and learning is centuries slow.

After more than four years of ambivalence, I now am ready to send this volume of essays out into a world that continues to debate "the woman question" in terms at least a century old, in the expectation that it will help teachers, students, scholars, parents, publishers, and policy-makers to find new terms in which to envision not only the past and the present, but especially the future. Even as lively audiences provoked many of the essays that follow, I expect to hear from readers.

Amagansett, Winter 1981
and Salt Lake City, Spring 1983

ACKNOWLEDGMENTS

In 1977, Susan Fernandez, then an editor at Indiana University Press, first suggested the publication of a volume of my essays. It is because of her patience and persistence that this volume has appeared. To many others I wish to acknowledge a debt for support, for the genesis of an idea, for the invitation to speak and to write on a variety of subjects I would not have touched without encouragement. To most of these individuals and institutions, I offer specific thanks in the headnotes that precede each essay or in footnotes that follow.

Here I want to thank several persons and institutions more generally: William Shawn, who told me I was a writer before I had written anything; Louis Kampf and the Modern Language Association, for giving me a platform and a topic on which to write; my colleagues on the MLA's Commission on the Status of Women, for their dynamic energy and commitment; The Feminist Press, for being an institution within which I could thrive as a writer. To many colleagues at The Feminist Press I am grateful for challenges and choices. Without co-director Maxine McCants and executive secretary Gerrie Nuccio this book could not have been finished.

For freedom to work on the history of women and higher education, I am especially grateful to Mariam Chamberlain and the Ford Foundation for a Fellowship for the Study of Women in Society; and to Carolyn Elliott and the Wellesley College Center for Research on Women for a Mellon Fellowship. I am indebted to many college and university archivists for their professional assistance, and especially, for the essay in this volume on Wellesley and Stanford, to archivists Wilma Slaight of Wellesley College and Roxanne-Louise Nilan of Stanford University. I wish also to acknowledge the advice and encouragement of historians Nancy Cott, Alice Kessler-Harris, Joan Kelly, Anne Firor Scott, and Amy Swerdlow.

Finally, I wish to acknowledge the ineffable, the civil rights movement and the women's movement that made my talents useful ones and that taught me to write with my voice. Two individuals from the women's movement did more, for they encouraged me to think of myself as a writer and to finish this book. Tillie Olsen and Shauna Adix, each in her own way, believed in me enough to help me believe in myself.

Myths of Coeducation

Mississippi's Freedom Schools

The Politics of Education
(1964)

This is the experience and the essay that changed my life. It is fitting, therefore, that this volume should begin with it, although the essay's theme is race rather than gender. And yet, of course, the language I use throughout illuminates the unconscious male-bias of my education, and hence the place from which I began to write. I wrote the essay because I was lonely for Mississippi, and sorry I had decided to return to my simple but privileged life in Baltimore. I wrote it also to explain to my friends what had happened to change me, for I felt changed.

No longer was I the junior faculty member, looking to friends and especially to elders for love and approval. I was an irritating "activist," and I had to learn to survive either alone or in new company.

The essay was published by accident. I had sent it to Howard Zinn and Staughton Lynd, two other freedom school teachers, as a gesture. When the Harvard Educational Review *editors began to search for an essay on the Mississippi experience, they wrote to Zinn and Lynd, who sent them mine. The essay was published in January 1965, and then reprinted in a special* HER *volume called* Community and the Schools *in 1969. It has also been reprinted in the following texts:* Society and Education *(Wiley and Sons, 1967);* Children and Poverty *(University of Chicago Press, 1968);* The College Reader *(Harcourt, Brace & World, 1971); and* Social Issues in Education *(Macmillan Company, 1974).*

ALL EDUCATION IS POLITICAL. In Mississippi, at least, it is impossible to find this trite. There, it is inescapable that the educational system furthers

1

the political, that the kind of learning the individual gets depends completely upon the role he* is supposed to live.

A thirteen year old Jackson, Mississippi girl, sitting within a Freedom School circle this summer, described the events of the last day, the previous year, in her public (segregated) junior high school. Students in a high school nearby had asked the students in "Shirley's" school to join them in a protest-demonstration against local school conditions and procedures. "Shirley's" (Negro) teacher had threatened the class with failure for the year, should they walk out to join the demonstrators. Most of the class was intimidated, but not "Shirley" and several of her friends. She left, she said, because she knew that she had not failed for the year, she knew she had earned good grades, and she knew that it was right to join the demonstrators. As she and her friends reached the downstairs floor, they met, head on, the (Negro) principal "who was coming at us with a board." They turned, fled, back-tracked through the cafeteria and out the back way to join the demonstrators.

The Negro school child in Mississippi, like "Shirley," associates the school he attends, in spite of the color of his teachers and principal, with the white world outside him—the police, the White Citizens' Council, the mayor or sheriff, the governor of his state. And the school child's instinctive vision is perfectly correct. His teachers are either timid and quiescently part of the system or they are actively extra-punitive, dictatorial, hostile, vengeful, or worse. Sometimes his teachers are badly-trained, misinformed, but even when they know just that, they remain fearfully bound to the system that made them. The teacher with the ruler or iron chain or whip is himself caught in a power structure that allows him to teach only by rote to rote-learners. You learn this, he says, and you too can learn to get along. Get used to the violence, get used to being struck, get used to taking orders, for that is the way life is on the outside. You too can learn to follow the rules and get to sit up here, ruler in hand, ready to strike out at anything out of line.

It is possible to sympathize with the middle-class Negro teacher caught between his own desire to rise from the poverty around him and his fear of the white power structure that controls his ability to rise. For the Negro teacher and his Negro principal are directed by white school superintendents, themselves under the direction of other white political forces. In Negro schools, the intercom is used by the principal to intimidate and harass the teacher. The principal, in turn, is harassed by others. And only

---

*Each time I have reread this essay in preparation for this book's publication, I have been tempted to change the pronouns throughout. After all, I wrote the essay as a woman writing about the experience of teaching students, most of whom were women. Temptation admitted, I leave the ringing male pronouns as a reminder of the history we share with those who have gone before us.

the "Shirley," finally, is able to stand up and sing, with her friends and associates in Freedom Schools:

> Before I'll be a slave
> I'll be buried in my grave
> And go home to my Lord and be free.

If the official public school system of Mississippi is geared and oiled to operate efficiently for the status quo, it is no wonder, then, that the civil rights movement should have conceived of the Freedom School. But would children for whom a school was an unpleasant training ground for a repressive society come, voluntarily, even to a "Freedom" school? Of course, voluntarily was the first clue. No one had to come, and once there, no "attendance" was taken. You came if you wanted to and you stayed if you were interested and you left if you felt like leaving. Your teacher, moreover, was "Tom" or "Leo" or "Gene," who shook your hand, called you by your first name, and said how glad he was to meet you. In your "class," your teacher sat with you in a circle, and soon you got the idea that you could say what you thought and that no one, least of all the teacher, would laugh at you or strike you. Soon, too, you got the idea that you might disagree with your teacher, white or black, and get a respectful hearing, that your teacher was really interested in what *you* thought or felt. Soon you were forgetting about skin colors altogether and thinking about ideas or feelings, about people and events.

As educators, we live in a fool's paradise, or worse in a knave's, if we are unaware that when we are teaching *something* to anyone we are also teaching *everything* to that same anyone. When we say we are teaching mathematics to Freddy, we also must admit that we are teaching Freddy what kind of person we are, how we live in the kind of world we control (or the kind of world that controls us), and how he can grow up to be one of the controllers or controlled. Teaching, we become, as so many people have said, a model for Freddy to learn from, quite apart from the mathematics or French or history we may be teaching him. And sometimes we are very "good" models. Sometimes, like "good" parents or "good" political leaders, we teach Freddy to love his neighbors, to honor honesty and integrity, to value the means as well as the ends, to abstain from using and controlling and killing human life. But sometimes we are not so inclined. Sometimes, at our worst, we educators resemble tyrants.

The idea of the Freedom School turns upside down particularly effectively the conventions of many public school systems that have to do with the role of the teacher. The teacher is not to be an omnipotent, aristocratic dictator, a substitute for the domineering parent or the paternalistic state. He is not to stand before rows of students, simply pouring pre-digested, pre-censored information into their brains. The Freedom School teacher is, in fact, to be present not simply to teach, but rather *to learn with* the students. In the democratic and creative sense that Wordsworth understood when he described the poet as "a man among men," the Freedom School teacher is a student among students. He does not have all the answers; his creativity is his ability to communicate with his students, to listen to them as much as they listen to him. The vitality of the teacher, as Freedom Schools would have it, lies in the student's and the teacher's mutual apprehension of life. A Freedom School teacher knows that education is the *drawing out* not of blood from stones, but rather of experience and observation from human beings. He knows that a thirteen year old who has survived his years in Mississippi understands, however fearfully or inarticulately, a great deal about the world he has survived in. The Freedom School teacher is there not as professional manipulator, but as concerned questioner—who really wants to hear what his companions will say, who really wants, himself, to be led by it. And thus he can turn the key to help the student break through the door that confines him—and all without recourse to the same means, authoritarianism, represssion, violence, that have kept him locked in.

For much of the month of August, I coordinated and taught in one of Jackson, Mississippi's nine Freedom Schools. Opened on the fifth of August, these were in addition to the more than forty others that functioned through the summer in more than twenty different towns. Like most of the schools around the state, mine was located in the basement of a church. The basement room was acoustically difficult for a single voice and yet many voices together filled it uncomfortably. How to get attention, even briefly for announcements or for the start of some activity, perhaps the breaking up of the group into small discussion units? On the second day, when my voice had begun to hurt and when clapping my hands had begun to seem ineffectual, I hit accidentally upon the Quakerly method of raising your right hand. The children saw me standing before them, my right hand raised, and for communication's sake, my left index finger against my lips. They began to nudge one another, to raise their own hands, and to place their own fingers on their lips. And very quickly, the room grew quiet. I said, "All hands down," and delighted that the method had worked, added, "Isn't this a lovely way to get silence?" Of course the children responded all together to me and to each other, and we had to begin all over again, right hands raised. But the method did work.

Also on one of the very first days, in the hot afternoon, with the teachers uncomfortable because they had had no lunch, and the children restless because we had not yet solved the problem of outdoor play space, two little boys began to fight. They were small enough so that I could forcibly separate them, but even in the midst of my hot, hungry exasperation, I had a vision of other fights and bigger boys whom I would be unable to pull apart. And from somewhere came the words: "Now, look here, we have few rules in this school, but we do have one important one and that is we do not hit each other—we talk. Understand? We talk here. This is a school for talking. Whenever you feel like hitting someone, remember to talk instead." The children looked puzzled and I said it all again. And then I sat down—in the midst of chaos—to talk with the two little boys about their fight. There were more fights in the next several days, but my words had begun to spread so that some of the older children were repeating them to the younger ones. And while we were never entirely free from an occasional blow—it was virtually impossible, for example, to keep older brothers from "punishing" their younger siblings—there were few or no fights after the first week.

The Greater Blair Street AME Zion Church, under the direction of Reverend R. M. Richmond, gave us not only shelter and equipment but most of all moral support and friendly protection. We drew our students, regardless of church membership, from the neighborhood. The families in a six to ten block radius ranged from lower-middle class to very poor (incomes from close to nothing to four thousand). The people in the neighborhood, like most of Jackson, were nervous about the arriving Freedom School teachers and were especially loathe to give us housing, for that would signify open support. Reverend Richmond convinced the people next door to give their empty room to the two male teachers. They, Gene Gogol and Tom Timberg, in the company of friendly students-to-be, had been canvassing the neighborhood during the time I was spending getting acquainted with the minister. When they reported back that they had had several offers of spare cots that could be moved elsewhere as well as of food—signs, of course, of a desire to help but without the attendant danger of housing a summer volunteer—we were able to make arrangements to move the beds into the empty room in the house next door to the church.

Our first impressions of the community were not incorrect: the parents continued to be cautious. With few exceptions, we had no contact with parents. But the children, of course, were different. They turned up, they turned out, they were willing to do anything, to go anywhere with us.

As Staughton Lynd, professor of history at Yale and summer director of all Freedom Schools in Mississippi, said, it was "a political decision for any parent to let his child come to a Freedom School." And many parents, in Jackson at least, avoided making that decision. I had assumed that parents knew that their children were attending Freedom School—until the day when I took up the question of sending a representative from our school to the state-wide Freedom School convention in Meridian. Expenses would be paid and the weekend program would be entertaining; I felt certain, that morning, that it would be difficult choosing the one delegate we were allowed to represent us. But to my surprise no one was willing to make a nomination—it was as if they all understood something I did not. I asked for volunteers and got no response again. Then I asked a thirteen year old girl, who had been particularly articulate the day before in a discussion, whether she would like to go. She said, first, only an abrupt "No," but when questioned in disbelieving tones, she admitted to, "Yes, but I can't."

"But why not, then? All your expenses would be paid, and you know you'd enjoy it."

She finally said that her father would not allow her to go, that he disapproved of her association with "the movement" in general, and that he did not approve even of her attending Freedom School. She was deliberately vague about whether or not he knew she was attending. When I asked whether it would help if I went to see him, she first laughed and then urged me most seriously not to. The story repeated itself, with certain variations, around the room.

Two young mothers, both of them relatively new to the neighborhood, were sympathetic enough to the movement and interested enough to issue invitations to us. The mother of a six year old, who sent her daughter to Freedom School, sent word also that she would like to see "the teachers" after school, at which point she invited all of us to a hot dinner the following afternoon at three. Later, she asked to be included in our evening activities. Another mother of a teen-ager, whose own family disapproved of the student's attending Freedom School, also sent for the teachers, whom she then invited to accompany her to a jazz concert. Later, this mother held a party for the departing teachers and announced her willingness to be of service to Freedom Schools in the future.

Freedom Schools were planned originally with high school students in mind. In most places around the state, when Freedom School opened, *all* children turned up, regardless of publicity about high school students. Eventually, around the state, community centers were founded, first to take care of the younger children, later to function in ways that Freedom School could not or would not. When we opened our Blair Street doors on Wednesday, August 5, at eight a.m., "children," ages three to twenty-three, began to arrive. And of course we turned no one away. They came in twos and threes, sometimes several from a family, the teen-agers holding the hands of their younger brothers and sisters. Fifty-one students arrived throughout that first day and fifty more during the next several days. Some stayed awhile and left, never to appear again. Others stayed that day and came every day thereafter. Some came and disappeared, and then came again to stay to the end.

Nearly half of any total number of children present at the Blair Street School were under the age of ten. For these children we ran a combined school and community center in one of the two basement rooms of the church. Luckily, on the day before school had opened, I had met Leo Reese, a magically personable reading specialist from Gary, Indiana, the father of eleven children, who had volunteered to spend one week in Jackson. Leo, a native Mississippian and a Negro, had been born and raised in Pascagoula, on the Gulf. In the few days that Leo was present, he organized a program for the younger children, and because of his skills, freed three of the four assigned teachers for work with the older students. Later, after Leo had gone, two young women, Shirley Logan, a Jacksonian and a recent college graduate, and her cousin from Chicago, Superior Walker, came to the Blair Street School for a visit and stayed for two weeks to carry on the program with the younger children.

Mornings at Freedom School began slowly without opening bells. On some days we sang freedom songs until the group collected. On one day, August 6, Hiroshima Day, I told the students about what had happened nineteen years ago. On another day, I read from Langston Hughes' poems and then listened to reactions from the students. By nine-thirty, we were usually numerous enough to break into smaller discussion groups. Those children under ten went off to their room, generally for the rest of the day, unless there was to be a special activity in the afternoon. The older students separated sometimes into several age groups for a discussion that occupied most of the morning. The Citizenship Curriculum, about which I shall have more to say later, is the core of the program shared by all Freedom Schools in Mississippi. There was usually time, an hour before lunch and one after, for two hours of "electives." Negro history, chemistry, biology, English, French, and typing were the subjects settled on by the groups' desires and their teachers' abilities.

The afternoons were particularly hot, and more and more frequent were the noisy visits to the drinking fountain and the lavatories at the back of the church. There was no outdoor play space, but, eventually, teachers began to take groups of students to the playground of a nearby Catholic school that the sisters allowed us to use. One of the older boys organized a softball team and both boys and girls were eager to play ball regardless of the heat. Late in the afternoon (called "evening" in Mississippi) some of the teachers and students joined the regular COFO precinct workers for voter registration work.

The best afternoons at Blair Street were those filled with special events. On opening day, for example, Pete Seeger, arrived at one-thirty in the afternoon to give us a private concert. With the whole school present, the very littlest ones asleep in any arms that would hold them, Pete talked first of his recent visit to twenty-seven countries around the world. He told us that all children were the same the world over and that music was a language that flew easily over even the highest walls. He demonstrated his statements by playing and singing Indian, African, Chinese, and Polynesian songs, in each instance allowing the rhythms to illustrate the emotion before offering a translation of the words. "Isn't this a happy song," he said, after singing, in African dialect, "Everybody Loves Saturday

Night." He taught the children to sing the foreign words of several songs, and though we didn't know it then, that was the high moment for them. The Blair Street students had no idea that Pete was a famous man, but they wanted to hear more of him and happily turned up that evening to be transported across town to Anderson Chapel where Pete Seeger sang for a packed and overflowing house until his voice gave out.

Films were also a good afternoon activity. On the day we showed the full-length *Oliver Twist* to an audience of more than one hundred, I heard one boy of ten mutter to himself about Oliver, "He sho' is white, but he's a slave just the same." The film ran too late in the afternoon for discussion, but the following morning was filled with questions and talk about child labor. Another group of films were part of a special, state-wide program arranged by Paul Lauter, a professor of English at Smith College. All bearing upon the connections among the struggle for civil rights, nonviolence, and the need for world peace, the four films were used by Paul to spark discussions. Two of these films were documentaries, one about Gandhi, the other about the Montgomery, Alabama, bus strike. The students were more interested in talking, however, about the other pair of films. One was a recent Polish film, *The Magician*. The other, an animated cartoon, *The Hat*, consisted of a dialogue between two soldiers (Dizzie Gillespie—whose music also filled the film—and the British comedian, Dudley Moore) who guard either side of a line, the hat of one falling onto the side of the other as they march. The students were quick to compare lines that divided nations with lines that divided people within nations. They remembered, during the discussion that followed, relevant details through which the film attempted to show that talking, in human terms, helps to erase lines.

Evening activities provided still other kinds of experience for the Freedom School student. Apart from concerts, there were mass meetings, at one of which, for example, A. Philip Randolph spoke along with leading Jackson ministers. Best of all was the Free Southern Theatre's production of *In White America*, which toured the state as part of a continuing program of special entertainment for Freedom Schools. Most of these students had never seen live theatre, and certainly not a play about themselves in history. Their response as audience was continuously energetic, especially since, as they reported the next day, they enjoyed recognizing incidents they had been reading of or discussing. One student, Kaaren Robinson, age fifteen, wrote the following as part of a review published in the *Blair Street Freedom Bugle*:

> It portrayed the brutal transportation of the Negro from his native Africa to a new country, the inhuman treatment upon his arrival, the confusing position of the political-minded white man with regard to his stand on the slave question and the continuous struggle of the Negro against overwhelming odds.

. . . . Because of his up-bringing, the new freedom put the Negro in a confusing state which naturally led him back into another kind of slavery. This slavery has lasted until now.

The author achieved these points through narration and conversation. Through this medium the Negro of today can better understand why the white man feels as he does toward him. However, this does not justify his feelings nor his actions. *In White America* is a great and moving drama which should be seen by black and white alike.

Though questioned, Kaaren resisted any attempt to enlarge upon the play's effect. From her point of view, the play allowed her to understand the white man's confusion; it told her nothing about the Negro she did not already know.

Charles Cobb, a student at Howard University before he joined the SNCC staff, was responsible late in 1963 for suggesting the idea of Freedom Schools. He has written cogently of their *raison d'être*, in a piece called "This is the Situation":

Repression is the law; oppression, a way of life—regimented by the judicial and executive branches of the state government, rigidly enforced by state police machinery, with veering from the path of "our way of life" not tolerated at all. Here, an idea of your own is a subversion that must be squelched; for each bit of intellectual initiative represents the threat of a probe into the why of denial. Learning here means only learning to stay in your place. Your place is to be satisfied—a "good nigger."

They have learned the learning necessary for immediate survival: that silence is safest, so volunteer nothing; that the teacher is the state, and tell them only what they want to hear; that the law and learning are white man's law and learning.

There is hope and there is dissatisfaction—feebly articulated—both born out of the desperation of needed alternatives not given. This is the generation that has silently made the vow of no more raped mothers—no more castrated fathers; that looks for an alternative to a lifetime of bent, burnt, and broken backs, minds, and souls. Their creativity must be molded from the rhythm of a muttered "white son-of-a-bitch"; from the roar of a hunger bloated belly; and from the stench of rain and mud washed shacks. There is the waiting, not to be taught, but to be, to reach out and meet and join together, and to change. The tiredness of being told it must be, "cause that's white folks' business," must be met with the insistence that it's their business. They know that anyway. It's because their parents didn't make it their business that they're being so systematically destroyed. What they must see is the link between a rotting shack and a rotting America.

The Citizenship Curriculum, the discussion of which filled most of our mornings, is frankly a response to the repressive society Charles Cobb has described. It is aimed at meeting two basic needs of students: first, a need for information; second, a need for identity and hence activity. The "facts" of history; in terms of dates, people's names, places, events, as well as the interpretations of history—all this has been denied to them, and denied particularly in relation to their own situation as American Negroes. Not only is Negro history unknown to them, but even the history of the current Negro revolution is known only in bits and pieces, largely through television, since their newspapers are notoriously uninformative. The second need, the need for identity and activity, is organically one with the need for facts. It has to do with what happens when an individual begins to know himself as part of history, with a past and a potential future as well as a present. What happens when an individual begins to assess himself as a human being? The aim of the Citizenship Curriculum here is to assist the growth of self-respect, through self-awareness, both of which lead to self-help. In this way, the curriculum at the center of the Freedom Schools is frankly and avowedly a program for leadership development.

In many different ways, the mimeographed curriculum makes clear the Freedom Schools' purpose: "to provide an educational experience for students which will make it possible for them to challenge the myths of our society, to perceive more clearly its realities, and to find alternatives, and ultimately, new directions for action." Or more briefly, "to train people to be active agents in bringing about social change." The curriculum itself, however, declares that "It is not our purpose to impose a particular set of conclusions. Our purpose is to encourage the asking of questions, and hope that society can be improved."

Because the chief tool is the question, the curriculum is hopefully "developmental," that is, one that "begins on the level of the students' everyday lives and those things in their environment that they have either already experienced or can readily perceive, and builds up to a more realistic perception of American society, themselves, the conditions of their oppression, and alternatives offered by the Freedom Movement." The seven units are as follows:

1. Comparison of students' reality with others (the way the students live and the way others live)
2. North to Freedom? (The Negro in the north)
3. Examining the apparent reality (the "better lives" that whites live)
4. Introducing the power structure
5. The poor Negro and the poor white
6. Material things versus soul things
7. The Movement

In addition, two sets of questions are to be constantly in the minds of the teachers and frequently introduced to the students:

The Basic Set of Questions:
1. Why are we (teachers and students) in Freedom Schools?
2. What is the Freedom Movement?
3. What alternatives does the Freedom Movement offer us?

The Secondary Set of Questions:
1. What does the majority culture have that we want?
2. What does the majority culture have that we don't want?
3. What do we have that we want to keep?

   Some of my own experience was with a relatively young group—eleven to fourteen-year-olds. After describing their own houses, they went on to describe the houses of whites in Jackson that they had seen, either because they had themselves worked as domestics, or because their mothers did. When asked what changes they would like made in their own houses, while their answers varied from additional rooms to more yard space, no one thought in terms as grandiose as the "white" houses they had described, and most of them thought of their houses as "comfortable." On the other hand, they were certain that their (segregated) schools were inferior, even when they admitted that the buildings were new. They resented their hand-me-down textbooks, they suspected the inadequacy of their teachers, and they complained particularly bitterly about the repressive atmosphere. In their schools, they reported that no questioning or discussion was allowed, except in rare instances when they and a particular teacher knew they were "taking a chance." Of course, they knew little or nothing of conditions in white schools, either in Mississippi or elsewhere, beyond their impression that these, somehow, were "better."

   High school juniors and seniors were especially interested in the subject of going north to freedom. On the one hand, many of them expressed a wish to go north to college, in part because they suspected that Negro colleges in Mississippi were as inadequate as their public schools, but also because they wanted the experience of learning in an integrated group. They were articulate about the need for communication between black and white. The freedom songs they sang each day—"Black and white together/ We shall overcome," for example—were not simply words to be mouthed. On the other hand, some of them had been reading with us from the works of Richard Wright and James Baldwin* of the Negro in Chicago or Harlem; and they knew they were living through a summer that had brought riots to northern cities, though not to Jackson, Mississippi. They questioned the condition of Negroes everywhere, and many of them concluded that it was probably better to stay in Mississippi and work to improve things there than to imagine that things were better in another place.

   The Freedom School curriculum's most substantial statement about values, "Material Things and Soul Things," takes as its central idea the society that is "humane" because it is "nonviolent." Negroes, of course,

---

*In 1964, I had not heard of Zora Neale Hurston, and the poets and prose writers I was prepared to discuss were all males. The literary curriculum I offered included e. e. cummings, William Carlos Williams, Langston Hughes, Richard Wright, and James Baldwin.

are no more naturally violent or nonviolent than any other group. But these students, brought up on the edge of a volcano, named as their heroes Martin Luther King and Medgar Evers, and, when they knew of him, Gandhi as well. At Blair Street, I asked the question about heroes because Paul Lauter had reported that when he asked the question at Freedom Schools throughout the state, those very three names occurred. It was also Paul's impression that as SNCC people became veterans at their jobs, nonviolence for them became not strategic manner but genuine conviction. For the veteran SNCC worker, Matt Suarez, who dropped in one afternoon at Blair Street for a visit and stayed for a discussion, nonviolence had become essential to life. Some of the students who listened to him had also experienced organized demonstrations within the discipline of the nonviolent movement. But their minds were far from decided. They questioned the theory; they suspected themselves of "violent feelings"; they talked about "strategy"; they asked for a "speaker"—and got more discussion!

Because the student needs to learn not only about the world he lives in, but also how to be free enough to live in it, the chief tool of Freedom Schools always was discussion. Ideally, discussion began with the question, "How do you feel about . . . ?" or "How would you feel if . . . ?" and moved on to questions about motivation ("Why do you feel this way?" or "Why would anyone feel this way?"). Once the discussion had begun, the questions could move on to students' reactions to each other's ideas. At first, of course, students were distrustful of the situation generally. Some were also shy before their peers as well as frightened of their teacher. But of course they all had feelings and they all had some words with which to describe them. And eventually the moment came, unnoticed and passed over, when a student could say easily to his (white) teacher or to a fellow student, "I disagree," and explain why.

The teacher's main problem was to learn to keep quiet, to learn how to listen and to question creatively rather than to talk at the students. He had to discard whatever formal classroom procedures he had ever learned and respond with feeling and imagination as well as with intelligence and good humor to the moods and needs of the group. Above all, the students challenged his honesty: he could not sidestep unpleasantness; he could not afford to miss any opportunity for discussing differences.*

I have no crystal ball, but I can submit two aspects of my own experience that suggest that the Freedom Schools of '64 spread more than transitory ripples in a huge Mississippi sea. The first was a discussion that led

---

*So strong was the power of the male-centered universe that, although I am describing my own experience, I use the pronoun "he."

directly to social action independently instigated by the students themselves. The second was an experiment that led directly to the students writing poetry.

The third week of Freedom Schools in Jackson was also the week of school registration for those Negro first-graders who were to attend previously white schools. Registration was scheduled for early Thursday morning; a mass meeting for interested parents had been called by thirty-six Negro ministers of Jackson for Tuesday night. This was Monday morning, and the group at the Blair Street School had begun, for some reason, to talk about the "myth" of Negro inferiority. At one point, when there was silence, I asked how many of the twenty students present (ages fourteen to twenty) knew some first-grader who was about to start school. Everyone did. Did anyone know any who were going to a white school? No one did. When I asked why, I got many different responses:

My sister thinks her son would be unhappy with white children.
My brother hasn't gone to kindergarten.
The white school is too far away.
My mother wants my brother to be with his friends.
My father says he doesn't like the idea.

None of the students had mentioned the word fear. They all looked uncomfortable and I felt my anger rise: "What am I going to say to my friends back North when they ask me why Negro mothers haven't registered their children in white schools? That they like things the way they are?" I could see the consternation on the face of Gene Gogol, my fellow teacher, who began, "I disagree, Florence, you just don't understand the situation." I felt that his rebuke was probably a just one, but then the students began to smile wryly and, one by one, they began to talk of the various fears that "perhaps" these parents were feeling. Personal safety. Economic security—the loss of jobs because they weren't being "good niggers." Failure in the white school—either because of social ostracism or because of poor training and possibly the alleged intellectual inferiority. But then suddenly, I do not know exactly what shifted the discussion, perhaps something about the white faces that Gene and I wore in the midst of the black ones, suddenly the students were talking about *positive* reasons for sending children into integrated schools. Then one of the sixteen-year-old girls suggested that perhaps we—meaning those of us in the discussion group—ought to go out into the neighborhood and talk with parents who were reluctant to send their children to white schools, that perhaps we were most suited for this job since we knew the value of good education and we knew there was really nothing to fear. When I suggested that we try one of the school's favorite procedures, role-playing, there were volunteers immediately for mother, father, child, and for two visitors from the Freedom School. The players were evenly matched so that the play-discussion rehearsed all the arguments we had heard. The role-playing father remained essentially unconvinced, but his wife assured the visitors that she had really changed her mind and that, after they had gone, she would "work on" her husband.

Gene and a crew of student-volunteers worked all the rest of Monday, Monday night, and all of Tuesday. They talked to more than seventy families and received from twenty-seven of these assurances that at least the mother would attend Tuesday night's mass meeting, perhaps would take advantage of the transportation we would provide. Disappointingly, only one mother kept her promise. But on Wednesday morning, Gene and some students began their visits again, and by Thursday noon, all of Blair Street's Freedom School were boasting that eleven of the forty-three Negro children in Jackson who actually registered to attend previously white schools had done so as a direct result of Gene's and the students' talks with parents.

Thus the students had direct evidence that their school experience had led them to create something that was lasting and profound. Additional evidence—this of a more personal nature—followed their reading and discussion of poetry.

We had begun with poems by Langston Hughes. They knew immediately that when Hughes, in a poem called "As I Grew Older," mentioned a "thick wall" and a "shadow" growing between him and his childhood "dream," he was talking about walls and shadows they knew every day in Jackson: the barbed wire around the parks, for example, or the hate in white men's faces when they tried to go to a movie downtown. I did not need to be a teacher showing the difference between literal meaning and what was "symbolized." There *was* curiosity about forms. Do all poems rhyme? What is rhyme, anyway? Can poets use any words they like? The students, who had never heard of Langston Hughes, were surprised by his slang, by his use of jazz expressions. They listened to the occasional irregularity that made rhythms interesting, especially in a Hughes song-poem like "The Weary Blues"—which they never tired of.

One day, when discussion had flagged, I suggested a "game." Let's divide into four groups of five and try writing a "group" poem. I even offered a subject: try writing about yourselves and Jackson—we had just been reading about Hughes and Harlem. When I returned, half an hour later, cries of "Listen to this" greeted me. With one exception, the poems were not group products—the groups had stayed to watch individual members create. The best poem came from a sixteen year old girl, a visitor to Jackson from Pascagoula, who had just come for the first time to Freedom School, and who was to continue attending thenceforth. This is Alice Jackson's poem called "Mine":

I want to walk the streets of a town,
Turn into any restaurant and sit down,
And be served the food of my choice,
And not be met by a hostile voice.
I want to live in the best hotel for a week,
Or go for a swim at a public beach.
I want to go to the best university
And not be met with violence or uncertainty.
I want the things my ancestors
Thought we'd never have.
They are mine as a Negro, an American;
I shall have them or be dead.

In the days that followed, we read poems by Sandburg and Frost, two poets the students had heard of, but the greatest excitement came from their introduction to e e cummings, especially to the poem "Anyone Lived in a Pretty How Town." One day, after two hours of a discussion of cummings' poems, I asked the eight or nine students present—ages fourteen to seventeen—whether they wanted to try writing again. When I asked whether they wanted a suggested subject, I heard an overwhelming series of no's. No subject . . . let us write what we feel like writing.

Within twenty minutes, Shirley Ballard, age seventeen, was reading aloud to me a poem called "Time." She read it slowly, emphasizing the individuality of certain words and phrases. Its feeling was clearly fragmentary. But then she showed me the page on which she had written the poem: four long lines, resembling her reading not at all. She had read it in a manner that suggested something else, and I showed her cummings' page. She caught on instantly, took her page, and returned in several minutes with the following version:

Time goes by so slowly
my mind reacts so lowly
        how faint
how moody
        I feel,
                I love not
        I care not.
Don't love me.
Let me live.
        Die
        Cry
        Sigh
All alone
        Maybe someday I'll go home.

Another seventeen year old, Sandra Ann Harris, quickly produced a cummings-like poem—even to the elimination of all capitalization:

why did i my don'ts
why did i my dids
what's my didn'ts' purpose
is it to fulfill my dids

what isn'ts have i proclaimed
what ises have i pronounced
why can't i do my doings
my couldn'ts do renounce

my wouldn'ts are excuses
my couldn'ts couldn't be helped
my weren'ts were all willful
my words of little help

the haven'ts were just there
my didn'ts did believe
that all my won'ts are daring
my wills to receive

If it is startling to consider how much these students learned so quickly, it is also instructive to consider that in Freedom Schools all over Mississippi this summer students were becoming both social activists and poets. An impressive volume of poetry (which may soon be published) appeared in Freedom School newspapers. And a Mississippi Student Union has been formed. The connection between poetry and politics should surprise no one who has read the Romantics or, more recently, the poets of the Irish Renaissance. What is surprising is that, in some ways, it took *so little* to accomplish so much in the Mississippi Freedom Schools.

Consider the discussion circle, the union of teachers and students in a status-free ring. Consider too the position of these students—blacks in a white culture—as outsiders who were now, in 1964, *conscious* outsiders, youngsters seeing new possibilities ahead of them and, at the same time, young adults with the wisdom to see what Negro slavery has been. Under these special new conditions, one could talk and think about what it was like to be a slave and what it might be like to be free. One could even try *being* free. Under these special conditions—the consciousness of being suppressed combined with the proffered opportunity to base education on that consciousness—creativity was the natural response.

What have we to learn from Freedom Schools? The politics of education. That our schools are political grounds in which our students begin to learn about society's rules. That, therefore, if we wish to alter our students and our society, we must alter our schools. That if we would have strong and creative minds we must remove chains both from bodies and spirits. That we as adults and educators have to listen and respond rather than preach. That we need to share with our students a sense of being open to what each uniquely experienced companion can reveal. That this perspective of equality is itself a revolution that goes far beyond the surface movement of Negroes into white society. And that if Freedom School teachers in Mississippi society know themselves as unwelcome and harassed outsiders, not unlike the Negro students, then authentic teachers anywhere must face a similar knowledge.

The Freedom School students and teachers who heard Langston Hughes' "As I Grew Older" understood that Hughes' prayer was theirs too—for strength and wisdom to break through all spiritual prisons of self and society and so to reach freedom:

> My hands!
> My dark hands!
> Break through the wall!
> Find my dream!
> Help me to shatter this darkness,
> To smash this night,
> To break this shadow
> Into a thousand lights of sun,
> Into a thousand whirling dreams
> Of sun!

Why Educate Women?

(1968)

*In 1968, after teaching about women for four years in fresh-
man English courses, I had begun to consider the assumptions
behind the education of women, although without a knowledge
of history, nor a vision of the possibilities for change. What I report on here emerged from the experience of my classroom and
from reading male thinkers on women. By then, I could have
cited Virginia Woolf and Simone de Beauvoir, but I chose not to.
They would have added nothing to my still unformed consciousness, for I could see only men speaking to men about the other
half of the human race. Since I had been educated in that male
stream, I had no sense of the waters that had fed Woolf or de
Beauvoir: I had not yet read Mary Wollstonecraft or Margaret
Fuller, nor the writers they had read.*

*The theme of this essay—career versus family—came di-
rectly out of my teaching experience. That classroom honed my
consciousness, not only about gender, but about its intersection
with class. The critical idea was "work": what was a "girl" to do
with her life after college? This theme—that college led women
to marriage, men to vocation—has been integral to all the writing I have done.*

*One measure of the change that has occurred in the years
since this essay was written is that young college women assume
that they will work for all or most of their lives, married or not,
with children or without. Whether or not they are conscious of
the revolution that has occurred at least in the purpose for which
college women are currently educated, women as well as men expect a college degree to prepare them for a job.*

*I wrote this essay first as a lecture, though I cannot remem-
ber the occasion on which I first read it. It was published first in*

Liberation *(August/September 1969), under the title, "The Education of Women." It has been reprinted under that title in three books:* Liberation Now: Writings from Women's Liberation Movement *(Dell, 1971);* The American Sisterhood: Feminist Writings from the Colonial Times to the Present *(Harper and Row, 1972); and* And Jill Came Tumbling After: Sexism in American Education *(Dell, 1974).*

RECENTLY, ON A TRAIN, a Goucher College student met the editor of a relatively new magazine. "Why don't we get your magazine?" she queried.

"Isn't Goucher a girls' school?"

"Sure, but what's that got to do with it?"

"Well, we didn't think you'd be interested—it's about careers."

This is a perfectly commonplace attitude. Even in 1969, it is assumed that women who go to college are generally sitting out four years of their lives before becoming wives and mothers. During my nine years at Goucher, I have found little encouragement for any other view. Unfortunately, statistics bear me out only too well. Though more women than ever before go to college, and even receive degrees, fewer proportionately go on to graduate school. The faculties of colleges and universities naturally reflect this condition: there are fewer women on the faculties of women's colleges than there were in the 30s; the percentage of women on the faculty of the University of Chicago has dropped from 8 percent at the end of the nineteenth century to a recent low of 2 percent; and a number of university departments are searching currently for their token female. And as studies continue to show, when men and women of comparable education and experience are employed, women's salaries and rates of promotion are significantly inferior to men's. In spite of a century of sporadic hue and cry about women's rights, and in spite of our rhetoric about the equality of women, even in spite of the pill and the recent outburst of women's liberation groups, women remain a passive majority of second-class citizens.

Our education is chiefly to blame, but of course after one has said that, one must add at once that education reflects the values of our society and is to a major extent controlled by those values. That is to say that we do not think of our girl students as we do our boys—and this is true from the beginning of their school years as well as on to graduate school where women are openly discriminated against for reasons which I do not here need to list. What would happen to men if women were, indeed, allowed to compete in a system equally open to them? This is, of course, a rhetorical question, since it is not likely to happen. We do know that white men, in our culture, are by and large loath to compete with black men, and our friends tell us that women will have to wait until those male racial and economic problems are solved.

Economic and political problems cannot, obviously, be solved by educational institutions. But colleges can educate their students quite deliberately to those problems, and even, if they will, to work toward their solution. Generally speaking, the purpose of those responsible for the education of women has been to perpetuate their subordinate status.* There is a hoary story still being told about the difference between educating men and women. It goes like this: "When you educate a man, you educate an individual, but when you educate a woman, you educate a family." Obviously, the story is meant to compliment women as traditional carriers of culture. But more to the point is the role that woman is channeled into by her culture. The question of purpose in education is dependent upon a prior notion of hierarchy. Put another way, education is prophecy fulfilled: imagine women educated for a push-button household and a consumer's life and you create institutions to effect that. To illustrate, I want to look at the views of five men—I choose men because for the most part they have been responsible for our history and our education.

First, Plato and Aristotle, who illustrate two poles: the revolutionary believer in equality between the sexes and the conservative believer in the inferiority of women. Plato, as revolutionary, writes in the *Republic* that, "There is no occupation concerned with the management of social affairs which belongs either to woman or to man, as such. Natural gifts are to be found here and there in both creatures alike; and every occupation is open to both, so far as their natures are concerned." He concludes, therefore, that "we shall not have one education for men and another for women, precisely because the nature to be taken in hand is the same." When he describes roles for women, he allows them "their full share with men" in all areas of life, "whether they stay at home or go out to war." He continues, "Such conduct will not be unwomanly, but all for the best and in accordance with the natural partnership of the sexes." Obviously, Plato's notions have not only not prevailed; they are hardly known today.

To read Aristotle on the same subject is to learn how little a student may learn from a teacher. For to the question "why educate women?" Aristotle would have answered, "Certainly not." This is his key statement, from the *Politics*: "We may thus conclude that it is a general law that there should be naturally ruling elements and elements naturally ruled. . . . The rule of the free man over the slave is one kind of rule; that of the male over the female another. . . . The slave is entirely without the faculty of

---

*Although I could not have substantiated this generalization with appropriate historical footnotes at the time I wrote it, as other, later essays in this volume make clear, the generalization is correct. The earliest admissions of women to higher education (or even to secondary education) were accomplished without challenging the assumption that women's work was appropriately maternal.

deliberation; the female indeed possesses it, but in a form which remains inconclusive. . . . It is thus clear that while moral goodness is a quality of all the persons mentioned, the fact still remains that temperance—and similarly fortitude and justice—are not, as Socrates held, the same in a woman as they are in a man." Aristotle thus offers no education to woman. Or if we think of her in a category close to the slave's, only such education as will make her more useful to man, her master. The defining of capability—or "role definition"—controls education. And Aristotle's voice has prevailed. He and the early Church fathers settled the noneducation of women for nearly two thousand years.

Milton's is a useful voice to illustrate the perpetuation of woman's subordinate status in a form somewhat more subtle than Aristotle's. In fact, Milton is my favorite example of such a view, one that I find still dominant today. To Goucher students, I usually say, study him closely: he is the enemy. You must understand your enemy if you are to defeat him. Women are teachable, Milton says, though just barely and only under careful conditions. Certainly, they need to be observed and looked after constantly or trouble may follow, as it did for Eve in the garden. But the order is plain enough: God teaches man and man teaches woman, just a bit of this or that, enough to keep her in her place. Milton's main idea is hierarchy: woman is subordinate in status, inferior in intellect, and even less reliable than man in matters of the heart.

In matters of the heart, Jonathan Swift has argued, either sex might claim distinction—for foolishness and corruption. "I am ignorant of any one quality," he writes in "A Letter to a Young Lady on her Marriage," "that is amiable in a Man, which is not equally so in a Woman; I do not except Modesty and Gentleness of Nature. Nor do I know one Vice or Folly which is not equally detestable in both." If women are more full of "nonsense and frippery" than men, their parents are to blame for failing "to cultivate" their minds. "It is a little hard," Swift continues, "that not one Gentleman's daughter in a thousand should be brought to read or understand her own natural Tongue, or be judge of the easiest Books that are written in it. . . ." Swift's remedy is to offer himself as tutor for the young lady in question; in *Gulliver's Travels*, he recommends education for both sexes.

When I asked my students what they thought of Swift—expecting at least some delight or surprise at his modernity–one sophomore said, "Why, he's insulting. I didn't like him at all." She added that his attitude was patronizing and demeaning: "He doesn't care anything about the girl. All he cares about is that she please her husband. That's why he wants her to be able to read. So that she can carry on a conversation with him."

Marianne's sharp disgust surprised me and some of the other students present, one of whom commented gently and slightly in wonderment: "But that's just why I'm going to college and taking English courses. My boy friend is at college and I think that I should be able to keep up to his interests and his friends. You know, I want to know what he's talking and thinking about."

Both students had in mind a passage in which Swift offers his young lady a rationale for the education of her intellect: "to acquire or preserve the Friendship and Esteem of a Wise Man, who soon grows weary of acting the Lover and treating his Wife like a Mistress, but wants a reasonable Companion, and a true Friend through every Stage of his Life. It must be therefore your Business to qualify yourself for those Offices." That is, to function interestingly for one's husband—or children. The question of self or vocation is entirely absent, as it is from the concerns of the majority of women in college today.

About a hundred years after Swift wrote his essay, Harriet Taylor and John Stuart Mill began a long and complex intellectual relationship, one of the results of which was a book that Mill published in 1869 called *The Subjection of Women*. Like Swift, Mill believed that sexual differences do not entirely, if at all, control the intellect. Women are not a separate and lesser species but, as Mill put it, they are a separate class or caste, created and controlled by men through a process of socialization that includes depriving women of education.

I want to quote from Mill's book at some length because I think it is still the best single piece of analysis and because it is his only significant work not available in paperback.* First, his argument about the alleged inferiority of woman's "nature":

> Standing on the ground of common sense and the constitution of the human mind, I deny that anyone knows, or can know, the nature of the two sexes, as long as they have only been seen in their present relation to one another. If man had ever been found in society without women, or women without men, or if there had been a society of men and women in which the women were not under the control of the men, something might have been positively known about the mental and moral differences which may be inherent in the nature of each. What is now called the nature of women is an eminently artificial thing—the result of forced repression in some directions, unnatural stimulation in others. It may be asserted without scruple, that no other class of dependents have had their character so entirely distorted from its natural proportions by their relation with their masters. . . .

---

*Alice Rossi's significant edition of Mill's essay, *Essays on Sex Equality* by John Stuart Mill and Harriet Taylor Mill, was issued in 1970 (University of Chicago Press). The volume provided not only the unavailable text, but a historical context that reminded many academics, including me, that there was to be found a long tradition of thoughtful and articulate *women*—if only we would begin the search.

Women's relations with their "masters," according to Mill, are unique for an "enslaved class," for two reasons; their universality in time and space, their perpetuation seemingly without "force." "The subjection of women to men being a universal custom," Mill begins urbanely, "any departure from it quite naturally appears unnatural." On the other hand, most women accept their state. In fact, "All causes, social and natural, combine to make it unlikely that women should be collectively rebellious to the power of men." Thence follows an analysis by a "master" of the master's point of view: "Women," Mill begins,

> are so far in a position different from all other subject classes, that their masters require something more from them than actual service. Men do not want solely the obedience of women, they want their sentiments. All men, except the most brutish, desire to have, in the women most nearly connected with them, not a forced slave but a willing one, not a slave merely, but a favorite. They have therefore put everything in practice to enslave their minds. The masters of all other slaves rely, for maintaining obedience, on fear—either fear of themselves, or religious fears. The masters of women wanted more than simple obedience, and they turned the whole force of education to effect their purpose. All women are brought up from the very earliest years in the belief that their ideal of character is the very opposite to that of men; not self-will and government by self-control, but submission and yielding to the control of others. All the moralities tell them that it is the duty of women, and all the current sentimentalities that it is their nature, to live for others, to make complete abnegation of themselves, and to have no life but in their affections. And by their affections are meant the only ones that they are allowed to have—those to the men with whom they are connected, or to the children who constitute an additional and indefeasible tie between them and a man. When we put together three things—first, the natural attraction between opposite sexes; secondly, the wife's entire dependence on the husband, every privilege or pleasure she has being either his gift, or depending entirely on his will; and lastly, that the principal object of human pursuit, consideration, and all objects of social ambition, can in general be sought or obtained by her only through him, it would be a miracle if the object of being attractive to men had not become the polar star of feminine education and formation of character. And this great means of influence over the minds of women having been acquired, an instinct of selfishness made men avail themselves of it to the utmost as a means of holding women in subjection, by representing to them meekness, submissiveness, and resignation of all individual will into the hands of a man, as an essential part of sexual attractiveness.

Mill concludes this section of his book by summarizing:

> In no instance except this, which comprehends half the human race, are the higher social functions closed against anyone by a fatality of birth

which no exertions, and no change of circumstances can overcome; for even religious disabilities . . . do not close any career to the disqualified person in case of conversion.

The remedies Mill proposes are changes in law and the opening of educational and vocational opportunities to women. His ideal is "freedom of individual choice" regardless of sex:

If the principle is true, we ought to act as if we believed it, and not to ordain that to be born a girl instead of a boy, any more than to be born black instead of white, or a commoner instead of a nobleman, shall decide the person's position through all life—shall interdict people from all the more elevated social positions, and from all, except a few, respectable occupations.

It is a pity to spoil Mill's peroration with a sour note, but he makes, in the end, a nineteenth-century distinction between married and unmarried women. Whatever her talents and inclinations, the married woman ought to stay at home—for practical reasons at least. No housekeeper can replace her with economy and efficiency both. When he pleads for woman's presence in the university and at the bar, Mill is pleading for the unmarried woman alone.

Obviously, in 1969 we do not officially hold to Mill's distinction between married and unmarried women. And yet our suburban style of life institutionalizes Mill's notion of economy: by the time a woman pays for a babysitter and a commuter's ticket, she might just as well stay at home. In fact, though our forms may look different, essentials have not been altered for the majority of women since Mill's day. And some beliefs about us hearken back to Aristotle and Milton, though now they are part of the unconscious of college-educated females. For example, the basic assumption about women's biological inferiority, dealt what one might have expected to be a death-blow in the 1940s by Simone de Beauvoir, comes to college annually in the heads and hearts of freshmen women.

Four years ago, I began to use as a theme in a freshman writing course, "the identity of woman." Some of the corollary reading assigned has included D. H. Lawrence's *Sons and Lovers*, Elizabeth Bowen's *The Death of the Heart*, Doris Lessing's *The Golden Notebook*, Mary McCarthy's *The Group*, Kate Chopin's *The Awakening*, Simone de Beauvoir's *The Second Sex*, a collection of essays entitled *Women in America*, and Ralph Ellison's *Invisible Man*. In every class I have taught, someone has asked, "Why are our books only by women?" or "Why do we have to read mostly women writers—they're always inferior to men." Even in something as simple as athletics, girls have been eager to point out that female swimmers are inevitably inferior to male swimmers. Only once in all the classes I have taught did a student point out that males of some cultures, say Vietnam, may be physically "weaker" than females of another culture, say the Soviet Union or the U.S. And I have typically received lengthy essays "proving" that women must be inferior since in the whole length of recorded history so few have been truly great. At the same time, I should point out that a questionnaire I used did not verify the impressions I gained from class discussion and student themes. It was as though the students answered the questionnaire in terms of what was "supposed to be."

The same split occurred with regard to the question of women's social equality. On paper, the students indicated a belief in its existence. In class and in themes, they gave evidence that they lived their lives in the chains Mill described and analyzed. Their dependence on male approval came out particularly in discussions of coeducation, though with varying degrees of openness and consciousness. Close to the surface and freely aired was the question of dressing for boys. It was a relief, students said, to be able to live whole days at Goucher in jeans and no make-up. And they joked about looking very different—sometimes unrecognizably so— when they left the campus for a date or a weekend. Very few students said that they dressed in a particular way to please themselves. Much more difficult to get at was the deeper question of sexual role in the classroom's intellectual life. I have had only a few students able to say, as one did this year, at the beginning of an essay, "Men distract me." In fact, that was why she had come to Goucher. In high school classes, Virginia became aware of her unwillingness to be herself: either she was silly or silent. Here at Goucher, she said, she was able to say what she thought without worry about what boys would think of her. Moreover, she was going to be a lawyer because that was the most "male" occupation she could think of. She wanted to show that she could do what any man could. If she could manage that, then she could be "independent," and that, she said, was a meaningful goal.

Virginia is an exception. Obviously women go to college today in numbers that would boggle Mill's brain. But most come without genuine purpose, or, when they discover purpose, it is in Mill's or Swift's terms. About halfway through one term, students were talking about the motivation of a character in a story by Doris Lessing. Joan tried to make a point about the complexities of motivation by saying that she had come to Goucher only because her parents had wanted her to go to college and this was as good a place as any and that for nearly a whole term she had been wondering what she was doing here, but now she understood what her purpose might be, not only here but for the rest of her life. The class hung on her words, but she grew suddenly shy of naming her discovery. Finally she said, "Enjoyment. I think that I am here to enjoy not myself but life— and also later on, after I get out of college." Joan was immediately chastized for "selfishness." "The purpose of life," another student said, "is to help other people." Most of the twenty students sitting in the circle proceeded to take sides; a few tried to reconcile the two positions: "helping other people" might itself be "enjoyable." "If you enjoyed tutoring in Baltimore slums," one girl retorted, "then you weren't doing your job properly." The discussion raged as few classroom discussions do. I said nothing, except at the end when we had to stop for supper. Then I commented that no one had mentioned, in more than an hour, earning money or having an ambition or vocation; no one had talked about the fulfillment of her identity in terms of satisfying and useful work. The students were not particularly astonished; my terms meant very little to them, at least at that time. Those who were most numerous and most vocal thought that "service" or "helping people" should be performed for its own sake, because that was morally right, not as an enjoyable act for the individual to perform or for any other reason. This is the woman-slave mentality that Mill was describing a hundred years ago.

It is clear that a social order sends young women to college who are generally unconscious of their position in that society. And on the whole, colleges do very little to sort out the conflicts they feel. How can they please themselves and please their (future) husbands and/or satisfy the demands of class and society? Their conflicts have grown sharper, more fierce and destructive, since Mill's day. For women a hundred years ago, the problem was to fight for the right to an education or to be allowed to vote. Women have these rights. But in fact a woman is—unless she closes her eyes completely—pulled terrifically in two opposing directions. They are not parallel lines: marriage and career.

On the one hand, she is still playing with dolls, dressing to suit boys, and pretending to be dumb in a coed high school class. She is still a continual disappointment to her mama if she returns from college each term without an engagement ring. She wants—and naturally so—to get married and have children. To assume that a career would not conflict with marriage and child-rearing, at least as our present society is arranged, is an error.

On the other hand, her college education assumes that even if she is not going on to a career or graduate school, she should specialize for two years in some particular area of knowledge. The curriculum, moreover, doesn't help her to work out the dual roles she may have to assume, that is, if she is not simply a housewife. It assumes, largely, that the problem doesn't exist. The curriculum is geared to vocation, however narrowly conceived. An English major will send you to graduate school, for example. But nothing I can think of at Goucher prepares women for marriage or motherhood.

Why do we educate women? Cynically, I might answer, to keep them off the streets. Certainly, we are not thinking of them even as we do think of men—as the future engineers and administrators of a complex bureaucracy. Then why design curricula for women that are remarkably similar to those for men? Why, especially when they and their teachers assume a lesser degree of serious intellectual commitment from female than from male students, even from those avoiding the draft. I have heard a few male professors at women's colleges candidly admit either the "ease" with which it is possible to teach women or the "bore" it is. And women like me fret about the "passivity" of our students. But mostly we do little to promote a reawakening or an altering of students' or faculty's consciousness. "There, there," one professor was overheard saying to a weeping freshman, "don't cry about that paper. In a few years, you'll be washing dishes and you won't even remember this course."

I have spent a lot of time on the purpose of education because I think that we must be conscious of our motives. Are we, as one student put it recently, educating women to become "critical housewives?" I for one am not, not at least any more than Hopkins' professors are educating "critical husbands." We can do better than that for our students and I think we should. Women and men both need work lives and private relationships. Women need to be educated for consciousness about themselves as members of a society they can learn to change. Even if women are to spend some years of their lives at home with small children part or all of the day, these are few years when compared to a lifetime. Without what I call a "work-identity," moreover, women, their families, and society generally lose a great deal.

Identity and Expression

A Writing Course for Women
(1970)

In the spring of 1970, The Chronicle of Higher Education, *reporting on the women's movement as it had begun to touch the university campus, described me as teaching "consciousness" to my students at Goucher College. By June, I had received 48 letters asking me to describe exactly what I was doing in the classroom. In July, therefore, I wrote and mimeographed a reply: about seven thousand words. It described a writing course that I had developed since my return from Mississippi in the fall of 1964.*

Later in 1970, I gave a lecture based on this mimeographed "letter" at Wesleyan University in Middletown, Connecticut. Susan McAllester, editorial associate of College English, *and responsible for editing* A Case for Equity, *heard the lecture. She persuaded me to allow the publication of portions of the "letter," which she turned into the essay that follows. It appeared first in* College English *(October, 1971), and then in* A Case for Equity (1971). *Through the decade, teachers who have read it have continued to write to me for the original "letter."*

I have cut the list of resources originally attached to the bibliographical section, since many of the organizations and almost all of the addresses are now different. But I have left the bibliography as a measure of the distance we have come in the years since I wrote the essay. One would not need to rely, for example, on Invisible Man, *but could use a host of fiction by black women writers, including the novel by Paule Marshall,* Brown Girl, Brownstones, *to name but one appropriate* bildungsroman; *similarly, one would not have to use* Sons and Lovers *alone or at all, for one now has Agnes Smedley's* Daughter of Earth.

I

MY WOMEN STUDENTS consistently consider women writers (and hence themselves, though that is not said outright) inferior to men. If women believe themselves inferior writers, so it will be. Why should naturally inferior writers attempt anything ambitious? How to convince young women that their self-images grow not from their biology but from centuries of *belief* in their inferiority, as well as from male-dominated and controlled institutions? How to convince them of this when even the brightest of them reviews the past in a lengthy essay and concludes that since there have been few great intellectual women, women must be inferior as a biological group?

A device I began to use two or three years ago was helpful in that it allowed me to bring the problem directly to my students, as well as to assess some of its depth and complexity. On the first day of class, after I had talked about the course a bit, enough to establish the beginnings of a nonthreatening atmosphere, I asked students to write for ten minutes on their assessment of themselves as writers: do they like to write? what are their "hangups" about writing? I read the papers and returned them the next day marked only with + or − signs, or occasionally with + − or a − +. I was attempting to gauge, crudely of course, their self-images as writers. If there was a sign of pleasure or achievement, I rated them + ; if there was none—only a legend of pain or failure—I rated them − . Some of the pain ranged from "I never enjoy writing" to "When I have to write anything, I get a headache for the whole day before." More serious still were the self-indictments: "My English teacher last year said I can't think logically"; or "I don't have any ideas"; or "I don't have any imagination"; or "I can't write anything really interesting." I have never had more than six "positives" from a group of 15 or 20; in my last group of 15, there were 14 "negatives." I have used this device to initiate discussion about why students feel as they do: do such feelings reflect the alleged inferiority of women? do they indict the teaching of composition? etc. Such discussions have led to admissions from many students that they secretly want to write, that they should like to have "ideas" and "imagination," but that they feel it's too late for them. They are asking to be told, of course, that it is not too late, and I certainly oblige.

There was some correlation between those students who liked to write and those who could; also between those who liked to write and those who kept some sort of journal or wrote lengthy and elaborate letters daily. For several terms I asked the students to bring a journal-notebook to class each day and to spend the time from arrival to ten minutes past the bell writing in that book. I used the time in the same way. In another term, I asked that students write for ten or fifteen minutes each day in a journal outside of class. In still another variation, I asked that students keep a journal that recorded what went on in each hour of class, though they were to write in it in the evenings. In all cases, students were not obliged to show me their journals, though some wished to do so; in conference, we usually discussed the effect of journal-writing. And in all cases, students reported at least a notable rise in fluency: those students able to write only twenty words in the first ten-minute session, for example, were writing several pages before the end of the term.

The group experience for women is a particularly crucial one for several reasons. If they have come from coed classes, they have experienced the domination by men of intellectual discussion; if they have come from a women's high school, they may still never have had serious discussion with their peers, and with an adult present, about the nature of women's lives. In either case, they have been taught to dislike each other, to regard other women as competitors for men's favors. Intense group discussion about their lives is meant to build students' respect for one another even as it should allow them to trust themselves to sustain intellectual discussion—and hence to attempt it in writing.

There are several associated problems in this regard. The passivity and dependency of women students—these characteristics are of course not innate but socially conditioned in schools and the culture at large—need special attention, as does their avoidance of conflict. The role of the teacher in the open-ended group discussions is, therefore, important. Obviously, it is helpful for students to have before them a model of a strong woman teacher-intellectual. At the same time, given the social conditioning of freshman women, a strong woman may arouse negative reactions. Assuming a relatively unobtrusive role in the classroom, on the other hand, may also arouse some negative reactions, especially from those who want what they have been accustomed to: directions that tell them clearly "what the teacher wants" so that they may continue their passive-dependent patterns. Since it is important to break those patterns, I have risked the anger or bewilderment of students, calculating that it may be of benefit to the group as well as to individuals. On the whole I have been correct, though I was not always wise enough (especially in the beginning) to rescue those students for whom independence was terrifyingly traumatic.

Once women students feel confidence in the possibility of their functioning as intellectuals, they can choose whether they wish to commit themselves to the work involved. Writing is hard work; thinking is hard work. Women are trained in school and out to follow directions well—which means passivity. It is not that passive-dependent people don't work conscientiously at a given job; but such people find it easier to be told what to do than to figure it out for themselves, or even to decide what they really *want* to do.

If the first aspect of the theory of teaching women to write involves the breaking of passive-dependent patterns and assumptions of inferiority, the second has to do with informing them about the processes of social conditioning, helping them to analyze sex-role stereotyping and to grow conscious of themselves as women. Hence the theme of the course is explicitly "the identity of *women*." In the sections that follow, I shall describe course materials as well as procedures. Here I will add only one more note about theory. Consciousness or knowing fosters power and control: all of these terms are essential for the writer, even as they are also political terms. None of a teacher's theory, therefore—at least if she is intent upon helping her students to free themselves—should be a secret from them. I did not know this to begin with, nor did I know all the "theory" that I have presented here—it has grown into theory from the five years and fifteen courses of experiences. But from relatively early on, I have tried to be open about why I asked students to do particular things; or why I was interested in experimenting with the journal-writing, for example. While I do not tend to spend time lecturing about anything in this course, I have taken some of the first hour to explain at least my theory about the ways in which reading and discussion are related to writing. I also state such facts as: I do not put grades on themes; no themes are ever classified as "late"; the class is to agree on a schedule, though individuals can establish their own deviations from it or even their own patterns; I do not take attendance; no reading is required; there are no exams; etc. At the same time, I try to explain that a writer learns to write by writing, that the class and individuals in it are responsible for arranging a schedule that will spread themes through the term and so allow for rewriting and improvement.

II

How the Course Works: Just as the material above summarized what was in fact a cumulative development, what follows is a summary of fifteen different classroom patterns. The individual pattern is always a result both of what I have learned from previous experiences and of the particular nature of any single class. Thus, when I have had two sections in one term, their patterns have been different. In each case, however, my purpose has been identical, and in each case I have told the class as much of it as I then understood: to improve their ability to write through helping them to understand their own social identities as women and their potential as feeling and thinking people. I shall describe the three aspects of the course—reading, discussion, and writing—separately, but of course in practice they are always going on at the same time.

About the Readings: (Section III contains an annotated bibliography). In the beginning, I relied on readings to begin discussions and as early subjects of themes. Of late, I have been freer to begin with the lives of students. In the beginning, I could count on a negative reaction from women students to the reading list: "too many lady writers" was a typical comment, often stated sneeringly. Of late, particularly this past year, I have felt a decided shift in attitude, less hostility and more interest in the subject. This past year, for the first time, I used underground literature from women's liberation; this past year also, students brought in those issues of national magazines that had devoted special attention to the subject of women. Some of this provoked, I might add, some analytical papers on women's magazines.

To students bored with the readings, I suggested looking at children's books or school texts, and from them I had papers and reports on such subjects as sex-role stereotyping in third-grade arithmetics.

No readings have been "required," in the sense that students were to be tested on content. It was clear enough, however, that discussions died or had to be diverted when an insufficient number of people had read what the group had decided to read. If that was the case, we usually talked about the reasons: if the text agreed upon was declared "boring," we talked about why and decided whether to try it again or to go on to something else. When students decided to read Kate Chopin's *The Awakening*, not one turned out not to have read it to the end; when students decided to read James's *Washington Square*, on the other hand, only a few had read far into the novel on the day it was to be discussed. We spent perhaps half a dozen hours on the Chopin book, and only one on the James. Almost all students wrote essays on the Chopin book; one or two on the James. I have ordered as many as ten paperbacks for a ten-week course—a procedure that allows students some choice.

About Writing: The English Department has, in the past, set flexible guidelines for the number and length of themes. Students in my courses have generally written up to twice the amount set by guidelines. Those with special problems of dependency know that they have at least to meet the guidelines. When there were ten weeks to the term and five papers suggested, the class usually agreed on a schedule of a paper every two weeks. Dates were mandatory, not for my convenience, but for the convenience of those writing on the same subject and for those whose job it was to select papers for class discussion. Students were also quick to learn that some writing each day or each week brought rewards they could feel: greater ease and fluency and, especially in rewriting, a sense of control about the development of paragraphs, for example, that they had not had before. I should add also that many students discovered that, under non-threatening conditions, they enjoyed writing; they were willing to experiment, even to "fail," since the worst they might expect was a note from me saying they ought to revise this or that. Thus some students who had never dared to try writing a story or a poem were eager to do so. Others who had never dared to try a difficult intellectual subject—their thoughts about religion, for example—did that. Most were eager to write what some of them began to call an "ideas" or "argument" paper: most had never tried to take a "position" on a subject and literally debate it. This was terribly difficult for many since, typically, women students try to see "both sides," possibly to avoid being part of some "conflict." It is safer to be neutral or "open-minded" if you are a woman. But of course it is difficult, if not impossible, to be a neutral writer.

Since students write at will or at class-arranged will, and with no punitive deadlines established by the teacher, one obvious sign of trauma is the absence of any writing at all from particular students. They need individual attention in conferences, special support, and encouragement. Even so, such students may not begin writing until mid-term. Their pattern has been to write prolifically in the last half or even the last third of the term and to end the term wishing it were the beginning. By the term's end, the writing of these students will not have improved as much as others', but generally the students and I have felt that their gain in self-direction was at least as important an achievement.

If, on the other hand, the course offers freedom and independence to experiment with both form and subject, it also asks women to write several serious essays on themselves and the social conditions of being women. Early essays have been focused either on their own lives or on the lives of characters in novels or on some combination of the two. Usually, students have written "identity" papers during the concluding weeks of the term. But once I asked students to write identity papers early, and the results sparked another set from that group. Several of the students had written very intimately; others had avoided dealing with their lives by theorizing about the idea of identity; and still others had disguised their views in a story or a poem. After discussion, students were interested in trying modes they had not tried before. Discussion served particularly to evoke from those students who had avoided the personal both admiration for those who had not and confessions that they tended not to trust people, especially not a group of women.

On Open-ended Discussion and Open Questions: The purpose of reading is different from what it might be in a literature course. I am not teaching students an interpretation (mine or anyone else's) of literature. I am not leading them—through skilfully arranged questions—to conclusions that I have reached about a novel. I am not conducting Socratic dialogues. Instead, I am establishing a classroom tone and organization in which students may learn to react to literature as well as to analyze those reactions. "React" means to respond to such questions as "Do you like this story?" or "How did the ending make you feel?" or "Did you identify with a particular character?" These are questions designed to evoke affective responses rather than solely cognitive ones—a process that is more difficult than it may seem, since students are school-conditioned not to respond at all but to guess the cognitive response that the teacher is searching for. Even when there is a response, when students learn what this teacher "wants," they are typically puzzled that I expect them to "explain," develop, or defend that response. I want to know "why" they feel as they do, a question that leads both back to the piece of literature and into their own experiences, assumptions, etc. More importantly, the process connects feelings and thoughts and is essential to analysis.

There are problems galore in this kind of discussion: How to keep it from becoming a dialogue between a student (who then feels "picked on") and the teacher? How to keep it from wandering into trivia? How to keep it from petering out altogether? How to decide where to begin on which day? Should the teacher begin each day? How to know which leads from students to follow? How to know when or whether to interrupt a discussion? And so forth. Briefly, the secret for the teacher is to experiment and to be as conscious as possible during the period, even to keep a journal immediately afterwards of what happened. For example, silence is extraordinarily difficult, embarrassing for a group of students, sometimes shocking as well. Try silence for a minute or two. Try it and eye contact at the same time. The purpose of such efforts is not "sensitivity-training" in the ordinary sense, but rather to establish that the teacher is not totally responsible for thought and movement in the circle of discussants. As the term continues, students ought to begin to initiate discussion, either because of something that interested them in the reading—e.g. "I found Edna less appealing as the book went on, and I just couldn't believe that she'd kill herself. What did you think about the ending?"—or because of writing problems—"I found that the topic we'd decided on is impossible, and I have started something else. Is that all right?"—or personal/social problems of possible interest to the class either for discussion or as a possible subject for writing or both—"I invited my brother to come to this class, and the first question he asked me was, 'Have you a man or a woman teacher?' "

An open question is one that facilitates discussion. "How did you feel about . . . ?" is perhaps the most open question of all; "Do the rest of you agree?" is another. It is different from a "closed question" in that the answer is not known in advance. Thus, I ask no questions about factual events in a novel. If in the course of discussion someone offers an inaccurate piece of information, another student will usually challenge the error; the issue is settled by referring to the text. The text is authority. If I am asked a question, I answer it, attempting to be precise about whether I am stating "fact" or "opinion." Generally, I conclude by asking what others in the group think. If possible and polite, and if the question is clearly one of opinion, I try to turn it back to students in the group. I still find myself asking "closed" or "leading" questions occasionally; when I do, I stop, explain what I have been doing, and offer the piece of information or opinion instead, as though I were simply a member of the group. As teacher, my problem is to find a role for myself somewhere between the traditional person of authority and a "member of the group." My position depends usually on the relative strength or dependency of the particular group of students.

A Final Note on Attendance and Class Tone: Students do not take notes in this class, nor do I keep attendance records, nor are they ever "tested" on anything that goes on. Why, then, do they attend with special regularity? The question itself has come up with regularity, generally midway through or late in the term. Sometimes the student who poses the question does so with some hostility, sometimes with curiosity, sometimes as a joke. The replies have not essentially varied. They amount to the outburst of one student a couple of years ago: "It's just *interesting*—I'm afraid I'm going to miss something if I stay away." My guess is that students are really commenting also on the experience of controlling a classroom. Many of them understand the relationship between that classroom experience and the papers they are writing. Others, struggling with the writing, find the classroom experience rewarding—they can talk even if they cannot write! When classes have begun to function as "groups" they have not wished to part. Thus, there are typically scheduled "extra classes" in the last week or weeks of term, as well as lunch sessions or a "party." For some students, the class has become a "reference group," in which they feel free either to try out pieces of writing or to talk of a particular problem or decision. Obviously, this latter has happened relatively rarely, and only of late, when I have known better how to conduct the class.

III

Annotated Bibliography

D. H. Lawrence's *Sons and Lovers* has been very useful for starting the course, since students enjoy reading the book and are therefore interested in initiating discussions on such topics as the relative guilt of mother or father in their bad relations with each other and with the children; or for identification with either of the two young women in the novel.

Doris Lessing's *The Golden Notebook* proved too complex for the kind of student-initiated discussion that I wanted. Lessing's stories in *A Man and Two Women* were much better for this purpose, even though students by and large considered several of them "horrid" or "unpleasant." I plan to use *Martha Quest*, since it has recently become available again.

Ralph Ellison's *Invisible Man*: For several years in a row, no matter what other books I had ordered or what discussions or readings students initiated, I left a week or two at the end for reading and discussion of this book, accompanied by a request for an "identity paper." I used the depth of the papers as a personal gauge of my "success" in raising the consciousness of students. Often, as one might expect, they contained the best writing of the term, since students generally combined in them their own term's experience as well as their ability to analyze what had occurred. Interestingly, students read *Invisible Man* as though it were written about them, not about a black male. They found the concept of invisibility particularly apt.

I experimented with other texts, chiefly *The Group* by Mary McCarthy and some essays and novels of Virginia Woolf. *The Group* aroused more negative feelings than I could deal with except through coercion, possibly because the identification of Goucher students with students in the novel is a potent one. I gave up the struggle with that one after two attempts, but I may return to it. The Woolf materials seemed remote to their lives, and I finally gave them up too.

In the last two years, I have begun to use, as openers in the course, Ibsen's *A Doll's House* followed immediately by Kate Chopin's *The Awakening*, and then later, as students asked for it, *Sons and Lovers*. In the fall of 1970 I began with Hardy's *Tess of the D'Urbervilles*. Obviously, I do not believe that a particular group or order of books needs to be fixed. In fact I believe rather that some books need to be changed to suit changing students, but also to relieve the teacher from potential boredom.

Poetry: I tried several volumes of Denise Levertov last year, especially because she was to be on campus for several days. Students were very interested in reading and discussing poems, and in writing them. I found much of this valuable and will repeat the attempt—using other poets coming to campus—although it becomes difficult, if not impossible, to keep students to essay writing!

Non-fictional Materials: Although I have ordered Simone de Beauvoir's *The Second Sex* for class after class, until last year it was largely unread by students. Students never chose to discuss this book in class and rarely brought references from it into their writing or discussion; and yet no class voted to abandon it when I asked at the end of term for suggestions about reading lists for the next term.

For the past three years I have ordered *Women in America* (ed. R. J. Lifton, Beacon Press, 1970), and occasionally I have asked students to read particular essays for discussion when particular factual questions have come up, especially about sociological or psychological questions. But again there was little independent use of this text before this past year, although students would not vote to abandon it.

This past year I used *Born Female* (Caroline Bird, Pocket Books, 1970) for the first time, and found that students read it rather disbelievingly. It provoked lively discussions and, in a few cases, papers. More surprisingly, students in another section read and demanded detailed discussion of *The Second Sex*. Both groups shared each others' books and were eager for more material. Anne Moody's *Coming of Age in Mississippi* (Dell, 1968) has recently proved valuable. (From the reactions of my class in the fall of 1970, I suspect that autobiographical materials will be more useful than fiction.)

I put on library reserve—since there was not time to order and no available resources here—copies of all the underground women's liberation literature I had.

IV

Conclusion: The story of this course has no conclusion, but I should like to indicate one of its possible directions. The growth of my own feminist consciousness has led me back to the theory of teaching composition. As a student and teacher, I learned and then taught conventional methods of organizing papers. I grew skillful at analyzing a student's research and especially the paper she had written, and directing her into a revised outline. I taught many students how to proceed from note-cards to outline to paper-writing. But as I began to write (and the period of my own writing coincides with the period of experimentation I have been describing), I noticed that I did not follow my own precepts. In fact, I could not follow them. Why not? When I began to collaborate on a book with a man, it was clear that we had two different modes of working. He spent from days to weeks staring into space with a pad before him, working out a detailed outline—all before writing a line. I wrote sometimes as much as 40 or 50 pages—most of which I threw away—before I "knew what I was doing"—which sometimes amounted to an outline. Sometimes the form grew very naturally from the associative process I allowed to develop at the typewriter. At any rate, I began last year to describe both processes to my classes and to ask that students grow conscious of which was theirs or whether theirs was still different. If an understanding of "identity" contributes to "expression," might not a conscious sense of the writing process lead back into the self? and forward again to the written page?

Teaching in the
Modern Languages

(1970)

*In 1969, I became the first chairperson of the Commission
on the Status of Women set up by the Modern Language Association. In that job, I surveyed the more than five thousand English and modern language departments, and asked questions
about the employment of women. With the help of two dissertation students at Johns Hopkins University, Laura Morlow and
Richard Burke, and with the help of other Commission members, I designed a questionnaire, and spent much of 1970 engaged in bringing in and analyzing the responses.*

*I wrote this essay as a lecture in order to introduce the first
major forum sponsored by the MLA's Commission on the Status
of Women, held in New York in December 1970. The occasion
filled a large hall with more than a thousand persons, many of
them male. It was my task both to introduce the diverse subjects
of the panel, which included the male-bias of the literary curriculum and of literary biography and criticism, and to report on
the newly-completed survey. The news about the status of wom-
en in departments was gloomy, and I was able to place it within a
historical frame that clarified but did not relieve the gloom.*

This essay was published in a special issue of College English *in May 1971, along with the papers of the other three panel-
ists. The National Council of Teachers of English then published
the special issue as a monograph called* A Case for Equity:
Women in English Departments *(1971). A rather different, more
technical report of the same study appeared in* PMLA *in May
1971, under the title, "The Status of Women in Modern Language Departments: A Report of the Modern Language Association's Commission on the Status of Women in the Profession."*

WHEN VIRGINIA WOOLF addressed a historic meeting of professional women in the 1930s, she described her struggles with "The Angel in the House," who would slip behind her as she began to write and say, " 'My dear, you are a young woman. You are writing about a book that has been written by a man. Be sympathetic; be tender; flatter; deceive; use all the arts and wiles of our sex. Never let anybody guess you have a mind of your own. Above all, be pure.' " The Angel "died hard. Her fictitious nature," Woolf reports, "was of great assistance to her. It is far harder to kill a phantom than a reality."[1]

Whether Woolf was correct in her estimate, women have still both phantoms and realities to fight. We have the phantom woman job candidate, for example, who is, we are told, quite unreliable. If employed, she is certain to leave for marriage or for pregnancy. What is more, if she is a proper woman, she will not be driving, ambitious, or even possibly arrogant and intelligent enough to publish and thus bring fame to the department; nor is the passive, quiet but chatty creature likely to become a charismatic Kittredge. And so what can she do but teach—and probably freshman composition or French 100 at that.

Thanks to a new book by Helen Astin[2] and to several similar briefer studies of the woman doctorate, I may attempt to throttle that phantom at once. While it is true (and to their credit) that women Ph.D's spend significantly more time than men teaching (50 percent to 31 percent) and less time in research (25 percent to 41 percent), it is not true that women are unproductive as scholars. Astin studied women eight or nine years beyond their doctorates, more than half of whom were married and had families. She reports that 75 percent had published at least one article—the typical woman doctorate had published three or four—and 13 percent, eleven or more. It is also untrue, Astin's study indicates, that women do not "use" the doctorate. Ninety-one percent of the women she studied were in the labor force, 81 percent of them fulltime, and almost half of them still in their first job, another 30 percent having changed jobs once. This is hardly the record of an undependable, unstable work force. Astin kills more phantoms than I can report here, but one is especially worth noting to this audience: those women who report instances of discrimination, she writes, are "active professionally and publish frequently." She speculates that the same characteristics ("aggressiveness, candor, or competitiveness") that may account for "greater productivity" account also for those women's "readiness to voice their opinions and express their disapproval of discriminatory practices."

"Disapproval of discriminatory practices," you remember, led two years ago to the formation of the MLA Commission on the Status of Women in the Profession. The commission's newly completed study of departments reveals the realities of the woman doctorate's world. For example, 55 percent of our graduate students are women; no more than one out of nine or ten of their teachers is a woman. Or if one looks at a group of institutions, the prestige of which ranges from low to high, the proportion of women diminishes as the prestige rises. Or if one looks at salary and tenure, women are to be found earning lower salaries and holding proportionately fewer tenured positions, especially at institutions of high prestige. Even if one looks at who teaches freshman English and French 100, and who teaches graduate courses, the same pattern stares back: the percentage of women among the teaching faculty declines as the course level rises. In short, women are at the bottom of our profession in rank, salary, prestige, or all three.

Almost all the women on the commission, for example, earn lower salaries than the one male among us, who is, I should add, younger than most of us and an associate professor. Four of the seven women on the commission are assistant professors, though we have all published widely and though I am the solitary older member without the doctorate.

I am a Ph.D. dropout. That is, I left Wisconsin in order to comply with the demands of a husband who wanted to move to New York. It was not then, as it is not usually now, possible to transfer credits to another institution. But I was not going to be a professor anyway, I thought, I was going to be a professor's wife. I would teach part-time or when I could find a job, and wherever I happened to be. I liked teaching, but I did not think of myself as a "professional." One day, when marriage brought me to Baltimore, I was conveniently able to fill in for someone going on leave at Goucher College. I grew interested in that teaching job, and finally freed myself from marriage, and even began to write the dissertation, though I did not finish it. For teaching was still my main interest, and through teaching I became involved in the political struggles of my students, first blacks in Mississippi and in several inner cities of the north, then women. Because of these struggles, I went to Mississippi in the summers of 1964 and 1965 to work in the civil rights movement; and instead of finishing my dissertation, I began to write and even to publish essays and a book, about education, politics, and literature. But it was not the sort of traditional scholarship generally appreciated by departments of English.

So here I am: still an assistant professor at age forty-one, in my eleventh year at a women's college, in my fourteenth year of full-time teaching, still enjoying two or three sections of freshman English a year, and three or four upper division literature courses besides. I have never had a paid sabbatical year; I have never taught a graduate course. On the other hand, I have taken steps "down" the professional ladder to work in the Baltimore city high schools, on a project aimed at improving the teaching of high school English. Along with my rank, my teaching, and my interests goes a salary in keeping with my status, or should I say "place," in the profession.

And what has been my response? Until four or five years ago, silence: that was the way things were, I thought, if I thought about them at all. I had been naughty not to finish the degree, and I would be punished accordingly. More recently, I have worn a wry smile and remarked coyly that remaining an assistant professor "kept me honest." And anyway, I explained, I enjoyed my life. Though I was not rewarded in material ways, I could and did invent new courses and proceed even with major experiments in teaching.

But eighteen months as commission chairwoman has eroded that wry smile. I feel now a growing anger as I come to realize that a) I am not alone in my state—indeed, the sorrier aspects of my life are rather typical of too many women in the profession; b) there are many women worse off than I by far, many even who have followed the traditional route, who hold the "proper" credentials and who can find work only part-time; and c) our profession still rings with the male laughter that signifies only discomfort, not even fear, much less respect for women. Most important of all, I have come to realize our large numbers. It is as though, to borrow Ralph Ellison's image, we have been invisible even to each other—at least until now.

Our numbers, compared to most male-dominated professions, are startling. Nationally, the proportion of women on college and university faculties is usually cited as between 18 percent and 22 percent. The comparable figure for the modern language fields is 37 percent—a statistic that accounts for 33 percent full-time, 54 percent part-time. Most political science departments, to cite a field different from ours, have no women faculty. Ninety percent of all departments in our fields report employing at least one woman. And of course, even if you are a member of a graduate department where women are rare, you know how many women there are in the profession (at least potentially) if you look around at your graduate students. A 55 percent majority are women. And there might be more still, judging from a study of undergraduates by James A. Davis. Using a huge sample of college seniors—33,982—Mr. Davis found that women were 69 percent of those planning graduate work in languages, 65 percent of them in English. [3]

And why not? Who reads books more avidly than little girls age six and seven? Or my Goucher students? Helen Astin tells us that women in the arts and humanities make the earliest career choices. An explanation is not hard to find. In the language of social psychologists, the idea of *enjoying* art and literature is sex-linked to women. A team of researchers at Worcester State Hospital recently published the results of an ingenious experiment. [4] Three groups of male and female clinical psychologists—that is, the sort who practice on human patients—were given three identical lists of 122 items previously verified as either "male" or "female-valued." Each group was given a different set of instructions: choose those traits, one was told, that characterize the healthy adult male; another, the healthy adult female; the third, a healthy adult, a person. As you may expect, and to our mutual horror, the healthy adult and the healthy male were identical, and totally divergent from the clinically healthy woman. But perhaps to our delight, the clinically healthy woman, unlike males and "persons" in our society, "enjoys art and literature very much."

The picture one gets from the study we have done is of a mass of women choosing literature, language, and writing as their interest; and a minority of men making the same choice. The minority of men sweep on to the Yales and Harvards, and into the large coeducational universities to dominate and control the profession. How is it that the study of language and literature, which attracts two-thirds women and one-third men, winds up as a profession with the statistics reversed? How is it that even the 37 percent who are women are not spread equitably through the profession?

There is very little to prove that women are discriminated against in admissions to graduate school or in awards of stipends. Studies indicate that of those who apply, men and women are accepted or awarded grants in equitable proportion. But the catch lies in the words "of those who apply." Many more women apply for M.A. and M.A.T. programs, for example, than for doctorate programs. Sixty-five percent of those in M.A. programs were women; and a healthy majority of such degrees—55 percent of M.A.'s and 62 percent of M.A.T.'s—were earned by women during the past five years. But women are "cooled out" of the profession as early as possible, so that by the time one gets to doctoral programs the percentage of women graduate students has fallen to 49 percent. Other studies show that women who apply as doctoral candidates are not only fewer than men, they are better qualified, at least in terms of their college or high school records, than many of those men.[5] If women applicants to graduate schools are more highly qualified than many male candidates, then the rate of women accepted and granted stipends should be *greater* than that of men. To find no sex differences among the proportions applying and being admitted reveals that for women the standards of admissions are actually higher than they are for men.

Once into graduate school, women have still to continue "proving" their "seriousness," even in fields traditionally of interest to them and socially acceptable for them. "Why is a pretty girl like you thinking of burying yourself in a library?"—that is what Leonard Woolf once said to me, and that question continues to haunt women graduate students. Or other questions: "do you expect to be married shortly?"; or "do you plan to have any children?" We must grow conscious of these matters, since recently announced cutbacks in graduate departments could, if we are not alert, conspire to cut down the numbers of women willing to meet the demands of doctorate programs and thus reverse the upward trend of female Ph.D.'s in the profession. That would be extremely unfortunate, not only from the point of view of equity and legality, but because of the quality of female professionals.

What if women are not "cooled out," what if they persist and complete the doctorate? What awaits them? If they are full professors, our study reveals, women are four times as likely to be teaching in two-year or four-year colleges than to be in departments granting the Ph.D. In community colleges, the proportion of women teaching in our field is incredibly high for academe: 39 percent of doctorates who teach English and other modern languages in community colleges are women. Other figures for women teaching in such institutions are larger still—most above 50 percent. But the proportion of women diminishes as one looks at B.A., M.A., or Ph.D–granting departments, until one finds a scant 12 percent of women doctorates holding full-time appointments in graduate departments. Even that proportion drops to 8 percent if one considers faculty who teach only graduate students.

It is difficult to explain away that distribution of women faculty, especially if one accounts only for those who hold the Ph.D., in the manner of one part of the Commission's study. It is impossible to explain the distribution away if one knows also that in the period between 1920 and the present, the proportion of Ph.D.'s granted to women has never fallen below 17 percent, which is its lowest point, and has usually been closer to 30 percent than to 20 percent. For other modern languages, where the pattern is somewhat more erratic, the lowest point is well above 20 percent and there are several highs above 30 percent. In short, if we look at the proportion of doctorates granted women during the last fifty years of the profession, that figure is on the average well over 25 percent. It is clear enough, therefore, that there has been a supply of women doctorates sufficient to fill those associate and full professor ranks proportionately, and in all kinds of institutions.

How, then, do we account for the pattern? Large scale admission of women to graduate schools; widespread distribution of women to high school departments, to community colleges; moderate distribution to some four-year colleges, though at lower ranks, and only token appearance in university departments. It is the inevitable product of a successful series of interlocking social, political, and economic arrangements. Women, convinced of their inferiority long before they get to graduate school, find further verification for these feelings in the scarcity of women professors with whom to study. Without such models of possibility, women have for fifty years kept their alleged "place" in the profession by passing through male-controlled graduate departments, absorbing the explicit lessons of the superiority of traditional scholarship over teaching, the implicit lessons of male dominance and female inferiority.

I am not arguing, in case there is any doubt, in favor of the traditional scholastic values of the profession: publish, diminish your teaching load, aim at graduate courses. But it is obvious enough that even in terms of those values, women have faced serious discrimination. More important for all of us, I believe, is that demeaning attitudes toward "women's work" in the profession—the teaching of freshman and sophomore courses—may help to perpetuate those outworn scholastic values. Since the publication of Nevitt Sanford's *The American College* in 1962, and certainly since Berkeley in 1964, we have all given at least lip service to platitudes about the importance of teaching. Yet no one can seriously maintain that the reward system in the profession—money, mobility, prestige, even a job—has begun to reflect the value placed on teaching. Quite the contrary: in Maryland, for example, English department faculty in the university teach three courses, a civilized load, it is said; at the state colleges, the load is four; in community colleges, it is five courses, generally including three sections of composition. And I need not tell you which institutions employ the greatest proportion of women, and which institution is able to offer the highest salaries and best facilities.

If the pattern of distributing women in the profession helps maintain its established values, it is also a useful way to gain cheap labor for an essential job: the teaching of English and other modern languages. For let no one tell me that the teacher of language and literature is a trivial vestige of another era: she is powerful, whether she is tool or instrument, and she can learn to be instrument. When I accepted the job as chairwoman of the Commission on Women, I made it clear to the MLA council that I was not interested in promoting a few more token women in the profession. I was not really interested in professionalizing masses of women either, if one understands professionalizing to include the ruination of good teachers through forced publication and research. I was interested in changing the lives of women, and I considered the English and language teacher second to none in importance, if that job is to be done. The English teacher—from primary grades through graduate school—helps control an individual's sense of identity and meaning as well as the concept of culture that individuals carry around with them. Literature and language, as we sometimes forget, do teach values, do shape images and perceptions of self, of society, and of how these are related. Even if the teacher is silent about such values, the literature, of course, is not. Writers, literary critics, editors, and teachers have, in fact, helped to misshape our perceptions about the nature and roles of women.

We have three complex needs to satisfy together in the next several years, perhaps the next decade. First, to prevent backsliding, especially in relation to the admission of women to graduate programs, but also in relation to whatever small gains women have made in the late sixties—and this in a period that will continue to reflect the general overproduction of Ph.D.'s. But even as the job market tightens, discrimination against women can only increase their anger and militancy. Letters like this one are still being posted on bulletin boards of major universities:

> The Department of Foreign Languages . . . seeks a young (26–40), married male Ph.D. in French with substantial residence in France, and with some publication, or promise of it, to head the French section of this department. He must be truly scholarly and seriously interested in French literature and enjoy teaching it, but he must also be willing to teach at lower levels. . . .

Last year I did not have such letters in hand; and this year I am omitting the name of the department and the chairman; but he will be informed that such letters are not only in bad taste—they break the law.

Second, in the next several years we must also work to change the study of literature so that it does not continue the sex-role stereotyping of its tradition. Third, and most important, we must work to change the education we offer to masses of people, men and women alike. The profession represented here in the MLA rests (and often uneasily) on a base of women teachers of English and other modern languages in public schools and in community colleges. And if they are in difficulty, if the curriculum they offer is not all it should be, if graduate students are badly prepared for the world beyond the campus, some of the burden of responsibility falls upon us, or at least upon those who control, or who could change, graduate departments.

Even as we in the MLA must acknowledge responsibility for discriminating against women, women must also now begin to assume new responsibilities in the profession. For too long we have apologized for our pleasure in teaching or in our students. For too long we have foregone our own literary tastes, our ideas of significant scholarship, looking to men in the profession to write the textbooks, edit the anthologies, editions, and selections, even of women writers. For too long we have ourselves ignored women writers and offered to our students a male-dominated curriculum and a male-centered criticism.

In the next decade, I expect that we will discover other Kate Chopins, women like Rebecca Harding, perhaps, to add to the curriculum; we will rescue not only Emily Bronte but Margaret Fuller from the hands of male critics. As our own status changes, as our understanding of the social role of women grows, we will help not only those women who happen to be in our profession, or those who happen to be our students, but because our work is in language and literature, we will be able to reach all women, everywhere. Perhaps we can spread these radical words of Margaret Fuller:

> I believe that at present women are the best helpers of one another.
> Let them think, let them act, till they know what they need.

We only ask of men to remove arbitrary barriers. Some would like to do more. But I believe it needs that Woman show herself in her native dignity to teach them how to aid her their minds are so encumbered by tradition.

Notes

1. "Professions for Women," *The Death of the Moth* (London: The Hogarth Press, 1947), pp. 149–54.

2. Helen Astin, *The Woman Doctorate in America* (New York: Basic Books, 1970).

3. James A. Davis, *Great Aspirations: The Graduate School Plans of America's College Seniors* (Hawthorne, N. Y.: Aldine, 1964).

4. Inge K. Broverman *et al.,* "Sex Role Stereotypes and Clinical Judgements of Mental Health," *Journal of Consulting and Clinical Psychology,* 34 (1970): 1–7.

5. Davis, *Great Aspirations*; Lindsey R. Harmon, *Careers of Ph.D.'s: Academic versus Nonacademic.* Career Patterns Report no. 2 (Washington, D.C.: National Academy of Sciences, 1968).

Feminism, Fiction, and the Classroom

(1970)

With the trepidation characteristic of those who return to their graduate campuses to perform their first professional act, I wrote an early version of this essay as a lecture for an English department audience at the University of Wisconsin, Madison in October 1970. I returned not only as a "dropout" who was not about to complete the still-missing dissertation, but as a feminist activist, chair of the Modern Language Association's Commission on the Status of Women, and newly-engaged in a study of sex-bias in the literary curriculum.

The lecture was not my first effort to talk with an audience on this topic, but it was the first occasion on which I dared to name as "male" a major writer of distinction. More than a decade later, this seems harmless enough. But it was then an incredible provocation to literary scholars—to call W. B. Yeats, James Joyce, D. H. Lawrence "men" reduced them from the "universal" gods they were held to be.

A new assistant professor, who later became the national coordinator of the National Women's Studies Association, Elaine Reuben challenged me to be more direct and less delicate. The Soundings *editor, Sallie TeSelle, urged me to take more space and be more specific. Thus, this essay, which first appeared in the winter 1972 issue of* Soundings. *It also appeared that year in* Images of Women in Fiction: Feminist Perspectives, *edited by Susan Koppelman Cornillon (Bowling Green University Popular Press).*

THE CONNECTIONS between feminism and literature are deep and abiding, if only because literature has been one of the few vocations open to women. The century that saw what Ian Watt calls *The Rise of the Novel* also saw numbers of women for the first time writing and publishing books. At about the same time that Jane Austen was beginning to conceal from her father and his congregation the fact that she was attempting novels, Mary Wollstonecraft was writing her first feminist tract. Inspired by the prose of Tom Paine and by the ideals of the French and American revolutions, Wollstonecraft in 1792 questioned whether half the human race were to be denied liberty, equality, and fraternity. More than fifty years later, across the Atlantic, another woman writer, Margaret Fuller, tried again. *Woman in the Nineteenth Century*, like Wollstonecraft's *A Vindication of the Rights of Women*, was a book ahead of its time. Both volumes have suffered similar fates: they shocked and irritated contemporary readers; and except for a small feminist following, they disappeared from general view. Both volumes have been derided, treated condescendingly, or ignored by historians, literary critics, and publishers. Indeed, until late last year, *Woman in the Nineteenth Century* was unavailable in the U.S. as a volume in paperback. Because they were feminists as well as writers, moreover, both women have suffered extraordinary abuse or neglect, both as subjects of biographies and as writers.

In our own century, two novelists—Virginia Woolf and Simone de Beauvoir—have illuminated our consciousness perhaps more brightly than any other feminists. They have had longer and perhaps happier lives and wider audiences than Wollstonecraft and Fuller. Yet, of course, compared to male contemporaries or to non-feminist women writers, they have been treated shabbily. Their feminist works—*A Room of One's Own* (1928), *Three Guineas* (1938), *The Second Sex* (1949)—bewildered or irritated reviewers much as had the earlier tracts. For all four women, the feminist books were "natural" ones to produce: they, like most women with time to read, were consummate readers; but they were also writers and reviewers, journalists and literary critics when most women were wives and mothers.

In their feminist volumes, Wollstonecraft, Fuller, Woolf, and de Beauvoir make connections between their lives and their work. While their books may be described as feminist tracts or ideological treatises, they are also something else. They are *apologias*: justifications or explanations of their own lives and work. They explain the states of their minds: their perceptions about the social attitudes of men toward women, not only but including intellectual women like themselves; their understandings of the ways in which women learn to be women; their attitudes toward each other. And of course, their volumes are "personal" as well as philosophical or ideological: sometimes they are "emotional," shrill, angry, or even embarrassingly intimate. These exceptional women—and their lives do distinguish them from the mass of women who were born when they were—are trying to explain both their own lives and those forces that control most women's lives.

That may seem to be a simple and rather harmless idea, but it is not. Traditionally, a man's life is his work; a woman's life is her man. That a woman's life might have connections with her work is a revolutionary idea in that it might—indeed, must—lead her to examine and question her place as woman in the social order. The idea may be especially revolutionary when it is not simply in the head of *a* Wollstonecraft, *a* Fuller, *a* Woolf, *a* de Beauvoir, but an idea in all our heads.

I want to begin to demonstrate the power of that idea by tracing the discontinuities between my own life and work. I use my life because it is an ordinary one and because I have been mainly not a writer but a teacher of literature. I begin with autobiography because it is there, in our consciousness about our lives, that the connection between feminism and literature begins. That we learn from lives is, of course, a fundamental assumption of literature and of its teacher-critics.

I

When I was seven, my grandfather, a dispossessed orthodox Rabbi from Galilee, decided to teach me Hebrew and Yiddish. He was growing old, he said, and he had to teach a grandchild before he died. My brother was only four, and so he had no choice but to begin with me. Each day after school, as I brought my books to the kitchen table, my Zaida, a pale, thin man with a scholar's stoop, would mutter, as if to comfort himself, "Because she is a girl, I am wasting my time. Ach, but I must teach someone. There is no one else." I would pretend not to hear; I never responded to his remarks, certainly I never thought of challenging or even questioning his statements. Yet I have always remembered those words, along with the only compliments he ever offered: at the close of most lessons he'd say, sometimes grudgingly, other times cheerfully, "For a girl she's not bad." Of course I was "not bad": I never failed *to learn the lesson*: And he'd tell me to study twice as hard for the next lesson—and as long. And I would. I would always learn the lesson. By the time of his death, three years later, he had taught me to read and write Hebrew and Yiddish; but at his death, all such lessons ceased for me. Since girls were not considered by orthodox Jews to be teachable or worth teaching, I escaped, and happily, I should add, from the torments of Hebrew lessons that my brother was forced to endure.

I forgot the Hebrew and Yiddish as quickly as possible, but not the atmosphere surrounding those lessons from my Zaida. I was a slavish student through high school, college, and graduate school. I did what I was told, I followed the lines laid out by the teacher, I *learned the lesson*, whatever it was.

The lesson that orthodox Jewry had taught me was extreme only in its frankness. One could say that I knew early where I stood. Other young girls and women, even today, get the same message disguised or indirectly, in the American way. The lesson is simplicity itself; there are rewards for good women students, but to get them they must keep their place. Education prepares women well for submission or stupidity.

My college major was English literature, and my heroes were male: Shakespeare, Chaucer, Wordsworth, then Swift, Shaw, and Yeats. I cannot remember reading a woman writer during the four years at Hunter College, although it was a woman's college then and three of my five most influential teachers were women. I have realized only recently how unusual it was to have had several strong women teachers. It was they who encouraged me to try to go to graduate school, where, in my first year at Smith College, I continued to study Shakespeare, Chaucer, Swift.

I should say something more about these women as models. While I admired them, I did not want to be like them. They were spinsters; even a dean I loved at Hunter was a spinster. I could not connect them with the women I read of in fiction; or the women men wrote poems about. Nor could I connect them with my mother or other mothers I knew. They were some strange form of being: neither male nor female. Or so I thought in my ignorance.

In 1951 I came to the University of Wisconsin as a graduate student and teaching assistant. I loved teaching from the first and the desire to teach kept me at graduate school. I studied hard and got all A's in my courses, at least in part because I did what I was told and *learned the lesson*; but in my deepest feelings, I was at graduate school only as a means to an end—teaching. Teaching, but never with the assumption that I would be a professor. For example, when a male teaching assistant in a Tennyson seminar turned his term paper into an "article" for publication, I marveled and applauded his daring, but I never imagined doing the same. In my free time, I didn't write articles. I gave potato pancake parties! When male teaching assistants talked about where they might apply for jobs, I tuned out of the conversation: I would go where my husband went and look for a job when I got there—probably part-time or at the last minute. Let me be perfectly clear: I was not discontented. On the contrary, I have always described those three years at Wisconsin as among the happiest of my life. I was very nearly completely without what we now call "consciousness."

An anecdote may help to clarify what I was like at twenty-two. Toward the end of my first year at Wisconsin I read George Eliot's *Middlemarch*. In the novel the heroine Dorothea, a very bright, sane, human young woman approximately my age then, chooses to marry a dusty old professor. She reasons thus: I must marry, that's all a woman can do; but I'd like to do something really useful with my life; so why not marry a man whose work is important and, since I am intelligent, put myself at his service; then I'd be part of something important and useful. Not a bad rationale; perhaps one familiar to all of us. When I was twenty-two, I thought Dorothea was a fool; not because of her rationale, however, but because she had made so poor a choice. Her husband was a pathetic drudge, without either common sense or genius. What was wrong with Dorothea, I thought then, was that she hadn't found herself a *bright* and *young* man to serve. I would not make her mistake: I could recognize dullness; I would seek the bright young man. And I did. That is, for more than the first ten years of my post-graduate life—from 1950 to 1963, I did not take myself seriously as an intellectual woman, I could not think of myself as a potential professor. In spite of all my school and college honors, in spite of eight years of hard study, what I wanted was to marry a professor, to be a professor's wife, to cook a professor's dinners, entertain his students, bear and raise his children, type his manuscripts, inspire his great critical books.

By late 1963, when my ex-husband was about to move from Baltimore to Berkeley, I chose not to go with him. I remember seeing myself in the glass doors of Van Meter Hall one morning after I had made that decision and thinking, "You are a professor. No, you are *the* professor." And then rather melodramatically, perhaps, "The professor's wife is dead." I felt more frightened than glad. I didn't know what it meant to be a professor other than to be like a man. And I was sensible enough even then to know I wasn't a man.

In the summer of 1964 I went to Mississippi to teach in a Freedom School. I date this experience as the turning point in my life. In Mississippi I continued to teach mostly women students, but they were black and poor, not white and middle-class. In Mississippi I learned a few new things about teaching—only one of which I'll mention here. The subject of the summer was liberation: Freedom Summer it was called, and for many of us, teachers and students, it was just that. To liberate *oneself*—and no one else can do it for you—you need not only the belief in the value and possibility of freedom—without that nothing else is possible, but you need also an understanding of those social forces that have oppressed you. Without such knowledge powerful enough to include the means of change, freedom or consciousness is meaningless—head-stuff only. And in Mississippi, the aim of Freedom Summer and Freedom School was to change the consciousness of students *and* the social and material conditions of their lives. A phrase that has become trivialized through its misuse was not stale then: teachers and students were "agents of change" in Mississippi. We moved from the classroom into the streets and back again to our books. The education of that summer changed lives, revolutionized people. And it was meant to.

When I returned to Goucher in the fall of 1964, it was with reluctance. Until the leap in my own consciousness occurred. Why had those Mississippi students been better writers than Goucher undergraduates?

Why had teaching in Mississippi been a living experience rather than the plastering of the living with dead culture? It was not simply a question of curriculum, though there was that. It was more a matter of purpose. How could I expect who thought of themselves and other women as inferior to write well or to live out their education? Mary McCarthy's *The Group* had caught the experience of college women who learn quickly enough to leave their ideals back in those ivy halls. I had lived that life myself. College is one thing; the life of a woman another. But it had taken Mississippi to make clear to me the need for a new connection: between learning and life. Black students needed to feel and love blackness, to want liberation enough to struggle, even die for it. Maybe it would have to be the same for women.

But how does one *love* "being a woman"? You know the words of pop songs on the subject. In the language of the women's movement, such songs tell us to love "being a sex object." What is there in life for women beyond pleasing one's grandfather, father, or husband? And looking forward to caring for children? What is there for women to love?

Although I had been a teacher for more than a decade, I could not answer those questions in 1964. But I could continue *to ask the questions* of myself, my students, and the books we read together during the next five or six years.

II

When I returned from Mississippi in 1964, therefore, I began very tentatively and timidly to learn to teach what people now call "consciousness-raising," and of course my own consciousness was growing at the same time. Before I turn to the classroom and the reading I was doing, let me emphasize that political consciousness about my own life and the lives of black people preceded my efforts to change my classroom. We all know women (and some men, too) today who are changing their classrooms because of the women's movement. I want to emphasize the line of that educational development because I regard it as healthy not only for women and literary criticism but for education generally, and for social change. It makes sense to me that the classroom should function in response to the real needs and questions of students and teachers, and, on the other hand, that out of the classroom should flow some lively literary and aesthetic debate rooted in the lives and understanding of women.

Beginning in 1964, I felt the need to read all books anew, though I did not change the syllabus of my literature courses and they continued to include mainly male writers. I will choose two examples from that reading—James Joyce and D. H. Lawrence—because they are well known and hence will allow me to move rapidly to conclusions.

One of the few literary judgments I can take some pleasure in today is my early response to Joyce. Except for *Dubliners*, I remember feeling bored by his books, though I regret never having the courage until recently to admit to my views. I regret also that I assumed the boredom to be a failure of taste—after all, who was I, a mere woman student, to judge that god Joyce? I could not even argue his vulgarity, as Virginia Woolf had, for my origins were as lower-class as his. No, I must be incorrect, I used to think.

But rereading *The Portrait of the Artist as a Young Man* for the fifth or so time in 1967 or 1968, I noted the places that interested me. One was the opening chapter; another Stephen's epiphany on the beach, just before he makes his decision to abandon family, church, and nation. I focused on the vision as Joyce gives it to us:

> A girl stood before him in midstream, alone and still, gazing out to sea. She seemed like one whom magic had changed into the likeness of a strange and beautiful seabird. Her long slender bare legs were delicate as a crane's and pure save where an emerald trail of seaweed had fashioned itself as a sign upon the flesh. Her thighs, fuller and softhued as ivory, were bared almost to the hips, where the white fringes of her drawers were like feathering of soft white down. Her slateblue skirts were kilted boldly about her waist and dovetailed behind her. Her bosom was as a bird's, soft and slight, slight and soft, as the breast of some darkplumaged dove. But her long fair hair was girlish: and girlish, and touched with the wonder of mortal beauty, her face.[1]

Why, I asked myself, should a young Catholic Irishman look at a young girl on the beach and think not of loving or marrying her (or of other things) but rather of flying away—of rising as a "hawklike man" and evading family, church, nation? I had never asked the question before, nor had it been asked of me. The socialization of women, and the conventions of the classroom, not to mention the sanctity of Joyce, combine to prepare women to ask few questions. We are, moreover, accustomed to being contemplated as objects of men's visions. We usually accept such contemplation, sometimes even gratefully. There is, after all, "The Solitary Reaper," a source of lovely inspiration for William Wordsworth, or Daisy Fay for Jay Gatsby. Is Joyce's Stephen not enjoying that sort of experience? Perhaps, but perhaps not.

The ambivalence of the passage is remarkable: the girl is both "mortal" and a "magic" bird. And yet not a bird, not the sort of bird one imagines flying over vast spaces at all, but a "seabird," like a crane, a species imagistically without motion or power: cranes are fragile and still; they pose; they barely breathe. And yet, even as a magical, delicate object/bird, the girl exists for Stephen/Joyce in moral terms, again ambivalent ones: she is not altogether "pure"—a piece of vegetation besmirches her, beautifully, to be sure, a piece of the "emerald" isle itself (or its waters); more than that, there is the word "boldly" used to describe the manner in which she had managed her skirts, pulled back to reveal "flesh" and "thighs, fuller" than those of any crane in life or art, as well as "the white fringes of her drawers" that remind Stephen again of a bird, but this time of the feathers, "down"—used to stuff bed-pillows. Stephen's eyes linger on the girl's "bosom," and here again, cranes won't do, since they can hardly be said to have them. "Her bosom was as a bird's, soft and slight, slight and soft, as the breast of some dark plumaged dove." The repetition and inversion suggest Stephen's watching the girl take several breaths: her breasts are mortal ones as are, finally, her "girlish"—twice repeated too— hair and face. Here she is woman, not bird at all. And yet Stephen doesn't approach her.

He stares at her for some time, we are told, and she tries to stare back, "without shame or wantonness." "Long, long she suffered his gaze," but she cuts off first and begins to wiggle her toe in the water. There is one final clue to her mortality: "a faint flame trembled on her cheek." And then Stephen's exclamation of "profane joy"—"Heavenly God." He has had his vision. What is this girlish woman for Stephen? Why does the youthful male artist have to see a *girl*, not a bird or a young man in order to make his decision, to know that he must split from his family, church, nation, to feel "the riot of his blood"?

He has felt his power, or one could say his *difference*. Here is a woman he doesn't know whose beauty attracts him, whose sexuality pushes through his attempt to view her as an object. What might she mean to him? A few moments of carnal bliss? Marriage and a family, *his* family? Ugh. Unless, of course, she is a bird, an aesthetic image. But he can only half manage that. Psychologically and sociologically, of course, a woman can't fly away—it is Stephen who will fly, Stephen the artist. What the experience confirms for Stephen is his maleness, his energy; "the riot of his blood" sends him flying—away from the girl. He even takes the measure of maleness against the girl's biological potential as a woman: "Her image had passed into his soul for ever," Joyce reports to us, and a few sentences on, then Stephen, too, will be able "to recreate life out of life." Not as a biological woman, but as an artist, an image-maker.

What can we learn from the study of a brief paragraph, a few pages? It would be possible to demonstrate, at greater length, the manner in which the scene we have been describing functions in several other respects as pivotal in the novel. To understand Stephen's inability to relate humanly to a young girl is also, of course, to understand the attitudes he was taught by Catholicism, by his class and national background. The ambivalence toward the young girl is at once a combination of his earlier idealistic view of women and his experience with a prostitute, as well as his way of moving past that to declaim himself a man and an artist. We do not wish him otherwise. But to see the scene and the novel with this point of view is also to make specific the *maleness* of Joyce's view rather than its alleged universality.

Of course, I had come to my view—one I can label "feminist"— through questions and assumptions I have thus far taken for granted, or noted only indirectly. At the beginning of this paper, for example, I mentioned the names of women artists and the titles of their feminist books. I had come to read Joyce this time with the consciousness of women's lives, artists, and others, my own included. According to the maleness of such views as Joyce's, women are land-bound. The artist can fly and create, even in motion. We women are of the earth, we are the earth, we are the earth-mother. Even in birthing—read William Faulkner—we are passive. The male artist, whether he is Stephen or Joyce or someone else, must conceive his power, or his difference from women, must take his measure against them, must finally define the two sexes as different species, active and passive, master and servant. Defenders of Joyce might argue that he is but representing social reality as he knows it; indeed, I would agree. But I should add at once that Joyce's vision of reality is specifically male-centered. Perhaps he should have been more precise about his title: Portrait of *an* Artist, not Portrait of *the* Artist as a Young Man. But of course Joyce was neither reformer nor visionary.

Unlike Joyce, Lawrence was both reformer and visionary. When I first read *Sons and Lovers*, I was not bored. I was a young woman and I thought I was in the presence of a god. I wept openly at Mrs. Morel's death in that novel, and I marveled that Lawrence could know so much about people, could be so enlightened about sexual relationships. For once I was prepared to quarrel with Virginia Woolf's taste, and I remember feeling, several years later, when I first read de Beauvoir on Lawrence, that she was a bit "excessive" in her views. I did not understand why she should "dislike" him so.

Lawrence's popularity has continued unabated from my student days until now, and for several reasons. For one thing, Lawrence helped to liberate parts of the western world from a Christian/Puritan ethic that regarded sexuality as unclean, and we owe him gratitude on that score, especially since women have for centuries been regarded as the prime source of that uncleanness. In Laurentian fact, without blood-knowledge, that is, without the consciousness of one's deepest bodily functions, *man* is merely a dying or a dead machine. And Lawrence certainly has left us a body of writing that honestly and convincingly portrays sexual man. But not woman. Not that I didn't believe Lawrence when I first read him. I did, and many women do. But I don't now.

Lawrence's "love ethic" calls for something he names "star-equilibrium." That is, man and woman, in an intellectual/sexual relationship, ought to meet as separate individuals with separate identities, in an ideal balanced orbit. They ought not to melt into one another or merge into conventional marriage: that notion conveys the obliteration of one by the other. Equilibrium, a delicate balance between conscious individuals: not a sentimental blurring of identities into a married couple. As theory, "star-equilibrium" is very appealing, especially to women seeking equality in relations with men. But it is also a snare and a delusion, since if it functions at all (and it does only rarely even in Laurentian settings) it never functions on levels beyond the personal: women are wives and men are writers, thinkers, coal miners, farmers, or other workers of the world.

When we look at Lawrence's novels, it is always man who instructs woman and it is always woman who winds up in service to a man. If she does not, if she is intrepid enough to decide against marriage, to say no to a man, she is dealt with harshly. If she is an artist like Gudrun in *Women in Love*, then she is death-dealing. If she is a would-be intellectual like Hermione in *Women in Love*, if she attempts to think as Birkin does—and Hermione does do that—she is told off for not being womanly enough. Or if she turns to teaching, as Miriam does in *Sons and Lovers* after being educated by Paul Morel, her male teacher warns her that while work may be all a man needs, work can be for a woman only a small part of her life. A woman, a Laurentian woman at least, needs a man, needs marriage and a monogamous heterosexual relationship to be complete.

It is not that Lawrence is insensitive to the pressures on women, to the boredom and frustration of his own mother, as depicted, for example, in Mrs. Morel in *Sons and Lovers*. Indeed, he is extraordinarily sensitive. That is precisely why it is also important to note how his maleness, his male egocentricity, operates in conjunction with his sensitivity and social awareness. A particularly clear case has to do with Lawrence's attitudes toward homosexuality. Birkin, in *Women in Love*, longs for a similar star-equilibrium-like relationship with a man and justifies the need for male relationships, even playing suggestively with the notion of a homosexual relationship with Gerald. But nothing disgusts the Puritan in Lawrence more than *female* homosexuals. And as a matter of fact, though *Women in Love* begins with a close relationship between two sisters, the novel effects their alienation from each other. A married woman, Lawrence insists in this novel and in others, does not need even a blood-sister; she ought to be content with her husband's friendship and love, period. Remember Swift's injunction to the young woman just married to have nothing to do with other women? Lawrence seems to be warning women similarly: don't trust other women. Your husband will provide what you need, at least if he is sexually virile.

A student once came to me with a plan for an honors thesis on Lawrence's view of women. First she would look at all the women characters alone; then she would look at them in relation to men. Wickedly I said, "Go and outline the first part, and let me see it before you begin part two." She returned in a week, bewildered. "I can't find a woman who exists alone—can you help me?" she asked. And I admitted to my wickedness. In a Laurentian world we women exist by prescription in relation to men—or we are doomed, damned, and dismissed. It is not only that his male view is partisan; it is a partial view and leaves much of our lives untouched.

The questions I put to Joyce's and to Lawrence's work may be put to most male writers. Conclusions might also be similar: Lawrence's view is partial; Joyce writes of and for only male artists. In several hundred women's studies courses in literature offered in 1970–71, students are searching for images of women or classifying the stereotypes they find—the bitch-goddess, the earth-mother, the patient housewife, the fallen woman. This is not, perhaps I should add, an effort to damage the reputations of male writers; that's not the point. A more interesting literary question is involved. Wendy Martin, a professor at Queens College who teaches a course called "The Feminine Mystique in American Fiction," puts it this way: "Since there are few women (in fact, no women) in American fiction whose lives are self-actualizing (i.e., who have identities which are not totally dependent on men), we will attempt to analyze the social, economic, and literary reasons why women are presented as passive creatures rather than human beings who lead challenging or even risk-taking lives."[2]

Martin could not have stated that thesis without another vision of female life apart from the one in the fiction most of us have read. Indeed, she follows her thesis with a hint of that vision for her students:

> In our discussion, we will contrast the lives of fictional heroines with the lives of Elizabeth Cady Stanton, Fanny Wright, Amelia Earhart, Margaret Fuller, and their twentieth-century counterparts in an effort to determine why, ever since the first best-seller was written by Susanna Rowson in 1798, American fiction has not reflected the lives of women as they really are or could be.[3]

In another essay I have written about the "reality principle"—that children's books ought to reflect at least the truth of our lives: women do work and men are fathers as well as workers. Martin's synthesis of American fiction—that it "has not reflected the lives of women as they really are or could be"—leads us to basic questions about the nature and purpose of literature.

It is terribly puzzling, even to someone as old as I, let alone to young students, to read a group of novels or poems and discover oneself nowhere in sight. Especially with regard to women, literature is very conservative, even reactionary. Mostly the fiction we have in print and thus available to us* has reported the condition of domestic life: the excite-

---

*At the time I wrote this essay, I did not know, and had hardly begun to envision, the fictional riches then beginning to become available to us, both from the work of writers lost to our view and from new work.

ment of the premarital romance, and the dullness of woman's lot afterward. As Ian Watt has put it, fiction was usefully directed to support the socialization of women; it has done its job well thus far. But from a feminist's point of view, literature has a significant social function for the future.

III

One of the social functions of literature occurs in the classroom, and it is to that place that I want now to turn. In a recent and still unpublished essay, Nancy Hoffman, a professor at Portland State University, describes her work as a "social" act:

> For those of us who are teachers, reading poetry is not only, or even primarily, a private act, but a social one. We give poems to our students because we know the poems and the students, because *in the public sorting out of a poem, we participate in a communal, often unacknowledged, process of sifting through our lives.*[4]

One of my students at Goucher once described as her purpose for reading fiction "to know what to do with my life." We read to change ourselves and others. Sometimes it is the students who are inspired with vision, sometimes the teacher.

I want to begin with a classroom experience that involved the consciousness of young black high school students participating in an experimental N.D.E.A. Institute in the summer of 1965. They were allegedly nonreaders, but they read with attention, even fascination, Richard Wright's novel of 1940, *Native Son*. The hero of Wright's novel, Bigger Thomas, kills two women: first a white woman accidentally, and later a black woman he has loved. The deaths come relatively early in the novel and Wright focuses attention on the aftermath, especially on the reaction of Bigger and others to the murders. Bigger's lawyer Max, an enlightened Communist of the thirties, defends him admirably and in the last pages of the novel visits him before his death. Max takes as his last responsibility an attempt to make Bigger understand why he is going to die. He talks mainly about the hatred that the rich and the poor feel for each other, minimizing the racial aspect of the conflict. He concludes by saying, "But . . . on both sides men want to live; men are fighting for life. Who will win? Well, the side that feels life most, the side with the most humanity and the most men. That's why . . . y-you've got to b-believe in yourself, Bigger . . . ."

Bigger's response in the next page and a half turns Max from a compassionate intellectual do-gooder into a man whose "eyes," Wright tells us, "were full of terror." What does Bigger say to frighten Max? Here is some of it:

Aw, I reckon I believe in myself . . . When I think about what you say I kind of feel what I wanted. It makes me feel I was kind of right . . . I ain't trying to forgive nobody and I ain't asking for nobody to forgive me. I ain't going to cry. They wouldn't let me live and I killed. Maybe it ain't fair to kill, and I reckon I really didn't want to kill . . . It must've been pretty deep in me to make me kill! . . .

What I killed for must've been good! . . . It must have been good! When a man kills, it's for something. . . .

and then the most crucial line of all:

I didn't know I was really alive in this world until I felt things hard enough to kill for 'em. . . .[5]

We had had four days of interesting but not especially focused discussion of the novel. On the fifth day, the last, I summarized some of what the students had been saying and asked a final question:

But why at the end does the kind white man, who has tried to help him, now feel terror? . . . You've been saying that what Bigger wanted was "to feel like a person" . . . At the end of the hour yesterday, we talked about this. We read what he said. We were all a little shaken about that: he said that if he did it, it must be good. Were these murders good, then? And why is Max in terror?[6]

Here are two responses from black sixteen-year-old students:

Luke: I believe that Bigger didn't feel like he was a man until he killed that woman. And Max knew that other Negroes held the same frustration within them and that they wouldn't be human, wouldn't feel like people— like men and women—until they killed. That released the frustrations. And that's why Max felt terrified.

Valerie: I think Max felt terror because he saw something in Bigger that maybe would be in a lot of Negroes and it scared him . . . If Bigger is just one of many, then maybe there'll be many killings . . . And it scared him, because it won't be just one person, but a lot of people.

None of these students had read Franz Fanon; most of them had read little else of what we call literature. They were Biggers with a difference: like him they had felt social refusals, some very immediately. During the course of the summer two black students who tried to get haircuts in a shopping center close to the campus were refused. Unlike Bigger, these students had other courses of action—they organized a picket line. Unlike him, too, they could generalize about their condition and his. They had words to explain the relationship between being "Negro"—this was 1965 and no one was saying "black"—and growing up in a world hostile to Negroes. As another student, Howard, put it, "Bigger does represent the Negro population" and "Bigger is just a symbol of how fear grows up in the Negroes."

To possess their history, their cultural selves, without fear or embarrassment, this was the accomplishment of those black students in 1965. They could read Wright's novel with skills that few literary critics have managed, at least in part because they were beginning to recognize their own historical and cultural tradition. After all, Bigger comes out of a well-hidden but nevertheless real enough history of armed black rebellion against slave masters. That such history remains hidden from Bigger is an added irony, even as his violence has embarrassed or frightened many readers of Wright's novel. But these students, engaged in their own modest struggle and at the beginning of their own self-consciousness, took him as their brother: life and art knew no bounds in their reading and in the classroom.

When I returned to this novel last year in a large class of women students, they accepted my lecture on the novel's conclusion without question. Many of them had read Fanon (first published in English in 1966), and besides it was 1971 and they were accustomed to the idea of racial hatred, even openly expressed. It was a very different atmosphere from 1965, when all the adults in the room, including me (my teaching that summer was observed daily by about twenty high school teachers and other visitors) were startled by the students' open statements about racial hatred and fear.

But I asked some new questions that had come out of my recent reading and thinking: why had Bigger not killed any of the men, black or white, in the novel, but rather two *women*? If killing is what might make him feel "free," why did he have to kill a woman? Why not a man? He had opportunities to kill several men either in anger or in cold rage. Why had he not done so? I offered two "clues":

1. When Bessie guesses that Bigger has killed Mary—she is the only person to guess the truth about that—she says next, "If you killed *her*, you'll kill *me*" [Wright's italics]. Bigger tries to reassure her by reminding her of Mary's skin color, but Bessie remains unconvinced. "That don't make it right," she says.[7]

2. When Max is questioning Bigger about why he killed Mary, he asks, "But what had she done to you? You say you had just met her." Bigger tries to explain that she hadn't done anything, but she had made him "feel like a dog." And then, Wright tells us,

> His voice trailed off in a plaintive whisper. He licked his lips. He was caught in a net of vague, associative memory: he saw an image of his little sister, Vera, sitting on the edge of a chair crying because he had shamed her. . . .[8]

In both instances, sex matters more than race. Bessie seems to be saying that even though Mary was white, and I am black, if you killed one woman, you'll kill another. Your loyalties won't hold to your race where women are concerned. And Bigger's "associative memory" leaps to connect his feelings toward Mary with those toward his own sister.

I can't do much more with these details, and I stirred little or nothing in my students by citing them (at least there were no lively responses at the time). But it is intriguing to consider whether Wright might have been alert to the possibility that sexual identification was sharper even than racial. Is sisterhood that powerful? Did Wright guess this or know it? The vision is probably more terrifying than most of us can manage, even with our feminist consciousness.

An equally terrifying novel has had quite another effect on groups of women students. For the past four years, I have included Kate Chopin's *The Awakening* in my courses. Before this year, my students were young, ordinary college freshmen, and we read the novel early in the first term, sometimes before anything else. Perhaps I should pause to describe the novel, for although Chopin is having something of a vogue these days, women writers are not as well known, unfortunately, as their brothers. In this novel a young woman in her late twenties, married to a successful New Orleans businessman and the mother of two young children, learns to swim during a summer holiday and finds herself awakened to life and to her own sexuality. Partly it is the sea, partly a young man she takes more seriously than he takes her. The novel was dynamite in 1899—the St. Louis *Republic* said it was "too strong drink for moral babes and should be labeled 'poison.' "[9] And it is still dynamite in the classroom today.

For Edna discovers that she is not a "mother-woman." Indeed, she sends her children to her in-laws, refuses her social responsibilities as the wife of a businessman on the rise, and moves alone to a cottage where she may be free to see her own friends and to paint. She even has a brief and not especially rewarding sexual affair. But then the man she loves returns; she leaves him briefly to attend to her friend's difficult childbirth; and when she returns to find him gone for good, she despairs. Shortly thereafter she returns to the scene of her original "awakening," undresses on the beach, and naked swims out to her death. Her awakening thus leads directly to her suicide. Consciousness kills her, and so it might still kill women who feel as Edna does.

Young freshman students several years ago (and for several years in a row) had little sympathy for Edna, and no empathy. They charged her with "selfishness," with being a bad mother and an extremely poor "manager." Why couldn't she divide her time between her children and her own interests? they queried. And if she could not, perhaps the "happiest" ending possible was suicide. After all, death put her out of her misery. There was always at least one student, however, who argued that the novel was really saying something else entirely. It was about "waste"—for example, "the waste of a person's life who just woke up too late to do anything to change her life." At twenty-seven. Too late.

And the novel supports this view well. Edna's awakening tells her that she has no existence apart from her children, her husband, or other men. And without "existence," there is no point in living. If she is not a mistress or a wife and mother, if she is unwilling to be a mistress or a wife and mother, what is she? Is she doomed to be nothing? Chopin says of Edna, near the very end of the novel, that "there was no one thing on earth that she desired." To want nothing is to feel utterly hopeless—indeed suicidal.

It is the political story of many women. This is not a beautiful and idyllic novel—though one male critic has called it that. It is the tormented struggle of a woman alone, without either a woman's movement or a social theory. She knows her feelings: she suspects herself of "selfishness." Indeed, she judges herself most harshly and finds herself wanting, and dies in despair, a wasted life. Or at least that was what I thought.

This year at Old Westbury I read the novel again, this time in the company of sixteen women mostly my own age, a few older, a few younger, most of them with one to eight children, and all from extremely varied backgrounds. And the class exploded as only rare classes do. As was customary, each student had prepared a brief "position paper" on one of several questions. But the central issue was clearly the suicide, and the first student who read her paper set the tone by declaring, "I don't believe it. I don't believe she killed herself. She couldn't. No one could who had been through that much and knew that much. The ending is a mistake."

Few people agreed with her, or with each other, but the papers were variations on a sense of outrage about the suicide. Somehow it cheated them; they were not going to accept it as finite, decisive. One woman read it as a new birth, not death at all but a deliberate move back to the beginning, to the womb and the source of all life, the sea. Most, like this student, were pushing beyond the novel's plot to the novelist's whole canvas. They liked Chopin's view of women, especially that she made room for mothers, for good marriages, and yet gave heart, they thought, to those women who might want other lives entirely.

I listened through the evening and did not argue my views. Occasionally I asked a question or for further explanation. Or I refereed their debates. Mainly I felt awed by the energy and vibrancy the novel had evoked in all of them. Some chord had been struck that touched their lives as it had not touched my younger students or me. I too had come to consciousness late, but I had never despaired, and perhaps I accepted too readily the possibility that some, like Edna, might do so. Perhaps I was wrong.

It is certainly arguable that, like black students who saw themselves as Biggers with a difference, these women recognized their relationship to

Edna and drew strength, not despair, from it. Their lives *would* be different from hers; and they were grateful to Chopin for drawing the picture that made theirs plain.

The current *possession* by women of literature by women writers is a phenomenon novel in my lifetime. I can remember when women students were annoyed with my syllabus because it contained mostly "lady writers." But now there are not enough Kate Chopins to satisfy. And when Tillie Olsen, whose stories we had read at the beginning of the year, was to visit the class, the anticipation was greater than anything I have known. Nor did the excitement abate when it was clear that Olsen was not very different in age, appearance, or speech from most of the members of the class. Indeed, the temperature rose.

Her visit inspired a communal supper, to which many of the women brought, unannounced, a daughter (one, a daughter-in-law). Several mothers introduced themselves and their daughters by saying, "This is my daughter. After I had read 'I Stand Here Ironing,' I gave it to her to read, and she wanted to meet you too." For those who don't know this story, it is a working mother's reflections about her eldest daughter, now a high school student whose teacher has sent a worried note home about her. There are no men in the story. The themes—poverty, a young girl's life, and a mother's anxious love—are rare in literature. The language is simple and moves with the rhythms of the mundane ironing board. Yet its language is the poetry of speech perfectly caught.

I cannot describe that evening: the circle of chairs, the people on the floor, the quiet voice that read "Tell Me A Riddle," a story I won't describe but urge you to read. Like *Sons and Lovers*, which is the only story I know in English as good as "Tell Me A Riddle," it tells of the slow death of a strong woman. But unlike Lawrence's story, there is more here than pathos and waste. Surprisingly, there is both humor and courage in the life of an immigrant woman who might have been a revolutionary leader or a poet but was "only" a wife and mother. It was impossible to talk about the story that had moved us to tears. But we could ask about the writer. "Tell us, Tillie," the students asked, "how you came to be a writer." "Who encouraged you?" "What made you decide you could do it?" Some of the women asking the questions were her age. How could she not tell them about her life? Especially since her life was like theirs. Indeed, her life, she said, was in the stories. She had written "I Stand Here Ironing" on the ironing board, in between chores. She knew that immigrant woman. Her life was in those stories and we must not be embarrassed to announce that we recognize the life as our own.

Before I close I want to mention two directions for the future. First, I hope that we are going to discover anew and find among ourselves and encourage among our children and students many more Kate Chopins and Tillie Olsens. Let me name some we are reading already: Tess Slesinger, Christina Stead, Harriette Arnow, Toni Morrison, Rebecca Harding Davis, Agnes Smedley, Paule Marshall, Olive Schreiner, Elizabeth Madox Roberts. And I have confined myself to fiction; a list of poets might be longer still. Second, I hope that we are going to write anew the history of our past and especially the biography of our lives. The Feminist Press, with which I am associated, has begun part of that gigantic task: to restore our past; to answer the questions, How does one love being a woman? What is there in life for women? What do women want? Margaret Fuller, the first American to write a feminist tract, tried one answer you may enjoy:

> It is not the transient breath of poetic incense that women want; each can receive that from a lover. It is not life-long sway; it needs but to become a coquette, a shrew, or a good cook, to be sure of that. It is not money, nor notoriety, nor the badges of authority which men have appropriated to themselves . . . it is for that which is the birthright of every being capable of receiving it,—the freedom, the religious, the intelligent freedom of the universe to use its means, to learn its secret, as far as Nature has enabled them, with God alone for their guide and judge.
>
> Ye cannot believe it, men; but the only reason why women ever assume what is more appropriate to you, is because you prevent them from finding out what is fit for themselves. Were they free, were they wise fully to develop the strength and beauty of Woman; they would never wish to be men, or man-like. . . .
>
> Tremble not before the free man, but before the slave who has chains to break.[10]

Notes

1. Joyce, *Portrait of the Artist as a Young Man* (London, 1916), p. 195.
2. Florence Howe ed., *Female Studies II* (Pittsburgh, 1970), p. 33.
3. Ibid.
4. "The Will to Change: Women's Poetry and Patterns of Progression" (italics supplied).
5. Wright, *Native Son* (New York, 1950), pp. 390–91.
6. All the classes were taped. My comments and questions and the students' responses that follow are from one of the tapes.
7. Wright, *Native Son*, p. 168.
8. Ibid., p. 324.
9. Kenneth Eble, Introduction to Kate Chopin, *The Awakening* (New York, 1964), p. v.
10. *Woman in the Nineteenth Century* (New York, 1971), pp. 62–63.

Sex-Role Stereotypes Start Early

(1971)

Early in 1971, a telephone call from Columbia Women's Liberation informed me that the group had just concluded its "sit-in," and had won several of its major demands at Columbia University. These included the demand that, for the first time in nearly a century, a woman was to be invited to lecture to the illustrious Superintendents Work Conference held each summer for three weeks at Teachers College on that campus. "Wonderful," I acknowledged warmly, "congratulations."

"Well," the voice faltered for a moment on the other end, "I'm glad you feel that way, since we want you to prepare that lecture."

It was the kind of challenge I could not refuse, for by then I was not only engaged in the work of the MLA Commission: I was also interested in extending the purview of the fledgling Feminist Press, an institution that took as its domain the reform of schools as well as colleges.

The essay printed here is the lecture I read in July 1971, at 9:00 A.M. to approximately thirty-five superintendents of schools from all over the U.S.—most of whom went promptly to sleep at the sound of my voice. I read, in fact, to four pairs of eyes, all painfully aware of my dilemma. They were a young redheaded white man; an older black man; a middle-aged black woman; and another young white man who, it turned out, was a New York Times *reporter. Occasionally, a very loud snore in the first row would wake up a few persons nearby, but they would soon drop off again. As my voice ceased, nearly two hours later, all the heads reappeared, and there was a mild scattering of applause. "Any questions?" I asked, and a hand appeared at once to my left at the back of the room.*

"But after all," he began, as though he were continuing from where I had stopped, "isn't it true that it's all in the genes— girls are just born that way, and so are boys; there's not much that can be done about it."

What to do? I now had the attention of all the eyes in the room. Apparently, the morning nap had provoked alertness. Did I dare begin to read again, with only one hour until lunch? I decided not to, but instead answered the question in a temperate, even polite, manner, and relatively briefly, expecting that other, similar questions would follow. And they did. The questions allowed me to repeat the lecture during the next hour, in quite another manner, but this time to a live audience.

The Saturday Review *published the essay in October 1971. Since that time, it has been reprinted in 10 volumes:* The Study of Society *(Random House, 1973);* The Women, Yes! *(Holt, Rinehart and Winston, 1973);* The Sociological Perspective *(Little Brown and Company, 1974);* Changing Sexist Practices in the Classroom *(American Federation of Teachers, 1973);* Perspectives in Marriage and the Family *(Allyn and Bacon, 1973);* Readings in Psychology *(Kendall/Hunt Publishing Company, 1974);* Psychology: Search for Alternatives (Don't Read This Book) *(McGraw-Hill, 1975);* Undoing Sex Stereotypes *(McGraw-Hill, 1976);* Women: Portraits *(McGraw-Hill, 1976);* Issues in Feminism *(Houghton Mifflin, 1980).*

"I REMEMBER QUITE CLEARLY a day in sixth grade," a college freshman told me a year ago, "when the class was discussing an article from a weekly supplementary reader. The story was about a chef, and someone in the class ventured the opinion that cooking was women's work, that a man was a 'sissy' to work in the kitchen. The teacher's response surprised us all. She informed us calmly that men make the best cooks, just as they make the best dress designers, singers, and laundry workers. 'Yes,' she said, 'anything a woman can do a man can do better.' There were no male students present; my teacher was a woman."

Children learn about sex roles very early in their lives, probably before they are eighteen months old, certainly long before they enter school. They learn these roles through relatively simple patterns that most of us take for granted. We throw boy-babies up in the air and roughhouse with them. We coo over girl-babies and handle them delicately. We choose sex-related colors and toys for our children from their earliest days. We encourage the energy and physical activity of our sons, just as we expect girls to be quieter and more docile. We love both our sons and daughters with equal fervor, we protest, and yet we are disappointed when there is no male child to carry on the family name.

A hundred fifty years ago, Elizabeth Cady Stanton learned to master a horse and the Greek language in an attempt to comfort her father who had lost his only son and heir. No matter what evidence of brilliance Cady Stanton displayed, her father could only shake his head and murmur, "If only you were a boy, Elizabeth," much to the bafflement of the girl who had discerned that riding horses and studying Greek were the activities that had distinguished her dead brother from her living sisters. Only thirty years ago, at family gatherings, I remember hearing whispers directed at my brother and me: "Isn't it a pity that he has all the looks while she has all the brains." Others could contribute similar anecdotes today.

The truth of it is that while we in the West have professed to believe in "liberty, equality, and fraternity," we have also taken quite literally the term "fraternity." We have continued to maintain, relatively undisturbed, all the ancient edicts about the superiority of males, the inferiority of females. Assumptions current today about woman's alleged "nature" are disguised psychological versions of physiological premises in the Old Testament, in the doctrines of the early church fathers, and in the thinking of male philosophers, writers, educators—including some who founded women's colleges or opened men's colleges to women. In short, what we today call the "women's liberation movement" is only the most recent aspect of the struggle that began with Mary Wollstonecraft's *Vindication of the Rights of Women* in 1792—a piece of theory that drew for courage and example on the fathers of the French and American revolutions. It is, of course, only one hundred years since higher education was really opened up to women in this country, and many people know how dismal is the record of progress for professional women, especially during the past fifty years.

How much blame should be placed on public education? A substantial portion, although it is true that schools reflect the society they serve. Indeed, schools function to reinforce the sex-role stereotypes that children have been taught by their parents, friends, and the mass culture we live in. It is also perfectly understandable that sex-role stereotypes demeaning to women are also perpetuated by women—mothers in the first place, and teachers in the second—as well as by men—fathers, the few male teachers in elementary schools, high school teachers, and many male administrators and educators at the top of the school's hierarchy.

Sex-role stereotypes are not to be identified with sexual or innate differences, for we still know little about these matters. John Stuart Mill was the first man (since Plato) to affirm that we could know nothing about innate sexual differences, since we have never known of a society in which either men or women lived wholly separately. Therefore, he reasoned, we can't "know" what the pure "nature" of either sex might be: What we see as female behavior, he maintained, is the result of what he called the education of "willing slaves." There is still no "hard" scientific evidence of innate sexual differences, though there are new experiments in progress on male hormones of mice and monkeys. Other hormonal experiments, especially those using adrenalin, have indicated that, for human beings at least, social factors and pressures are more important than physiological ones.

Sex-role stereotypes are assumed differences, social conventions or norms, learned behavior, attitudes, and expectations. Most stereotypes are well known to all of us, for they are simple—not to say simple-minded. Men are smart, women are dumb but beautiful, etc. A recent annotated catalogue of children's books (distributed by the National Council of Teachers of English to thousands of teachers and used for ordering books with federal funds) lists titles under the headings "Especially for Girls" and "Especially for Boys." Verbs and adjectives are remarkably predictable through the listings. Boys "decipher and discover," "earn and train," or "foil" someone; girls "struggle," "overcome difficulties," "feel lost," "help solve," or "help [someone] out." One boy's story has "strange power," another moves "from truancy to triumph." A girl, on the other hand, "learns to face the real world" or makes a "difficult adjustment." Late or early, in catalogues or on shelves, the boys of children's books are active and capable, the girls passive and in trouble. All studies of children's literature–and there have been many besides my own—support this conclusion.

Ask yourself whether you would be surprised to find the following social contexts in a fifth-grade arithmetic textbook:

1) girls playing marbles; boys sewing;
2) girls earning money, building things, and going places; boys buying ribbons for a sewing project;
3) girls working at physical activities; boys babysitting.

Of course you would be surprised—so would I. What I have done here is to reverse the sexes as found in a fifth-grade arithmetic text. I was not surprised, since several years ago an intrepid freshman offered to report on third-grade arithmetic texts for me and found similar types of sex roles prescribed: Boys were generally making things or earning money; girls were cooking or spending money on such things as sewing equipment.

The verification of sex-role stereotypes is a special area of interest to psychologists and sociologists. An important series of studies was done in 1968 by Inge K. Broverman and others at Worcester State Hospital in Massachusetts. These scientists established a "sex-stereotype questionnaire" consisting of "122 bipolar items"—characteristics socially known or socially tested as male or female. Studies by these scientists and others established what common sense will verify: that those traits "stereotypically masculine . . . are more often perceived as socially desirable" than those known to be feminine. Here are some "male-valued items" as listed on the questionnaire:

very aggressive
very independent
not at all emotional
very logical
very direct
very adventurous
very self-confident
very ambitious

These and other characteristics describe the stereotypic male. To describe the female, you need only reverse those traits and add "female-valued" ones, some of which follow:

very talkative
very tactful
very gentle
very aware of feelings of others
very religious
very quiet
very strong need for security

and the one I am particularly fond of citing to men who control my field—"enjoys art and literature very much."

The Worcester scientists used their 122 items to test the assumptions of clinical psychologists about mental health. Three matched groups of male and female clinical psychologists were given three identical lists of the 122 items unlabeled and printed in random order. Each group was given a different set of instructions: One was told to choose those traits that characterize the healthy adult male; another to choose those of the healthy adult female; the third, to choose those of the healthy adult—a person. The result: The clinically healthy male and the clinically healthy adult were identical—and totally divergent from the clinically healthy female. The authors of the study concluded that "a double standard of health exists for men and women." That is, the general standard of health applies only to men. Women are perceived as "less healthy" by those standards called "adult." At the same time, however, if a woman deviates from the sex-role stereotypes prescribed for her—if she grows more "active" or "aggressive," for example—she does not grow healthier; she may, in fact, if her psychiatrist is a Freudian, be perceived as "sicker." Either way, therefore, women lose or fail, and so it is not surprising to find psychologist Phyllis Chesler reporting that proportionately many more women than men are declared "sick" by psychologists and psychiatrists.

The idea of a "double standard" for men and women is a familiar one and helps to clarify how severely sex-role stereotypes constrict the personal and social development of women. Studies by child psychologists reveal that while boys of all ages clearly identify with male figures and activities, girls are less likely to make the same sort of identification with female stereotypes. With whom do girls and women identify? My guess is that there is a good deal of confusion in their heads and hearts in this respect, and that what develops is a pattern that might be compared to schizophrenia: The schoolgirl knows that, for her, life is one thing, learning another. This is like the Worcester study's "double standard"—the schoolgirl cannot find herself in history texts or as she would like to see herself in literature; yet she knows she is not a male. Many women may ultimately discount the question of female identity as unimportant, claiming other descriptions preferable—as a parent, for example, or a black person, or a college professor.

Children learn sex-role stereotypes at an early age, and, by the time they get to fifth grade, it may be terribly difficult, perhaps hardly possible by traditional means, to change their attitudes about sex roles—whether they are male or female. For more than a decade, Paul Torrance, a psychologist particularly interested in creativity, has been conducting interesting and useful experiments with young children. Using a Products Improvement Test, for example, Torrance asked first-grade boys and girls to "make toys more fun to play with." Many six-year-old boys refused to try the nurse's kit, "protesting," Torrance reports, "I'm a boy! I don't play with things like that." Several creative boys turned the nurse's kit into a doctor's kit and were then "quite free to think of improvements." By the third grade, however, "boys excelled girls even on the nurse's kit, probably because," Torrance explains, "girls have been conditioned by this time to accept toys as they are and not to manipulate or change them."

Later experiments with third, fourth, and fifth-graders using science toys further verify what Torrance calls "the inhibiting effects of sex-role conditioning." "Girls were quite reluctant," he reports, "to work with these science toys and frequently protested: 'I'm a girl; I'm not supposed to know anything about things like that!'" Boys, even in these early grades, were about twice as good as girls at explaining ideas about toys. In 1959, Torrance reported his findings to parents and teachers in one school and asked for their cooperation in attempting to change the attitudes of the girls. In 1960, when he retested them, using similar science toys, the girls participated willingly and even with apparent enjoyment. And they performed as well as the boys. But in one significant respect nothing had changed: The boys' contributions were more highly valued—both by other boys and by girls—than the girls' contributions, regardless of the fact that, in terms of sex, boys and girls had scored equally. "Apparently," Torrance writes, "the school climate has helped to make it more acceptable for girls to play around with science things, but boys' ideas about science things are still supposed to be better than those of girls."

Torrance's experiments tell us both how useful and how limited education may be for women in a culture in which assumptions about their inferiority run deep in their own consciousness as well as in the consciousness of men. Although it is encouraging to note that a year's effort had changed behavior patterns significantly, it is also clear that attitudes of nine-, ten-, and eleven-year-olds are not so easily modifiable, at least not through the means Torrance used.

Torrance's experiments also make clear that, whatever most of us have hitherto assumed, boys and girls are *not* treated alike in elementary school. If we consider those non-curricular aspects of the school environment that the late anthropologist Jules Henry labeled the "noise" of schools, chief among them is the general attitude of teachers, whatever their sex, that girls are likely to "love" reading and to "hate" mathematics and science. As we know from the Rosenthal study of teacher expectations, *Pygmalion in the Classroom*, such expectations significantly determine student behavior and attitudes. Girls are not expected to think logically or to understand scientific principles; they accept that estimate internally and give up on mathematics and science relatively early. And what encouragement awaits the interested few in high school? For example, in six high school science texts published since 1966 and used in the Baltimore city public schools—all of the books rich in illustrations—I found photographs of one female lab assistant, one woman doctor, one woman scientist, and Rachel Carson. It is no wonder that the percentage of women doctors and engineers in the United States has remained constant at 6 percent and 1 percent respectively for the past fifty years.

Although there is no evidence that their early physical needs are different from or less than boys', girls are offered fewer activities even in kindergarten. They may sit and watch while boys, at the request of the female teacher, change the seating arrangement in the room. Of course, it is not simply a matter of physical exercise or ability: Boys are learning how to behave as males, and girls are learning to be "ladies" who enjoy being "waited on." If there are student-organized activities to be arranged, boys are typically in charge, with girls assisting, perhaps in the stereotyped role of secretary. Boys are allowed and expected to be noisy and aggressive, even on occasion to express anger; girls must learn "to control themselves" and behave like "young ladies." On the other hand, boys are expected not to cry, though there are perfectly good reasons why children of both sexes ought to be allowed that avenue of expression. Surprisingly early, boys and girls are separated for physical education and hygiene, and all the reports now being published indicate preferential treatment for boys and nearly total neglect of girls.

In junior high schools, sex-role stereotyping becomes, if anything, more overt. Curricular sex-typing continues and is extended to such "shop" subjects as cooking and sewing, on the one hand, and metal- and woodworking, printing, ceramics, on the other. In vocational high schools, the stereotyping becomes outright channeling, and here the legal battles have begun for equality of opportunity. The testimony of junior high and high school girls in New York is available in a pamphlet prepared by the New York City chapter of NOW *(Report on Sex Bias in the Public Schools)*. Here are a few items:

> Well, within my physics class last year, our teacher asked if there was anybody interested in being a lab assistant, in the physics lab, and when I raised my hand, he told all the girls to put their hands down because he was only interested in working with boys.

> There is an Honor Guard . . . students who, instead of participating in gym for the term, are monitors in the hall, and I asked my gym teacher if I could be on the Honor Guard Squad. She said it was only open to boys. I then went to the head of the Honor Guard . . . who said that he thought girls were much too nasty to be Honor Guards. He thought they would be too mean in working on the job, and I left it at that.

> We asked for basketball. They said there wasn't enough equipment. The boys prefer to have it first. Then we will have what is left over. We haven't really gotten anywhere.

Finally, I quote more extensively from one case:

> MOTHER: I asked Miss Jonas if my daughter could take metalworking or mechanics, and she said there is no freedom of choice. That is what she said.
>
> THE COURT: That is it?
>
> ANSWER: I also asked her whose decision this was, that there was no freedom of choice. And she told me it was the decision of the board of education. I didn't ask her anything else because she clearly showed me that it was against the school policy for girls to be in the class. She said it was a board of education decision.
>
> QUESTION: Did she use that phrase, "no freedom of choice"?
>
> ANSWER: Exactly that phrase—no freedom of choice. That is what made me so angry that I wanted to start this whole thing.

> THE COURT: Now, after this lawsuit was filed, they then permitted you to take the course; is that correct?
>
> DAUGHTER: No, we had to fight about it for quite a while.
>
> QUESTION: But eventually they did let you in the second semester?
>
> ANSWER: They only let me in there.
>
> Q: You are the only girl?
>
> A: Yes.
>
> Q: How did you do in the course?
>
> A. I got the medal for it from all the boys there.

Q: Will you show the court?
A: Yes (indicating).
Q: And what does the medal say?
A: Metal 1970 Van Wyck.
Q: And why did they give you that medal?
A: Because I was the best one out of all the boys.

THE COURT: I do not want any giggling or noises in the courtroom. Just do the best you can to control yourself or else I will have to ask you to leave the courtroom. This is no picnic, you know. These are serious lawsuits.

Such "serious lawsuits" will, no doubt, continue, but they are not the only routes to change. There are others to be initiated by school systems themselves.

One route lies through the analysis of texts and attitudes. So long as those responsible for the education of children believe in the stereotypes as givens, rather than as hypothetical constructs that a patriarchal society has established as desired norms—so long as the belief continues, so will the condition. These beliefs are transmitted in the forms we call literature and history, either on the printed page or in other media.

Elementary school readers are meant for both sexes. Primers used in the first three grades offer children a view of a "typical" American family: a mother who does not work, a father who does, two children—a brother who is always older than a sister—and two pets—a dog and sometimes a cat—whose sexes and ages mirror those of the brother and sister. In these books, boys build or paint things; they also pull girls in wagons and push merry-go-rounds. Girls carry purses when they go shopping; they help mother cook or pretend that they are cooking; and they play with their dolls. When they are not making messes, they are cleaning up their rooms or other people's messes. Plots in which girls are involved usually depend on their inability to do something—to manage their own roller skates or to ride a pony. Or in another typical role, a girl named Sue admires a parachute jumper: "What a jump!" said Sue. "What a jump for a man to make!" When her brother puts on a show for the rest of the neighborhood, Sue, whose name appears as the title of the chapter, is part of his admiring audience.

The absence of adventurous heroines may shock the innocent; the absence of even a few stories about women doctors, lawyers, or professors thwarts reality; but the consistent presence of one female stereotype is the most troublesome matter:

Primrose was playing house. Just as she finished pouring tea for her dolls she began to think. She thought and thought and she thought some more: "Whom shall I marry? Whomever shall I marry?

"I think I shall marry a mailman. Then I could go over to every-body's house and give them their mail.

"Or I might marry a policeman. I could help him take the children across the street."

Primrose thinks her way through ten more categories of employment and concludes, "But now that I think it over, maybe I'll just marry some-body I love." Love is the opiate designated to help Primrose forget to think about what she would like to do or be. With love as reinforcer, she can imagine herself helping some man in his work. In another children's book, Johnny says, "I think I will be a dentist when I grow up," and later, to Betsy, he offers generously, "You can be a dentist's nurse." And, of course, Betsy accepts gratefully, since girls are not expected to have a work identity other than as servants or helpers. In short, the books that schoolgirls read prepare them early for the goal of marriage, hardly ever for work, and never for independence.

If a child's reader can be pardoned for stereotyping because it is "only" fiction, a social studies text has no excuse for denying reality to its readers. After all, social studies texts ought to describe "what is," if not "what should be." And yet, such texts for the youngest grades are no dif-ferent from readers. They focus on families and hence on sex roles and work. Sisters are still younger than brothers; brothers remain the doers, questioners, and knowers who explain things to their poor, timid sisters. In a study of five widely used texts, Jamie Kelem Frisof finds that energet-ic boys think about "working on a train or in a broom factory" or about being President. They grow up to be doctors or factory workers or (in five texts combined) to do some hundred different jobs, as opposed to thirty for women.

Consider for a moment the real work world of women. Most women (at least for some portion of their lives) work, and if we include "token" women—the occasional engineer, for instance—they probably do as many different kinds of work as men. Even without improving the status of working women, the reality is distinctly different from the content of school texts and literature written for children. Schools usually at least re-flect the society they serve; but the treatment of working women is one clear instance in which the reflection is distorted by a patriarchal attitude about who *should* work and the maleness of work. For example, there are women doctors—there have been women doctors in this country, in fact, for a hundred years or so. And yet, until the publication in 1971 of two new children's books by The Feminist Press, there were no children's books about women doctors.

In a novel experiment conducted recently by an undergraduate at Towson State College in Maryland, fourth-grade students answered "yes" or "no" to a series of twenty questions, eight of which asked, in various ways, whether "girls were smarter than boys" or whether "daddies were smarter than mommies." The results indicated that boys and girls were agreed that 1) boys were not smarter than girls, nor girls smarter than boys; but 2) that daddies were indeed smarter than mommies! One possible explanation of this finding depends on the knowledge that daddies, in school texts and on television (as well as in real life), work, and that people who work know things. Mommies, on the other hand, in books and on television, rarely stir out of the house except to go to the store—and how can someone like that know anything? Of course, *we* know that half of all mothers in the United States work at some kind of job, but children whose mommies do work can only assume—on the basis of evidence offered in school books and on television—that their mommies must be "different," perhaps even not quite "real" mommies.

If children's readers deny the reality of working women, high school history texts deny women their full historical reality. A recent study by Janice Law Trecker of thirteen popular texts concludes with what by now must seem a refrain: Women in such texts are "passive, incapable of sustained organization or work, satisfied with [their] role in society, and well supplied with material blessings." Women, in the grip of economic and political forces, rarely fighting for anything, occasionally receive some "rights," especially suffrage in 1920, which, of course, solves all *their* problems. There is no discussion of the struggle by women to gain entrance into higher education, of their efforts to organize or join labor unions, of other battles for working rights, or of the many different aspects of the hundred-year-long multi-issue effort that ended, temporarily, in the suffrage act of 1920. Here is Dr. Trecker's summary of the history and contributions of American women as garnered from the thirteen texts combined:

> Women arrived in 1619 (a curious choice if meant to be their first acquaintance with the New World). They held the Seneca Falls Convention on Women's Rights in 1848. During the rest of the nineteenth century, they participated in reform movements, chiefly temperance, and were exploited in factories. In 1920, they were given the vote. They joined the armed forces for the first time during the Second World War and thereafter have enjoyed the good life in America. Add the names of the women who are invariably mentioned: Harriet Beecher Stowe, Jane Addams, Dorothea Dix, and Frances Perkins, with perhaps Susan B. Anthony, Elizabeth Cady Stanton . . . [and you have the story].

Where efforts have been made in recent years to incorporate black history, again it is without attention to black women, either with respect to their role in abolitionist or civil rights movements, for example, or with respect to intellectual or cultural achievements.

Just as high school history texts rely on male spokesmen and rarely quote female leaders of the feminist movement—even when they were also articulate writers such as Charlotte Perkins Gilman, or speakers such as Sojourner Truth—so, too, literary anthologies will include Henry James or Stephen Crane rather than Edith Wharton or Kate Chopin. Students are offered James Joyce's *Portrait of the Artist as a Young Man* or the *Autobiography of Malcolm X*, rather than Doris Lessing's *Martha Quest* or Anne Moody's *Coming of Age in Mississippi*. As a number of studies have indicated, the literary curriculum, both in high school and college, is a male-centered one. That is, either male authors dominate the syllabus or the central characters of the books are consistently male. There is also usually no compensating effort to test the fictional portraits—of women and men—against the reality of life experience. Allegedly "relevant" textbooks for senior high school or freshman college composition courses continue to appear, such as Macmillan's *Representative Men: Heroes of Our Time*. There are two women featured in this book: Elizabeth Taylor, the actress, and Jacqueline Onassis, the Existential Heroine. Thirty-five or forty men—representing a range of racial, political, occupational, and intellectual interests—fill the bulk of a book meant, of course, for both men and women. And some teachers are still ordering such texts.

It's not a question of malice, I assume, but of thoughtlessness or ignorance. Six or seven years ago I too was teaching from a standard male-dominated curriculum—and at a women's college at that. But I speak from more than my own experience. Last fall at this time I knew of some fifty college courses in what has come to be known as women's studies. This fall, I know of more than 500, about half of which are in literature and history. I know also of many high school teachers who have already begun to invent comparable courses.

School systems can and should begin to encourage new curricular developments, especially in literature and social studies, and at the elementary as well as the high school level. Such changes, of course, must include the education and re-education of teachers, and I know of no better way to re-educate them than to ask for analyses of the texts they use, as well as of their assumptions and attitudes. The images we pick up, consciously or unconsciously, from literature and history significantly control our sense of identity, and our identity—our sense of ourselves as powerful or powerless, for example—controls our behavior. As teachers read new materials and organize and teach new courses, they will change their views. That is the story of most of the women I know who, like me, have become involved in women's studies. The images we have in our heads about ourselves come out of literature and history; before we can change those images, we must see them clearly enough to exorcise them and, in the process, to raise others from the past we are learning to see.

That is why black educators have grown insistent upon their students' learning black history—slave history, in fact. That is also why some religious groups, Jews for example, emphasize their history as a people, even though part of that history is also slave history. For slave history has two virtues: Not only does it offer a picture of servitude against which one can measure the present; it offers also a vision of struggle and courage. When I asked a group of young women at the University of Pittsburgh last year whether they were depressed by the early nineteenth-century women's history they were studying, their replies were instructive: "Certainly not," one woman said, "we're angry that we had to wait until now—after so many years of U.S. history in high school—to learn the truth about some things." And another added, "But it makes you feel good to read about those tremendous women way back then. They felt some of the same things we do now."

Will public education begin to change the images of women in texts and the lives of women students in schools? There will probably be some movement in this direction, at least in response to the pressures from students, parents, and individual teachers. I expect that parents, for example, will continue to win legal battles for their daughters' equal rights and opportunities. I expect that individual teachers will alter their courses and texts and grow more sensitive to stereotypic expectations and behavior in the classroom. But so far there are no signs of larger, more inclusive reforms: no remedial program for counselors, no major effort to destereotype vocational programs or kindergarten classrooms, no centers for curricular reform. Frankly, I do not expect this to happen without a struggle. I do not expect that public school systems will take the initiative here. There is too much at stake in a society as patriarchal as this one. And schools, after all, tend to follow society, not lead it.

Women's Studies and Social Change

(1972)

*During the summer of 1969, I began to receive course sylla-
bi and bibliographies from faculty members teaching courses on
women. An undergraduate at Goucher College, now sociologist
Sally Burke at the University of California, Santa Barbara, organized a mailing list and a description of these, and wrote back
to anyone who sent in information with the information about
all the other correspondents. By the following summer, Sheila
Tobias had persuaded KNOW, Inc., a woman's press in Pittsburgh, to publish the seventeen course syllabi she had collected,
in a volume called* Female Studies No. 1. *The numbering proved
prescient, for Tobias persuaded me to publish those I had by
then collected, and she provided me with some secretarial assistance from her office at Wesleyan University where she was provost. Thus,* Female Studies II, *a collection of sixty-four course
syllabi, bibliographies, and essays, appeared in time for distribution at the 1970 meeting of the Modern Language Association.*

*Because of these publications and the more ephemeral list-
ings of what became women's studies courses distributed by the
MLA's Commission on the Status of Women, my office became
by 1971 when I moved to the State University of New York, College at Old Westbury, the clearinghouse on women's studies.
Carol Ahlum, undergraduate at Goucher and then graduate student at the University of Massachusetts, devoted herself to keeping the records on women's studies courses. She deservedly became second author of the following essay.*

*Alice Rossi, then my colleague at Goucher College, and edi-
tor of* Academic Women On the Move *(Russell Sage, 1973),
commissioned the essay. Published in that volume, it was the*

first scholarly essay to appear on women's studies courses and programs. An early version of this essay, much abridged, was used as a lecture called "Why Women's Studies? The Politics of Coeducation," delivered at the University of Delaware in February 1972. In April 1972, I read still another brief version of this essay called "Neither Bridge Nor Barrier—A Place to Work for Change," as the closing keynote of the Radcliffe College conference on women's education.

Introduction

THE MOST CONSPICUOUS SIGNS of the women's movement on campus are the women's studies courses and programs that have mushroomed during the past two years. By December 1970, there were one hundred ten courses, and two women's studies programs at San Diego State College and Cornell University.[1] Neither of these programs was degree granting, but each offered a roster of elective courses, and in each institution one or more women had been hired to develop the program. One year later, in December 1971, we knew of six hundred ten courses, more than a dozen of which were graduate courses, while a few were high school ones; and fifteen women's studies programs, five of which were degree-granting, one, in addition, was an M.A. program. The academic year 1972–1973 will see further rapid development: we have learned of approximately three hundred new courses in the months since December 1971; we know of seventeen institutions at which discussions about women's studies programs are underway; new master's programs have been established at Sarah Lawrence College (in women's history) and at San Francisco State College. More important, perhaps, are the courses beginning to appear in high schools and the curriculum being developed for elementary schools.

In short, it is hardly necessary to proselytize on behalf of women's studies: the phenomenon exists. A new and more insistent problem is how to organize, or institutionalize, the courses that are appearing as if by magic on campus after campus across the country; how to understand their appearance, how to gauge their direction.

What we are witnessing, of course, is a movement, and movements are political in essence. Movements may have unified organizational support or direction, but they do not always need them. The current women's movement is, in fact, a classical instance of a movement without unified organization or direction. Nationally, for example, there exists no single association of faculty women, nor of academic women in general. It is difficult if not impossible to find organized efforts that reach across professional disciplines or beyond the confines of individual campuses. No one person or group has said, "Let's organize women's studies across the country." Indeed no organization could have produced the proliferation that has occurred in the space of two years.

The ease with which the proliferation has occurred suggests several hypotheses: the tendency in higher education toward fadism; the relative flexibility of individual faculty offerings, within customary departmental guidelines—an improvement, perhaps, over conditions of a decade ago; the presence of women faculty on campus, sensitive, alert, even possibly committed to the women's movement; and of course, the power of that movement itself.

Particularly in departments of English, sociology, and history, individual faculty members have been relatively free to inaugurate new courses, with or without departmental or general institutional approval. The bulk of the eight or nine hundred courses currently being taught in women's studies are separate courses introduced into traditional departments or, in fewer cases, into law and other professional schools. Such an infusion—"The Role of Women in Economic Life," "The Sociology of Women," "The History of Women in the U.S.," "Images of Women in British Literature," "Women in Cross-Cultural Perspective"—can only enliven departmental offerings; indeed, in some instances, they have drawn students' registration beyond the wildest dreams of a chairman.

Women's studies *programs*, on the other hand, have been slower to develop. The term has been used to name any structure beyond individually instituted or department-instituted courses, and the range of existing programs is very broad: among the fifteen in progress on campuses, it would be difficult to find a pair that duplicate each other in aims, organization, relationship to the university, and so on. The best definition possible, therefore, is that a program exists when some body (either a group of women teaching women's studies courses or the institution itself) declares that a group of courses *is* a program. Since the idea of programs raises administrative and political as well as educational questions, we reserve such discussion for later in the essay.

It is important to underscore at the outset the pioneering nature of women's studies. Among the pioneers themselves there is ambivalence about goals as well as means. Shall programs and publications be called "female" studies, "women's" studies, or, increasingly these days, "feminist" studies? Skeptics have declared the movement a fad that will pass or, less flattering still, an effort at self-aggrandizement. Our sense is that campus feminists are explorers, often of the past as well as the present and future. We believe that the movement will divest itself of fadism, discipline itself against self-aggrandizement and continue to make strides as a serious movement for educational and social change.

What gives us confidence? We are encouraged by our visits to campuses; the seminars on women's studies we have attended on some twenty campuses; the several dozen conferences held this year and last or about to occur; our correspondence with hundreds of women engaged in research and new curricular design; and the essays feminists—women and men—are writing about their explorations in teaching (see bibliography). The emphasis on teaching methods and on the development of new curricular materials also strengthens our confidence. For the women's movement in its distinctive form—the small consciousness-raising group—is a *teaching* movement. The movement's primary aim has been to educate women and men about the stereotypic images they hold of themselves and each other. That institutionalized education in the United States should become conscious of the way in which girls and boys, later women and men, are socialized (often stigmatized) into roles seems to us essential. To change the education of women (and men) is one broad purpose of women's studies.

Feminists interested in change, however, have not neglected the past: women's history permeates women's studies at every level, in most disciplines. Students are reading Catharine Beecher, Mary Lyons, Emma Willard, and M. Carey Thomas, as well as suffragists, feminist labor leaders, and feminist writers. Again and again the same intellectual and political questions arise: Why did such splendid women not accomplish all they wished or might have? What happened to the energy of the nineteenth century feminist movement? Why are we having to "do it all over again today"? It is clear, for example, that nineteenth century feminists fought as hard and as long for education as they did for suffrage. At the beginning of the nineteenth century an ordinary woman could not go to high school and even an extraordinary one could not go to college, certainly not to a professional school. And most teachers were men. By the end of the nineteenth century, it was possible for middle class women to go to high school, most of higher education had opened to economically privileged women, and even professional schools had opened doors a crack. Teaching in elementary schools and, increasingly, in secondary schools had become a woman's profession. The accomplishments of nineteenth-century feminists with regard to education for women were profound.

Yet these institutional changes were accomplished without striking at the heart of beliefs about the nature of woman's inferiority and her second "place" or "role" in the social and political order. Educational institutions accommodated themselves to the presence of women, either alone or in the company of men, without changing their fundamental views of the comparative educability of women and men. We know now that education per se does not change the status of women with regard to men, but merely the status of women with regard to other women. Education has not served to change either women's images of their own inferiority or men's images of women as inferior creatures. The education of women thus far has produced accomplished or "successful" women who, if they function in a patriarchal social order as "tokens" of possibility, also serve to remind us of the severe limitations thereof. Women's studies may provide one useful corrective to tokenism.

Where Did the Idea Come From?

The Student Movement and Educational Reform

Women's studies is not an isolated phenomenon, although a decade ago those words were not on the lips of even the most disgruntled academic, whether student or teacher, female or male. A decade ago students and faculty were complaining of irrelevant courses and especially of the fragmentation of the curriculum that left students feeling untaught and faculty feeling ineffective. The division of knowledge into arbitrary capsules called history or economics, psychology or sociology, and the organization of specialists into structures called departments were two essentials of the modern multiversity and even of the liberal arts college. As student or faculty member you had to fit yourself into one of those cubicles; you were a "nineteenth century British" member of a college or university English department, you were a major in "macro-economics" or "social psychology." Connections between economics and literature or psychology were not a proper subject for the aspirations either of student or professor. Boxes were boxes and labels were labels.[2]

It is possible to trace the complaints about curriculum made by students and faculty through the first half of the sixties, but it is not until 1965 that the first "free universities," organized by Students for a Democratic Society (SDS) and similar groups, began to function on such campuses as San Francisco State College, the University of Pennsylvania, Bowling Green, and the University of Washington.[3] The free university movement that flourished for several years on several hundred campuses fed into the academic world a number of educational reforms, including the idea of the "experimental college" harbored by the university or created anew in the wilderness. For our purposes, the most essential contribution of the free university and experimental college movement is curricular innovation and reform.

It was not only boredom that drove students at Berkeley to complain of feeling like IBM cards. It was not simply the size of the multiversity nor the remoteness of the faculty from teaching. It was the experience first of direct participation in the civil rights movement, especially in southern Freedom Schools where the curriculum engaged students and teachers both with the necessities and realities of social change. What *were* living conditions in Mississippi? Courses engaged students in factual reporting, statistics-gathering in neighborhoods and surrounding regions. And why were black people in Mississippi living in poverty? Thus, the study of history aimed at understanding a current social disorder. On the heels of Mississippi summer came the war. Why could students learn nothing on their campus about black people and less than nothing about the Far East and a strange place called Vietnam? This is what students were asking in 1965, in free university literature and in leaflets written to promote "teach-ins." Early in 1966 courses sprang up on the war, on conscientious objection and pacifism, on black history. As early as 1966, at the Free University of Seattle (founded by University of Washington students) there was a course on women's history.[4]

Free university courses were distinct from "regular" college courses chiefly in their source and function, but also in their teaching and learning styles (antiauthoritarian, nondirective, collective rather than competitive). These matters are of importance to women's studies, as we shall make clear later in this essay. The courses grew out of the interests of students; they were meant to serve the needs of those students. Such needs might be intellectual: why are we in Vietnam? what *is* the history of pacifism? Or they might be practical: how to throw pots, fix an engine, stay out of the draft, write a television script, organize a free school. Obviously they might also become courses in long-range strategies for change, as are some current women's studies courses. To read today the titles of courses offered in a free university catalog in the mid or late sixties would surprise few of us, for much of it has been absorbed into the "regular" curriculum, whooshed up by the vacuum of traditional departments, when it has not resulted in the creation of new ones. We may now take for granted courses on China, the war, peacemaking, Marxism, the Far East. Students may "get credit" for writing workshops or other "applied" courses, as well as for what has come to be known as "field studies"—the course that may be an activist project off campus in the community.

As the academic arm of a student political movement, free universities also focused substantial attention on black or other ethnic minorities in the United States. The history and culture of blacks, Chicanos, Caribbean peoples, Asians, working-class people, and, eventually, women, appeared with regularity in catalogs across the country. In some free universities, such courses were related to organizing efforts among the population in nearby communities. At San Francisco State's Experimental College, for example, courses in black history and culture and involvement in black communities led to demands for a black studies program and for other institutional reforms. In short, the free university movement's interest in third world and ethnic studies, and the increasingly vocal demands of a black political movement in the 1960s, preceded the development on campus of black studies departments. It is also perfectly clear that these and other ethnic studies departments reflect the changing social order in the United States and pressures to alter the elitist content and form of college education. If we are a democratic, open society of diverse people, students, blacks, Chicanos, and now women have been saying, let's see some of this openness, democracy, and diversity.

It is possible to understand the movement for educational reform as a movement to reveal the diversity within American society, to counter the uniformity of white, middle-class, male-dominated institutions and models.[5] It is possible also to understand the movement for educational reform as an attempt to gain at least intellectual control of the complex society in which we live, that is, by focusing the learning process on connections and interrelationships rather than on separate "disciplines." If we are talking of studies that prepare students not for particular jobs but rather for living a life, it makes as much sense to define an area of undergraduate study as "black studies" or "women's studies" as it does to define that area as "history" or "literature." Certainly size of subject area or intellectual scope has little to do with distinctions between the two types of categories. The primary distinctions are the ones that students hit upon a decade ago when they talked and wrote about the evils of specialization that prevented ordinary people from solving problems or understanding complex social issues.

Departments of history or English, for example, are organized to be as inclusive as possible. Undergraduates in literature choose a random series of courses that may range in time through a thousand years, if the geographical limitation is Britain and the United States, or twenty-five hundred to three thousand years if the offerings include "world" literature or history. Rarely does a student of literature pick up more than a thin sense of chronology; more often, the message in literature courses is of "timelessness," as though literature did not spring from the particulars of people's lives, their class, race, national origins and religion, and of course their sex. Similarly, history departments are caught between "coverage" of bodies of historical data and teaching students how history is written, from whence history springs. Of course, the source material of history is frequently "literature." Similarly, it is difficult to understand the emergence of "the novel" in the eighteenth century without a review of a changing social order in Europe.

Students of women's studies or black studies will face other equally complex problems. The intellectual "cut" is diametrically different. To study the history and culture of black people or women in the United States is to confine yourself to a narrow geography, a relatively brief unit of time, and to one major issue, race or sex. But of course these issues are connected to all others, as are the issues of class for example; and hence, studies move properly into other disciplines. This emphasis is strikingly similar to the old liberal arts notion of a "rounded" course of study; at the same time, the focus is distinctive and eliminates the effects of fragmentation. Students do not move from course to course gaining a "smattering" of introductions to traditional bodies of knowledge; rather, they use tools and perspectives of various "disciplines" to understand at least one aspect of the social order, say women's history and social role in the United

States. But, of course, even with so narrow a definition, the perspective is broad and may extend itself indefinitely, even as does the study of literature. For example, one may study Indian women, black women, working-class women in the United States, or one may focus on comparative, cross-cultural studies. In short, the intellectual ordering of area or ethnic studies may be different from the study of literature or history per se, but many of the same patterns of focus and perspective apply in both cases. To argue that literature, sociology, and political science are definable, distinct, limited, and hence legitimate areas of study, but that area or ethnic studies are too broad and impressionistic, is unsound.

The immediate problem confronting institutions developing women's studies programs is the need for trained faculty, both with respect to curriculum and methodology. Our graduate schools still are producing narrow specialists in traditional disciplines. The pressures on young faculty members to conform to departmental standards, to publish in the usual journals, is still strong. It is not surprising, therefore, to find among young women teachers the anxiety of those taught to be psychologists, say, or historians, and hence, allegedly unable to think about or deal with literature, much less with connections between psychology and literature. For some time to come, team-taught courses will have to compensate for the narrowness of traditional training and provide interdisciplinary approaches to curriculum.[6]

The "Politics of Coeducation"

If it is possible to view women's studies as part of a general attempt to reform college curriculum, it is also clear that the women on campuses have been quick to seize the opportunity. And of course they were present to do so. For more than a century, United States higher education has been characteristically coeducational: we have preached the rhetoric of equality for women in our colleges and universities as we have not (until recently) for blacks and other minorities. Whatever their status, however they may be regarded by themselves or others, women in the United States attend college at proportions unusual for Western countries. The number of women *employed* by a college or university is typically greater than the number of men, if one considers not only faculty (20 percent) but secretaries, clerks, librarians, housekeepers, cooks, maids, and the wives of graduate students, faculty, and administrators. In short, the presence of women in mass numbers (however invisible they may have been, and felt themselves to be in the past) provides a powerful force for change. Women do not have to be "recruited" to campuses; in most cases, they are an overwhelming presence.

The first effect of the women's movement on campus was to cause women to study their status there. While discriminatory patterns were evident both in hiring and promotion, such studies also pointed to the presence of more complex problems. The attrition rate among graduate women students, for example, could not be explained simply by charging "discrimination." The fact that women high school graduates enter college with higher achievement records than male students, and yet set lower vocational goals for themselves clearly can not be dealt with by an Equal Opportunity Employment officer. Indeed, when one sets side by side the increasing proportions of women who do complete high school and go on to college, with the diminishing proportions who go on to graduate or professional schools, the question of "discrimination" in higher education becomes a problem for relatively few women. The massive problem is a more complex one altogether: the control not over whether a highly motivated woman can get a job but over the processes of education whereby only relatively few women emerge as highly motivated when and if they graduate from college. The crucial issue in women's education, therefore, is their aspiration.

While aspiration is a function of multiple social factors in the development of young women, important among them is the total school and college experience.[7] College officials, like public school officials, maintain that girls and boys, women and men, are treated exactly alike in classrooms and by educational institutions. Indeed, in most classrooms, females and males hear the same lectures, read the same books, do the same assignments, take the same examinations. But the *content* of the curriculum is male-biased; women are absent or are presented in passive, limited, and limiting roles. In addition, the treatment of males and females is distinctly different with regard to such subjects as physical education, and with regard to student activities outside the classroom, and health, housing, or counseling policies. In effect, the "sexual politics" of schools is no different from that in the world outside.

Let us consider the classroom first. When history is taught, it is the history of male warriors, rulers, tradesmen, investors, explorers. When literature is studied, it is the literature of male writers recording *their* lives, *their* perspective—*Huck Finn* and *The Portrait of the Artist as A Young Man* are classic examples. Psychology reflects the male experience and male points of view. Until recently, most courses in social inequality examined inequality with regard to race, religion, ethnicity, and class, but not sex. Courses on marriage and the family assumed the inevitability of the maternal role. The perspective of theology, art, history, music, political science is parallel. The implicit curricular message to women students has been simple: *men* work, write, and make history, psychology, theology; women get married, have babies, and rear them.

Women's studies is part of a broad effort to develop interdisciplinary studies. In particular, it is related to ethnic studies in its focus on the history, culture, and the status of a social group. The rapidity with which women's studies has developed on campuses can be ascribed both to the presence of women in relatively large numbers, especially among graduate students and junior faculty; to numerous studies of the status of women on campus and in the professions; and to the failures of curriculum and other aspects of collegiate and university life. The immediate justification for women's studies is the narrowness of the traditional male dominated curriculum, geared to support the life goals of men and to undermine the idea that women might hold similar life goals or might wish to explore new directions for human achievement and social reward. The alleged equal treatment of women in the classroom itself is one of the causes of women's inferior social role and condition. Women and men have been taught, by example and by the content of the curriculum, that men strive and succeed; but that with rare exceptions, women do not. All men on campus are potential achievers and one would not wish to take that away from them. One would only wish for women the same privilege of hope and achievement.

Courses

We would not have written this essay at all, were it not for one unique aspect of the academic women's movement. From the very beginning, women were interested in and willing to share syllabi, bibliographies, and general plans for courses and programs. In our office alone, between 1970 and 1972, there has been a lively correspondence with some 500 people. Indeed, the press of such correspondence in the spring and summer of 1970 led us to the idea of publishing lists of those people teaching women's studies courses so that they might correspond with *each other*, but the list doubled and tripled almost at once, so that by October of 1970, we knew of 110 courses. The original idea of individuals circulating their own syllabi to a small group of women around the country no longer seemed practical. The need for a "clearinghouse" was inevitable.

The review of curriculum that follows is based, therefore, on three sets of materials. First, we have a list of course titles and associated information, published most recently as *The New Guide to Current Female Studies*. From this list one can derive gross statistics (610 courses, 200 institutions, 500 instructors, and so on), and further categorical data (there are 163 courses in departments of English, 52 in sociology, 84 in history, and so on).[8] But the most valuable materials are the syllabi themselves and the essays written by teachers of women's studies courses. A total of 137 course syllabi have been published in *Female Studies I, II* and *III*. In our files we have an additional 250 syllabi plus those for most courses offered by women's studies programs. A total of eleven essays have been published in *Female Studies II* and *IV*. Another large group (fifteen essays) were prepared for a conference entitled "Women and Education: A Feminist Perspective" held at the University of Pittsburgh, and published as *Female Studies V*. A dozen discrete essays have been published during the past two years, and our files contain another dozen unpublished papers. Like the total number of courses that have appeared in so brief a period, the number of essays is astonishing.

Some 610 courses are distributed across 197 institutions, about half of which are located on the east coast, nearly a quarter in the midwest, and a somewhat smaller number on the west coast.[9] Twelve institutions are located in the south. The number of courses at individual institutions ranges from one or two (the most numerous category) to thirty-three at the State University of New York at Buffalo where there is a "college" of women's studies. Nearly one half of the institutions offering women's studies courses are universities granting the doctorate; a quarter are four-year coeducational colleges. The final quarter is divided among women's colleges (thirty-five); men's colleges (three); and two-year colleges (fourteen).

There is no hard data on the numbers of students attending women's studies courses. But it is our impression from correspondence, visits to campuses, and essays that registration is generous, ranging from the three hundred students in the opening Cornell course, and one hundred fifty in a sociology course taught by Arlie Hochschild at Santa Cruz in the spring of 1971, to courses and seminars of thirty or fewer. Syllabi rarely are specific either about the level of the course or the number of students anticipated. Most of the students are women, although in large "general" courses men may constitute 10 percent of the class. Many courses include "token" males and at several male institutions (Dartmouth, Rutgers, M.I.T.) women's studies courses have been organized exclusively or predominantly for male students.

There is also no hard data on the status of teachers of women's studies courses, but again it is our impression that many, if not most, are graduate students or junior faculty. We also know that for some dozen of these teachers, professional careers have been disrupted by their interest in developing new courses and by their ability to attract numbers of students thereby.[10] On the whole, these courses are taught by women in just under nine out of ten cases (532 out of 600).

The subject of teaching styles merits a separate essay. We can do little more than report our impressions (culled from correspondence, visits, and essays) that, in general, teachers are transfigured by the experience of teaching even *one* women's studies course. They report shifts in their views of a discipline, as well as changes in their teaching styles and their *ability* to teach. They also report a strengthened commitment to the women's movement, to the lives of women beyond the campus. Finally, they report a heightened intellectual and political understanding of the multiple aspects of women's studies. Quite naturally too, while women's studies teachers feel a heightened sense of their own creative *power*, they sense also a certain polarization of attitudes of other faculty and administrators toward them.

In large courses, lectures are a necessity, but these are usually accompanied by small group discussions, often quite deliberately intended as consciousness-raising experiences. Indeed, if one generalization were called for, we would say that the trend is to substitute, wherever possible, groups and group processes and cooperative ("collective") projects for the individual competitive ones so familiar to us in academe. None of this is surprising, given the emphasis in the women's movment on *sisterhood*, antielitism, leaderless consciousness-raising groups, and the power of collective decision-making and activity. What is surprising is the speed with which the movement's priorities and principles have been extended into the classroom.

Finally, a cautionary note is probably in order. Most women's studies courses were offered for the first time in the 1971–1972 academic year; many more will be offered in the academic years to come. The impressions recorded above are based largely on conversations and correspondence with those who are two-year (or longer) veterans of women's studies. Within the next several years, we will need to use some survey techniques to review and revise what we have offered here as impressions.

The Curriculum

The central idea of women's studies is sex bias and the status of women. Major curricular energies have focused on definitions and analyses of sex-role stereotypes in institutional life (discrimination in hiring, marriage and divorce laws, women and the church, etc.) and in history, literature, film, and other aspects of the culture; on the processes of socialization and education through which stereotypes are perpetuated; and on the idea of innate sexual differences or tendencies. This focus holds true across courses in specific disciplinary departments as well as in introductory and interdisciplinary courses.

Implicit or explicit in women's studies courses is a critical vision of the social subordination of women. At the very least, teachers theorize that when women (and men) become conscious of sex bias, they will be motivated to plan means of appropriate social change. Many courses focus on affecting changes in the lives of women and men. How is it possible to break the processes of socialization not only for the student studying the materials (which is what happens) but for others currently in elementary schools or others still unborn? Some courses are organized with a "coda" on the future; others actually involve making that future happen.

The clearest examples of the latter are new courses in law schools, in some of which law students research proposed changes in legislation or prepare arguments in defense of individual women's cases.

"Introductory/Interdisciplinary" or "General" Courses

Of necessity a women's studies curriculum assumes an interdisciplinary approach; that is, it is difficult, if not impossible to consider sex-role stereotyping, status, and social change without reference to multiple aspects of women's lives, including, of course, their relationships to men. Indeed, the first courses to be organized consciously as "women's studies" courses were "general" ones. Either taught by a team of women from several departments or done as a series of lectures coordinated and integrated by a generalist or by one who taught her speciality, these courses have usually attracted large enrollments. Given the departmental nature of higher education, such courses have had to find homes in exceptional places. Continuing education programs and extension divisions have provided some space, and in several universities (Pittsburgh and California at Irvine for example), courses were offered as a special program generated by a friendly divisional dean's office. At Cornell, the former School of Home Economics (now called Human Development and Family Studies) permitted the organization of "The Evolution of Female Personality," a course that drew more than two hundred students (of whom 30 were men) and an additional 150 auditors.

The 1970 Cornell course, revised in the following years, remains one model for a rapid general survey of the area. Approximately four lectures were offered on each of six major topics: Status of Women (law, marriage, socialization, biology); History of Women; Image of Women (in popular and high culture); Family Roles, Social Ecology (urbanization, architecture and planning, black women); Prospects for Change. Nineteen lecturers contributed to the course, including members of the departments of sociology, biology, English, art, and history, as well as six visiting scholars (a professor of gynecology and obstetrics, an attorney, a member of the New York Human Rights Commission, Joyce Ladner, and Kate Millett). The emphasis in lectures, as well as in extensive readings assigned, was on the facts—what do we know—and on varieties of interpretations and points of view. Although there was some attention to concerns of black women, there was generally little or no discussion of class differences or political perspectives. The concluding lectures emphasized the future for educated or "independent women" (through discussion of Mary McCarthy, Simone de Beauvoir, Doris Lessing).

Quite a different model for a large introductory course is "The History and Social Role of Women," a course offered at the University of Pittsburgh in the spring of 1970. This ten-week course focused on economic and political issues, on work rather than the family. The curriculum was organized by three women from the English, Spanish and history departments around the following topics: General Concepts of Women in Industrial Society; Nineteenth and Twentieth Century Views of Women; Class-Determined Roles of Women; Sexual Politics; The Meaning of Women's Liberation. Readings included Engels, Mill, Gilman, G. Myrdal, as well as literature by Lawrence, Lessing, Woolf, Albee, and Ibsen. The course was organized to clarify class differences among women as well as racial differences, reflecting the diversity of Pittsburgh's student body. The concluding segment of the course focused on Doris Lessing's *The Golden Notebook*, Margaret Benston's "Political Economy of Women's Liberation," and other essays from recent movement publications.

These two courses illustrate two modes of organizing general introductions to women's studies and illustrate as well several recurring patterns of most women's studies courses. The readings are remarkably diverse—for academe, that is. Typically, fiction or some other form of "literature" is mixed not only with standard women's movement works (Friedan, de Beauvoir, Millett, O'Neill) but with readings in psychology, biology, history, sociology, and so on. In both courses, students kept journals; they met weekly for lectures and in small discussion groups that sometimes functioned as consciousness-raising sessions.

Such courses have continued to emerge, initiated by members of departments, divisions, schools, or entire institutions. In the fall of 1971, at a small experimental college (State University of New York/College at Old Westbury) such a course seemed the best way both to test students' interest and to initiate a faculty new to women's studies. At the University of Wisconsin, where there had been several discrete women's studies courses taught by members of the English department, Joan Roberts of the School of Education organized a graduate course called "Education and the Status of Women" in the fall of 1971. Twenty-five women professors, all "tokens" in the university's departments or schools, lectured on such topics as "Women in Philosophical Perspective," "Women in Literature," "Law," "Minority Groups," and so on. The curriculum may be compared to Cornell's: variety is the key, required readings are extensive, and written critiques required. In addition, Roberts describes an interesting term project. Students may work alone or in groups, but the group option seems favored, or at least it is the one described in most detail. Students who prefer "to read extensively, to discuss their thinking, and to raise their levels of awareness about women, [may form] *small discussion groups* of four or five students." Individuals are expected to "keep a cumulative *idea and attitude log*" weekly, in which they record "evidence that your reading, your thinking, and your feelings changed or did not change in ways that make sense to you as a person *and* a scholar." Students who prefer "action research" may form groups of from two to six, define a research problem, its methodology, implications, and so on, and proceed. Again, a report is required.

On some campuses, an initial women's studies course was offered by an individual faculty member as part of her regular teaching load in a particular department. Whatever the title of the course and whatever the department, in most cases the course served to introduce women's studies to the campus. When Gerda Lerner, an historian at Sarah Lawrence, designed "The Many Worlds of Women," she set out "to explore women's role, status, self-image, and history." "It was, frankly, an experiment," she writes, "in that it did not confine itself to a strict 'history of women in the United States' approach, but sought to approach the subject in a freewheeling, interdisciplinary way. This proved to be its greatest strength . . . ." Similarly, Lillian Robinson's literature course at M.I.T., called "The Sexual Order," focused on sexual identity, sexuality, and political relations between the sexes through the use of popular and literary materials, as well as readings in Freud, Marcuse, Reich, Engels, Mead, Masters and Johnson, Mill, Wollstonecraft, Woolf, and latter-day feminists. Just as Gerda Lerner concluded that her students could think about the history of women more clearly after they had been provided with a generous frame of reference, so Robinson acknowledged that her approach to literature, "influenced by cultural anthropology," called for an examination of "some central sexual myths." "Literature," Robinson continues, "is both the source and the reflection of those myths."

"Introductory" courses in women's studies also are offered under the titles of "Philosophical Issues of Contemporary Feminism," "Sex Roles in American Society and Politics," "Psychology of Women," "The Role of Women in Economic Life." It is, therefore, unwise to generalize about women's studies courses from a cursory examination of titles alone. Understandably, in a developing area of study and research many courses may seem (or be) "introductory," especially when they function also to initiate women's studies on a campus.

Introductory courses are probably more "political"—or at least more potent—in intent and effect than other individual courses. They may, in fact, lead to the development of other courses or even to programs. Moreover, feelings of "solidarity" have been generated by large classes of women and feelings of intimacy in small groups. Equally important, perhaps, is that faculty are brought together by an interdisciplinary course. Individually, faculty members experience an increase in sensitivity and consciousness. In addition, as a University of Wisconsin syllabus pointed out, team-taught courses "provide numerous possible role models for women students."

In short, the message to students is: look here, there is a body of material, research, and theory, probably unknown to you because it is not included in the general college or university curriculum. Women have begun to look into such matters; you may do so too. Indeed, you may begin in this course, and your project may take you into a number of fields. Thus an introductory course in women's studies is political in its effect, if it sends students on to other courses with new questions.

"Disciplinary" Courses

By and large, the general pattern of curricular development has been from the "general" or "introductory" course to the "disciplinary." Half of the forty-five syllabi in our file of history courses, for example, are compensatory courses in United States history; they move chronologically through the centuries from the arrival of the *Mayflower* to the publication of *Sexual Politics*; most typically, the focus falls on the nineteenth century suffrage movement. Other history courses survey a larger historical period or European history alone. In all cases, the materials students read and the subjects they study are new to them, despite a decade or more of history courses in schools and college. The discovery of women's lives and accomplishments produces, in and of itself, an effect beyond the normal expectations of the classroom. We can describe it as *contagious energy*, both intellectual and emotional in its source and appearance. It is as though women students, reading the lives of such women as Anne Hutchinson, Lucretia Mott, Sojourner Truth, Margaret Fuller, "catch" their vital purposes, their fire and commitment. There is also some anger, as Wendy Martin writes and as our own experience has confirmed, when materials on women's lives are either difficult to find or wholly unavailable. The bias in history texts and biographies provides further justification for study and research. Characteristic is the compensatory use of feminist writings (Wollstonecraft, Mill, Gilman, for example) and histories of feminism (Flexner, O'Neill, Sinclair, Lerner), as well as new source books (Kraditor, Schneir).

On the other hand, the writings of several feminist historians emphasize another view of history altogether, one that would not focus on major historical leaders of either sex, and would not be limited to politics or economics. "We have to create a history in which man is no longer the measure," Lerner writes, "but *men* and *women* are the measure." The "new questions" we have to ask of the past are "interdisciplinary questions." Similarly, Linda Gordon writes;

> We need histories of many social phenomena for which there *are* sources available, but of which historians have not before seen the importance: a history of birth control, of sexual reform movements, of childraising, of women's work in their homes, of courtship, but above all we need histories of general economic, political and cultural developments from a feminist point of view.

Gordon's program in women's history at the Cambridge-Goddard Institute reflects her views, and Lerner has organized a program in women's history at Sarah Lawrence College. It is interesting that both programs offer M.A. degrees. At the undergraduate level, another curricular sign of new feminist thinking about history is the handful of courses on the history of the family offered not by sociologists but by historians.

Unlike courses in history, traditional literature courses are noteworthy for the presence of women as fictional characters or the subjects of men's poetic fantasies. Of ninety-six literature syllabi, fifty-eight survey stereotypes of sex roles and images of women in traditional bodies of literature, mainly fiction, and mainly American and British. A fairly frequent ploy is the contrast between nineteenth and twentieth century writers, male and female. Usually, there are more male than female writers considered; usually, the female writers are predictable (Austen, Eliot, Woolf, Plath, Lessing, and Olsen are favorites). Only rarely does the list exclude women writers entirely. Most reading lists include ideological writers, especially Friedan, Millett, and de Beauvoir, and in several syllabi, topics are organized thematically to follow de Beauvoir's chapters.

Just as most history courses are compensatory, most literature courses are consciousness-raising. The line between the two is probably impossible to draw, and obviously both kinds of courses accomplish both ends. But on the whole, women learn to read not new texts or those on new subject areas (as in history), but with new perceptions. Students (and teachers) may be heard to exclaim, "Now I have to go back and reread all those books I read last year—and everything else besides."

More than history, at least as it is commonly taught, literature is about the lives of fairly ordinary people. For that reason, it is a primary source for cultural definitions of women. Carol Ehrlich, for example, describes her course at the University of Iowa: "depictions of the female will be related to the prevailing legal, social, sexual, and political status of women in American society." Wendy Martin is more explicit:

> because [there are] few women (in fact, no women) in American fiction whose lives are self-actualizing (i.e. who have identities which are not totally dependent on men), we will attempt to analyze the social, economic, and literary reasons why women are presented as passive creatures rather than human beings who lead challenging or even risk-taking lives.

In Martin's course, students contrast the fiction they read with the lives of such "real" women as Stanton, Wright, Fuller, Earhart. The significant *literary* questions—about the absence of "self-actualizing" women—is also an important social question. Students must think about their own lives, as well as those of historical figures and fictional ones. As Selma Burkom, formerly of Kirkland College, now at San Jose State University, puts it, literature courses in women's studies foster the "explicit linking of literature and life" and for that reason their impact on students is profound. The awareness of students moves them to increased consciousness about the lives of women and men in society, including their own personal lives; and to increased understanding of literature as a strong social, even political, force on people's lives.

Relatively rare to begin with, there are now some twenty-one courses that consider only the woman writer. Some of these also focus on stereotypes or attempt to generalize about "women's consciousness," or to "explore female experience" or "personal (as opposed to political) views of feminine problems." Several are particularly interesting augurs for future developments. Bernice Zelditch's course on women poets attempts to answer questions about the "topics" and "forms" women choose, and whether or not women write "important poetry." Priscilla Allen's "Rediscovery of American Women Writers" focuses on Kate Chopin, Christina Stead, and Tess Slesinger, three women with new or no reputations who may be "superior to nearly all of the lesser lights (e.g., Bret Harte, Hamlin Garland) and to many of the greater ones (e.g., Stephen Crane, Frank Norris, W. D. Howells)." "And if they are," Allen continues, "how many other female artists remain forgotten . . .?" Courses like Allen's and Zelditch's move us into the "nature of literary criticism, especially the content of the established canon."

Within the social sciences, women's studies courses are both compensatory and consciousness-raising. Even more than history and literature syllabi, those written by sociologists (fifty-one), economists (six), political scientists (nine), and psychologists (fourteen) are strongly interdisciplinary. A course in economics includes units on the family and (unpaid) household labor; a course in political science includes a section on marriage and property law; a course in psychology focuses on marriage; and a course in sociology is called "The Family." Any one of these courses, moreover, might include some or all of the following topics listed in a single (sociology) syllabus: Differences between Men and Women (biological, psychological, cross-cultural); Varying Patterns of Male and Female Roles and Relations (by class, race, ethnicity); Sex Roles and the Division of Labor (economic and family institutions); the Segregation of the Sexes (friendship networks, single-sex gatherings); Relations Between the Sexes: Which Conceptual Framework? (power relationship, class, majority-minority); Attempts to Transform Sex Roles (alternatives, problems, and prospects).[11]

One third of the sociology courses, and most of the other courses in the social sciences are, not surprisingly, "general" courses, introductions to the status of women in the United States. A handful of "cross-cultural" courses broaden the survey to include women in other parts of the world. Other small groups of sociology courses focus more narrowly on "The Family—And What of Its Future?"; "The Social Dynamics of Sex Roles"; "Socialization of Women"; "The Sociology of the Women's Movement." Several psychology syllabi focus on biological and psychological theories of sex differences, some of which are openly critical of "instinct-based theories." But most survey as well such associated areas as the family, socialization, adolescent behavior, sexuality, discrimination in employment and education, and so on. By and large, syllabi in the social sciences are far lengthier than those in literature, sometimes even those in history. It is not simply the presence of detailed course outlines and itemized reading assignments; often course materials include a bulky bibliography and an elaborate list of research and action projects. In addition, such syllabi may begin with a statement of perspective or a series of strategic questions:

> What are the goals of this struggle—for women and for society? What are the explicit and implicit barriers to a breadth of alternative spheres for women? What are the prospects for social change or the possible advantages for society of the expansion of women's roles? Is equality a realistic goal? Can society reconcile the implementation of equal rights of women with the responsibilities attendant upon the female of the species?[12]

In addition to their significant focus on the future and strategies for social change, the general impression of these syllabi is of "heaviness"— lengthy reading assignments, detailed written analyses required, and complex projects. A typical undergraduate course calls for the reading of ten books and a dozen or more journal articles, the ubiquitous journal keeping ("in which the sociology and social psychology of their own sex-based status may be recorded and interpreted"), and a research paper or project. As a group, these courses are more research-minded than literature or history courses.

New Developments: Courses in Professional Schools

While initial courses in schools of law, education, social work, nursing, theology, and medicine have taken the form of "general" introductions to women's studies, a significant number are specialized and research and action oriented. Law courses are most interesting in this respect and far ahead of the rest. As Aleta Wallach writes of a course developed at UCLA, "We consciously tried to avoid a purely legalistic approach because we learned from the failure of 'Law, Lawyers, and Social Change,' a compulsory first year class on racial discrimination, that strict case analysis was an empty exercise." The seminar, which included nine women and six men, was organized, therefore, around "two material or product goals":

> 1) To bring materials to the law library as the start of a permanent collection of materials on women and 2) to prepare individual papers which would also be added to the library collection for further reference.

In other law courses, students work as research teams, not only on employment, family and criminal law, but on constitutional law, laws concerning "control of the body," government benefits, media, education, and public accommodations. In a course offered on the UCLA campus by Riane Eisler, students were asked to group themselves into research teams to work on such projects as the following:

> Five hundred family dissolution cases under the new (post 1970) California family law will be chosen at random. The files will be examined to determine the results (e.g. child custody, division of property, child and spousal support). Students will follow up the women in the cases. A questionnaire will be devised by the students dealing with such matters as financial credit problems, insurance, child support, child care, employment readjustment, personal readjustment, etc. The resulting evaluation of the new law should consider such questions as the husband's present exclusive control of the community property, the possibility of state funding for vocational retraining for housewives, as well as specific legislative recommendations to improve California family law.

In every case, students were asked to produce "specific legislative proposals."

Graduate and undergraduate courses in schools of education seem firmly committed to research projects. Students are "encouraged to conduct a field project" and to report on progress to their peers. Such projects may involve observation of teachers in classrooms as well as investigation into parental attitudes or children's behavior. Similarly, the single example of a course offered by a school of social work (State University of New York at Buffalo, School of Social Policy and Community Services) emphasizes the word "practice" without scanting theoretical considerations. Topics for reading and discussion include: Caseworkers as Models for Identification; The Psychology of Women; The Female Caseworker—Problems of Self-Definition; Casework and Reproduction; Special Groups of Women—The Adolescent Girl, the Middle-Aged Woman; The Advocate and Social Worker Roles in Casework. The instructor, Mary Schwartz, describes her dual goals:

> The purpose of this course will be to explore the significance of certain new perspectives on women for social work practice. The emphasis is on the word "practice." Students will be expected to examine their own work in field placement. This will involve an exploration of attitudes and values and a broad look at agency practice. Casework materials will be analyzed with a view toward reexamining basic social work concepts from newly-emerging points of view. Articles from the women's liberation movement will be looked at critically.

Courses in other professional schools have been slow to develop. We know of only one women's studies course in each of the following schools:

nursing, medicine, home economics, city planning. Graduate courses are, thus far, similarly occasional.

Additional Trends: Some Conclusions

A handful of new undergraduate courses suggests that additional departments will continue to inaugurate women's studies in foreign languages (including classics), in art history, music, theater, film, and speech. The latter is especially interesting when combined with the history of women's speech making. Students in a course taught by Martha Weisman of The City College of New York are studying the "Rhetoric of Women Activists in the United States," past and present. Other efforts at isolating more sophisticated interdisciplinary curricular segments for "advanced" or "specialized" courses have come chiefly from professors of literature and history. Maureen B. Flory, of Mt. Holyoke's Latin Department, for example, offers a course called "Roman Women: Fictional and Historical"; Annette Baxter at Barnard offers a history course called "Autobiographies, Diaries, Letters"; Jenny Knauss at Mundelein gives a history course on feminist ideological writing (from Wollstonecraft to Firestone). In a few instances—Anne Driver (history) and Florence Howe (literature) at Old Westbury, Adele Simmons (psychology) and Zella Luria (history) at Tufts—such courses are team-taught, and cross-listed in two departments.

To summarize so fluid a movement may be futile. Yet certain conclusions seem obvious, and others plausible, even though we are reporting a scant two-year development in women's studies courses. First, there is little sign of consciousness-raising courses per se; yet all courses are invariably consciousness-raising. Second, most courses are rigorous in traditional (and some in nontraditional) terms—readings, reports, papers, projects. The general tone is of an intellectual feast long denied adherents hungry for its goodies, whether historical or statistical reports or experimental studies or novels and poems by women. In our own field, where ennui tends to dominate through and beyond graduate school, the discovery or rediscovery of women writers and the review of traditional (male) literary texts currently provides the chief excitement. In a recent essay, Wendy Martin insists upon the importance of "intellectually solid" women's studies courses "to give feminism academic legitimacy." In sum, whether because of the inherent interest in or novelty of the subject matter, or because of the need for "legitimacy," women's studies courses have raised the consciousness of participants chiefly, although not exclusively, through the study of particular texts, reports, experiments, issues, and ideas. At the same time, through many of the syllabi and all of the essays (and our conversations with teachers and students), there is another note:

courses depend upon the participants, and courses are arranged intention-ally to affect those lives further in some significant manner. As Ruth Cowan recently put it, her interdisciplinary women's studies course at State University of New York at Stony Brook was judged by its partici-pants as successful "*academic* consciousness-raising." As a descriptive term, "*academic* consciousness-raising" will probably please few parti-sans of women's studies, and fewer movement women or academics. We believe it is a useful term, nevertheless, despite the negative connotation of "academic" (meaning without effect or empty of value, as pejorative-ly: "just an academic exercise"). We think it is useful because it describes in a single phrase the tensions of women's studies that may either split the movement or provide its strength.

One reason for the ease with which the opening wedge of women's studies courses was achieved is the essential conservatism of higher educa-tion: it is always easier for departments and individuals to *add* the "new" to the curriculum than to *re-form* the "old." On the other hand, there is also in academe a tendency to control the power of the "new." We have often been asked whether we see women's studies courses as a temporary stopgap, filling a need for compensatory education only long enough to allow faculty to incorporate new materials, writers, studies, into their "regular" courses. Several years ago, we might have viewed this prospect as pleasantly inevitable. We believe now that such a view was at best short-sighted.

The predominantly male faculty and administration has not looked with favor upon women's studies, nor will it, we believe, once it is clear that such studies may change people's lives, at least by altering their ex-pectations and demands. We think that it is realistic to expect reluctance either to incorporate women's studies materials into "regular" courses (or possibly, an incapacity to deal well with such materials), as well as a di-minishing willingness to allow the proliferation of separate women's stud-ies courses.

In one respect, clashes between advocates of women's studies courses and other faculty are inevitable. Since women's studies focuses distinc-tively on problem-solving (rather than on a discrete area of knowledge for its own sake), its effect should be manifest: the more "successful" the course, the more profound its impact on the lives of students going on to other courses or out into graduate school or the community. Given the maleness of higher education, as well as the male biases for the nonaffec-tive domain and against change, women's studies advocates ought to be prepared for at least several years of suspicion if not neglect and hostility.

On the other hand, there is an additional, if pleasanter, tension. If academics are suspicious of "consciousness-raising" and "activist" ele-ments in women's studies courses, movement women are equally suspi-cious or sometimes scornful of "academics" and their work. We regard this tension as necessary, inevitable, and even healthy for women's studies, for we believe that knowledge ought to be responsible to people and relevant to social issues. Students and teachers need to be jabbed with questions about how they are spending their time, to what problems have they given priority, whose research are they doing. Are they working for an administration or a government interested in pacifying demands or for women interested in change? Many feminist scholars whose syllabi, essays, classes, and conversations we have come to know understand this tension creatively. Whether they can manage to balance their scholarly and activist concerns and at the same time sustain and increase their base and power on the university campus remains to be seen. To a very great extent, the future lies in the direction of programs.

Programs

The geography of women's studies programs follows closely the geography of the women's movement up the west coast from San Diego to Seattle, Washington; down the east coast from New England to New Jersey and as far west as Cornell, Buffalo, and Pittsburgh. And this is no happy coincidence, for unlike single courses, women's studies programs are political as well as educational entities. Their existence usually means official recognition and physical space, often funds, and sometimes the technical status of a department, with the accompanying powers to hire personnel, organize curriculum, and recommend students for degrees. Such a program with close relationships both to the women's movement and to the general community of women on campus and off might be a formidable vehicle for educational and social change.

We say "might" for two reasons. First, the precedents for this vision of social change are not altogether auspicious; second the strategy itself may be suspect. The strategic theory for a separatist program like black studies or women's studies depends on a belief in alternative structures or parallel institutions. A similar conception lay behind the free university and experimental college movement. If the host institution cannot be changed, build a smaller one beside it, or even inside it: the alternative institution should thus be able to succor its inhabitants (students) in ways that are especially strengthening and thus turn them into "agents of change"; at the same time the alternative institution should provide its host (the university, or other departments) with a model for imitation, perhaps making change more likely. We have written elsewhere and at length about the misfirings of parallel institutions conceived as vehicles for changing large, host institutions. At San Francisco State's Experimental College, for example, the prevailing motto of the students was "blackmail the institution with quality." Needless to say, it did not work. Theoretically, the larger, traditional unit would simply "wish" to imitate the novel, younger, obviously "superior" experiment. The theory is suspect for several reasons, but chiefly because it imagines that institutional change can occur without struggle, even without collision.[13]

What the model accomplishes is separatism, a goal that may be useful for certain short-range purposes. With reference to black studies, Nathan Hare calls these purposes "therapeutic," that is, building "ethnic confidence." It is possible to argue the necessity of separatism as a primary step toward social change. Groups need "turf—a piece of "liberated territory"—and the space and time with which to plan for the future. Two dangers are obvious, however. First, running an "experimental college" or a department is a full-time job; second, it seems to be more difficult for an established department than for an insurgent one to maintain vital relationships with the communities around it.

For some of the reasons above, women's studies programs, in their first year of operation, do not appear to be moving toward separatist models. Perhaps they have learned hard lessons from previous educational reformers or from the experience of black studies programs. In any event, they are trying to have the best of both worlds: some separatism for the sake of building strength and community; but a continuing presence in all aspects of university life and structure.

The dominant model of organization among programs may be described as "interdepartmental," or what Sacramento State College women call "decentralized." The pattern has been for individuals teaching women's studies courses in various departments to come together and declare themselves a "program." In several instances students, staff, and community people, including faculty wives, have joined faculty in their deliberations concerning the program's structure or center.

At Portland State University, for example, a group of women and men teachers and students met last spring to discuss the women's studies courses then being offered as part of regular departmental work. They decided to publish a "catalog," announcing courses as a group, and in effect establishing "a shadow or underground department of women's studies which was student-controlled and free of administrative interference." When the university asked the "Ad Hoc Women's Institute and Resource Center" to request official recognition, a lengthy debate preceded their sensible conclusion:

> In the end, we decided that since our proposal for a certificate program in women's studies was not likely to reach the appropriate committee of the Oregon State Board of Higher Education for at least one year, and more likely two, that we would submit a proposal *pro forma*, but would put our efforts into continuing to build our independent Women's Studies Program organically, and according to our needs.

Even where programs have not been so dramatically insurgent—at Pittsburgh, Washington, Richmond, San Francisco State, and Buffalo, for example, where they asked for and received official recognition, funds, space, and some staffing—organization remains decentralized. At the universities of Pittsburgh and Washington, where women students and faculty pressed this year for official recognition of women's studies programs, they won the votes needed in committee after committee throughout the university hierarchy.[14] At Pittsburgh, the College of Arts and Sciences requested sufficient funds from the university's instructional budget for the appointments of five feminists to provide the nucleus of a women's studies program. The five would be appointed to particular departments by a joint decision of those departments and a women's studies search committee. All but the director of the new program would teach half-time in women's studies, half-time in a department. As of late spring, three women had been appointed, none at senior level.

At the University of Washington the women's studies program is located in "General and Interdisciplinary Studies," a division of Arts and Sciences that incorporates some dozen interdisciplinary programs. A search is on for a director, to be appointed jointly to a department and to women's studies. The director will coordinate the program, recruiting teachers from feminists on the faculty or among the graduate students. She may also, as in a number of programs, influence the recruitment and hiring of feminists useful both to departments and to women's studies. At the University of New Mexico, where a search is also on for a director of a new program in women's studies, the president has notified departments and deans that new female appointments are to be made only after consultation with the women's studies search committee.

At Sacramento State, where the women's studies program was given ultimate control over a full budget line and three-quarters of another budget line, the program has attempted, with only moderate success, to influence the selection of new faculty members. In several instances, departments preferred to appoint nonfeminist or antifeminist women to the candidates proposed by the women's studies program. Similar departmental behavior has been reported by other programs as well, and it is clear that if the decentralized or interdepartmental model of organization is to work, women's studies programs must gain the power to negotiate with departments about new appointments.

At Buffalo, where programs are called "colleges," the "College of Women's Studies" provides first, "a focused place" on campus where women can come together not only for community and solidarity but "to exchange perspectives and develop new ideas . . . new directions for research"; second, it functions also as a "base" from which "to support efforts in all the departments and professional schools to improve their curricula with respect to the needs and realities of women's lives." The goals of programs are dual: *to draw into* their centers, courses, and research activity students, faculty, and members of the general community; *to move outward* to affect other areas of the institution. Thus, the internal structures of women's studies programs must necessarily be somewhat fluid, a decentralized *network* rather than a traditional bureaucracy.

We find this organizational model attractive because it avoids stuffing women into a corner of the campus (or the society) "to do their own thing." Women's studies courses need centers and programs, but they need also the structures or networks that allow them to do their work in the world. Such networks might extend not only into all areas of the campus (nonacademic as well as departmental ones) but also into the community—into schools, libraries, parents' groups, and so on. Given the notion of networks, women's studies programs might organizationally avoid the isolation that academic departments ordinarily suffer; at the same time, they might also be more realistically equipped to manage their educational innovations.

Most programs have not been established with degree-granting power. The notable exceptions are the University of Washington (which conferred its first A.B. degree in June of 1972), Richmond (City University of New York), San Francisco State, and Douglass (Rutgers, New Jersey). Several California programs (Sacramento, Long Beach, and Fresno) have recently applied for the power to offer "minors." In general, however, the aim of programs has been to provide a group of elective courses, the chief educational function of which is both consciousness-raising and compensatory: to compensate for the deficiency of regular course offerings and to raise women's levels of aspiration.

Barnard's programmatic statement justifies its eleven-course program of electives:

> The question arises whether the inclusion of courses on women might upset our balanced curriculum and weaken its professional approach. If we acknowledge that the purpose of a liberal arts curriculum is not merely to provide preprofessional preparation for our students, but also to give them an appreciation of their cultural heritage, then, in an institution where women are educated, it is our duty to give them an awareness of their legacy as women. The nature of that legacy is riddled with problems of sexual definition. Since positive answers cannot be supplied, it is even more urgent to place the "women question" within many scholarly perspectives. In so doing, our students will become aware of the variety of roles women have played, of the social and economic necessities which prompted them, and also of the dilemmas women have faced and the resources they have called upon.

To make a similar point, feminists at The State University of New York at Buffalo quoted from the undergraduate catalogue—"Education must be designed to liberate students from the confines of a narrow vision, to reach full potential"—and called for the establishment of a "College of Women's Studies" that will "begin to meet our needs as women." Whatever their tone, the programs state more openly than individual courses their educational mission and/or activist commitment. Portland, for example, aims to produce women who are "intellectual activists"; Goddard, women "able to act." And at Sacramento, Portland, Washington, and Richmond the connections between programs and local women's movements are clearly announced, although the details of such relationships are not characterized.

At the same time, whether the programs are collections of discrete "electives," or whether they are organized to constitute a "major," the curricular demands on students are, characteristically, rigorous. Portland's threefold description of academic purpose is typical: first, scholarly research with an emphasis on an interdisciplinary "problem-centered" approach; second, the development of new perspectives in teaching and class participation; third, the encouragement of new feminist writing and criticism. At Buffalo, the three-pronged curriculum calls for "integration" between "knowledge" and "action": first, theoretical courses, organized around problems, history, and social change; second "study and field work courses" resulting either in research or the development of strategies for change or alternate institutions; third, "basic skills" for women—especially in "male technology traditionally denied to them." (Such skills courses—in auto mechanics, self-defense, audiotape machines, etc.—also are offered at Goddard, Laney, Richmond, and Sacramento.) In most programs, an introductory course initiates students both to an interdisciplinary approach as well as to "sisterhood," and especially into "collective" ways of working both as intellectuals and activists.

Although individual courses may be innovative, a women's studies program is an additional learning ground for students, since most programs are attempting novel governing structures. Instead of operating through the usual departmental chairperson or by vesting authority in tenured members of a department, such programs have organized decision-making "boards" or "committees." Indeed, in the several instances of Sacramento, Portland, and Buffalo, there has been an agreement *not to* name a single person as "director" or "coordinator," however inconvenient or startling that may be for the university. On the Sacramento board, students have three votes, faculty two, and staff one. Portland began with a one person, one vote rule for major decisions, with meetings open to all; but as it grew in size (an enrollment of over 1,500 students during the academic year 1971–1972) they decided upon a seven-person board, and chose members by drawing out of a hat the names of those who had volunteered for such duty. At Buffalo, the governing structure is part of the experiment in innovation, with a "council of elected representatives" drawn complexly from among students in courses, from "course collectives" (i.e., groups of teachers who work together), and from staff. It is difficult to generalize about the effectiveness of the variety of governing boards in operation, especially at the end of the first (or at most the second) year of operation. But the issue is a critical one not only for internal growth and development of programs, but also as a means of ensuring the type of decentralization useful for social change.

Faculty appointed jointly to a women's studies program and to a traditional department must be prepared to expend the political energy necessary for functioning in both worlds, as part of a network for change. Some students find themselves similarly divided and their commitment strained. In a couple of instances, attempts at new governing structures have resulted in serious "splits" within programs and decreased effectiveness in community and campus activities.[15] In all cases, the reports we have had confirm the difficulties of innovation—lengthy, time-consuming meetings, debates, strained energies and relationships, and a relatively slow process of decision making. The energy for such effort, nevertheless, has not waned.

Do we recommend working toward programs? Yes, in part because women on campuses need organizational structures within which to work for change, and not simply on short-term goals. Resistance to most forms of organization is profound both from women on campus and off. The suspicion of women in the movement about the allegedly inevitable elitism of organizations, their tendency to spur competitive drives among people, whether male or female, has in part been responsible for the erosion or demise of such large urban liberation groups as there were even a year or two ago. And while academic women are not averse to elitist organizations—indeed, they must function in them—they need more than their numbers if they are to effect institutional change in their own departments, let alone the campus as a whole, or the community. Hence, we recommend not only working toward programs, but conceiving of them in deliberately nonbureaucratic, antielitist forms.

A June 1972 release from "Women's Studies at California State University at San Francisco," reports a neatly negative decision of the "Advisory Committee" (their form of governing board): "To *not* work toward a separate 'Women's Studies' department since our major purpose is the recognition of women's important 'place' at every level in all disciplines rather than its 'special' character." And yet the same release announces not only an interdisciplinary major "with a *Focus on Women*" (twenty-eight courses from which to choose), but a similar master's program. The Advisory Committee also functions to "sponsor research proposals"; to advise "in the area of affirmative action for women faculty"; to support several adjunct organizations—the Women's Alliance (faculty) and Independent Campus Women (a student action organization). In addition, the

Advisory Committee has begun to function off-campus in "related activities," a "newly organized Bay Area Consortium on Continuing Education for Women," and, with twenty colleges in the Bay area, "in the development of a center or clearinghouse of information and referral for women students." In less than two years, then, women's studies at San Francisco State has begun to take on the appearance of a "network" without diminishing its role as an intellectual center for students' new curricular interests and needs.

In general, small or moderately large campuses have sparked programs more quickly than multiversities, at least partly because of the availability of feminists on faculties and their relationship to local or national women's movements. One useful strategy for the future envisions affirmative action officers (on large university campuses especially) working closely with departments and with women's studies programs to facilitate the hiring (rather than the firing) of feminists with the energy to organize for change.

At Buffalo, the women wrote of their educational goals: "This education will not be an academic exercise; it will be an ongoing process to change the ways in which women think and behave. It must be part of the struggle to build a new and more complete society." Goddard's feminist studies program concludes with the hopes that their students will "leave . . . not only with a body of knowledge, but a reason for learning it, a context to fit it in, but most important, a strong sense of an inner core of self that most women never develop. We want them to be able to act on the world, and in the world."

We choose to conclude on the rhetoric of idealism because that is where women's studies is at the end of its first few years. Such rhetoric will seem distinctly familiar to those who have survived the efforts of the sixties to change higher education, to place it at the service of people who need knowledge to solve their problems. Women in the forefront of academic change today build on that decade of work and hope. Because of their numbers, their willingness to learn from the past, their energy, and the breadth implicit in the feminist perspective, they may succeed where others before them have failed.

Notes

Author's Note: We wish to acknowledge the assistance of grant number RO-5085-72-54 from the National Endowment for the Humanities. Florence Howe is project director and Carol Ahlum research associate; the title, "Literature, History, and the Education of Women."

1. The Modern Language Association's Commission on the Status of Women in the Profession published, for distribution at the December 1970 convention, a list of those courses under the title "Current Guide to Female Studies."

2. The exception to the generalizations maintained is American studies, although it, too, is a relatively recent phenomenon and its reputation has been not unmixed. The existence of American studies programs and departments, it should be noted, has provided an institutional precedent for newer ethnic or area studies. Alternatively, at some institutions, black studies and women's studies have been subsumed under the department aegis of American studies.

3. Indeed, *The American College*, published in 1962 (ed. Nevitt Sanford), is a product of a decade's work—the fifties. It reports, in essence, the "failure" of higher education to make an impact on the students that pass through its doors and out into the world. Coincidentally, Students for a Democratic Society published also in 1962 *The Port Huron Statement*, a sixty-page pamphlet that reaches a similar conclusion. For a full discussion of these reports as well as the free university movement see Lauter and Howe, *The Conspiracy of the Young*, chap. 4.

4. We understand, of course, that on a few campuses in the sixties several women were teaching such courses as women's history—Annette Baxter at Barnard is a prominent example. We would argue, however, that her action was then a private, rather than a public or "movement" concern.

5. For an enlightening discussion that supports this thesis indirectly, see Alice Rossi, "*Sex Equality: Beginnings of Ideology*," pp. 3–6, 16.

6. Of the 610 courses listed in *The New Guide to Current Female Studies* (ed. Ahlum and Howe), 71 are team-taught by 174 faculty members, 20 of whom are male.

7. It is not possible here to review the literature on sex bias and the public schools. See Florence Howe, "Sexual Stereotypes Start Early," *Saturday Review*, October 16, 1971, pp. 76–82, 92–94; also *Report on Sex Bias in the Public Schools*, New York Chapter of National Organization for Women, 1971; also the entire February 1972 issue of *School Review*, 80(2).

8. While we have received information about some two hundred additional courses, these are not yet organized for publication.

9. The listing in *The New Guide to Current Female Studies*, on which we have based our statistics, is a good example of eastern chauvinism, or at least of poor communication between east and west coasts. A recent trip to the west coast has brought to light several facts, too late unfortunately to do more than include them here. There are twice as many programs on the west coast as on the east coast.

10. The sentence describes euphemistically the fate of women "pioneers" in women's studies at such institutions as Fresno State College, Wayne State University, The University of Wisconsin at Madison and Whitewater, Goucher College, etc., though it is also fair to add that several of these women have been welcome elsewhere. It may be surprising, but women have lost their jobs for developing and teaching successfully women's studies courses.

11. From an unpublished syllabus by Barrie Thorne, Michigan State University, winter 1972; course title: "Sex Roles in Contemporary Society," Sociology 866, section 1.

12. From an unpublished syllabus by Beatrice Bain, San Francisco State College, spring 1971, course title: "Women as a Social Force."

13. See Lauter and Howe, chap. 4.

14. It is interesting to contrast this achievement in 1971–72 with the experience of graduate students at Northwestern University who in 1968–69 attempted

to take a women's studies program proposal through appropriate committees where it was stripped, bit by bit, of its purpose and being.

15. See, for one account of such a split, Roberta Salper's essay on San Diego State's program: "Women's Studies: San Diego State College."

Bibliography

Ahlum, Carol, and Howe, Florence, eds. *The New Guide to Current Female Studies*. Pittsburgh: KNOW, Inc., 1971.

Arnesen, Nancy. "Teaching Women's Studies in Community College." Paper read at Modern Language Association Convention, Chicago, 1971.

Barauch, Grace. "Research in Psychology Relevant to the Situation of Women." Paper read at the conference on Women and Education: A Feminist Perspective, November 5–7, 1971, sponsored by the University of Pittsburgh and the Modern Language Association Commission on the Status of Women, 1971.

Bart, Pauline B. "Why Women's Studies?" In *Female Studies V*, edited by Siporin, 94–99.

Benson, Ruth Crego. "Pittsburgh Diary: Reflection on USOE Institute;" "Crisis: Women in Education." In *Female Studies IV*, edited by Showalter and Ohmann, 1–7.

Chamberlain, Kathleen. "Women Students at Manhattan Community College." Paper read at Modern Language Association Convention, Chicago, 1971.

Chapman, Gretel. "Women and the Visual Arts." In *Female Studies V*, edited by Siporin, 38–39.

Chmaj, Betty E., ed. *American Women and American Studies*. Pittsburgh: KNOW, Inc., 1971.

Clarenbach, Kathryn F. "Human Status for Women." Paper read at Midwest Association for Physical Education of College Women, 1970.

Cohen, Audrey. "Women and Higher Education: Recommendations for Change." *Phi Delta Kappan*, 53 (1971): 164–67.

Davis, Devra Lee. "The Woman in the Moon: Towards an Integration of Women's Studies." In *Female Studies V*, edited by Siporin, 17–28.

Farians, Elizabeth. "Institute for the Study, Redefinition and Resocialization of Women: A Program for Colleges and Universities." Unpublished paper, 1971.

Ferguson, Mary Anne. "The Sexist Image of Women in Literature." In *Female Studies V*, edited by Siporin, 77–83.

Foster, Ginny. "On Being 'Femmes des Lettres.' " Unpublished paper, 1971.

Ginsburg, Ruth Bader. "Treatment of Women by the Law: Awakening Consciousness in the Law Schools." *Valparaiso Law Review*, Symposium Issue, 5 (1971): 480–88.

Gordon, Linda. "Why Women's History?" In *Female Studies V*, edited by Siporin, 49–52.

Greenwald, Maurine. "Women's History in America." In *Female Studies II*, edited by Howe, 65–73.

Hare, Nathan. "What Black Studies Means to a Black Scholar." *Integrated Education*, 8 (1970): 8–15.

Hoffman, Nancy Jo. "A Class of Our Own." In *Female Studies IV*, edited by Showalter and Ohmann, 14–27.

Hoffman, Nancy Jo. "Reading Women's Poetry: The Meaning and Our Lives." *College English*, 34 (1972): 48–72.

Howe, Florence, ed. *Female Studies II*. Pittsburgh: KNOW, Inc., 1970.

Howe, Florence. "Identity and Expression: A Writing Course for Women." *College English* 32 (1971): 963–71; abbreviated version in *Female Studies II*, edited by Howe, 1–4.

Howe, Florence. "Feminism, Fiction, and the Classroom." *Soundings: An Interdisciplinary Journal* 55 (1972): 369–89.

Howe, Florence, and Ahlum, Carol, eds. *Female Studies III*. Pittsburgh: KNOW, Inc., 1971.

Knowles, Mary Tyler. "All Male Students and Women's Liberation." *In Female Studies IV*, edited by Showalter and Ohmann, 35–39.

Krouse, Agate Nesaule. "A Feminist in Every Classroom." In *Female Studies V*, edited by Siporin, 1–6.

Landy, Marcia. "Women, Education, and Social Power." In *Female Studies V*, edited by Siporin, 53–63.

Lauter, Paul, and Howe, Florence. *The Conspiracy of the Young*. Cleveland: World, 1970.

Lerner, Gerda. "Teaching Women about Women." In *Female Studies II*, edited by Howe, 86–88.

Lerner, Gerda. "On the Teaching and Organization of Feminist Studies." In *Female Studies V*, edited by Siporin, 34–37.

Lewis, Eleanor J. "What Women's Studies Can Do for Women's Liberation." Paper read at the conference on Women and Education: A Feminist Perspective, November 5–7, 1971, sponsored by the University of Pittsburgh and the MLA Commission on the Status of Women, 1971.

Martin, Wendy. "Teaching Women's Studies—Some Problems and Discoveries." In *Female Studies IV*, edited by Showalter and Ohmann, 9–13.

Miller, Lindsay. "Newest Course on Campus: Women's Studies." *New York Post* (series), (May 22–27, 1972).

Oltman, Ruth. "Campus 1970: Where Do Women Stand?" Washington, D.C.: American Association of University Women, 1970.

Reeves, Nancy. "Feminine Subculture and Female Mind." In *Female Studies V*, edited by Siporin, 84–93.

Reuben, Elaine. "Feminist Criticism in the Classroom, or 'What Do You Mean *We*, White Man?' " Paper read at Midwest Modern Language Association Convention, Detroit, 1971.

Robinson, Lillian. "The Sexual Order." In *Female Studies II*, edited by Howe, 42–43.

Rossi, Alice. "Sex Equality: Beginnings of Ideology." *The Humanist*, (September/October 1969): 3–6, 16.

Salper, Roberta. "Women's Studies: San Diego State College." *Ramparts*, 10 (1971): 56–60.

Salzman-Webb, Marilyn. "Feminist Studies: Frill or Necessity." In *Female Studies V*, edited by Siporin, 64–76.

Schmidt, Dolores Barracano. "Sexism in Textbooks." In *Female Studies V*, edited by Siporin, 29–33.

Sherwin, Susan S. "Women's Studies as a Scholarly Discipline: Some Questions for Discussion." In *Female Studies V*, edited by Siporin, 114–16.

Showalter, Elaine. "Introduction: Teaching about Women, 1971." In *Female Studies IV*, edited by Showalter and Ohmann, i–xii.

Showalter, Elaine. "Women and the Literary Curriculum." *College English*, 32 (8): 855–62.

Showalter, Elaine, and Ohmann, Carol, eds. *Female Studies IV*. Pittsburgh: KNOW, Inc., 1971.

Siporin, Rae Lee, ed. *Female Studies V*. Pittsburgh: KNOW, Inc., 1972.

Somerville, Rose. "Women's Studies." *Today's Education*, 60 (1971): 35–37.

Stimpson, Catharine R. "Women as Scapegoats." In *Female Studies V*, edited by Siporin, 7–16.

Strong, Brian. "Teaching Women's History Experimentally." In *Female Studies IV*, edited by Showalter and Ohmann, 40–47.

Tobias, Sheila, ed. *Female Studies I*. Pittsburgh: KNOW, Inc., 1970.

Tobias, Sheila. "Female Studies—An Immodest Proposal." In *Female Studies I*, edited by Tobias.

Tobias, Sheila. "Female Studies for State University of New York." Paper read at Second Caucus on Women's Rights at State University of New York at Albany, 1970.

Tobias, Sheila, and Kusnetz, Ella. "Teaching Women's Studies: An Experiment at Stout State." *Journal of Home Economics*, 64 (1972): 17–21; also published in *Female Studies V*, edited by Siporin, 100–113.

Trecker, Janice Law. "Women in United States History High School Textbooks." *Social Education*, 35 (1971): 619ff.

Trecker, Janice Law. "Women's Place is in the Curriculum." *Saturday Review*, 54 (1971): 83–86, 92.

Trecker, Janice Law. "The Amazing, Invisible Woman." Paper read at New York State Conference on the Social Studies, New York City, 1972.

Wallach, Aleta. "Genesis of a 'Women and the Law' Course: The Dawn of Consciousness at UCLA Law School." *Journal of Legal Education*, 24 (1972): 309–53.

West, Anne Grant. "Women's Liberation or, Exploding the Fairy Princess Myth." *Scholastic Teacher Jr/Sr High*, (November 1971): 6–19.

White, Barbara A. "Up from the Podium: Feminist Revolution in the Classroom." In *Female Studies IV*, edited by Showalter and Ohmann, 28–34.

Literacy and Literature

(1973)

Following a write-in campaign, organized by Carol Oh-mann, professor of English at Wesleyan University, I became second vice president in 1971, first vice president in 1972, and then president of the Modern Language Association in 1973. At the end of that year, I delivered the following essay as the presidential address of that year's annual convention. It was published in PMLA in 1974.

IN A NOVEL by Ernest J. Gaines called *The Autobiography of Miss Jane Pitman*, the fictional author explains his motive for investigating the hundred-year life of his heroine, born a slave: "I teach history," he says, "I'm sure her life's story can help me explain things to my students." In answer to my question, "Why do you read fiction?" a female college student said, five years ago, "Because I want to know what to do with my life—I want to learn how to live." Before I could begin to discuss *Native Son* with a group of black high school students ten summers ago, one of them asked, "Is it true? Is this a true story? Did it really happen to him [meaning Richard Wright]?" In a recent discussion of Kate Chopin's *The Awakening*, I was startled to hear adult women insisting that the novel's conclusion was "incorrect," "probably a mistake," one student said, or "only symbolic," another offered. In their view, anyone with Edna's knowledge could never choose voluntarily to die. They—my students—would have written the novel differently, and they were deeply disturbed by its image of the hapless woman.

I begin with these vignettes for several reasons. To make palpable not only why some writers write, but why many students read. Literature, in its most ancient and in its most modern forms, illuminates lives, teaches us what is possible, how to hope and aspire, especially as we grow up.

111

Though most of us are teachers, it is all too easy to forget that we touch directly the lives of people in the process of growing up, of deciding how to live, what work to seek, and with what purpose. Because I believe in the importance of the lives we touch, I am glad of this opportunity to talk not only to the members of this Association in its ninetieth year, but also to that larger profession of teachers outside the MLA.

And I speak out of some urgency, not simply as part of the annual ritual of a professional association. This is not a festive year for the teaching of modern languages and literatures. Nor is it a year of anger and protest—against the Vietnam War, against an association bent on meeting in Chicago, against that same association for its indifference about its members' needs and interests—I'm sure some of you remember 1968. Perhaps that was the last fat year for the teachers of modern languages and literatures. Not only at the college and university is this true: 1968 was the last year in which the demand for elementary and secondary teachers exceeded the supply. Tens of thousands of would-be public school teachers are waiting tables this year or clerking in shops, answering phones or monitoring laboratories. English and foreign language teachers are among the most in excess.

Few of us in 1968 recognized the signs that we read painfully today. More Ph.D.'s than jobs, thousands more, and more on the way. Plans for cutting back whole faculties at private and even public colleges, especially in the humanities, even if it means letting tenured faculty go, or encouraging them to retire early. Plans for increasing teaching loads and the size of classes; plans for tenure quotas; plans for the eventual demise, through neglect, of English, French, or other literature majors. And even administrative plans, as at my own new branch of the State University of New York, for a decade of disciplinary development without either English or foreign language departments, without any humanities or arts at all. How do we read these signs today? As paranoia, passing nightmare, or portent of inevitability?

We have all heard administrators say that a surplus market provides institutions with the opportunity to upgrade the faculty, to clean house. It also provides teachers with an imperative to reconsider our direction: to learn to shape the future.

It's not the first time that teachers have attempted to persuade themselves and others of the value of their work and thus, effectively, to hold on to their jobs and gain the power to teach others. The founders of this association in 1883 attempted to promote the teaching of English and modern languages in colleges at a time when the primacy of the classics had not yet been seriously threatened. While carefully avoiding an open competition with those who taught Greek and Latin, the founders believed that "a young man" ought to have "the option of studying any language he pleases," even, presumably, his own. But as they won their polite battle for students, courses, and departments, the gentlemen of the association (who in English began as teachers of rhetoric and composition) became literary scholars first, teachers second. By 1903—only twenty years after the founding of the MLA—the New England MLA was established especially for the discussion of pedagogy, and before another decade had passed, the National Council of Teachers of English had been formed. According to George Winchester Stone, the MLA by 1911 had become "so absorbed in the advancement of research in its field that it was ready to leave to others all talk about teaching and enrollment,"[1] even though, as Stone notes, foreign language enrollments, threatened by the rise of interest in the social sciences, had already begun to decline. Through this century, of course, the teaching of English has grown in importance, not because of any single association, but rather because of the steadily widening base of mass education. English teachers were necessary if an immigrant population was to be made literate, melted into the Anglo-American, and carried into the traditional "mainstream"—though the exact relationship between teaching literacy and the more recent notion of teaching literature and literary analysis remained undefined.

In 1946, Percy Long's resolution to the General Meeting called for a return to the association's "original purpose"—"the advancement of the study of modern languages and literatures"—along with a devotion to research. Under pressure because of declining enrollments, the association also announced its opposition "to curtailment of those subjects [English and foreign languages] in the curricula of colleges and secondary schools." And finally, the resolution called for "the mutual understanding of peoples through understanding of their languages and literatures as essential to the implementing of the social international obligations which our country has undertaken" (*PMLA*, 73, 1958, 37). Thus, more than sixty years after its founding, the MLA rediscovered teaching and, in the process, social utility as a defensive posture. The question, of course, becomes useful for what and for whom.

A wholly historical paper would review that period between 1946 and today: In those twenty-seven years, did this association manage to reestablish the importance if not the primacy of modern languages and literatures? Whose interests were they serving? And did teaching become as central to the association's concerns as scholarship? But the answers to these questions, in broad outline, are obvious, even from our own experience. Despite the massive Foreign Language Programs of the fifties, foreign language departments are in deeper trouble today than they were then. While the MLA's membership has grown in ninety years to thirty thousand, the NCTE's, shorter by twenty years, is two hundred twenty-five thousand. Presumably, the teachers are there, the scholars here. And it is only by some extraordinary series of historical coincidences that I, primarily a teacher rather than a scholar, stand at this podium. I shall use that vantage to attempt what may be only a straw in the winds of educational change.

Perhaps I should interrupt myself to say that, as the year has worn on, and the mail I have had from job-seekers has grown more desperate, I have thought about abandoning my subject and reading from that correspondence. The credentials—including extensive publications—of many being denied tenure this year are awesome; the new crop of Ph.D.'s is impressive, even with regard to teaching experience. And the horror stories about conditions in particular English and modern language departments could fill my time. I shall offer only two particular examples. At a prestigious, private eastern university, all the nontenured faculty in one literature department will be gone in the next several years, all freshman and sophomore courses are in the process of being dropped from the curriculum, and students will, henceforth, crowd into those upper division courses that the tenured faculty will teach. At a large state college, where the teaching of literacy is a pressing need, and where the teaching load is four courses, the faculty will be allowed one elective course each, whether or not those will combine properly to support the existing English majors in residence. If there are not enough courses for a major, the major may be allowed to perish. In addition, no new faculty will be hired, except to teach skills courses, and then on a per-course basis. The principle in both cases is simple: cut costs by cutting humanities, especially literature; where the teaching of composition is a necessity, use your faculty for that purpose; chop away at nontenured faculty and hire "adjuncts" on a per-course basis to teach what additional courses become necessary. Clearly, then, this becomes the fate of those being denied tenure or those bright new Ph.D.'s: if they are lucky, next year they may teach four "skills" courses a term as "adjuncts"—at two or more colleges—and earn the grand sum of $5,600 a year. I do not exaggerate: there are people doing that right now this year. We will see more of it before we see less.

Because the signs I read are bleak, I see no point in hand-wringing or in prescribing band-aids like emergency fellowship programs. I do not think that, unorganized as we are, we can stop the forces that would cheapen higher education for masses of students. Unorganized, we cannot hinder efforts to cut the necessarily rising costs of educating more people; nor perhaps can we prevent even our own demise at the hands of educational managers whose measures are cost-benefits, not learning. As one tiny pulley in a complex economy, we must not offer false hopes to our students, our friends, and colleagues in and out of work. Whether we decide to organize ourselves, and how we do so, and with what allies and purposes—these are not questions I will talk about today in detail. Rather, I would focus on the prior questions—are we worth organizing, caring about? The problem of jobs aside, should English and modern language departments be allowed to atrophy? Are there good reasons why the teaching of literature and language should continue? I want to focus on the question of belief in the value of our work because the failure of conviction, an embarrassment about the value of our teaching and scholarship permeates and demoralizes this profession above all others in academe.

What are the charges against us? The chief charge is irrelevance. We would be fools not to admit that there is basis for that charge, not merely at the level of doctoral dissertation topics and some scholarly research—how often do we ask about the intellectual value of our work?—but also at the level of curriculum. It is not only administrators who are cutting back departments; students are also declining to become our majors, or even to fill our regular courses in their customary numbers, though they will swell special courses in white women or minority writers.

The charge of irrelevance is really, then, two charges, the first from educational managers. As professors of literature, we are allegedly peripheral to a technological world, expendable because literature is merely one of several arts, none of particular significance except to fill leisure time or, in the words of an administrator I know, to expand "intellectual horizons for personal gratification." The humanities thus become useful only for "self-improvement," not essential to people's work, lives, and futures. Again, we would be fools to deny that we have contributed to this view of the humanities by allowing, indeed encouraging, the separation of the teaching of literacy from the study of literature. We may not consciously consider the elementary school teacher a colleague, for example, and yet she is responsible for primary literacy. We assume no responsibility either for her training in literature or for the subliterary texts she offers to children.

Historically, the separation of literacy from literature has rationalized the hierarchal structure of the profession. At the top, the university professor of literature; at the bottom, the elementary school teacher of reading and writing. Their paths may never cross. Between them and similarly separated from each other stand the high school teacher and the two- and four-year college teachers. High school teachers used to be responsible both for continued training in literacy and for the introduction of the student to literature. Increasingly, however, they are assigned to "regular" literature or "remedial" writing courses; increasingly also, as Janet Emig has been discovering, less and less teaching of composition occurs in the high school.[2] Teaching literacy, in our time, has fallen to two-year college teachers, or to the communications department at four-year colleges, while the teaching of literature has become the province mainly of separate English departments, as well as of university professors. If our job market is panicked, it is at least in part because we have trained increasing numbers of highly skilled specialists in literary studies, without equipping them for a world that needs teachers of literacy.

The separation could be justified as a necessary and useful division of labor. After all, one could argue, it is not possible for everyone to know everything, we need specialization and we need some order as well in the learning process. I agree, but I find the order we have established not only ultimately suicidal for the profession, but destructive for students. If professors of literature are, in fact, altogether different people from teachers of literacy, and if only teachers of literacy are necessary for a technological society, it is a simple matter to separate the two groups, especially since they are already made antagonists by a profession that values one above the other. Further, the jobless professors of literature cannot easily become teachers of literacy, since, as graduate students, they learn to be snobs about the very people who might hire them, as well as about those they might have to teach.

Thus, college teachers of communicative skills, like the elementary school teachers in the public school hierarchy, become the necessary proletariat: they cannot be eliminated, but they can be overworked and paid badly. The professors of literature, on the other hand, can be chopped off or cut back in times of economic stringency.

Thus far, the most prestigious graduate school departments have felt the pain only vicariously, through their inability to place graduate students in jobs and, increasingly, through their graduates of four and five years ago, now loose on the job market as well. But it is only a question of time before even those graduate departments must feel the pinch firsthand. If there are no jobs, there must be fewer graduate students; if there are fewer graduate students, there must be fewer jobs for their professors.

The gulf between the teacher of literacy and the professor of literature measures the ill-health of the profession. It is not only a matter of elitism, though that badly divides us. It is also the incapacity of many who have chosen literary study to face the hurly-burly of the remedial writing classroom. Teaching literacy is exciting precisely because it cannot be programmed. Before I could say anything about *Pride and Prejudice* in a class last year, I had to answer a series of questions: "Who provides?" my students wanted to know. "Where does the money come from—even the men in this book don't have to work." We searched the novel for servants and shopkeepers and talked about entailed estates and landed gentry. But in the terms in which I was taught literature, we were "distracted from the central concerns of the novel." The fact is that there are some good reasons for the spread of separate remedial English or communications or skills departments. On the whole, professors of literature have not wanted the job, and not only because it is untidy and full of surprises. Mainly, our qualifications for the job have been insufficient: familiarity with the subject matter called literature is not by itself a key to unlocking students' verbal skills and imaginations. On the contrary, the overrefinement of our professional concerns into narrowing literary specialties (called genres or periods) may cut us off from the contemporary power of language, the current interests of students.

When I teach both literacy and literature in a single course these days, I am part of a women's studies program. I spend less time on form and more on the values embodied in the work. I ask my students to compare their lives to those in the novels, poems, autobiographies, or histories we read. I ask them to listen to the voices in essays and describe the persons they hear. I ask them to listen to their own voices and describe those persons they are. Deliberately, I choose works in which students will and will not find themselves: deliberately, I place male beside female, black beside white, U. S. beside British or European. (I want to be able to place Western beside African or Eastern.) I am neither a teacher of literature nor a teacher of composition—at least not in the old sense in which I once learned to be those two people. I ask my students whether or not they are Paul Morel in *Sons and Lovers* or Marie Rogers in Agnes Smedley's *Daughter of Earth*: we talk and write about the characters' incompatible parents, rival siblings, unhappy love affairs, difficult economic circumstances, longings for education, work, direction, and purpose. I ask my students to project themselves into the lives and minds of Harriet Taylor and John Stuart Mill, or Mr. and Mrs. Ramsay, or of Mariah and Jacob Upshur in Sarah Wright's *This Child's Gonna Live*. My students become literate not simply because they can write sentences or compose paragraphs, but because they learn to write about who they are, where they came from, and where they want to go. They write "identity" papers sometimes, but these are social histories. Literature is not the only way to accomplish my end, but I find that without literature, I could not touch students as I want to.

The second charge of irrelevance has come from students, especially during this past decade. They have queried what we teach and how: the white, middle-class maleness of the curriculum; the isolation of literary from social and historical study; and the pretense of neutrality, that failure of conviction to which I have earlier referred. Our students today are no longer the young men of 1883. Indeed, more than 70 percent of our majors and more than 60 percent of our first-year graduate students are women. Their complaints have led, during these past five years, to reviews of the curriculum. I shall touch only one aspect of that review, specifically to demonstrate that the curriculum has never been and can never be neutral.

It was at first surprising to discover how insistent were the stereotyped patterns of sex-segregated behavior allowed to males and females in books written especially for children. Less than three years ago, for example, no children's book existed in this country in which a woman appeared as a physician, despite the fact that women have been midwives from the earliest times and physicians for more than a hundred years. Less than three years ago, only one picture book, Eve Merriam's *Mommies at Work*, communicated that idea, despite the fact that half of all mothers are part of the paid work force in this country. What version of reality, then, lay in children's books? Careful studies of thousands of children's books—several important ones by members of this association—forced us to acknowledge the consistency of images that help limit the aspirations of women and the potential for expression of men as well.[3] It is no accident that we remember Sleeping Beauty, Cinderella, Little Red Riding Hood, and Snow White. Little girls are supposed to learn to be patient, to wait for the prince to telephone, to expect the kiss that leads to the suburban dream house and the blissful life. Of course little boys learn something from these stories as well: they may be Prince Charmings, but they may also be wolves—it's their choice. The girls in either event are not in control of their lives. And the pattern persists through the most trivial texts to the most elaborate award-winning picture books and fiction. The scholarly studies demonstrate that the curriculum here is not ideologically "free" at all: not that publishers, writers, and teachers have conspired against women, but rather that they reflect unthinkingly the values of a patriarchal culture.

One of the very rare studies of the high school English curriculum effectively illustrates both its similar bias and its socializing power. I cannot take the time to describe the brilliant work of Mary Beaven, but I wish to quote from some of the Cook County, Illinois students who responded to her questions about "Feminine Characters in Literature."[4] She asked girls, "What female character that you have read about in English class would you like to resemble?"; boys, which "would you like to have as a (future) wife?"; and both, which "would you like to have as mother?" Somewhat less than half of each group said "none" to all three questions, I am happy to report, since their choices were so limited: from Scarlett to Juliet for wife, from Melanie to Hester for mother. They offered unsolicited comments instead. From the girls, a sampling:

1. "Since sixth grade, I can't recall reading about any women I admired."

2. "Have never read a book in English class with a strong female character."

3. "In the majority of English classes I've been in, all or most of the literature has been geared toward what the guys in the class would most enjoy as my teachers firmly believed, 'The girls will read anything.' Thus, in class we read of very few female characters."

From the boys, a sampling:

1. "Come to think of it I haven't read many books with strong female characters."

2. "I don't ever recall reading a book which had a woman which impressed me that much."

3. "We have read about so few women in English class that they are hardly worth mentioning. The few we have read about I would not care to have for a wife or mother."

Beaven argues convincingly that the literature programs she has examined "do not present girls with feminine characters with whom they can identify." "Nor do they present boys," she continues, "with feminine characters to whom they can relate." And she concludes by deploring that adolescents do not have "more opportunities to identify with a healthy, feminine role." Indeed, with all the riches of literature—by women as well as men—it is infuriating to consider the poverty of choices offered high school students during four impressionable years, especially when they live in a wasteland of TV, pop music, and film devoted to transforming the banal stereotypes of children's books into the violence of pornography and murder.

The college and university curriculum in English and modern languages from freshman through graduate courses, familiar to most of us here, offers little relief from what I have already described, and with even less excuse, for our majors and graduate students are chiefly women. I am not talking about those special courses we offer in minority literature or in literature by or about women. There are in 1973 more than four hundred women's studies courses in literature alone.[5] And of course that response—the flexibility of departments willing to offer still another elective course—has been exceptional. Still, one course is no substitute for an entire curriculum. Let me tell a story on myself here.

With a male colleague, more than a decade ago and at a women's college, I designed a new sophomore survey course, required of majors but elected by many others as well. I was proud of that course and continued to teach it through the first half of the sixties, despite the fact that (a) all the authors were male; and (b) most of the works described the coming of age of male characters—Wordsworth in *The Prelude*, for example, or Pip in *Great Expectations*; and (c) the only attractive female characters to be found in all the texts assigned were Glumdalclitch and Samuel Butler's Alethea. Any dispassionate review of that curriculum—from *Dr. Faustus* to *The Waste Land*—would declare its maker(s) misogynist. And I should have to agree.

It does, indeed, matter what we teach.

One special power belongs to this profession—and I use that word in its broadest sense here to mean all of us from elementary school through the university. The power of language and storytelling is the power over identity and history, or, as Ellison has said, of "face and race." Literacy is not learning to read *Dick and Jane* or the essays in a freshman reader. Literacy is the power to name the world through the word—as Paulo Freire has put it. He is talking about the Brazilian peasant who, in the process of becoming literate, becomes conscious of the place and power of peasants in the social order, of their history and their future. I would not argue that literacy must necessarily be taught through literature rather than through the study of history or other "disciplines." As I have indicated earlier, the definition of literature is far from settled, and I at least would prefer a broad rather than a narrow one. At the same time, however, for women, for working-class students, and for those who are members of minorities, fiction, autobiography, and poetry are especially powerful: they cannot locate themselves—their "face and race"—in the study of history or philosophy which has, at least until now, ignored them. But the intense passion with which students search for veracity in works of literature—as I indicated in my opening remarks—charges us with special responsibility. As teachers, we have the power of the literary curriculum in our hands.

If we have not used that power well, it is perhaps because most of us are part of a generation taught to think in terms of literary "universals," as though English or French or German—or Western literature together— were all of literature; as though English or French were the only essential languages. If we are still narrow and provincial—chauvinist is the current term—it is not surprising, given our own rearing and education.

From the day I entered kindergarten in the mid-thirties and heard another child chastised for speaking a Yiddish word, I willingly dismissed my heritage—even the word seems old-fashioned now in my mouth—and willingly lost my second language. I lost not only the language but also the literature as well as the culture. I became truly American, without second language, ethnicity, even religion. In college I became an Anglophile, the young Wordsworth my first love, the older and perhaps more misogynist Swift my second. Of course it occurred to me from time to time that I was "only a girl." But I read literature second-guessing a point of view that seemed sexless and without particular bias.

Students now know better. The legacy of the sixties is their consciousness—and ours—of the reality of bias. We are not "one world," nor were we ever. Students are also conscious of the value of their diversity. They feel and can talk about racial hostility, about sexism, about class bias: they know about "point of view" even before we lecture on that topic—it is part of the real world they live in. The hegemony of the white, male, middle-class world, at least in literary studies, will never be again as it was before the sixties. We must help bid it good-bye, and as we do, carrying with us what in a new age with new students will prove of value, we will need as well to bid good-bye to the presumed objectivity with which we have learned to treat literature.

Admitting that all the books assigned were interesting, a black woman (who works as a teacher's aide and is finishing her last year of college at night) wrote at the end of her examination, "The one book I preferred reading above the others was *The Autobiography of Miss Jane Pitman*. The main and most important reason is that all my school life I have been asked to read mostly about white people. In this book, I was able to read and understand things more clearly because it reflected a set of people that I not only identified with but am a part of." A younger white man also singled out that book: "Maybe the book meant something extra to me," he wrote, "after growing up in a black neighborhood and now teaching in a predominantly black grammar school. Sometimes I look into a black child's eyes and wonder if times have really changed so much."

Earlier, I mentioned my students' unusual reaction to Kate Chopin's *The Awakening*. They knew that the novel had been published in 1899, and I had described the limited choices then open to a twenty-eight-year-old middle-class mother of two, in New Orleans where there was no way to "join the women's movement" or look to it for support. They understood all of that intellectually, but today, they were saying, they would write a different conclusion to the story. They were taking the measure both of the novel's place in history and of their own contemporary state of consciousness, not merely as individuals but as a group of women. As a piece of literature becomes significant for personal and social understanding, so does the process enhance the significance of the study of literature. My students were influenced by *The Awakening*, as I had meant them to be.

But many of us are afraid to admit that we can and do influence our students. We cultivate a certain self-irony as we protest that "we really do nothing significant." Or we emulate "scientific objectivity" by imagining that we are merely conduits for information or disinterested guides to the values and attitudes that joust within a literary work. For that simple-minded view of the teacher, for the refusal to think honestly and clearly about the fact that we teach a world view, a perspective, an ideology, that we teach "what we are," as Emerson said—each day we stand before a class and talk on any subject; for the refusal to acknowledge that the choice of subject is itself a political decision, since our courses do not cover *all* knowledge, or all *literature*, or even all *good* literature; for burrowing our heads in the sand, we may be said to deserve the charge against us: we are useless and hence expendable.

But of course it is a lie: traditional literary study embodies and dignifies certain Western and American values, largely those of a particular sex, race, and class. We have been useful in fostering those values; we can be useful in challenging them. We make significant choices each time we order books for our students—when, for example, we substitute *The Narrative of the Life of Frederick Douglass* for Franklin's *Autobiography*; or when we place beside Dickens' *Hard Times* Rebecca Harding Davis' *Life in the Iron Mills* or Engels' *The Condition of the Working Class in England*. We shape our classes around what we would have our students understand as important.

As a guide to literary study, I offer a letter my colleague Roslyn Baxandall found in the December 1911 issue of *Life and Labor*. It was signed "A New New Yorker," and it focuses on an area largely ignored by literary criticism: the impact of books on their readers. I want to read the letter to you:

> At our League meetings every time we are asked to write to you and tell you what we think of Life and Labor. And that is why I write to you today. I am a Jewish girl, and I like Life and Labor, but the girls in our factory are not interested in Life and Labor, and I will tell you why. They do not know much—they have not much learning; they cannot do much thinking after the day's work, and no one can do any thinking "speeding up" at a machine, and only when they see something written by someone they know, like Pauline Newman, will they take the trouble to read it. What they need is stories, but stories that will stir them.
>
> I do not know if I can tell you in English, but I will try, to tell you why I think the stories of Life and Labor do not mean much to the Jewish girls. You see, they are all pleasant stories, and we Jewish people have suffered too much to like just "pleasant stories." We want stories that tell of struggle, and that tell of people who want justice—passionately. You see, with the people in your pleasant stories we have no fellowship. They do not seem real.
>
> Last night I was with some of our factory girls, and they begged me for a story and I told them the story of Jean Valjean, and they all listened eagerly, and when I finished they said, "So long, so long have men and women struggled for justice and it is not here yet. We too, must struggle." And so they went on with more courage in their hearts for the struggle, and then I thought why not have Life and Labor give us the story of Jean Valjean, so that we may all take new heart and courage.

It is difficult to follow the cadences of that letter. But I want to conclude by suggesting that our curriculum does not yet provide "courage in their hearts for the struggle," or the tools of language necessary to carry it forward. Courage and tools: these are not unreasonable goals of literary study—for our students as well as for ourselves. A defeated cynicism pervades higher education, fostered no doubt by a more general social malaise that will not disappear even with the impeachment of the president. We have our own houses to clean: Shall we continue to organize our profession to foster elitism and competition? Will our courses continue to serve our own specialized interests, rather than our students' futures? Dare we admit that literature also matters to our lives?

Courage and tools: the needs of teachers and students are not far apart. Whether we renew our responsibility for literacy or work cooperatively with interdisciplinary programs—whichever route we choose—with it we must choose also to reevaluate and change the canon of literary study. Two years ago here in Chicago, Adrienne Rich described that work. "Re-vision," she called it, "the act of looking back, of seeing with fresh eyes, of entering an old text from a new critical direction—is for us more than a chapter in cultural history: it is an act of survival."[6] It is also an act of great joy—the discovery of Anne Finch and Margaret Walker, of Shi Ming (Yang Ping) and Ama Ata Aidoo, of Mary Wilkins Freeman and Mary Austin, and I could fill another hour with new names of women and men, alive and dead, whose works we now have the pleasure of reading.[7]

Many young people in this association (and a few in my generation) have begun this enormous and joyous task, and some of them have lost jobs in the process. But their work is the hope of the profession—its thread of vitality. I could have spent my time on this work of restoration and discovery, and perhaps in another year another president will. We are still in the early stages of that process of survival—all of us who have been omitted from literary study and from the curriculum in general: not only women but most of the invisible masses that have always peopled this earth.

I should like to conclude with a poem that names one of us, Pablo Neruda's "Cristobal Miranda (Shoveller at Tocopilla)." I read Robert Bly's translation.

> I met you on the broad barges
> in the bay, Cristobal, while the sodium nitrate
> was coming down, wrapped in a burning
> November day, to the sea.
> I remember the ecstatic nimbleness,
> the hills of metal, the motionless water.
> And only the bargemen, soaked
> with sweat, moving snow.
> Snow of the nitrates, poured
> over painful shoulders, dropping
> into the blind stomach of the ships.
> Shovellers there, heroes of a sunrise
> eaten away by acids, and bound
> to the destinies of death, standing firm,
> taking in the floods of nitrate.
> Cristobal, this memento is for you,
> for the others shovelling with you,
> whose chests are penetrated by the acids
> and the lethal gases,
> making the heart swell up
> like crushed eagles, until the man drops,

rolls toward the streets of town,
toward the broken crosses out in the field.
Enough of that, Cristobal, today
this bit of paper remembers you, each of you,
the bargemen of the bay, the man
turned black in the boats, my eyes
are moving with yours in this daily work
and my soul is a shovel which lifts
loading and unloading blood and snow
next to you, creatures of the desert.

Notes

*This Presidential Address delivered at the 88th Annual Convention of the MLA, in Chicago, 27 Dec. 1973. The talk could not have been written without the women's movement, the MLA's Commission on the Status of Women, the Women's Caucus for Modern Languages, and the special support of my friends at The Feminist Press and of Louis Kampf. I want to dedicate the talk to my students, to Paul Lauter, and to Tillie Olsen, the teacher of us all. Her fiction, her life, and her learning sustain us and inspire us to continue the work she has begun.

1. "The Beginning, Development, and Impact of the MLA As a Learned Society: 1883–1958," *PMLA*, 73 (1958): 33.

2. Janet Emig is Associate Professor of English Education at Rutgers Univ.; her work is in progress.

3. For a bibliography of such studies, see *Feminist Resources for Schools and Colleges*, a publication of The Feminist Press, Box 334, Old Westbury, N.Y. 11568.

4. "Responses of Adolescents to Feminine Characters in Literature," *Research in the Teaching of English*, 6 (Spring 1972): 48–68.

5. In a new publication, *Who's Who and Where in Women's Studies* (Spring 1974).

6. "When We Dead Awaken: Writing as Re-Vision," *College English*, 34 (1972): 18.

7. See, as representative samples of the work of recovery, *By a Woman Writ: Literature from Six Centuries by and about Women*, ed. Joan Goulianos (Indianapolis: Bobbs-Merrill, 1973); *American Voices, American Women*, ed. Lee R. Edwards and Arlyn Diamond (New York: Avon, 1973); *Fragment from a Lost Diary and Other Stories: Women of Asia, Africa, and Latin America*, ed. Naomi Katz and Nancy Milton (New York: Pantheon, 1973).

The Future of Women's Colleges

(1974)

In the spring of 1974, I was invited to lecture on the topic of this essay both at Simmons College and Wheaton College. It was a coincidence that surprised me, since I was feeling remote from the concerns of women's colleges by then, and since only Barnard College had shown any interest in women's studies. It was also not clear that the rush to coeducation by single-sex colleges was over. The late Esther Westervelt convinced me that Simmons was serious about being a "new" kind of women's college, that she and others at Simmons wanted to hear what I might see in its future; and a faculty committee at Wheaton expressed the same view.

Ten years later, women's colleges are becoming the kinds of institutions I suggested was possible. By 1980, Wheaton had a feminist president, and provost, and was embarked on an ambitious federally-funded three-year project to transform the male-centered curriculum into a coeducational one.

A brief selection from this lecture was published in the Wheaton College Alumnae Magazine *in August 1974.*

I HAVE, AS YOU KNOW, spent most of my teaching life with women. As if in unconscious preparation for that experience, I spent eight years attending a women's high school and two women's colleges, Hunter and Smith. From 1960 to 1971, I taught at Goucher College; for the past three years I have taught at a public college, SUNY/Old Westbury, on Long Island, but chiefly in a women's studies program. The differences between these two experiences make the case for the feminist classroom and curricular program. These differences may be summarized concisely: they are 1) consciousness; 2) knowledge; and 3) power. I shall discuss them in that order,

125

drawing on my experience both at women's colleges and in women's studies. I use the word "power" to mean the power to change not only one's self, but others and, with them, such institutions as colleges. I am most interested in the power of the curriculum.

First, then, consciousness, a state of awareness essential for meaningful learning. Let me explain what I mean.

I was, like many women, a diligent pupil through school and into college. In college I was, to my surprise, not the solid "B" student I had been at Hunter College High School, but an "A" student. Yet through college, as in high school, I cannot remember asking a searching question of any teacher in any course. I learned what was presented to me, learned it relentlessly even, but without the drive, imagination, creativity of someone who wants an answer to a question. If ever there was a passive receptacle capable of whooshing into its nozzle batches of details—and feeding them back in orderly fashion—that was me. I can recall some curiosity, I am glad to say, and it sent me to anthropology courses, but I was dabbling, and I knew it. It was foreign, exotic stuff, like the countless novels I read in order to find out what happened to the characters I became interested in.

I should add at once that I was not at college to find a husband, but rather, as a working-class woman, I had been sent to college by a mother determined that her daughter would become the elementary school teacher her orthodox Rabbi father had not allowed her to be. I entered kindergarten with the concept of becoming a teacher already firm in my head. And so, through high school and college, the question was simply, what kind of a teacher was I to be?

I was a physiology major to begin with, largely because of a high school biology teacher I admired. I enjoyed my freshman year of human physiology, and managed to get through the mathematics, and even to deal successfully with the scientific German I was obliged to take. But during my second year, I struggled less successfully with chemistry, and my mathematics teacher caught on to the fact that I was simply memorizing equations and attempting to apply them without understanding their function. I made few errors but those were quite illogical ones apparently, and finally I was summoned for a talk with her about my future as a science major. That occurred at about the same time that my chemistry teacher was wondering why I could not manage to catch on to inorganic chemistry, although surprisingly I understood the concepts of organic. Both teachers suggested separately that science was not my cup of tea. And I agreed, not only without a fight, but without a murmur. My grades in chemistry and mathematics, I should add, were "B" rather than the "A's" in physiology and German.

Now why did I give in just like that? Midway through college, I switched fields with ease and without struggle. From science to English.

Why? I remember how, in high school, I had devoured those marvelous stories of Paul de Kruif called *Microbe Hunters*; how disappointed I was to learn that there were no more of them. And then I turned to Hans Zinsser and other medical and scientific biographies. But all of these, with the exception of Madame Curie, were about men. I am not suggesting that I was conscious of that fact; after all, my teachers at Hunter High were women, as were most of my teachers at Hunter College. You could argue that I was incredibly fortunate to have had so many role models throughout my high school and college life. But the curriculum did not support those role models. I had certainly never imagined myself a scientist.

Despite two years of work in the science concentration—which meant in those days a number of required courses—I switched to English. It was, you might say, a "natural" choice. I had already received four A's in required English courses; and had I not been told since my earliest days at school that I was a good reader and a competent writer? So I would be an English teacher and not a science teacher; somehow, it did not seem to matter. Even writing this now, saying it, boggles my mind. Because, of course, things matter very much to me now. And the perception of that eighteen year old I was disturbs and pains me.

My vocational goal, remember, was higher than my parents' had been for me: it was teaching in a high school I was aiming at, not an elementary one. But if I had been a boy, my parents would not have aimed me at teaching at all, but dentistry probably, or law or medicine. A profession.

My former husband's experience provides an interesting parallel to mine. We did not know each other in our student days, but he too switched from science to English. Physics had been his field of interest, even from his days at the Bronx High School of Science. But he switched to English because it was the early1950s and he did not want to make atom bombs; English seemed to him a more humane area of study. How I envy that decision when I think of the difference between us. I was told I could not do science well and accepted that diagnosis; he decided he would not participate in race suicide. In truth, we each could have decided to do anything we wanted; the difference was that he knew it and I did not. It never occurred to me until I was past thirty that I could decide what to do with my life, and, more than that, that my work was important to me and might be of value to others.

I tell you all this because I want to make a particular point about the curriculum. In at least two respects, I did not have the ordinary female's experience of high school and college: first, most of my teachers were women—that is, I had a more than adequate supply of immediate female teacher role models; second, I had a mother who was ambitious for me to achieve, and a family atmosphere, therefore, supportive of study, even though I was a woman, not a man. A woman today who had been to an average high school might easily find that most of her teachers were male; and at most colleges in the country, even in 1974, she might find that less than 20 percent of her teachers were women, and most of those young instructors or assistant professors. A woman today might find that her parents are more interested in her chances for a good marriage than in her ambitions for a career.

But what I and most college students, including those at women's colleges, would have in common today is the curriculum.

Nowhere in my four college years, although my teachers were mainly women, did I learn anything about women either in history (exception: three British queens) or as writers or painters, let alone as scientists or as mathematicians. Now that I am thinking of it, it occurs to me that I did read Ruth Benedict and Margaret Mead in those days: maybe that was why I elected several anthropology courses. Maybe. It is hard to tell now how much I longed for—although I had no words and certainly nothing of what we would now call consciousness. I was not angry—I would not have known what to be angry about. But I was also not alive, not in the way students are today, or even in the way they were a decade ago.

In the mid-sixties, I was teaching at a women's college. On the first day of a freshman writing class, with my fifteen students in a circle, I asked what people wanted to be—why had they come to college? What would they be doing ten or more years hence? One young woman responded quite simply: "I am going to be a U.S. Senator," she said. At which the other fourteen students laughed helplessly. And the student who had spoken closed her mouth and was silent for the next six weeks. Andrea—that was not her real name—had not passed through our public school system. She was the daughter of a state department official and had been educated abroad. College was her first experience with U.S. education, and that class her first shock. Later in the term, she chose to do her long paper on the question of women's potential. She consulted a number of traditional sources in history and literature, some in sociology and psychology, and wrote a brilliantly executed paper in which she came to the following conclusion: since there have been no outstanding women political leaders or thinkers and relatively few artists, and even fewer scientists, or discoverers of any kind, one must conclude, however reluctantly, that women as a group are inferior to men. There were individual exceptions, perhaps, but on the whole women had no potential.

I was appalled by that paper. It argued flawlessly—and my standards were very high—a case I had probably unconsciously accepted. Yet to read it was devastating. In those days, I could not argue the case: in those days, I too had not read Mary Wollstonecraft. I had not heard of Elizabeth Cady Stanton. I was as ignorant of my heritage as Andrea. But I had read Simone de Beauvoir the year before, and Virginia Woolf's feminism a decade earlier. And I sent Andrea to those sources. Indeed her paper, her experience of reading those sources, made me add de Beauvoir and Woolf to the freshman feminist curriculum I slowly developed in the late sixties at Goucher.

Both my student and I had had, in one respect, essentially the same experience. It could be summed up in an aphorism: the more education we had, the less value we placed on women. In my own case, I had been raised by working-class parents and in a small but nevertheless extended family. I knew the strength of both my immigrant grandmothers firsthand. And I knew very well that while my father worked hard, he could come home and collapse; my mother, who also worked hard, came home and did another day's work in the house, cooking, cleaning, listening to my brother and me, looking after our clothes, hers and my father's and so forth. I knew the strength of women firsthand. But especially after my years at women's colleges, especially when I began to do my graduate work at the University of Wisconsin, that notion of strength dimmed. What was valued in the academic world were intellect and power, and where were the women of intellect and power? What had women ever *done* that mattered? At college and graduate school, you did not think of the strength of women in families, but rather of the intellect and power of men in government or in science or even in literature and art.

Andrea had been reared in a cocoon of privilege that had one special virtue: she had not been through the rigid sex-stereotyping of U.S. public schools; she had also missed the peer group pressures and the media. When she said she wanted to be a U.S. Senator, she was saying what in her family was a not unusual notion. The curriculum she began to survey in her very first term at college told her otherwise: it told her what I learned especially at graduate school. That intellectual women or women of achievement were rare or exceptional persons who were declared not part of the normal run of women; they were deviant in relation to other women, and in terms of the curriculum, they were also inferior since they were not male.

By 1966 or 67, my own consciousness had allowed me to offer my students at least a couple of resources outside the normal curriculum. And my own work at Goucher had begun to shift somewhat. I was teaching introductory composition courses organized around the identity of women, and offering my students readings almost entirely by women, despite their disdain or repugnance. In my private political life, however, I was dismayed by those women activists leaving the civil rights or antiwar movements to organize their own feminist groups. I had not joined NOW and was not interested in its work. Indeed, to all those "separatists" I would have made the same speech, could I have gathered them together to hear me. "Wait," I would have told them, "wait for the time when we have gained more rights for minorities in this country, and wait also until we have managed to end the war in Vietnam. Then we can look after women's rights." I would not have known then that I was saying in the mid-nineteen sixties precisely what abolitionists had said in the mid-eighteen sixties to our feminist foremothers. How *could* I have known? Not one of the courses I had ever taken through sixteen years of school and college had ever mentioned feminism, much less the suffrage movement, much less anything else about women's history. And so, even as an assistant professor of English at a woman's college with a distinguished feminist history (all buried of course), my consciousness was minimal.

A number of events altered that consciousness, and I will not take the time to describe any of them. What I want to make clear, however, is that it was not only personal experiences—with women and with men—that honed my awareness of feminism (and needless to say, much of this comes out of an awareness of sexism). It was information, knowledge. In fact, although I have separated consciousness from knowledge for the sake of neatness and clarity, it is clear enough as well that the two are tightly intertwined. I had little consciousness, not because I had had no unpleasant experiences with sexist males, females, or institutions; I had had at least my share. But my response to them had been very limited: either I accepted, hence "internalized" the sexism (you could not be a scientist unless you were either a male or an exceptional female); or, on rare occasions, I burned with indignation over "unfair" treatment. In either case, I never considered the possibility that something might be done about such views or treatment. My general response was to "work harder." What changed my consciousness deeply, irretrievably, was knowledge—of my history as a woman, of the art women have created, of achievements in abolition, in struggles for women's education and other rights; in short, of women's subjection and the long and remarkable history of efforts to overcome that subjection—a history filled with achievements despite barriers.

If I seem to emphasize this matter of knowledge, it is that the term consciousness-raising has come to mean simply the raising of emotions, strong feelings against the sexism of the society, agitational feelings, anger, even fury. But that is not an adequate definition. Consciousness comes out of knowledge, some of which may be experiential. Indeed, the strongest, firmest consciousness is built on the conviction, the passion even, that comes from the joining of experience and information. That is precisely why education is so crucial for women. Precisely why it is not enough for any institution that educates women to focus its attention chiefly on improving extracurricular life. *The center of consciousness in an educational institution is the curriculum.*

On campuses about five years ago, we began to feel what is now called "the rebirth of feminism," that movement that in this country was a rich part of nineteenth-century history, although none of us had heard about its past till recently. We began by looking at our own status as women faculty and hundreds of studies were done, hundreds of legal complaints filed with HEW, and, as you may know if you read Carnegie Commission reports, the entire effort of the past five years has resulted in an increase in women faculty of .9 percent—obviously, of little consequence.

The studies, however, had another result of more consequence. They revealed a pattern so massive in proportion that it could not be explained by discrimination alone. It is perfectly true—and both the Newman Report and the more recent Carnegie Commission study state this outright—that there is abundant evidence to establish widespread overt discrimination against women, a punishable offense these days, and institutions as prestigious as Howard, the University of Michigan, Columbia University, and now the whole California system have felt the pinch. Also there is a growing list of cases won by women in court or by State Human Rights Commissions or by precourt pressures from HEW or EEOC. On the other hand, if you think of the relatively small proportion of women who have chosen to go to graduate school in the first place, and to stick it out in the second, and I am thinking of the women who apparently *choose* a less ambitious path or leave before writing the dissertation, as I did, then discrimination, bad as it is, does not explain those cases.

So in 1970 different kinds of studies got underway—of the curriculum both hidden and overt. I shall talk only of the actual curriculum, although I am willing to answer questions about the hidden curriculum in schools and colleges. Because these studies focused on the public school curriculum as well as on higher education, I shall review a series of them with a focus on readers for children and literature for older students. Since literature is my own scholarly domain, I feel free to criticize its shortcomings.

When books are school texts, of course they gain additional authority. The message of those books, from elementary through high school, is simple enough: boys and men lead adventurous lives, struggle for achievement and recognition, usually gain it, and with heroism; and even if they wind up carrying an attache case to the office each day, in children's readers, they are, as fathers, playful, resourceful, and heroic in relation to their children. Girls and women, on the other hand, when they are not in the background, are limited both in thought and deed. Two images, apart from the incessant apron, pervade children's picture books and older children's readers: the girl without arms—her arms disappearing because her hands are joined together behind her back dominates in full figures of girls; and the girl behind windows, I nearly said bars, wistfully looking at the real world out there, or waiting for that prince to rescue her. Women are simply mothers, and motherhood, of course, is never heroic, difficult, painful, or an important achievement.

Instead of looking at the high school and college curriculum in some detail, I would like to offer you several items not in it. I do so, frankly, because I am tired of that dull story, tired of reciting the horrors of the English or history curriculum, the more devious sexism of mathematics texts and assumptions, and the dangerous poses of sociologists and psychologists. So I shall offer you several "what if's": what if we had read these letters as high school or college students?

Abigail Adams to husband John Adams as he began to write the laws of a new government. March 31, 1776 from a letter, "Remember the Ladies, and be more generous and favourable to them than your ancestors. Do not put such unlimited power into the hands of the Husbands. Remember all Men would be tyrants if they could. . . ."

John Adams to Abigail, April 14, the same year: "Depend upon it, We know better than to repeal our Masculine systems."

John Adams to James Sullivan, late in May, the same year, with the same subject still on his mind. He wrote on the question of the electorate for the new nation, and he asked, in his letter, "But why exclude women?" And he answered: It is not because of their alleged "delicacy," not because they are mostly occupied with the "necessary nurture of their children" and other "domestic cares." For obviously, some men too may be declared less physically strong than others, John Adams was realist enough to know that most men will also be busy with their own affairs, rather than with the concerns of government. So he settled the question of women's suffrage in quite another way: "Such is the frailty of the human heart," John Adams wrote, "that very few men who have no property, have any judgement of their own. They talk and vote as they are directed by some man of property, who has attached their minds to his interest." He added, to make his point perfectly clear, "women and children have as good judgements and as independent minds, as those men who are wholly destitute of property; these last being to all intents and purposes as much dependent upon others, who will please to feed, clothe, and employ them as women are upon their husbands, or children on their parents. . . ."

What if we had read those letters as we learned U.S. history and could begin therefore to understand the close relationship between property, status, and power as the U.S. framers of the constitution understood what they were about? Why, a person might ask even at this moment, if the question was owning property, why then could women not own property?

Obviously, as you know, that rule was changed before the rule about the franchise.

What if as students we had read the transcript of the case of Susan B. Anthony before the bar of justice, on the charge of voting illegally at the Presidential election in November 1872. Before pronouncing sentence, Judge Hunt asked Anthony whether she had "anything to say why sentence shall not be pronounced," and she responded: "Yes, your honor, I have many things to say; for in your ordered verdict of guilty, you have trampled under foot every vital principle of our government. My natural rights, my civil rights, my political rights, my judicial rights, are all alike ignored. . . ." She continued, and the judge said that "The Court cannot listen to a rehearsal of arguments. . . ." But Anthony continued anyway, "Your denial of my citizen's right to vote, is the denial of my right of consent as one of the governed, the denial of my right of representation as one of the taxed, the denial of my right to a trial by a jury of my peers as an offender against law, therefore, the denial of my sacred rights to life, liberty, property, and—" Again, the Judge interrupted her: "The Court cannot allow the prisoner to go on." But Anthony went on. And the Judge once again—after half a paragraph—succeeded in interrupting her. And again she continued—this time managing a lengthy paragraph:

> All of my prosecutors, from the 8th ward corner grocery politician, who entered the complaint, to the United States Marshal, Commissioner, District Attorney, District Judge, your honor on the bench, not one is my peer, but each and all are my political sovereigns; and had your honor submitted my case to the jury, as was clearly your duty, even then I should have had just cause of protest, for not one of those men was my peer; but, native or foreign born, white or black, rich or poor, educated or ignorant, awake or asleep, sober or drunk, each and every man of them was my political superior; hence, in no sense, my peer. . . .

To the Court's insistence that Anthony, and I quote, "has been tried according to the established forms of law," Anthony replied, "Yes, your honor, but by forms of law all made by men, interpreted by men, administered by men, in favor of men, and against women. . . ." And she continued by reminding the Court of the laws that once "declared it a crime . . . to give a cup of cold water, a crust of bread, or a night's shelter to a panting fugitive as he was tracking his way to Canada. . . ."

What if, as impressionable adolescents, we had heard that exchange? I will tell you what happened when one of my students read it aloud to my class this term—it was part of her report on Anthony. She read this piece of the transcript—about two thousand words; and students in my class— most of them over the age of thirty—cheered. It was as though they were present: the drama was their own drama.

Before I move on to the final portion of my lecture, I shall attempt some summary statements about the curriculum: about the "knowledge" we offer especially to women students:

1. Women's education cannot be described as "equal" to men's if the curriculum is entirely or mostly the story of male accomplishments, male lives, the thoughts and aspirations of men.
2. Such a curriculum is not simply unfair to women (and men too); it is distinctly harmful to their growth and development.
3. The traditional curriculum has a negative effect on the aspirations of women; and while it is supportive of men's aspirations, it prepares them not at all to live in an egalitarian manner with women. It prepares

men to devalue women, to discriminate against them, and to support sexist institutions.

4. It is not enough to focus on the need for curricular change in higher education. Elementary and secondary education are as bad or worse and revision must begin there as well, if we are ever to be able to talk honestly about equal opportunity for women.

Five years ago, as you know, women on campuses across the country began to teach what we now call women's studies courses. In 1970, we knew of sixty-six courses; in 1974, we know of more than four thousand. In 1970, there were two incipient programs—at Cornell and San Diego; in 1974, there are more than one hundred, and a little less than a third of them offer degrees or minors. Six offer M.A.'s. That suggests a power to me, a new and vital resource: all those academic women (and a few men) teaching about women.

What are its goals? Those involved in women's studies usually list several or all of the following:

1. to raise consciousness
2. to compensate for prior deprivation
3. to encourage the production of useful research
4. to restore the lost culture and history of women
5. to work actively toward social change

I would state them with a different emphasis today. First, we need women's studies because without a change in the content of the curriculum—from elementary school through college—we shall continue to lose the best female minds of each generation, and we shall continue, instead, to force professional ambitions onto males, interested or not, capable or not; and on to the rest of us, some relatively mediocre professionals. That is one argument. We need, not only the tiny handful of women who become achievers; we need all those talented women the educational system and social pressures send to the kitchen or typing pool.

Second, we need women's studies because the bias in the curriculum reflects a bias in knowledge, and promotes a general continued ignorance. It is not simply that we need to add women to the history curriculum: rather, a study of women's role on the frontier, for example, or on the plantations during the civil war, *changes our conception of those historical periods, issues, or circumstances*. It is not simply that we have omitted almost all women artists; we have taught students to believe that there were none, not even second rate ones, much less first rate. It is not simply that we have failed to mention women in child development or developmental psychology courses; it is that we teach male development as though it were generic. We do not teach students about sex-role socialization, unless we are giving a women's studies course, and why should that be? Certainly, the socialization of females and males is a perfectly acceptable, even necessary study, for prospective psychologists, sociologists as well as all who would be teachers.

When this movement first began, I was one of those who expected it to last only for a relatively short period, less than a decade I thought, maybe no longer than five years. But I was wrong. For two reasons, women's studies programs will continue to develop and grow. First, the intransigence of my own generation of teachers and scholars. And second, the complexity of the knowledge being uncovered and still untapped.

There is still a third reason: it has always been easier in higher education to add to the curriculum than to change it. Even in a time of tight money, this is true. Changing a course in any discipline for example, requires commitment to the idea of change and a good deal of new knowledge. To change male-centered and biased history or literature courses, for example, an institution would probably have to invest in consciousness-raising courses for its faculty; professors would have to read and begin research in areas new to them; and both the institution and the faculty would have to value women students sufficiently to turn their attention to these goals.

In nearly every institution of higher learning across the country, there are young faculty members committed to the goals I have outlined. Many of them have done doctoral dissertations in the area we call women's studies. Others have shifted the focus of their research because of new awareness and interest. By and large, thus far at least, they have not been especially rewarded for their efforts. Indeed, some of them have lost jobs, promotion, tenure, or all three for their troubles. The faculty of my generation and those older than I are not especially friendly to these young scholars.

But the chief reasons why women's studies will continue to grow as it has, largely unaided by foundations or universities themselves, are 1) the momentum of the women's movement outside the campus and 2) the fascination of the new discoveries themselves.

What is the role of the women's college in this and the next decade of revision and revitalization? As I have indicated somewhat, my experiences at women's colleges were not particularly inspirational. Indeed, at Goucher, I pressed for coeducation, arguing that, aside from the special abundance of women role models on faculties, women's colleges provide no exceptional benefits for their students. Although I will not stop to outline the details here, I was convinced that most of the exceptional qualities of women's colleges were harmful to their students. I cheered coeducation on as it advanced onto male and female campuses in the sixties and even in the very early seventies, destroying what I felt were meaningless, purposeless ghettoes, remnants of other times and needs. I should add also that by 1971, I was also very worried about the separatist nature of women's studies on campuses; I could see new ghettoes being created, even as the old ones were breaking up. And in 1972 I wrote optimistically about new models for separatist programs: networks, not departments; a temporary or partial separatism, not fully institutionalized, or hardened into permanence.

At high peaks of social movements, however, polarization is not uncommon. And I think we are going to have to read both the development of women's studies and the halt in the spread of coeducation on women's college campuses as part of the power of the women's movement that has pressed us in the direction of polarization. For healthy reasons, let us assume, women's colleges are beginning to reconsider their special missions as colleges, recover their feminist histories, and plan for the future development of their students in a changing world.

I should like to contribute to that venture by offering some advice. As I said at the beginning, the advice comes out of my experience of women's studies as compared with my prior experience at women's colleges. I would work toward five goals, the first of which is a temporary one—planning a bridge to the other four.

1. *Initial Planning*: using those faculty currently capable of initiating women's studies courses, a planning group could begin to discuss curriculum, methodology, and a women's studies core as a nucleus for revision of the whole curriculum. They might decide to emphasize history, literature, and sociology, as well as art history and economics.
2. *Faculty Education*: through the use of summer institutes and sabbaticals, visiting professorships, team-teaching, and other devices, a women's college might institute a three-year plan for the education of the entire faculty and the revision of curriculum.
3. *Research Support*: The establishment of a research center or of special research facilities to support the work of some facet of women's studies, perhaps one especially important to either the history of the institution or its geographical location would signify the institution's commitment and contribute to its changing climate. For example, women's studies at the University of Alabama will probably declare itself a special center for the study of southern women. A women's college in New England might consider a focus on Puritan women, or early factory workers or New England women writers. Whatever the choice or choices, a women's college is an appropriate institution for housing and organizing burgeoning research on women's history and achievements. Such a research program or center would, of course, attract visiting scholars.
4. *Diversification of the Faculty*: Bringing onto the campus such feminists as lawyers, physicians, elementary school teachers, parents, ac-

tivists, and others, equipped to teach the faculty (and augment it by giving some courses or lectures to students) would also help to spur the new mission on.

5. *Diversification of the Student Body*: Through special recruitment efforts, a women's college might begin to attract older and minority women; the college might offer them opportunities both for "life experience" credit and for work as occasional adjunct faculty in particular aspects of the educational program.

The first three items are obvious enough: the force of my remarks through this lecture speaks to the revision of the curriculum and the concommitant development of new knowledge. It would seem perfectly appropriate to me were women's colleges to assume leadership in this area. There are models to follow, not only among women's studies programs, but also at at least one women's college: at Alverno College, in Milwaukee, for example, Sister Joel Read, the president, organized internal education programs for the faculty so that, as she writes, "the whole of our curriculum is, in an analogous way, 'Women's Studies.' History classes do not negate women; literature classes do not overlook them; religious studies courses investigate the effects of patriarchy upon them; science classes utilize women as models, as contributors, as text writers, and so on. *Infusion* is our method."

The last two items are not so obvious. Opponents of women's colleges, like Alice Rossi, have argued that "The last thing in the world young people between 17 and 21 need is segregation of the sexes. These are critical years in human development," Rossi continues, "when a primary task is the development of ability in establishing intimate ties with the opposite sex. If the man-woman relationship is not to be narrowly based on sex, young people need a wide range of encounters with each other in a wide variety of contexts." She may be correct: I have tended to agree with that view. But young women and men have another set of needs that even coeducation does not fulfill. They need to know adults, in situations other than the parental or teacher/student ones. No single feature of my teaching experience these past three years in Old Westbury's women's studies program has been more important than the mix of ages. In each class, the range has been from under 20 to over 50, and spread rather evenly. "Older" women feel comfortable at Old Westbury because they are not "freaks"; there are enough of them so that they can form their own "subgroups." In classes, it is not one of them against all the rest, but rather, younger students have the opportunity to measure their aims and fantasies against the experience of their classmates. And the mix is good for older women too, for they find the brightness of the younger students exhilarating and challenging; at the same time, they learn not to devalue their own life experiences. For the teacher, it is a delight to read social and political history or literature with a group of people, whose memories include the late thirties, the forties, and the fifties as well as the present.

Well, you may be asking at this point, why would I recommend all this? What would I hope to accomplish? The conventional cant for several Goucher commencements went like this: if you educate a man, you educate one individual; if you educate a woman, you educate a family. Neither vision of education is adequate to the world we live in: we need to be more than individuals, we need structures larger than the nuclear family; at least if we plan to live in a nonsexist world. Women's colleges will, I hope, work to educate women who will work to educate many others; whether they do that work as teachers or social workers, as architects or lawyers, as department store buyers or financial executives, they need the courage that their history and literature will provide, as well as the tools of their particular line of work. As an anonymous letter-writer has said, we need institutions to provide us with "more courage in [our] hearts for the struggle."

Women and the
Power to Change

(1973–1974)

Women and the Power to Change *was written early in the seventies by four women. It was my job to write the introduction and the title essay. On campuses, where we worked or studied, we had been energized by the power of the women's movement at the end of the sixties, and of course we were signs of that power. Small signals, perhaps I should more accurately say, since the four voices that came together to write the one book were the only women's voices in a large series of books on higher education produced by the Carnegie Commission. A decade later, we might write a different book, but then we were writing close to the scene, trying to sort out not only the strands of the feminist revolution on campuses, but its directions for the future.*

A decade later, the book strikes some especially prescient notes: the awareness shown by Adrienne Rich that pressure for a woman-centered university would arouse hostility we had not yet begun to feel; the awareness by Arlie Hochschild that to tune the university to women's lives would necessarily make some or all men uncomfortable, and that this would arouse hostility; the awareness by Aleta Wallach that her basic observation about the rule of law being in fact the law of men would arouse extreme hostility; and my own note that without a national organization and without some coherent attention to the female professions, we would be ultimately unable to deal with these hostilities and move forward, since by the eighties, we would be running harder and harder just to keep the few university places we had gained by the mid-seventies. All these notes forecast the backlash of the eighties. All are also essentially optimistic notes, since they project the power of women to continue working for change, and they understand that backlash is the response to such power.

Perhaps the single most important feature of this book (and the one most dismaying to our male editors, which probably accounts at least in part for the poor dissemination of the volume) is that we wrote not only analytically, but autobiographically. We wrote about our coming to consciousness, perceiving personal experience as the essence of political experience. We read and meant the title of the book ambiguously: women and the power to change their lives; and through that power, to change the institutions that shaped lives. We said that, thus far, we had set out to change ourselves, individually and collectively, and joyously we had begun that enormous task. Where there was pain, it was not from disappointment but the pain-mingled-joy characteristic of coming to consciousness.

My own essay conceived of power as deriving from Ghandian conceptions, as instrumental, not controlling, as an essential strategy for change: a feminist instrument born out of consciousness and knowledge and used most effectively to empower other women to free themselves and still others.

IN THE SUMMER OF 1964, when northern activists arrived in Jackson, Mississippi, we found there an organization called Womanpower Unlimited. Founded by Clarie Collins Harvey, a black businesswoman and church leader, Womanpower surprised me, not because it was an organization of women, but because it was integrated. Black women and white had come together to change racial relationships in their community. Meetings were relatively open in Jackson, but private elsewhere in the state. Several northern white women accompanied Ms. Harvey to the Gulf Coast on the occasion of one meeting, secret even from the husbands of women attending. A first experience in social integration for these women, the meeting's ambience was memorable: the triumph of achieving an unauthorized meeting; the anticipation of whether and how to go "public" and what might be achieved thereby; the excitement of discovering that, despite the racial lines, women had mutual concerns about their children's education and the general welfare of their communities.

No one talked more coherently about the "power" of women than Ms. Harvey, although without any threat to male dominance. While black women could be natural leaders, as her behavior demonstrated, they drew power from their inferior status. Women were less visible than men; therefore more movement was possible for them. Even if their private meetings had been discovered, as they had been in Jackson, what could it matter that some black and white women were talking together? A few husbands might be irritated, but women's meetings suggested no threat to the principled segregation of the community that a parallel meeting among their husbands might have signified. Nor could it evoke the kinds of sensationalized fears that meetings among younger women and men of both races had provoked that hot Mississippi summer. The strategy was designed to accomplish change slowly and without provoking fear, hostility, or confrontation: it relied upon patriarchy. After all, what could a few women do? Charity was their line and had been for decades. Charity—not change. Yet of course, these were women using their "womanpower" for change.

I begin with this isolated instance of a decade ago in part because I can think of no other recent instance in which the word "power" has been publicly used by a group of women either to name an organization or to promote one. Indeed, I can cite one instance in the late sixties in which the word was deliberately avoided. After the first public meeting of the Professional Women's Caucus, a small but representative group assembled to discuss, among other things, a new name for the organization. One possibility offering the acronym of "POWER" was immediately and utterly rejected. Discussion was hardly necessary, except to explain how unsuitable a term "power" was, especially for professional women who, by virtue of their status, had more power than most other women.

By the late sixties, black power and student power were part of the common parlance. Why *not* woman power? Interestingly, those suggesting the acronym were among the group's conservative, prestigious, and nonacademic members. But they were new to the women's movement, and they had not caught the pulse of its grass roots energy, where the word "power" was to be avoided at all costs, though the principle slogan was "sisterhood is powerful." It is important to understand why POWER alone as slogan and ruling concept has consistently been anathema to a women's movement interested not as much in its relationship to the outside male world as in its ability to organize other women.

In one sense the explanation is remarkably simple: the word power suggests control of one group by another, and hence, its use by a subordinate group may evoke in the dominant one a fear of insurrection. The letters of Abigail Adams and John Adams illustrate that notion amusingly. In March 1776, Abigail wrote to her husband John, who was beginning to write the laws of a new government:

> Remember the Ladies, and be more generous and favourable to them than your ancestors. Do not put such unlimited power into the hands of the Husbands. Remember all men would be tyrants if they could. If perticuliar [*sic*], care and attention is not paid to the Laidies [*sic*], we are determined to foment a Rebelion, and will not hold ourselves bound by any Laws in which we have no voice, or Representation.

John responded two weeks later,

> Depend upon it, we know better than to repeal our Masculine systems. Altho they are in full Force, you know they are little more than Theory. We dare not exert our Power in its full Latitude. We are obliged to go fair, and softly, and in Practice you know We are the subjects. We have only the Name of Masters, and rather than give up this, which would compleatly subject Us to the Despotism of the Peticoat, I hope General Washington, and all our brave Heroes would fight.

While invoking an insurrection of "peticoats" suggests Pope's delicate satire on women's foibles written 50 years earlier, it also lays out the ideology of patriarchy, even with some of its complexity. The "Masculine system" is named, but it is alleged to be merely a theory: "in Practice," women are so powerful that only the "Name of Masters" allows men any power at all. While this is obviously the wildest exaggeration, it is formed on the basis of commonly held assumptions: male power is allegedly controlled by hidden, female power (wives, secretaries, assistants, even mothers); if men were to lose the facade of power, they would have nothing else. Obviously again exaggerated, even this kind of logic excludes at least three other possibilities: first, that men might themselves try the use of secret (husband, male secretary or assistant, even father) power over women; or second, that power might be shared; or third, that power might *not* be conceived as a finite commodity through which one person or group controls another, either secretly or openly.

But the issue of women and power has generally been raised in a framework that insists upon a competitive struggle with men. Rousseau, for example, put the problem into one sentence: "Educate women like men," he said, "and the more they resemble our sex the less power will they have over us." Behind this sentence lie several complex assumptions: education is directly related to power; the education of women and men, like the power of each in relation to the other, must be distinctive and distinctly related to the patriarchy in which they exist. The sentence also suggests the possibility that education might undo what Rousseau and others of his time (and since) believed were innate differences accounting for man's superior and woman's inferior abilities and achievements. Mary Wollstonecraft's answer to Rousseau significantly directs the woman's movement even to this day. It is a delightfully simple response: "I do not want them [women] to have power over men," she wrote, "but over themselves."[1] Margaret Fuller, writing more than fifty years later, made almost the identical point: "Were they free, were they wise fully to develop the strength and beauty of Woman; they would never wish to be men, or manlike. . . ."

In one sense, Wollstonecraft and Fuller mean to be reassuring to men: we do not want your turf or your power; we simply want a room of our own, a space in which we can develop our potential, whatever that may be. Nineteenth-century feminists were modest enough about possibilities, admitting openly to man's greater physical strength, for example, and suggesting that it was impossible to "prove" whether or not women's intellectual capacity was precisely equivalent to men's. On the other hand, it was clear enough that whatever the potential of women, their education and their inequality before the law, to take only two elements, contributed significantly to their inferior status. What nineteenth-century feminists asked for, therefore, was equality before the law, and even more difficult to achieve, equality in the human consciousness that would allow women to develop whatever capacities they might have.

But things are never as simple as they seem. To insist that a woman wished to control her own life—and, in the twentieth century, her own body—may, on the surface, seem to be nonthreatening to men. To demand equality for women even in the nineteenth century was to insist that laws be changed, for example, or that colleges be opened to women. To suggest that such change would not also affect men's lives was either naïve or tactful. Obviously, I believe that the movement has not only attempted to be tactful; it has also tended to operate within the boundaries created by its own state of oppression. That oppression has taught women certain techniques for survival, among them the idea of cultivating their own garden, without infringing on male territory. To a significant extent, this has been the history of women through the past two centuries of struggle.

Even the seventy-year battle for suffrage was not, in itself, an infringement on male territory, though it was certainly fought as an infringement on a male prerogative. For suffrage was not linked to office-holding, or to sharing the power for decision making at the legislative, executive, and judicial levels of government. (It is also true that granting suffrage to women when they did helped preserve the power of established males over challengers to that establishment—like workers.) Thus, allowing women the right to vote was allowing them to vote for this man or that one, exactly as men in the society did. Similarly, admitting women to higher education did not alter the power relationships between women and men: women either filled subordinate slots in the hierarchy or filled entire ghettos of professional life, the elementary school, for example, or nursing and social work. Even in totally woman-dominated academic and professional areas, male power has consistently been at the top.

It is not surprising, therefore, that men assume that women might want power in order to move "up" and replace them, or that "giving" women power would in effect reduce the power of men. Indeed, the view is based on the traditional concept of power as a finite quantity of control that one person or group exercises over another person or group. If a husband has power, theoretically a wife does not; if the leader of a group is powerful, theoretically the members of that group must be without power.

It's a view of power as commodity: they who control the oil reserves have it, or he who owns the factory. Such a conception of power extends itself deeply into the society and hence into the thinking of its members: some one person or group *must be* better, stronger, smarter, more beautiful than the rest. An anecdote may illustrate this kind of thinking.

In 1967, at a community meeting in Washington, D.C., a small group of middle-class white mothers of a tiny minority of children attending an elementary school in a relatively poor black neighborhood were protesting the addition of new texts focused on the lives of black children. "If you teach these children to be proud of the fact that they're black," one white mother cried out *in extremis*, "where will that leave my children?" When several black mothers, in their astonishment protested, and others wept openly, and still others walked out, the white women could not understand or believe that they were responsible for the despair and disillusion that followed—or the anger. From their point of view, at least in 1967, if black were to be beautiful, clever, strong, then white must become ugly, stupid, weak.

In 1974, the terms are replaceable by male and female. I have heard mothers and female elementary school teachers say that if you "raise girls' self-esteem," you will necessarily "threaten the boys'." Again, the assumptions are drawn from the traditional view of power as a finite commodity that some, and not others, possess. According to that view, power becomes the object of a struggle to gain and hold superiority: the fulcrum can never be truly in balance. Indeed, a change of power in this sense—as we have heard people say time and again—changes nothing really, since power, the exercise by one group of control over others' lives, continues under a different face.

It is not surprising also, therefore, that inside the women's movement, probably only one word has carried more negative affect than "power," and that word has been "male." Indeed, the two words have tended for obvious reasons to become synonymous. Male power, private or institutionalized, has traditionally controlled most aspects of the lives of women, whatever their color or class, not only through the rule of law and coercion, but more subtly through the promise of love or the threat of its loss. John Stuart Mill, more than a century ago, wrote movingly about the power of husbands over wives:

> Whatever gratification of pride there is in the possession of power, and whatever personal interest in its exercise, is in this case not confined to a limited class, but common to the whole male sex. . . . it comes home to the person and hearth of every male head of a family, and of every one who looks forward to being so. The clodhopper exercises, or is to exercise, his share of the power equally with the highest nobleman. . . . In the case of women, each individual of the subject-class is in a chronic state of bribery and intimidation combined.

. . . Men do not want solely the obedience of women, they want their sentiments. All men, except the most brutish, desire to have, in the woman most nearly connected with them, not a forced slave but a willing one, not a slave merely, but a favourite. They have therefore put everything in practice to enslave their minds. . . . When we put together three things—first, the natural attraction between opposite sexes; secondly, the wife's entire dependence on the husband, every privilege or pleasure she has being either his gift, or depending entirely on his will; and lastly, that the principal object of human pursuit, consideration, and all objects of social ambition, can in general be sought or obtained by her only through him, it would be a miracle if the object of being attractive to men had not become the polar star of feminine education and formation of character. And, this great means of influence over the minds of women having been acquired, an instinct of selfishness made men avail themselves of it to the utmost as a means of holding women in subjection, by representing to them meekness, submissiveness, and resignation of all individual will into the hands of a man, as an essential part of sexual attractiveness.

Mill's view is important for its emphasis on what we now call socialization: the use of power to effect *internal* acceptance of external authority. As a result of the power of men, women have learned to believe in their own inferiority; indeed, as mothers and teachers of the young, women become instruments of "male" power.

The problems for women who understand the male use of traditional power are complex: How to break away from a force so all-encompassing? How to do so without assuming its guise and thus reversing patriarchal relationships and simply substituting females for the men in charge of institutions? In other words, how to change the power that controls women's lives without extending oppression either to other women, to groups of minorities, or to men themselves. In this essay, I want to answer those questions especially as they relate to academic women and the institutions in which they work. I am especially interested both in the manner in which teachers exercise their authority in the classroom and in the ways in which groups of teachers might begin to work together to change the education of women and men. I shall explore an alternative concept of power that has developed within the women's movement.

Conventionally conceived, power is the control exercised by one person or group over others. Whether the controlling person is a husband, a political leader, a school principal, a department chairman, or a classroom teacher, the exercise of power is typically elitist, hierarchical, authoritarian, and manipulatively dependent on reward and punishment. Whether the powerless are wives, citizens, teachers, or students, the exercise of power thrives both on their fears and on their acceptance, through socialization as well as through more direct means of control, of their permanent subjection. Obviously, such power is debilitating to those under its sway. Obviously also, power thus conceived has been identified as "male."

The expression, "the power of women," conjures up something different: witchcraft, for example, including conception and childbirth, thought to be original "powers" of women, mysterious in origin and frightening in practice. The power of women's beauty to inspire male genius is a commonplace of literature and the other arts. The power of women's virtue, especially her virginity, was enough to inspire the gods. With the possible exception of witchery, these were powers rooted in female biology; they were also transient. Most important, they functioned only in relation to individual men (or gods)—not with respect to the organization of society. Obviously, the powers of female beauty, witchery, pregnancy, and chastity, confined to women as they are, could not substitute for legal or political power. Indeed, offered as substitutes in a society that values legal and political power—as well as money, work, accomplishment, position—they become a means to keep women powerless.

Whatever the conceptions of women's power, in reality it has been covert and private: an exercise in cunning and winsome guile, practiced on allegedly unsuspecting husbands, lovers, fathers, brothers, sons. As Rousseau describes it, "A woman who is naturally weak, and does not carry her ideas to any great extent, knows how to judge and make a proper estimate of those movements which she sets to work, in order to aid her weakness; and those movements are the passions of men." Rousseau prescribes for a woman's education the thorough "study" of "the dispositions of those men to whom she is subject." Like John Adams who wrote after him, Rousseau also attempts to disparage the powers of male supremacy: "The mechanism she employs," he says, writing chiefly but not only of a woman's ability to provoke men's sexuality, "is much more powerful than ours; for all her levers move the human heart." Powerful or not, women's chief role and purpose in life was to please men. As Rousseau describes the education of women, it is consistently "relative to the men":

> To please, to be useful to us, to make us love and esteem them, to educate us when young, and take care of us when grown up, to advise, to console us, to render our lives easy and agreeable—these are the duties of women at all times, and what they should be taught in their infancy.[2]

Thus woman's "power" is confined to her private life and her education prescribed to maintain her ability to "please" that man to whom she owes her status as wife.

The power of women as a force for change in the nineteenth century was built on their perception of themselves as individually powerless: to change that condition, they adopted strategies they had learned in the abolitionist movement and in other contemporary movements for change, including that of moral reform and temperance. Essentially, they organized masses of women into large national organizations capable of accumulating millions of signatures on a petition, turning out thousands of marchers in a demonstration, or writing countless letters to Congress. They built their movement not on public denunciations of men, though they expressed their disappointments on that count privately in correspondence, but on the "rights" of women, even as announced officially in the 1848 "Declaration of Sentiments." The nineteenth-century movement built on the vision of a righteous and energized population of women— half the nation—strong in their conviction that they deserved "equality" before the law and in the minds of men. The seventy-year struggle to convince men of women's right to vote is evidence of both the determination of women and the reluctance of men to change the nation's legal patriarchy.

Like its nineteenth-century counterpart, the contemporary women's movement began with a concept of mass organizing of women to gain legal rights, not to suffrage, but primarily to equity in employment and salary scales. A second strand of the movement, begun almost simultaneously, grew out of the civil rights and antiwar movements. These women did not attempt national organization, but focused on building networks of small consciousness-raising groups in particular cities. They also attempted a number of visible "actions," one of which gained for women's liberation the indelible label of "bra-burners."[3] By 1969, the slogan "sisterhood is powerful" dominated both segments of the women's movement and expressed its main direction: to organize women around issues that connected rather than divided them: birth control and abortion; child care; education; work. Such groups as the National Organization for Women (NOW, founded in 1966) aimed to gather numbers of women as a potent pressure for change on many issues. The Women's Equity Action League (WEAL, founded in 1968) focused both its membership and its concerns on bringing class action suits against higher education for its treatment of women. The dominant mode through which organizing was eventually accomplished both for the large national organizations and for the radical feminist groups was the small consciousness-raising group.

"The concept of 'consciousness-raising,' " according to Juliet Mitchell, "is the reinterpretation of a Chinese revolutionary practice of 'speaking bitterness'. . . . Like Chinese peasants who took a step out of thinking their fate was natural by describing the conditions of their lives to each other, middle-class women in the U.S. brought the facts of their own lives to the surface."[4] "The first symptom of oppression is the repression of words," Mitchell writes; "the state of suffering is so total and so assumed that it is not known to be there." "Speaking bitterness" brings to consciousness the barely conscious; when the process occurs publicly, in a small group, "one person's realization of an injustice brings to mind other injustices for the whole group."[5] Both in China and in the United States, the process is part of an educational strategy.

In the United States consciousness-raising groups turned the women's movement into a teaching movement that was functionally both massive and yet totally decentralized—even into tiny splinters. Spread across the nation, the process was codified not only for the purpose of raising the consciousness of women about their relations with men, but also as a means of establishing new relationships among women. To be "sisterly" rather than competitive and backbiting was not only personal but political, since cooperation and supportive behavior enabled otherwise powerless women to work together toward change. One did not simply "make friends" with women; one became political "sisters" in a growing women's movement.

That movement openly eschewed "male power" in all its forms. In their place, women substituted the allegedly leaderless group. Theoretically, if no one person was "in charge" of a consciousness-raising group, then all were "equally" in charge. In practice, at least one person in the group probably had had experience enough to inform others of the "rules." In practice also, of course, all groups develop their own leadership, although the structure may remain covert. The rules called for an atmosphere of loving and supportive acceptance of all women in the group, whatever their experiences, ideas, values, or problems. Direct criticisms of or challenges to another woman's statement were not acceptable "sisterly" behavior, nor were dependence on outside authorities, deference to a woman's particular "status," or domination of the group by any one or more persons. One technique widely adopted attempted to encourage both the shy to speak and the bold to speak briefly: on an agreed-upon question, experience, or topic, each person in the group would speak in succession, with no fear either of interruptions or of cross-examination or debate-like challenges. Thus, a group of twelve might spend more than an hour—each of them in turn—describing an early sexual encounter or last week's most unpleasant sexist experience. The circle completed, one person might attempt a sisterly comment or question: "Alice, what you said was very moving. How would you handle the same experience today?" And Alice's response might make a connection to Laura's experience, or perhaps she or Laura might ask others how they would look at such an experience today. The process is not a showy one—there are few or no flashes of brilliant strategy; the gestures tend to be quiet, sharing ones that open the talk to those who are unaccustomed to speaking their thoughts out loud.

From the talk and the sharing come discoveries familiar to social science: alleged personal deviance is, in fact, social reality. Guilt about wifely or motherly boredom, desires for a working life or an education previously denied are common to middle-class women, not because they are personally maladjusted but because they were socialized to accept their insufficient social roles. The second stage in the educational process occurs when some member of the group takes the leap from consciousness to action. She might ask a husband or a lover, for example, to share some aspect of housework or child care, and if successful she might thus learn that it is possible to alter the pattern of her life. Successful, too, she becomes a "model" of encouragement for others in the group. When this leap occurs, the consciousness-raising group becomes a "support" group for women who are in the process of changing their personal lives and becoming thus at least part of a women's movement engaged in similar efforts.

It is easy to underestimate the importance of these consciousness-raising groups. They are open to various criticisms and have felt them from those both inside and outside the movement. For one thing, feminists have been concerned lest the illusion of "leaderless" groups perpetuate systematic manipulation within the movement, as well as a continued ignorance about the nature of power and leadership. For another, the groups have seemed, both in their singular introversion and in their isolation from each other, relatively unimportant, and hardly "political." Originally conceived, groups were thought to be capable of educating women whose raised consciousness would give them the power not only to change their personal lives but to join forces as part of a movement to change institutions in their communities. For many complex reasons, consciousness-raising groups succeeded only for a relatively short period in building networks for activist projects in major cities. Most of these networks—in Boston, New York, Chicago, and Washington, D.C., for example—are now dead, their members either out of the organized movement, or more likely, swelling the membership of NOW, WEAL, and the National Women's Political Caucus.

Politically, the consciousness-raising groups are very important, especially if one wishes to understand an alternative concept of power promulgated by the movement. The emphasis on "sisterhood," despite additional consciousness about class and race differences, allows the movement to function as a "mass." It allows trade-union women to feel a sense of "solidarity" with college professors (now increasingly, of course, joining those labor ranks). And so, despite the isolation of individual groups in particular communities, the message is one of importance for national movement building, because it allows for precisely what the nineteenth-century movement accomplished through its emphasis on the "rights" of women. While the traditionally powerful assert the possession of power as a commodity, to be exchanged for other commodities like money, approval, service, and time, and organize the acquisition of power through competition, an alternative view, built on sisterhood, makes an effort to diffuse power.

Power diffused in the group, and even into many thousands of groups, of course, is not to be confused with the power to make significant changes in institutions. The chief contribution of the consciousness-raising group continues to be an educational one: women learn not only about the sexual politics of their own lives but about the power potentially present in "sisterhood." The large step, from controlling one's own life to working with others on some ultimate political goal, is, of course, not an automatic one, though I think it would be fair to state that even if the consciousness-raising group does not motivate women to work actively in the movement per se, it often sends them into the work force or back to college, where they may also encounter the movement in the form, for example, of trade-union caucuses or women's studies programs.

Most women in the movement on campus and off have had the experience of consciousness-raising groups. They bring a new ambience to committee work, to leadership, and to political organizing generally. The variety of power exercised by such women is neither covert power in Rousseau's sense, nor the traditional, authoritarian form of "male" power previously described. Despite the media's image-making effect, the tone of rank-and-file feminist leadership is low-key but firm. In male circles, its openness may, indeed, be disarming. I have seen women, for example, move formally that the chair request that all persons on a committee successively state their views openly on a particular matter; and I have seen that request become an established pattern in the group.

The practice of feminist leadership is, of course, of special significance if one believes that leaders set the tone of groups by acting as role models for others. That is, authoritarian leaders may build authoritarian followers, so that up and down the line of hierarchy there is no possibility of an interchange between subjects and rulers, leaders and followers. Or leaders may be, as in the case of the charismatic Martin Luther King, Jr., symbolic or strategic role models for followers who are neither subject to him nor in his "control."[6] The experience of "leaderless" groups convinced many feminists of the need for open and democratically shared authority, and especially for *public* decision making. When leadership is covert, its control depends on additional meetings (or telephone calls) outside the established ones, and it is possible therefore for certain members, systematically excluded from such relationships, to be controlled, even as in the traditional manner of patriarchy. Knowledgeable feminists will insist, therefore, on democratic procedures for establishing leadership, and either on the systematic rotation of that power or on procedures for ensuring decentralization. Feminist groups may function entirely through a committee structure that depends upon one or two "coordinators" to convene the group for decision making.

While an open system of decision making is important, it is also dependent upon maintaining the broadest possible "base" of *informed* support. Perhaps the single most important lesson that feminists have learned both from critiques of the male establishment (including the male *left* establishment) and from the manipulative exercise of power by covert feminist leadership is the need for sharing information. Thus, in the first few years of its existence, in what was appropriately called the "mushroom effect," the women's movement spawned some two thousand publications, many of them newsletters published by local consortia of consciousness-raising groups or by chapters of NOW. In addition, most feminist organizations or groups I am acquainted with, including women's studies programs, also publish, for a broad constituency that typically extends beyond its immediate participants, elaborate "minutes" of meetings or monthly or annual reports of their accomplishments and goals. These efforts make manifest the continual importance of building a broad-based movement, for while consciousness and knowledge are not to be confused with power, they are both essential to its exercise.

I am not of the feminist school that believes in the moral superiority of women or in the superiority of any group of people. Nor do I believe that women possess any special "power" or capacity.[7] But I do believe that it is possible for a group of people who have been historically subjected to adverse conditions and treatment to develop alternative cultural forms of survival and political strategies for change. The consciousness-raising group and open forms of leadership and information sharing are two important political developments. Between 1969 and 1974, these have become influential on campuses, especially where women's studies programs have functioned as the academic arm of the women's movement. But a viable political strategy depends on numbers, on large organizations, and on long-range planning. For the kind of change to occur that feminists envision—not simply replacing a male authority figure in or out of the classroom with a female one—women need both patience and persistence. Since feminists are interested in changing not only the concept of power as a finite commodity but the manner in which power is exercised, the process of such change becomes important.

In the next section, I shall trace the process of such change for one academic woman who did not join the movement until the movement reached the campus—in 1969. While I was involved in other movements before 1969, it is fair to say that the women's movement changed the direction of my life, indeed gave my life the meaning it had not theretofore had.

A little more than ten years ago, several students introduced me to political activism through an innocent enough request for a lift from their suburban campus to the city where a picket line was in progress at a segregated movie theater. Instead of dropping them off, I joined the picket line, and, in a manner familiar enough to those academics who have survived their activism, became a "campus radical" at a rather conservative women's college. My reputation changed slowly during the course of the next several years, in part because I attempted, with relatively little consciousness about the effort, to continue my old style of life even while donning the new. I cannot now remember the context, but I do remember one day on which I knew that something had changed for me forever, and it is from that time that I chart the decline of my powerlessness. A male colleague, observing my unhappy expression through a lengthy interchange with two other male colleagues, commented afterward, "You can't please people and be 'political' at the same time. Some people are bound to disagree with you; you're going to offend others; and you'll have to get used to being disliked—or give in."

I was, of course, defensive: I did not *need* to please people, I protested. But the conversation in the narrow hall outside our offices flags my earliest consciousness of how sharp the contrast was between my need to please not only superiors but peers and my growing commitment to self-determination and activism. The theme is typical enough for women, academics or not: we are socialized in a manner quite distinct from males, so that we develop a need for "affiliation," not "achievement."[8] What a woman might want to do or to learn is second to another critical question: what is it desirable that she do or learn? The process of socialization leads to a feeling of powerlessness, or, more precisely, pleasing others expresses the powerlessness of women in our culture. Women learn to measure themselves against others' standards or needs—parents', teachers', husband's, or lover's—registering value in their eyes. I took my cues especially from teachers; ironically, it was in discovering a different role for myself as teacher that the decline of my powerlessness began.

Toward the end of my sophomore year at college, I switched from science to English without so much as regret, much less anger, about the two years spent on human physiology, mathematics, "scientific" German, and chemistry. My chemistry and mathematics teachers both urged me to leave science, and without further ado or discussion, I did. Discrimination? In the ordinary sense, I should have to dismiss that charge, for this was Hunter College in the late forties, when all the students and most of the faculty were women, and when there were, of course, many women science majors. But what these two women were saying to me was that women had to be not simply good or mediocre in science, but excellent; and that a female who had grown up afraid of mathematics and science, and who was hence somewhat backward conceptually, could not be reeducated, not even at the age of 18.

And I, at 18, accepted their diagnosis as I would the reading of an x-ray machine: no tears, no anger marked the scene for me. I would be an English teacher and not a science teacher. What mattered was becoming a teacher and so fulfilling my mother's own thwarted ambition. From the day I entered kindergarten, the idea was fixed in my head that I would become, some day, that teacher at the head of the room. Part of the curriculum for me each year was studying how to become "teacher."

I might never have had that two-year interlude in science had it not been for a high school English teacher who told me, confidentially, after long hours of work on the Hunter High School literary magazine one day, that I was one of the students she most liked working with. I was, she continued, the ideal "good" student, one who could write straightforward prose, but who had not a "creative" bone in her body. I believed that teacher, accepted her diagnosis again without a pang or murmur. She was the teacher; she knew. And I crossed English off my list.[9]

I do not think I am exceptional in this matter, but my class background contributed additional fears and feelings of inadequacy to the ordinary female socialization. Until I left Brooklyn's Jewish ghetto for Hunter College High School, I had had no difficulty making my way, for I was bright and hardworking, and exceptionally sensitive to satisfying other people's desires or needs, especially teachers'. At Hunter High, however, I didn't speak for one entire year, and my academic record was only mildly above mediocrity. The first teacher to hear my diction sent me to a speech "therapist" who pronounced me "defective," handed me a small mirror, and assigned me to special afterschool classes to rid me of dentalization, nasality, and other venial crimes. In that year, I wiped out my Brooklyn working-class accent, but I never again spoke freely in a classroom until, at the University of Wisconsin, I became a teaching assistant.

Thus, in choosing my major, my speech, even my "career," I looked outward to satisfy others' demands upon me. My mother set the goal, and my teachers became the rods against which I measured the possibility for accomplishing that goal. Pleasing others reflected an approach to schooling and to study that began with decisions and standards not my own. When a professor suggested that I was "good at ideas" and offered me a thesis subject, I slavishly followed his suggestion, grateful that it saved me the trouble of finding one for myself. It was not that I was entirely uncritical of teachers, rather, the teacher who influenced me became, in each case, my unquestioned authority.

As a novice instructor, I taught in a style I had grown accustomed to seeing as a student. I was a direct, clear, organized, and controlling teacher who told students what she wanted and who expected to be pleased by their doing as they were told. Most of my teaching at Wisconsin lent itself well enough to that scheme, since freshman composition was the funnel through which all high school graduates had to pass in order to remain at the universities.[10] In that class, I taught a standardized curriculum of grammar, punctuation, sentence style, and prose organization, designed to train competent essay writers of the style that Hunter College High School had defined for me. The essays these students produced were utterly unrelated to their racial, class, or ethnic origins, or to whether they were male or female. I was interested only in turning out people, who, like myself, had learned to bury even their local accents, to become that middle-American male voice that one hears on news broadcasts and reads in weekly news magazines. As I reconsider my training—and thinking—I feel most astounded by this particular failure: to assume that one can teach writing without understanding that feelings and thoughts arise out of particular personal and social conditions. And it helps me to comprehend why I was not a particularly astute or confident critic of literature, and why, as a graduate student, I was careful to choose only "straight research" topics, never "creative" or evaluative ones.

Literature as I had studied it and as I later began to teach it was a "subject" to be learned as I had learned formulas. It was also to be worshipped as the best that had ever been thought and written down, as a kind of religion *cum* philosophy, a substitute for moral guidance and for "universals" about the major "facts" of life, which, as I reflect upon them, were mostly suffering and death. Thus, Andromache's pain at the loss of Hector was every woman's pain at the death of a husband killed at war. And Hamlet's heroic efforts, excesses, and suffering were the model for those who would expose and punish sin and corruption. While this is not an impossible reading of literature, it is not especially helpful for students who would learn to write it or even to read it with some independent judgment of its values or portrayals of life. Nor is it a reading of literature that is particularly interesting or thought-provoking, since it asks no questions, sets no problems. It is conventionally moralistic and assumes that all can agree on "rational values" and that all readers are one reader. Most important, it sets up the teacher as authority on the meaning of literature.

That I read and taught literature in this fashion is not surprising, since I had spent more than two decades of a lifetime denying my own identity. I was a Jew and had avoided both the language of my childhood as well as its literature and culture. As an American immigrant's granddaughter, I had painfully learned proper voice, diction, and syntax, as well as a "correct" prose style, but I had avoided American literature and culture, preferring British medieval, renaissance, and eighteenth-century literature and history. I was a woman of working-class origins, but it never occurred to me to inquire whether women or working-class people generally had produced literature. In short, I chose to study literature distant from me in time and space and read, as Elaine Showalter has suggested that most women do, as an anthropologist investigating a strange (male) culture.[11]

By 1960, I had become so much a part of that male culture that I sneered openly at the idea of teaching on a women's campus. But my interest in teaching made me accept a temporary one-year appointment at Goucher College. As I had at Smith (where I had earned a master's degree), I worried about my clothes, my lack of "good" jewelry, family name, and academic connections. I still could not play tennis or ride a horse, and it was becoming increasingly difficult for me to admit, much less explain, those lapses. The snob in me won out. I was cold and aloof as a teacher. Students described me as "formidable." My behavior, of course, was also precisely what was expected by peers and superiors on the faculty and in the administration. There I became a most pleasant "daughter," especially to the male faculty a decade or so older than I, and to the dean. When it was clear that I was to stay on campus at least for another year, I was assigned the responsibility (with a young male teacher) of redesigning the required sophomore course for English majors. With utter disregard for our women students, we chose a series of "major" and "universal" works—from *Dr. Faustus* and *Paradise Lost*, through *The Prelude* and a half dozen others, to *The Waste Land*—in which there appeared not a single woman author nor a single admirable woman as central character.[12] I stayed at Goucher to teach that and other male-centered courses for nearly half a decade, and I might have continued to act the misogynist English teacher had I not volunteered, in the summer of 1964, to teach in the Mississippi Freedom Schools.

I arrived in Mississippi nervous to the point of anxiety and yet eager for my work to begin. I was nervous because I had expected to teach black history and literature, and although I had been cramming, I was not even a novice in those areas. Nevertheless, I wanted to begin at once. Much to my dismay, there was a weekend of "orientation," aimed mainly at keeping the summer volunteers alive through teaching them rules for survival, as well as procedures to follow if harassed or arrested. Another two days of meetings followed, in which I began to act as a rapid-talking, impatient know-it-all northerner, who wanted to cut through the seemingly aimless talk and get to the work of teaching. I remember being taken aside by Tom Wahman and Staughton Lynd, codirectors of the Freedom Schools, and asked, kindly but firmly, to abstain from speaking for the afternoon, and instead to listen to local black people and some younger black and white students try to work things out for themselves. I was, they said, older and more experienced than most, and I could not put my head on their shoulders.

I took their advice (anxious to please as always), and when I was impossibly bored, I read the curriculum materials that had been handed out earlier at Tougaloo. They were a revelation, for they specifically forbade "teaching" as I had until then understood it. Even the physical arrangement of the "classroom" was to be different from any I had ever sat in: no rows of chairs with the teacher at the front of the room; only "circles," with the teacher inside them. No "body of knowledge" that the teacher was to deliver to the students, but another procedure altogether: the teacher was to draw out of the students the knowledge of the world each of them lived in and the one they may have dreamed of; shared, this information could then be checked, through surveys or statistics, against the world beyond the church basement. Thus, for example, the question of inside plumbing: how many students described inside plumbing as they told about the houses they lived in, or those their mothers worked in? And according to surveys and statistical charts, who in Mississippi had and did not have inside plumbing in their houses?

The curriculum was organized to raise black students' consciousness of themselves as part of a separate "minority culture" that had its own identity, strengths, and weaknesses, its language and history, and that could decide its values and directions for the future. Thus, students attempted to define those aspects of their lives (the "minority culture") they wanted to keep and those they would change; in addition, they defined those aspects of the "majority culture" they would or would not want to adopt. In contemporary terms, we should describe the curriculum as interdisciplinary, problem solving, and very demanding. When we tried a unit on black history, for example, we tried to figure out whether Marcus Garvey's strategy was applicable in the 1960s. When it was clear that young black Mississippians looked to Chicago or New York rather than to Africa, we talked about why black people were "rioting" in those Northern cities. Even as we speculated, asked, and attempted to answer questions, we worked from a base of human experience—the knowledge these students had of black lives in Jackson, Mississippi.

As a teaching strategy, the curriculum was disarming for both teacher and students. Despite my age, race, and status, I could converse with teenage Mississippians in a manner that encouraged them to speak freely, in part because I did not have the information they did, and in part because my role had been defined differently from the traditional controlling teacherly one. If this was a "freedom school," my role as teacher was to create an environment in which students could decide to investigate this problem and not that, in which I was a resource but not an authority. Indeed, my authority was usefully bound, at least to help me learn a new role, by my whiteness and my visibility as a middle-class lady professor. I had no choice but to accept my differentness, and I learned that summer, through the creative writing of black students, that out of a sense of one's own identity can come rich expression and thought.

The teaching strategy is built on the assumption that the person who talks and who makes decisions about the direction of the conversation, or about what topic is to be investigated, learns; that talking is at least as important to learning as listening; and that, in a group, people can learn both to listen and to talk, whereas in a conventional classroom, the students learn to listen in order to memorize what the teacher has said. The strategy has two purposes: to break the hierarchical pattern that binds the traditional classroom (and in the case of a white teacher and black students, the hierarchy of race as well); and second to encourage young blacks to understand that they have knowledge of value to themselves and to others. The strategy thus involves seeking out the knowledge and strengths people have, and building on them, rather than holding people

up against a predetermined standard by which they must measure themselves (and find themselves wanting).

In the process of that summer I probably learned more than my students, especially about the politics of teaching. At Goucher, that fall, I began to apply what I had learned, moving my chairs into a circle, asking
questions that only students could answer, and attempting to find a curriculum that would meet the needs and interests of white, middle-class female students. Trying to learn how to teach women what eventually was
called "consciousness" became the chief means of raising my own.
Through most of the rest of the decade, I had to fight the hostility and suspicion of some students and faculty.

It is interesting to speculate about the refusal of faculty at a women's
college to admit the legitimacy of devoting one whole course to women's
lives. Even as late as 1970, I could not use the word "women" in the official description of the writing course I finally called "Identity and Expression."[13] By then I had demonstrated at least to my own satisfaction that
good writing was the product of consciousness about one's personal and
social identity, and that such consciousness could come out of a teacher's
efforts to choose literature related to women's lives and to share her power in the classroom. Shared classroom power energizes and activates students and may turn them into leaders who wish to share their power with
others—as well as into good writers.

Looking back, however, I can see that a social movement is helpful,
if not essential, to the process. The civil rights movement in Mississippi
provided a supportive context for change. Black students wanted to study
black history and writers; they were interested in themselves and in comparing their lives to those of white students. They did not need the motivation of grades, nor did they expect them in a "freedom" school. Goucher
women, on the other hand, were defensive about being women: " 'Lady
writers' were third-rate," one intrepid freshman said with some pique at
finding herself holding my syllabus. She and others like her had no intention of talking about their lives: "Women were boring"—they wanted to
read D. H. Lawrence and James Joyce. Thus, it is possible to understand
the slowness with which women students took both to the strategy and to
the curriculum: there was until 1969 no social context in which they and I
could find support. On the contrary, they lived on a campus that valued
only the most conservative paths for women, at a time in their lives when
the pressures of peers and parents were harshest on them to conform, and
when their own sexuality and that of Hopkins and Annapolis males were
omnipresent. Thus, to ask them to assume the consciousness of their power as women was, at that moment in time, probably an unreasonable request.

And I, too, was slow to consider the potential power of an organized
women's movement. I neither joined NOW nor interested myself in its
work. Nor did I join a consciousness-raising group: I raised my conscious-

ness, I continued to maintain, by teaching women. I had changed my life, and in the classroom, I would attempt to change students' lives. And I continued to deplore a "separatist" women's movement that had seemingly abandoned both the civil rights and the antiwar movements that seemed to me of primary consequence.

But in the spring of 1969, several women and I were appointed by the executive council of the Modern Language Association to a Commission on the Status of Women. Quite suddenly, I was not the individual teacher in a classroom, or even part of a band of volunteer teachers in Mississippi, but head of a group responsible for establishing "equity" for women in English and modern languages. I had, as Kate Millett used to say comically, arrived at the supreme position for women—the token. With other tokens in other professions, many of whom formed caucuses and were appointed to commissions during 1969 and 1970, we began the double task of charting the professional discrimination against women and raising their consciousness about their own condition.

Because of the Mississippi experience and my own decade of change, I emphasized, from the first, the importance of changing the education of women. Overt or simple discrimination was less than half of the problem. I knew from my own life and from the last five years of teaching women that most of the problems of inequity were more difficult to solve because of how they shaped what went on in women's heads. Thus, that was one place to begin. We had no word for it in 1969, but by 1970 women's studies had various labels. In the manner of the Mississippi Freedom Schools and the consciousness-raising group, and the experiments of my classroom, women's studies builds on the social reality of particular lives. Unlike traditional study, which begins from the standards of the "majority" class, race, and sex, as organized into "bodies of knowledge," this alternative process aims at developing consciousness about one's life in contrast or comparison to the norms that prevail. Organizing a process and curriculum called women's studies challenges traditional "bodies of knowledge" not only by replacing them (at least for a time), but more significantly by attempting to disestablish their authority. Consciousness about one's particular life and experience is the primary knowledge one needs not only to begin to investigate "bodies of knowledge," but to establish them in the first place. Thus, education becomes a key strategy to social change. As a singular movement, without organized head or agreed-upon strategy, women's studies has, nevertheless, begun a long and difficult task.

A 32-year-old mother of three children was explaining, as part of a panel on lifestyles, that when she and her husband were first married, she decided to use a small inheritance she had just received to send him to law school. "Why did you decide to do that with your money?" someone else on the panel asked. The student answered readily: "Because it was a good investment." And of course the class laughed. In response to the next question, "But why didn't *you* go to law school on that money?" she simply shrugged. There was no simple or comic answer to that question.

Listening to this interchange were forty-five students in an introductory course in women's studies at the State University of New York/College at Old Westbury, in the fall of 1973.* Their ages ranged, in an even spread, from 17 to 57; there were 5 males in the group, 8 black people, and several Puerto Rican women. The course was organized into five units of study:

1. The family and socialization, with special focus on mother/daughter or mother/son relationships
2. School and socialization
3. Adolescence and sexuality
4. Choices: Marriage and other lifestyles; college or work; career, vocation
5. Feminism and the future

Students were aware of two goals the teacher projected for the course: to raise the consciousness of the participants and to add measurably to their knowledge about the maturation of women and men. Texts included short stories and other literature of experience, essays, and research studies written by social scientists, as well as statistical graphs and charts and some historical material. Students were expected to keep a journal reflecting both their experience of the two ninety-minute classroom sessions and two reading assignments each week. The journal was to record their intellectual and emotional growth through the semester. Students were also expected to complete a group project of an investigatory nature. While the diversity of this particular group of students may not be typical, the curriculum taught, the teaching strategies, and the goals of the course are characteristic of a new national educational movement.

The thrust of this movement has been to change the education primarily of women, though men have been involved from the first, both as teachers and as students. The major instrument has been the sharing of knowledge, resources, and teaching methods through the development of a network that has published bibliographies of courses and programs; syllabi, reading lists, and essays about teaching women's studies; and more recently, the *Women's Studies Newsletter*. To share knowledge is, as I have made clear earlier, to allow for the development of many leaders, and thus for the rapid spread of a political movement.

*I wish to acknowledge the assistance of a grant (1971–1973) from the National Endowment for the Humanities (RO-5085-72-54) in gathering information for this section.

Women's studies began informally on approximately forty-seven campuses with the initiation usually of a single course in the academic year 1969–70. I say "informally," since there had been no prior discussion or planning, and few of those pioneers in curriculum change had been in touch with each other before the late fall of 1970. During the previous spring, Sheila Tobias and I—in two separate places—began to receive course syllabi and reading lists from teachers of women's studies courses and requests from others who wanted to begin such courses. In each case, the correspondence that accompanied the syllabi or requests assumed, naturally, that women were willing to share such materials. Totally absent was the conventional paranoia that fosters academic secrecy, even about reading lists. In the main, early courses were taught by junior faculty and graduate students at such prestigious institutions as Cornell, Wesleyan, Stanford, Yale, Princeton, Smith, and Barnard, as well as at Douglass, San Diego State, American University, the University of Pittsburgh, and the College of St. Catherine in St. Paul, Minnesota.[14]

In the fall of 1970, Ms. Tobias published seventeen course syllabi, all but one in history, the social sciences, and "interdisciplinary" areas, under the rubric *Female Studies*; she was especially foresightful to call the volume "No. 1." In December 1970, under the aegis of the Modern Language Association's Commission on the Status of Women, *Female Studies II* offered sixty-six syllabi and reading lists, thirty of which were in literature, the remainder in history, social science, and "interdisciplinary" areas. Both volumes and those that followed (the ninth and tenth volumes of the series appeared in 1975) provided a growing group of interested teacher-scholars not only with ideas and resources, but also with some political clout: If Harvard, Princeton, Smith, Yale, and Barnard could offer women's studies courses, why not the University of Pennsylvania or Indiana? If San Diego State, why not Long Beach, or Sacramento, or any of the other California campuses? A little less than four years later, one can list over forty-six hundred courses that have been offered in women's studies, approximately twenty-five hundred of which were offered during the academic year 1973–74.[15]

Courses have developed in every area of university study, although there are still relatively few in the hard sciences, and more in literature, history, and sociology, or in interdisciplinary combinations of these, than in all the other disciplines combined. There are also more courses in law than in other graduate or professional schools. Whatever the course, however, two or three patterns are significant. First, the rediscovery of nineteenth-century history and literature runs throughout the curriculum, regardless of the disciplinary origin or title of the course. Thus, in speech, courses focus on the "rhetoric" of nineteenth-century feminists, either alone or in contrast to their twentieth-century counterparts. A singular course in journalism also takes a historical perspective and rediscovers feminist journalists of the nineteenth century. Courses in economics or politics, as well as in sociology, are sometimes difficult to distinguish from courses in history. Similarly, many social science and history courses depend for materials on newly recovered or discovered autobiographies, memoirs, diaries, letters, or other writings of nineteenth-century women. Stories by such writers as Mary Wilkins Freeman and Rebecca Harding Davis are used in both history and literature courses. Indeed, the interdisciplinary nature of most women's studies courses makes disciplinary identification sometimes nothing more than a function of the title or the department from which a course derives.

As significant as the interest in nineteenth-century feminist history and literature is another in sociological and psychological implications of sex-role development. No literature or history course, no art history or philosophy course begins without defining sex roles as learned, not innate. Introductory courses are often devoted to aspects of socialization, and more advanced courses in the social sciences to new research in this area or to cross-cultural studies.

One additional curricular pattern is the emphasis on the future. If students begin to understand that they have a history, and if they also understand that sex roles are developed, not innate, they may naturally begin to think about change. Thus, many teachers' designs include codas on the future: What kinds of marriage contracts will partners write in 1980? What kinds of child-care centers should be instituted? How could housework be industrialized? How does an idea become implemented? Of what use is the passage of a law forbidding discrimination on the basis of sex? Answers to such questions insist upon the students' knowing the past as well as the present, but putting such knowledge to work for the future.

Three teaching strategies are as politically significant as the curricular items I have just mentioned. They are responses to and adaptations of the movement's consciousness-raising groups, and an emphasis on "sisterhood" and on action. With a trained student leader, the small group functions cooperatively rather than competitively. It is not a place where one advances one's own grade: for one thing, the teacher is rarely present. It is, rather, a place in which one learns to work with others, either to learn from their experience or their understanding of the material under discussion or to make a contribution to the group. In addition, groups often function as vehicles for term projects or papers. Group grades are not uncommon in this instance, and part of the learning process is the experience of dealing with those problems that group research raises: distributing labor equally; making use of various kinds of talents and resources; encouraging the shy to participate and the domineering to relax. Obviously, such projects require skilled leadership, and the teacher's job is to provide that by training a group of students to lead such activities.

The action project that substitutes for the library paper is also a commonplace of women's studies courses. While this activity is related to such innovations as field studies or internships, established in many institutions since the sixties, in a women's studies program it is likely to be related to the women's movement, or to women's needs on or off the campus. In law courses, for example, students take on research for actual cases as aides to lawyers or they attempt to rewrite legislation in connection with the work of an interested legislator. Other women are engaged in community health projects, or in counseling, or in developing nonsexist curricula for public schools. At California State College/Sonoma, students in a women's studies course began to collect information about forgotten or neglected women artists, made slides of their work, built up a collection about some two hundred artists, and have shown the slide show at high schools in their area and colleges across the country.

Such work is obviously useful, even as it is academically impeccable. It is also politically potent, since it both satisfies the needs of the women's movement and, in the process, trains future leaders of that movement. Leaders are trained not only through the development of their skills, consciousness, and knowledge, but through the successful application of these in the course of their education.

One additional teaching strategy deserves special attention. I leave for last the journal writing that fills most women's studies courses because it has not usually been understood as a political tool. Most students are required to keep journals at least in introductory courses, and often in others as well. Usually, instructions call for the student to reflect on the experiences she encounters in the course. The journal functions, in many courses, as an alternative to traditional examinations, and allows students to develop their own program of learning, even as they choose to comment on particular matters of significance. Thus, journal entries become a means through which students develop and record their own growing political awareness. As a composition teacher, moreover, I suspect that the act of writing it down is more indelible than the acts of thinking or speaking the same message. The need to write it down may also force more organized thinking. Interestingly, even those students who complain about the requirement usually confess, by the end of the semester, that they have found the journal useful for their own development. Students often report continuing a journal through other courses, though they may not be fulfilling a requirement. I consider the journal as potent a political tool as the activist group project, for it fosters confidence in a necessary skill, as well as the significant growth of consciousness about one's own and others' lives.

As the educational arm of the women's movement, women's studies has three particular tasks to accomplish, the first two of which are clearly under way. In an institutional setting that has been traditionally careless of or hostile to women, the women's studies teacher has led the development of courses and teaching strategies aimed at changing the consciousness of women (and men), and at adding new knowledge to their ken.

Equipped thus with consciousness and knowledge, their students have brought fresh leadership to ongoing movements for change on campus and off. Second, both teachers and students have added significantly to areas of knowledge and new research developments in such fields as sex-role socialization and gender identity. The history of women, and literature by and about women, have spawned an extraordinary series of publications, including new scholarly journals and a host of "special issues" of established ones, hundreds of books, and scores of bibliographies.

A third task, dependent on the first two, is more elusive: to change the male centered college curriculum, with regard not only to women generally, but to women of various classes and races. The readiness of higher education for such change cannot be judged by the massive proliferation of women's studies courses and programs, since it is always easier to add to the college curriculum than to change it in any substantive way. To change the curriculum would be to change those teaching it: not only to affect their consciousness about the need for such changes, but to add to their knowledge. It is not simply that women should be added to the history curriculum: rather, a study of women's role in the development of the frontier, for example, or on the plantation during the Civil War, changes the conception of those historical periods. It is not simply that women artists have been omitted from the curriculum: we have taught students to believe that there were none. Admitting that error, reviewing the work, for example, of anonymous female artists as well as of those whose names are known, necessitates a review of aesthetic criteria on which admission to the canon of art history has been based. It is not simply that women receive no attention in child development or developmental psychology courses: it is that male development is taught as though it were generic. Revision of such curriculum is not a matter of scissors and paste, but of significant, holistic change. To accomplish such change, an institution would have to invest in consciousness-raising workshops or courses for its faculty; professors would have to read in and begin research on areas new to them; and both the administration and the faculty would have to value women students—and new knowledge, generally—sufficiently to turn their attention to these goals.

While it is far too early to utter predictions about women's studies' efficacy in attempting to change college curriculum, it is possible to explore the political levers and strategies for such change. Quite early in the movement, teachers and students came together to form "programs," though not usually for the purpose of accreditation via the granting of degrees or the establishment of "minors." Unlike individual courses, a women's studies program is an administrative unit, with a designated "coordinator" or "committee" to carry out its function.

Thus identified, women's studies programs in 1971, when there were approximately seventeen, issued manifesto-like statements of intent and strategy. Often, these aimed at both gaining administrative support and recruiting students. Included were the needs to raise the consciousness of women about themselves and their history and to compensate for the omission of women from the traditional curriculum. Some programs also announced their intention of working toward the discovery of feminist history and culture; others called for the support of new research. While all were obviously interested in changing the education of women, several programs openly called also for the need to change the ongoing curriculum of the university.[16]

As an *indirect* effort to change higher education for women, women's studies programs can be viewed as functioning in the manner of parallel institutions. Indeed, program offerings may look like mini-college catalogs—a smorgasbord of courses from many traditional "departments" or "disciplines," plus some novel and usually interdisciplinary ones. Parallel institutions rarely change their hosts directly, though they often produce leadership that may affect other institutions. Thus, while the Mississippi Freedom Schools did not change education for black students in Mississippi, the movement trained hundreds of northern college students and teachers who put their new knowledge of leadership and teaching strategies to work in their home institutions. Similarly, the free universities that proliferated in the mid-sixties did not change the institutions they were peripherally attached to. Rather, many of those students and particularly some of those teachers who functioned in the free universities took their new skills, consciousness, and knowledge and put them to work in traditional institutions.

This view of women's studies programs as parallel institutions anticipates their development as separate units within a given institution. From the beginning, however, perhaps forewarned by the experiences of black studies, women's studies leaders have sought institutional forms other than simple separatism. Thus, programs were thought of as interdepartmental or as "networks" rather than as traditional departments. In a number of institutions, women's studies has developed through the efforts of faculty who divide their time between traditional departments and women's studies. In some institutions, the universities of Delaware, Pittsburgh, and Washington, for example, new appointments in women's studies are contingent on the agreement of traditional departments. The political perspective behind such ambiguous forms of organization is that of change: rather than be cut off, or separated from, the centers of university life in traditional departments, women's studies leaders have attempted to straddle both worlds.

For many, this has become an increasingly frustrating experience. In a nondepartmental world of women's studies, who is responsible for gaining office space, a budget, faculty lines, a library, and other resources for students? In some institutions, a friendly divisional dean or an umbrella of interdisciplinary programs has been the helpful vehicle, but obviously funds must be shared among a proliferating number of interdisciplinary areas of study. And so, women's studies programs may turn in the direction of more formalized departmental structures. While I am sympathetic to the weariness of women who have worked for years without that departmental secretary, budget, and office, and without the power to hire and fire, I am also concerned lest a potent strategy for change harden into a new kind of ghetto for women.

The test of women's studies on campus will not finally be the proliferation of courses or programs, but their effect on the rest of the curriculum. If by 1980, the number of courses and programs has doubled or tripled, and if in freshman English the students are still reading male writers on male lives, and in United States history the students are still studying male-culture heroes, wars, and male political documents, then we shall have failed our mission, or at least not yet succeeded.

From the beginning, there has been still another mission for women's studies: to assist the reeducation of women outside the conventional undergraduate population. The extension of women's studies into women's centers, continuing education programs, schools of education, nursing, and social work, and into inservice education programs for teachers, is a newer development. In addition, there have been several hundred attempts to introduce women's studies courses, especially in English and history, into the high school curriculum; and at least one school system, Berkeley, has attempted to develop a women's studies curriculum (especially geared for a racially mixed population) in its elementary schools. Such developments are extraordinarily significant, for they suggest the ability of women's studies to affect the great mass of women outside the college population.

While women's studies as an addition to the campus is, of course, a lively reality, the test of its power to change the education of women has hardly begun. All that has been accomplished, moreover, has occurred without the benefit of national organization or strategic planning by those involved in the women's studies movement. While there are women's caucuses or official commissions in nearly every professional association by now, representatives of these groups have met together only rarely and briefly. The Professional Women's Caucus, an effort to unite women from the trade union movement with those from academe and other professions, has not, for obvious reasons, been able to focus on academic women alone. More recently still, a coalition of professional associations, caucuses, commissions, and other feminist organizations was brought together under a national umbrella. The National Federation of Women's Professional Groups will publish a newsletter and provide informational resources to groups that join. Like the Clearinghouse on Women's Studies itself, none of these efforts establishes more than a network. While networks are an indispensable prelude to national organization, they cannot substitute indefinitely for that organization itself. Without an organization the work of strategic planning will be left to others, including such groups as the Carnegie Commission on Higher Education.

The Carnegie report *Opportunities for Women in Higher Education* (1973) is subtitled "Their Current Participation, Prospects for the Future, and Recommendations for Action." Because I believe that the report is an important one—it may even be an influential one—I shall analyze and comment on the vision of its authors and, where relevant, offer an alternative view.[17]

The first function of the authors, to define the "various barriers that have existed in the paths of women," is managed with tact. "Academic recruitment procedures," for example, are described as "tend[ing] to be somewhat 'cosy.'" "Especially among the more prestigious departments," the authors continue, "openings are not publicized."[18] While the "barriers" to the equitable employment and advancement of academic women are not explicated as fully or as strongly as in *Academic Women on the Move*, it is impossible to avoid a similar conclusion: the academic world is responsible and restitution is certainly in order. In addition, the authors offer a briefer view of the more basic problem: the aspirations of women, as affected by family, school, and society generally, even before admission to college. They are to be commended for paying close attention to the differences in opportunity afforded working-class and middle-class women. Further, the authors report on "evidence of discrimination in undergraduate admission," and note the need for assembling documentation of a still more complex variety of discrimination against women graduate students.[19] The tone throughout is judicious: a balanced presentation of academic culpability accompanied by numerous guidelines for change. Taken as a whole, however, the net effect of the volume is not auspicious for academic women, nor for young women just entering school this year. While the authors are not to be blamed for reporting the depressing realities of the academic world as it currently exists, they may be criticized for softening that reality, especially with regard to the next thirty years.

The prognosis appears refrain-like throughout the latter half of the volume: "These changes will come slowly . . ." and for two reasons. The first of these may be shocking to those who do not know recent academic history: ". . . during the decade of the most explosive growth in the history of higher education—the 1960s—women lost ground as a percentage of members of regular faculty ranks in four-year institutions, especially at the associate professor level, and gained ground only at the instructor level."[20] At least once the authors allow themselves a plaintive sentence, as they declare that, "As in the case of graduate students, it would have been far easier to provide increased opportunities for women on faculties a decade ago, when enrollments were rising exceedingly rapidly." And they note also as "surprising" the fact that "both the relative representation and status of women have deteriorated over the last fifty years."[21] Thus, one can only conclude that, left to its own devices, the academic world would only continue its neglect of women (and minority groups).

But the depressing prognosis depends as well on the additional fact that although some institutional growth will occur in the 1970s, there will be little or none in the following decade, and nothing for many decades to come (if ever) to match the 1960s. Since women, in effect, lost ground on faculties and in administrations through the decade of the 1960s, and since the growth rate of the education industry is slowing and will presumably come to a halt by 1980, it will take considerable time for women to "catch up" to where they should be, even according to their current numbers and proportions in various disciplines. The best that can be hoped for, therefore, is to maintain the status quo in female-typed fields and to add a few women to male-typed fields. If *half* of all new faculty hired henceforth were women, by 1990 30 percent of faculties would be female. Not sanguine about that possibility, the authors of the Carnegie report try another prediction, and suggest that perhaps by the year 2000 women will be "included in the national professoriate in approximately the same proportions as they are in the total labor force." They urge solemnly that "this is a task for a generation of effort."

Behind these predictions lies an estimate that allows for the doubling of the percentage of women who earn the doctorate annually—to 30 percent; and a hope that these 30 percent will, in the course of the next 30 years, fill 30 percent of the faculty slots in four-year institutions. That is a modest enough goal. And as depressing as it may seem for people who want to see change occur more quickly, it is an optimistic view, given the specific projections (printed in the appendix) for the next two to five years by Harvard, Stanford, and Columbia.[22]

Hence, one is left with an equivocal impression: on the one hand, the report is forthright and unflinching in its view of discrimination against women, and it prescribes a number of specific strategies to repair the damage—affirmative action, improved high school counseling, women's studies, part-time flexibility, child-care services, etc.; but on the other hand, change is bound to be slow, and the supporting details of the appendix of the report make that change likely to be slower still.

In light of the prognosis, two strategies emerge from the Carnegie report. The most obvious of these is the emphasis on affirmative action guidelines and goals. The authors make an effort here to reassure male critics of affirmative action that "colleges and universities can achieve affirmative action goals without the lowering of standards . . . ." Their own rationale hinges on the key word "balance," as though that might appeal to departments hitherto and for a hundred years or more, presumably, "unbalanced" in their rosters of white male scholars. Despite the evidence of the 1960s, the authors emphasize voluntary compliance, a function no doubt of Carnegie's general distaste for the hand of the federal government in higher education, and a preference for more indirect methods of control. Whether one espouses direct or indirect methods, some means of enforcement beyond morality and goodwill are essential, especially since they have not been effective motivators of change in the past, or even in recent history. In their concluding remarks, the authors resort to optimism, suggesting the need only for "interim" "federal pressure for affirmative action and pressure from campus and professional women's groups," and hoping that "as attitudes change, aspirations of women toward participation in higher education on a basis of equal opportunity with men will come to be taken for granted."[23]

A second major strategy is more daring and progressive: it is based on recent analyses of an increasingly sex-typed academic and professional world, and projects the encouragement of women to enter "nontraditional" fields. Certainly many feminists would applaud this aim, since a major principle of the women's movement has called for integrating the work force. If I am dubious about the principle, it is that such integration has not been of particular benefit to women. Quite the reverse: Caroline Bird describes, for example, the integration of males into library schools that resulted in their rapid assumption of major administrative responsibilities in the largest, most prestigious libraries, where they were often trained by women.[24] We all know how deferentially males are treated when they enter such female work worlds as nursing or elementary education. For the young male kindergarten teacher, the pipelines are greased on the route to administrative jobs. For women, we know that integration has usually meant a place at the bottom as in the feminization of the bank teller's job, or the teaching profession itself.

What would it mean for women to enter nontraditional fields? Given the technological world of the late twentieth century, it would obviously be desirable for women to become true participants in science and related professions. But the issue of "true" participation gives me pause, especially when I consider the relationship between numbers and power. With the statistics projected by the Carnegie report, it is inconceivable that women entering nontraditional fields could, by 2000, be any more, still, than "tokens." Even if the percentage of women engineers or architects increased from the current 1 percent to 6, they should still be tokens. Indeed, the writers of the Carnegie report use this fact to comfort "white male academic critics" who "exaggerate the threat to employment opportunities for white men."

Granted we are facing a situation in which the rate of increase in the number of faculty members employed is slowing down, and faculty employment may well become stationary or actually decline for a time in the 1980s. The potential job shortage for both sexes is most serious in the humanities and arts, in which women tend to be relatively well represented, but there are so few female Ph.D.'s in some of the traditionally male fields that it will be a long time before the competition of women presents any real threat.[25]

Not only would there be no possibility for developing feminist leadership in those traditional male professions; there would be no base sizable enough from which to organize for change. With all that said, however, it is still possible to encourage women to enter nontraditional fields—for other, more long-range reasons—but only as one part of a two-pronged strategy.

The second prong seems to me both of more immediate and of more ultimate consequence. Instead of bemoaning the fact that women numerically dominate the teaching, nursing, and social work professions, why not consider that fact important strategically? Why encourage the most talented women to enter a physics laboratory rather than a school superintendent's office or a department of educational administration? Why is it more important to spread a thin tokendom of women through the nontraditional kingdoms than to attempt a transformation of the traditional ghettos themselves—especially if one of those, the public school system, is responsible for the perpetuation of sex stereotyping and the low aspirations of women? It is here that I would want to move the writers of the Carnegie report, again, one step further. In the Carnegie report, women emerge as victims of both discrimination and socialization, but not as potential agents of their own change, much less agents of social change more generally. Since numbers are obviously useful both for building a base of support for change and for providing a large pool of talent from which to draw leaders, I would concentrate major energies during the next decade on the female professions, especially public school teaching. If schools are the major social agency responsible for socialization of the young, and if these schools are populated mainly with women, themselves socialized to do the job, clearly it is essential to release those teachers from the treadmill. The process needed is one similar to that invented by teachers of women's studies: new teaching strategies and a curriculum that builds on the lives and experiences of those studying.

I do not mean to suggest that by substituting female for male principals of elementary schools that the stereotypic treatment of girls and boys in classrooms will automatically halt, or that by replacing men with women in the hierarchy we shall change the structure and process of that hierarchy. But each year that I have traveled, I have met intrepid feminist teachers, leaving or in the process of making plans to leave public education—either for law school or for a Ph.D. program, and often with a special interest in women's studies. Some of these women could have offered an alternative vision to traditional leadership, but to none of them had such a possibility occurred. I would like to put such thoughts into feminists' heads, and to see programs begun expressly designed for new leadership. The next decade may be especially crucial if, as males enter to integrate the female job world, energetic feminists leave to seek careers elsewhere.

But more than leadership is needed to change the professions dominated by women. The service professions, like housework and child care, have always been held in low esteem both by the male world and by women themselves. And yet, of course, a complex society like this one could not continue to function without such work. To teach children, to serve the sick, the troubled, and the needy—these are significant tasks. How they are accomplished has been decided not by the women who do these daily jobs, but by males sometimes far from that place of work in both space and time. A consciousness about the potential of "womanpower," a knowledge of women's use of power, and an analysis of the current work and status of public school teachers, nurses, and social workers might lead, as in the case of nurses recently, to an awareness that the job needs redefinition by the workers themselves. What if a school or system's elementary school teachers told their (male) administration and school board (and their male-dominated union) that they wanted to redefine the curriculum? One could not imagine a more desirable, less painful means of implementing the federal guidelines to Title IX than to educate skilled new feminist leadership and huge numbers of informed and conscious teachers. We should not need to enforce Title IX on physical education: teachers might decide for themselves that both girls and boys need sound and integrated programs from grade one forward.

The question of timing deserves a special note. In part because they have been ghettos for women, in part because feminists have tended to shun the traditionally female, these professions have been the last to feel the impact of the women's movement: they need the interest and support of feminists to encourage those initiatives already under way. From women's caucuses and programs in teachers' unions, for example, have come a variety of conferences and publications on the subject of sex-role stereotyping, and there is now a useful center functioning in Washington to promote continued efforts.[26]

At the beginning of this essay, I asked several questions about breaking away from the control of a male-centered world without assuming its guises and reversing its patriarchy, without extending new forms of oppression to other women, to groups of minorities, or to men themselves. One early strategy depended on the somewhat ostrich-like assumption that women could cultivate their own sphere, assume power over their own lives, without affecting men's. When that first wave of nineteenth-century feminism impinged on males, it was to ask for "equality" in the male world, without changing its essential maleness. The recent movement has also built on similar assumptions about women seizing power over their own lives, but the methods have been more self-consciously in opposition to patriarchy's own: "sisterhood" and the sharing of power aim deliberately to undercut traditional authority. How profound is this movement for change? Not the last five years but the next ten will begin to tell us.

Conclusion

The chief effect of the women's movement on higher education has been its impact on the lives of academic women. No doubt this effect will continue to be felt among new generations now in schools or colleges: increasing numbers of women will be motivated to organize their lives around careers and egalitarian relationships, and many of these women will choose nontraditional careers. But even optimists declare that the numbers of women entering such professions as medicine, engineering, and architecture will remain minuscule unless three coordinated efforts begin: at the elementary school level, where girls are not expected to succeed at mathematics and science; at the high school and college levels, where girls are discouraged from pursuing studies in science and technology; and in the professions themselves, where the "old boys' clubs" remain untouched by the past decade of the women's movement. In those nontraditional areas, the battle to be fought still is for entrance, not for equity or power. It will be several decades before women's caucuses can make significant changes in any facet of those professions.

But there is another and more immediate effort possible: the power of women to change traditionally female professions. It is not that I urge women to keep their "place." Indeed, I expect and encourage a perceptible shift of women toward the nontraditional professions. But at the same time, I am concerned about such professions as nursing, social work, and teaching, their esteem now demeaned by two labels—"female" and "traditional." In the current decade and in the next, I should like to see feminist energies in higher education focused on these areas.

If the strategy I suggest as most important for those next ten years seems to come full circle—to urge the development of women's power in those areas where they are most numerous—teaching, nursing, social work—it is not because I think of these as belonging only to women. They are critical for the lives of men and children as well as women. To focus feminist energies on them now would be to develop "womanpower" to change three of the most important service institutions in the society. Academic women have used this first decade to change their own lives; the next one will tell us whether those changes contain the power to alter the institutions in which they and large numbers of their students work.

Notes

1. Mary Wollstonecraft, *A Vindication of the Rights of Woman*, p. 107.
2. Ibid., pp. 76, 131.
3. I am sorry to say that there never was a bra-burning, but rather the symbolic disposal of such items and others in a trash can before the 1968 Atlantic City beauty pageant.
4. I do not suppose that most women who have been in consciousness-raising groups are necessarily aware of their analogy to Chinese forms. Obviously, there were several elements in the United States culture that allowed for the spread of such groups: the coffee klatch, for example, the quilting bee, and other forms of female social or work groups made the idea of discussion sessions quite natural, though the "rules" for consciousness-raising groups set them apart from such precedents. It is also true that in a society that places value on psychotherapy, such groups were seen as having potential therapeutic value, as indeed they do. In the southern civil rights movement, discussion groups, especially on the subject of racism, also provided a precedent.
5. Mitchell, *Woman's Estate*, p. 62.
6. Quite by accident, I met Iowa political scientist John McClusky in January 1974 at a work conference on educational leadership, where we were assigned to the same writing team. We produced a paper called "Hierarchy, Power, and Women in Educational Policy Making." McClusky's doctoral dissertation, focused on conceptualizations of "liberating" as distinct from "debilitating" forms of power, describes the political career of Martin Luther King in detail. McClusky's unpublished papers are available from him.
7. Aside from the biological capacity to conceive and bear children, that is. All people are born with capacities or "powers" that the world they live in may encourage or deny. Despite many efforts of researchers, there has still been no hard evidence that distinguishes between the innate capacities of humans by sex or race.
8. These psychological terms have become commonplace in the academic women's movement, especially following the work of Matina Horner (1969) on the "achievement theory" of McClelland and others (1953). For a brief summary, see chapter 10 of Judith M. Bardwick's *Psychology of Women*.
9. By the time I returned to English, I had learned that one did not need to *be* creative. But I had taken this teacher's judgment so to heart that, when at college I had been selected, on the basis of my work in freshman composition, for a creative writing class, I petitioned to avoid it and to do the regular critical writing course instead.
10. In those days before universities' "tracking" systems, a form of open admissions prevailed. Freshman English was one of the hurdles designed to thin the entering population, and teaching assistants were unwitting accomplices to the "cooling-out" system (see Clark, 1960).
11. Showalter, "Women and the Literary Curriculum."
12. Indeed, the only admirable female characters in all the books were Swift's Glumdalclitch and Ernest Pontifex's spinster aunt Alethea in Samuel Butler's *The Way of All Flesh*.

13. Howe, "Identity and Expression: A Writing Course for Women," chap. 3 in this volume.

14. While most of the early courses seemed to come from institutions on the East Coast, this was a phase of Eastern chauvinism, corrected the following year with a broadening of the communications network.

15. A grant from the Ford Foundation helped to survey the academic world and to produce *Who's Who and Where in Women's Studies*, Tamar Berkowitz, Jean Mangi, and Jane Williamson, eds. (Old Westbury, N.Y.: The Feminist Press, 1975). Note: this volume is now out of print. Annual updates of women's studies programs appear in *Women's Studies Quarterly*.

16. Howe and Ahlum, *Female Studies III*; Deborah S. Rosenfelt, *Female Studies VII*.

17. While the report is issued, like others in the series, under the joint responsibility of a prestigious panel of 16 men and 2 women (Patricia Roberts Harris and Katherine E. McBride), acknowledgments include the names of four staff members, presumably the text's writers and researchers (Margaret S. Gordon, Elizabeth Scott, Laura Kent, and Jane McClosky), as well as a roster of a dozen academic and foundation women (and one man), many of them prominent feminists, who read and commented on drafts. Such contributions by individuals cannot be viewed as substitutes for the ongoing discussions of the Carnegie Commission itself during the last half-dozen years, much less for national organization and debate among academic women.

18. *Opportunities for Women in Higher Education*, pp. 120, 165.

19. "There also remains the possibility that faculty members in leading research universities, who tend not only to be overwhelmingly male but also to have prestigious reputations, are more likely to discourage women from entering their fields than are faculty members in comprehensive colleges and liberal arts colleges. There is some evidence that this tendency is not confined to traditionally male fields" (p. 68). The tone is characteristic of the report.

20. Women lost ground, though not so dramatically, also at the full professor and assistant professor levels. The general percentage of women on four-year college faculties declined from 19.1 percent in 1959–60 to 19.0 percent in 1971–72, during a decade when some institutions doubled their enrollments and new ones opened their doors for the first time; ibid., p. 110.

21. Ibid., pp. 111–12, 125.

22. Ibid. If one compares the general hope—to achieve faculties on which 30 percent are women—with the plans of Harvard, Stanford, and Columbia, one can only conclude that *other*, less prestigious institutions (and women's colleges—which the authors encourage to continue) will make up for their deficiencies. Such dual standards will simply continue things as they are.

23. Ibid., p. 137, 165.

24. Bird, *Born Female*.

25. *Opportunities for Women in Higher Education*, p. 139.

26. The Resource Center on Sex Roles in Education, a project of the National Foundation for the Improvement of Education.

Bibliography

Ahlum, Carol, and Florence Howe. *The New Guide to Female Studies*, no. 1. Pittsburgh: KNOW, 1971.

Ahlum, Carol, and Florence Howe. *The New Guide to Female Studies*, no. 2. Old Westbury, N.Y.: The Feminist Press, 1972.

Bardwick, Judith M. *Psychology of Women*. New York: Harper & Row, 1971.

Bird, Caroline. *Born Female*. New York: David McKay, 1968.

Carden, Maren Lockwood. *The New Feminist Movement*. New York: Russell Sage Foundation, 1974.

Carnegie Commission on Higher Education. *Opportunities for Women in Higher Education*. New York: McGraw-Hill, 1973.

Clark, Burton R. "The 'Cooling-out' Function in Higher Education." *American Journal of Sociology* 65 (May 1960):569-76.

Fuller, Margaret. *Woman in the Nineteenth Century*. New York: W. W. Norton, 1971.

Horner, Matina S. "Fail, Bright Women." *Psychology Today* 3 (November 1969):36-38.

Howe, Florence. "Mississippi's Freedom Schools: The Politics of Education." *Harvard Educational Review* 35 (Spring 1965):144-60.

Howe, Florence. *Female Studies II*. Pittsburgh: KNOW, 1970.

Howe, Florence. "Identity and Expression: A Writing Course for Women." *College English* 32 (May 1971):863-71.

Howe, Florence, and Carol Ahlum. *Female Studies III*. Pittsburgh: KNOW, 1971.

Howe, Florence, and Carol Ahlum. "Women's Studies and Social Change." In *Academic Women on the Move*, edited by Alice S. Rossi and Ann Calderwood. New York: Russell Sage Foundation, 1973.

Howe, Florence, John McClusky, and Elizabeth Wilson. "Hierarchy, Power, and Women in Educational Policy Making." Unpublished essay.

McClelland, D. C., J. Atkinson, R. Clark, and E. Lowell. *The Achievement Motive*. New York: Appleton & Company, 1953.

McClusky, John. "Beyond the Carrot and the Stick: Liberation and Power without Control." Unpublished essay. Also "Adult Models' Liberating and Debilitating Influence on Young Women in the U.S. Educational System." Unpublished project proposal.

Miller, Joanna, Michelina Fitzmaurice, Tamar Berkowitz, and Carol Ahlum. *The New Guide to Female Studies*, no. 3. Old Westbury, N.Y.: The Feminist Press, 1973.

Mitchell, Juliet. *Woman's Estate*. New York: Pantheon Books, 1971.

Rosenfelt, Deborah Silverton. *Female Studies VII: Going Strong*. Old Westbury, N.Y.: The Feminist Press, 1973.

Rossi, Alice S. ed. *The Feminist Papers*. New York: Columbia University Press, 1973.

Rossi, Alice S., ed. *Essays on Sex Equality*. Chicago: University of Chicago Press, 1970.

Rossi, Alice S., and Ann Calderwood, eds. *Academic Women on the Move*. New York: Russell Sage Foundation, 1973.

Showalter, Elaine. "Women and the Literary Curriculum." *College English* 32 (May 1971):855-62.

Tobias, Sheila. *Female Studies I*. Pittsburgh: KNOW, 1970.

Wollstonecraft, Mary. *A Vindication of the Rights of Woman*. New York: W. W. Norton, 1967.

Feminism and the
Education of Women
(1975)

In 1974–1975, I held a Ford Fellowship for the Study of Women in Society. This essay grew out of an attempt to discover, through a search in the archives of nine colleges and universities, whether curriculum could be found that was not male-centered and male-biased. Although the search for curriculum that included women's history and achievements proved nearly fruitless, the research illuminated controlling feminist assumptions behind three phases of women's education: the seminary movement that established secondary education for women; the movement that established eastern women's colleges and coeducation; and the current women's studies movement.

I wrote this essay during a visit to the University of Utah in the spring of 1975, when I worked in the archives following a week's teaching to faculty and administrators of an intense introductory seminar in women's studies. The program, organized by Shauna Adix, director of the Women's Resource Center, included a comfortable residence in which I was able to write. Once written, the essay became a lecture for the 1975 series organized by Judith Stiehm of the University of Southern California, and was eventually published by that university's press as part of a volume called The Frontiers of Knowledge.

In the summer of 1976, when I was invited to guest edit an issue of Boston University's Journal of Education, *called "Toward a History of Women's Higher Education," I revised the essay. The special issue appeared in August 1977, and that version appears here.*

WHEN I WAS A STUDENT my least favorite course was history. I had not learned to ask two or three questions which might have made a difference:

175

why? who made that decision? and what were women doing? Indeed, I accepted history as given—a bland series of causes and results of wars. Even revolutions were uninteresting, the Civil War without human content, and the terms of U. S. presidents undistinguishable except for Washington, Lincoln, and the current (second) Roosevelt. I am not exaggerating. Although history repeated itself several times in the course of my education in New York City's public schools and Hunter College, I went off to graduate school without the slightest interest either in U. S. history or literature, and for the next four years, I read British literature and as little British history as I could manage. It never occurred to me that *people* wrote history, ordinary people. It never occurred to me that women were part of history and might write the story of their lives.

During my first year in graduate school, at Smith College, I chose to study Chaucer and Shakespeare, and to write my master's thesis on Jonathan Swift's poetry, especially those poems addressed to or about women. Twenty-five years ago when I made that choice I was not a feminist, nor could I ask any questions of history. Although I chose to write about Swift's poems *on women,* my thesis projected one message only: Swift was an underestimated poet; indeed, I urged that he was a fine poet. Somehow, I had become his admirer and defender. My thesis explicated his poems, pointing to their well-constructed rhymes and rhythms, and urging the cleverness of their content, even on occasion the appropriate wisdom of their views as expressed formally (aesthetically) by the poem. Never did I question the status of women in the eighteenth century, or seek information about the comparative privileges allotted to women and men, nor did I attempt to evaluate Swift's views of women as compared with those of other men. And while I had read other eighteenth century *men* of letters on women—it would have been difficult to avoid the Spectator and Tatler papers or Pope's Belinda or Dr. Johnson's view of a woman preacher—never did I consider searching for actual writings of *women.*

Feminist scholars today are saying that women's history, achievement, and future are important enough to be studied, described, analyzed, reported, worked for. A philosophical feminist says "I care about women and I believe that their history and ideas are important to all of us." When I call myself an ideological feminist, I am adding something to the philosopher's position: I am saying that I will put my research at the service of changing the status and conceptions of women. Indeed, my research project exists because I have very real questions to ask about where women's education is going, where it should go, and how it should get there. I am interested in history because I hope that it will shed some light on the present and into the future. I want to understand not only how we got into some of our current predicament but how we are to proceed from here.

The questions I began my research with have grown out of a decade of discovering that the curriculum I had been taught from, and the very one I was passing on to my students, was male-centered and male-biased. White middle-class, male-centered and male-biased. Countless studies and other kinds of analysis now exist to demonstrate the cultural sexist bias of the curriculum. But I should like to make clear that when I was in college or graduate school, I never once heard the names of Elizabeth Cady Stanton or Susan B. Anthony, much less studied their writings and achievements. I had not read Simone de Beauvoir until 1965, when I was also reading Betty Friedan and Doris Lessing. For me, and for other feminists of my generation and for those younger as well, Kate Millett's *Sexual Politics* was the ultimate "awakening." For people like me who need information as well as experience, Millett was, like de Beauvoir and Friedan, compelling.

Lost Masterpieces Regained

Because of those books and others that I was reading even as I was trying to teach women students about their histories and to move them to talk about their lives, hopes, and desires, I began to realize that if we were to change the education of women, to provide them with the history and role models they needed, we would have to write new materials or republish those that had been lost. The Feminist Press was born during this period and at the end of its first year, Tillie Olsen offered our first lost treasure, *Life in the Iron Mills* published anonymously by Rebecca Harding Davis. I mention this work because it is an admitted masterpiece, lost to us from its first date of publication in 1861, and hence until this time never part of the curriculum. If Davis had been lost, we speculated, how many others were there? That question began to haunt me, as The Feminist Press began to publish other lost American women writers: Charlotte Perkins Gilman, Agnes Smedley, Kate Chopin, and Mary Wilkins Freeman. Why had they been lost? Who had "lost" them?

I began to wonder, what if I had read these writers when I was young? How might I have turned out? And then again, other possibilities occurred; perhaps they had not been lost originally at all? Perhaps it is the history of these writers that has been lost? Perhaps young people, at some moment in time, had read these lost women writers? Perhaps, I speculated, young women in college late in the nineteenth century had read feminist fiction writers and other feminist prose writers as well. Perhaps they had also studied, as part of their history courses, the history of efforts to gain suffrage?

And perhaps you are beginning to see how I got from my dissatisfaction with the male-centered curriculum and my desire for a more balanced and inclusive curriculum to wanting to know whether there had ever been anything different. I need to add to this process one other factor. Since the women's movement touched the campus, an entire educational phenomenon known as women's studies had developed. I added to my list of questions about the history of the curriculum, others about the future of women's studies. Should women's studies courses and programs be developed into separate departments with their own faculties, budgets, majors, etc.? What *is* the future of women's studies? What is the best way to design a curriculum that reflects and is immediately responsive to the explosion of knowledge created by the academic arm of the women's movement?

What have I found? My research has made clear to me three phases of feminism—we are now in the third—each of which has involved a battle over the function of women's education and the content of the curriculum. They each involve separatism and considerations of vocational purpose as well as the ideas of marriage and motherhood. The first phase, in part because it's the earliest, is the most persistent and the most acceptable to men. For these reasons, it is still a force with us today.

The women who fought the first series of battles for women's higher education in the early nineteenth century were all interested in training teachers. They thought women ought to be educated separately from men, and for one specific vocational purpose: teaching. Three-quarters of the history of women's education in the nineteenth century—whether at single-sex or at allegedly coeducational institutions—is also the story of teacher education. We should all know these names: Mary Lyon, the founder in 1837 of Mt. Holyoke, Emma Willard, the founder in 1821 of Troy Seminary, Catherine Beecher, the founder of Hartford Seminary, and later of other schools for women in the midwest—they and others worked through the early decades of the nineteenth century to persuade men of the value of educating their daughters, and to raise funds for the establishment of permanent institutions for women. Abbott Female Academy, for example, was founded in Andover in 1829 for "young ladies who may wish to qualify themselves to teach." According to A. C. Cole, Mary Lyon's "original and primary objective," as she worked through the 1830's to raise funds for opening Mt. Holyoke Seminary, "was the preparation of teachers for the millions crying for education, especially in the great valley of the west." Mary Lyon's scheme was the education of very young women—admission to Mt. Holyoke at 14 was not unusual—who would teach two to four years "and then marry and become firm pillars to hold up their successors." This "circulatory system" (we would use the term "revolving door") she thought "would accomplish more for education than a smaller number of teachers who, by not marrying, could devote 20 or 30 years to the profession." So teaching was not only an appropriate profession for women; it was also work that might also prepare them for marriage, child-rearing, and the community support of education. In my archival research, I have found person after person, female and male, commenting or arguing that the education of women would not be wasteful, since even if women married and therefore had to resign from their teaching jobs, their preparation was also useful for their expected work as mothers. Such statements, appearing either in catalogues themselves, or in presidents' reports, justify to a board of regents or to a legislature or to parents the expense involved in educating women who, it was expected, could only work for a short period before marriage and motherhood. It is important to understand also that early feminists regarded teaching as the prime means of earning a modest livelihood in dignified and socially useful work—for women who could not or would not marry.

Developing a Differentness: Feminism's First Phase

The feminist ideology behind such views of women's education emphasizes women's separate and subordinate social role. Women *are* different from men, such feminists proclaimed, but women ought to be allowed to develop that differentness for the greater good of society. As Emma Willard, founder of Troy Seminary in 1821 put it, schools for women ought to be "as different from those appropriated for the other sex, as the female character and duties are from the male'." Cole writes that the purpose of such education is twofold: "implanting proper ideas and ideals in future mothers" and "furnishing properly trained teachers." The ultimate purpose is gloriously ideal: "to elevate the standards of morality and of public education." The ideological portrait is incomplete, however, until we add Catharine Beecher's belief in the value of self-sacrifice. All of these women were devout Christians. For them, teaching was an appropriate female activity, since it was the obverse, secular version of clerical ministerial work. Women teachers were the secular arm of the church. Teachers were missionaries, moral emissaries, shapers of young minds and destinies. The purpose of women's education, according to Catharine Beecher, was to enable women not to "*shine,* but to *act.*" And to *act,* of course, in a moral manner for its own sake, to act as well as a natural role model for others and also as a deliberate moulder of others' morality. Catharine Beecher believed that women were especially suited for the role of moral teacher, since women were a) "continually striving after purity" and b) "consistently" self-sacrificial in their own homes (as contrasted with man's domestic selfishness and generosity outside the home). The key ideas for this entire generation of feminist educators were sacrifice and service: women, they argued were better equipped than men for sacrifice and service. Mary Lyon described for her students the opportunity for sacrificial service by "going to destitute places in the West to labor" (meaning to teach in Ohio and Kansas). As to pecuniary rewards, she said, "Ladies should not expect more than a mediocrity—less than $100 a year usually."

Not surprisingly, a significant number of men including some in charge of education decided that it was in their interest to heed the pleas of these feminists. All the members of the boards of trustees and many of the financial supporters of early seminaries and later women's colleges and normal schools were men. And why not: these feminists were not challenging the status quo; they were simply saying we can do the child-rearing job better than men and even, on a massive scale, more economically. Not only are we women naturally more moral and thus more ready to maintain law and order; we are also self-sacrificing and thus we will do all this for the benefit of society and not our own pocketbooks. What has been called by Michael Katz "the feminization of the teaching force" satisfied both the nineteenth century's social need for an economical and efficient system of public education and the early feminists' need for work that could be rationalized without social offense.

Later in the century, with the extension of secondary education, and the growth of public education into large systems, once again the twin needs for "economy and improvement" continued the demand for women teachers. As Katz describes the process, a school committee in Quincy, Massachusetts., in 1874, called for the establishment of large schools of 500 students, in which "one *man* [italics added] could be placed in charge. . . . Under his direction could be placed a number of female assistants." "Females," the *male* committee explained in 1874, "are not only adapted, but carefully trained, to fill such positions, as well [as] or better than men, excepting the master's place, which sometimes requires a man's force. . . . " And as if that were not enough reason—and of course ideologically from a male point of view it is not—the committee added, "and the competition is so great [among women for these jobs and between women and men] that . . . [women's] services command less than one-half the wages of male teachers."

On reflection, perhaps none of this history is surprising. How then does a subservient population convince its masters to allow it an increment of social progress? Obviously, by convincing the masters of its usefulness for *them*. Thus women teachers offered both an economical means to accomplish public education and the willingness as well to do so within the terms of the society's patriarchy. Women were to be taught how to teach the moral code that kept them enthralled in the first place. As Catharine Beecher surmised, as early as 1829, therefore, "the most important object of education" is not the acquisition of knowledge, but rather, "the formation of personal habits and manners, the correction of the disposition, the regulation of the social feelings, the formation of the conscience, and the direction of the moral character and habits." These, she said, "united, [are] objects of much greater consequence than the mere communication of knowledge and the discipline of the intellectual powers."

If the function of such teaching was ultimately moral uplift for the nation, the curriculum had to reflect this goal. Teachers were the secular arm of the church; women as teachers could accomplish the moral reformation of character, a duty that the church allowed only to males. The curriculum that followed from such educational principles and goals supported patriarchy, and taught women that the home or, temporarily, the classroom was their appropriate domain. Catharine Beecher proposed a department of moral philosophy, one that would teach such principles to future teachers, as the center of her school.

The curriculum differed in kind and degree from the classical education offered to their brothers through most of the nineteenth century; it simply verified women's distinct, traditional roles as nurturant servers of domestic life, propagators, child-rearers, and teachers. Women had to learn enough mathematics, and later science, as well as other skills to enable them to be adequate teachers of young children and older adolescents, but their education was not meant to develop in them the capacity either to question knowledge or to investigate its outer reefs. They learned enough to teach rudiments to others, not to shape knowledge anew.

But education, as we know, is not entirely predictable, or controllable. We often do not teach students what we want to or what we think we are teaching. The relationship between the early feminist educators I have described and the later ones connected to the founding of women's colleges after 1870 has not yet been traced in detail. The differences between the two groups concern us here, since we are the inheritors of their battle, the second major educational battle for women's education in the nineteenth century. That battle was initiated by the feminists we know as suffragists.

The Drive for Equality: Feminism's Second Phase

Both Elizabeth Cady Stanton (who went to Emma Willard's Troy Seminary) and Susan B. Anthony (who was of course a teacher) believed that there were *no intellectual differences* between men and women and that therefore their education ought to be identical, just as their social, economic, and political rights ought to be identical. Their ideology insisted on equality, not on distinct and separate spheres. And the founders of such colleges as Smith and Wellesley, as well as the second president of Bryn Mawr, M. Carey Thomas, put this theory into practice by adopting for women's colleges a curriculum identical to that proscribed for the men of Harvard and Yale. Women, such educators announced, could and should do all that men do. So long as Latin and Greek were staples of that curriculum, women at Bryn Mawr or Smith did Latin and Greek. As the curriculum broadened at Harvard and much later at Yale, so did it at the elite women's colleges.

Here is M. Carey Thomas in 1901, arguing that the education of women must be no different from the education of men. "The burden of proof, is with those who believe that the college education of men and women should differ." She too focuses on vocation, but it is that of the professions themselves. Her argument rests on the assumption that "women are to compete with men" in these professions. "There is no reason to believe that typhoid or scarlet fever or phthsis can be successfully treated by a woman physician in one way and by a man physician in another way. There is indeed every reason to believe that unless treated in the best way the patient may die, the sex of the doctor affecting the result less even than the sex of the patient." She argues similarly for bridge-building. And for cooking. And she concludes on a high note of warm optimism: "This college education should be the same as men's, not only because there is, I believe, but one best education, but because men and women are to live and work together as comrades and dear friends and married friends and lovers, and because their effectiveness and happiness and the welfare of the generation to come after them will be vastly increased if their college education has given them the same intellectual training and the same scholarly and moral ideals."

But what of the coeducational colleges and universities, the Oberlin of 1837 and the land grant colleges after the Morrill Act of 1862? At Oberlin, the story is not an heroic one. Jill Conway, Smith College's president, tells it in an essay in *Daedalus:* Oberlin was a "manual-work school" aimed to fill "an ever-expanding need [in the west] for trained clergy":

> In its early informal manifestations young men would undertake to work the land of a minister with sound theological knowledge if he would instruct them in return for their labor. Oberlin was a formal institutionalization of such an arrangement since the college was linked to a five hundred-acre farm where it was hoped that the students would produce enough in crops to reduce the cost of their education considerably. No sooner was the experiment launched, however, than it became clear that another element of cost could be eliminated if there were women students who could carry out the domestic chores in return for instruction. Once admitted to the college, they duplicated there all the existing service roles of women within the domestic economy. Classes were not held on Mondays so that the women students could launder and repair the men's clothes. Cooking and cleaning were done on a careful schedule outside classroom hours, and the women students always waited on table. Thus, the effect of the experiment was hardly consciousness-raising, and those few feminists, like Lucy Stone, who were early Oberlin graduates were radicals on such questions before they entered college.

Women were offered a secondary curriculum, called "literary," and when one young woman wanted to study theology, she was not encouraged. Antoinette Brown, a close friend of Lucy Stone, attended classes in theology for an extra three years, though she was ignored, indeed was not ordained or graduated.

Kansas State Agricultural College, now KSU, one of the first of the land-grant colleges to be founded one year after the Morrill Act was passed, was a pioneer in practical education for an increasingly broad base of U. S. citizenry. Thus, in 1874, President John A. Anderson issued a *Hand-book* arguing the uselessness of a classical education in Latin, Greek, and Mathematics—a very daring departure—and calling for the establishment of three curricula: 1) agricultural; 2) mechanics [engineering]; and 3) women's. The women's curriculum, an early version of home economics, provided for classes in "Special Hygiene" appropriate to women, "Gardening" (mainly ornamental without the "manual labor that should be done by men"); "Household Economy" (including "Lectures upon household chemistry. . . . embracing cooking, domestic management, and kindred topics"); "Sewing"; and "Farm Economy" (including those operations which usually come under the supervision of the farmer's wife or daughter, and which are not included in "Gardening" or "Household Economy," such as butter and cheese making, etc.) as well as literature and other subjects appropriate to women. Kansas also pioneered courses in industrial arts, but these were also carefully sex-typed: printing, for example, in its English origins a woman's industry, was in the 1874 curriculum, labeled as being only for men. (It was delightful to find it open to both sexes by the president who followed in 1884.) At other coeducational universities, it is clear that women were channelled into the Normal course—teacher education—and not into mining and metallurgy or chemistry or other areas of hard science, law, or medicine.

And so there were two possibilities for women at coeducational institutions—and these are still possible today: first, women could and did study alongside men in such courses as United States history or the literature of Great Britain or introduction to psychology; in each case, the curriculum is designed for and geared to the interests and achievements of men—it is male-centered and male-biased. Second, they might "elect" to study in almost totally female "professional" ghettoes—elementary education, for example, or home economics, or nursing. In these courses, the curriculum is for the most part still either male-centered, or male-biased. That is, women studying home economics assume that the traditional patriarchal forms of marriage and family organization are desirable, inevitable and unchangeable.

Challenging Male Hegemony: Feminism's Third Phase

Through the early twentieth century, the education of women in women's colleges or in coeducational institutions continues to alternate between two poles: 1) that women need a separate, special education, for vocations especially suited to them—teaching, nursing, or social work, for example; and 2) that women are men's intellectual equals and may therefore study appropriately all that men do. In both cases women had to accept the traditional view of themselves as entering acceptable female-typed activities or professions; or taking the more daring position of M. Carey Thomas—that women were as good as men and therefore could do *men's* work. In neither case, however, had there been a challenge to male hegemony *over the curriculum or knowledge in general.* In neither case had women said, *no,* we are going to redefine the terms of the work world. We are going to look closely at the history of work and reassess job classifications in the rational light of social needs today. That is the crux for us today. In the past women either carved out for themselves an area that men did not want anyway—domestic science, for example,—or they studied within the purview of patriarchal knowledge, that is, history as males have seen it or known it, or science, with priorities established by males.

David Reisman, writing an introduction to Jessie Bernard's *Academic Women,* in 1964 conveniently summarizes the state of higher education for women with particular relevance for teacher education: "Women," he says, "prefer to be *teachers, passing on a received heritage* and responsively concerning themselves with their students while men of equivalent or even lesser ability prefer to be *men-of-knowledge, breaking the accustomed mold* and remaining responsive not to students but to the structure of the discipline and their colleagues in the invisible university" (italics added).

Just one decade later, this sentence sharply divides the past from the present. Yes, that was the way it was for 150 years. Now it is different. Women will no longer be content to pass on "a received heritage"; rather, women have become, are becoming—in Riesman's terms women-of-knowledge, "breaking the accustomed mold."

I am of course referring to women's studies which is truly a new third feminist development: for the first time, feminists in an organized manner are querying education's ultimate—the curriculum and the sources of that curriculum, knowledge itself. Unlike the work of earlier feminists like Catharine Beecher, moreover, the queries are not confined to women's domestic sphere, but encompass many of the traditional male bastions, especially history, economics, sociology, psychology, anthropology, law, even medicine, as well as literature and the arts. Indeed, without the perspective provided by what we call women's studies, I could not have traced the preceding historical patterns.

The new feminism is profoundly different from both forms of the old. We are not saying today simply allow us a piece of the turf (Beecher, Lyon, and others of the first wave), or let us into your castle (second wave: equality), but rather, let us reexamine the whole question, all the questions. Let us take nothing for granted. Most definitely, let us refuse to pass on that "received heritage" without examining its cultural bias. And since women are half the population, they are black as well as white, poor as well as rich; they include all religions, all national and ethnic origins; since one can not talk about women as a monolith, examining cultural bias becomes a complex task far reaching in its potential for education.

Let me give you one immediate and practical example of current feminist thought about the curriculum. The study of American literature is not as old as the history I have been describing. The formal study of both English and U. S. literature hearkens back less than one hundred years. A staple of such reading has been Benjamin Franklin's *Autobiography.* Why? Why have millions of us, female and male, members of minorities and whites, rich and poor, been handed Franklin and not Frederick Douglass, for example, or Elizabeth Cady Stanton? (I will not detour into questions of literary style, but both Douglass and Stanton are at least as interesting on that count as Franklin.) New feminists are not saying that Franklin ought to be dismissed, but they question his value as a single representative of *all* Americans. They are saying that the life of one white male is inadequate to represent us all. His life needs to be viewed in the company of at least one woman's life; moreover, white lives are, alone, inadequate: they ought to be viewed in the company of at least the lives of some members of minorities.

This is a very different kind of feminism from Beecher's or Thomas's. Beecher might have wished her students to study women's lives, but not Stanton's, for she was a rebel. Beecher thought that women teachers should learn their subordinate role exceedingly well. She did not think women ought to get into politics; their domain was the household and, temporarily, the classroom. M. Carey Thomas, president of Bryn Mawr shortly after its founding about a hundred years ago, would also not have argued for reading Stanton's life. She wanted her students to be prepared exactly as men were: that meant follow the leader; read whatever men decided should be read.

New feminists like me are saying, let us look closely at this polyglot. Let us review the hierarchy. Let us study not one life as an example of how we were or how we ought to be. Let us study many lives—and what is equally important—how these lives related each to each. Why could Elizabeth Cady Stanton in 1830 not follow her brother to Union College? What college could a black person, male or female, attend in 1830? And how did educational deprivation affect her/his life opportunities? More significant, read in the company of Franklin's life, Stanton's tells us that bearing and rearing seven children did not prevent her from accomplishments that can be matched by few males in any century.

Today we inherit both sets of ideas about the education of women. Many of us still see women as more honest, virtuous, self-sacrificing, and hence more willing to serve—meaning teach—than men. Others see women as potentially as capable as men in all their spheres. Those who hold this view will usually adopt males as models for female accomplishment. You have heard women say, we can do anything men can do. Feminists today may be found in both those camps still, though I believe that the central thrust of today's feminists needs to be different. Especially for those engaged in education, feminism in all its forms is once again of central importance. On the one hand, we live in a sex-role defined job world. The ghettoes of nursing, elementary education, office work, and social work are realities. On the other hand, we are urging students to enter "nontraditional"—meaning male—fields.

And now I would like to return to my original questions. Have I learned—am I learning—anything of immediate use for those of us engaged in women's studies? The answer is yes and no. Yes, it seems to me that for the first time I can see the logic of our feminist history and I can appreciate and understand those women who struggled for their modest goals. Without them, we could not now be insisting that we too have a history to study and learn from. Their achievements as well as their strategies and tactics are not inconsiderable and we have much to learn from them.

On the other hand, there is no clear model for the current development of women's studies. That is not difficult to understand. It means that we have not been, before today, convinced of our own hegemony over knowledge, our own power to decide about the curriculum. That is an awesome responsibility. We do not want Harvard as a model. We know its severe limitations. We do not have elder brothers, male patrons to establish institutions and guidelines for us. Remember, it was Henry Durant, the intrepid founder of Wellesley who not only said, "Women can do the work. I give them the chance"—but who made it possible. Today *we* are making it possible, and the revision of the curriculum, the explosion of knowledge in all fields, will effect men as well as women. Ultimately—perhaps I am describing still another century of struggle—we will live in a very different educational world.

So, you have heard my optimism, and I am sometimes attacked for it, especially by academics who are "naturally" cynical. Reading history has made me more, rather than less, optimistic. In 1938, when Virginia Woolf wrote a militant feminist and pacifist book called *Three Guineas,* she asked the key question that new feminists have been asking these past ten years. She looked at "our brothers who have been educated at public schools and universities" and asked other women, "do we wish to join that procession or don't we? On what terms shall we join that procession? Above all, where is it leading us, the procession of educated men?" Woolf concluded that the procession was leading us downhill to war and to the degeneration of the human race. Yet she saw no way out but to join the procession, even on its own terms, for women then were powerless—without education, jobs, professions, money. If I am optimistic today, it is because I think that a sizeable number of us with and without jobs, professions, money, are prepared, have begun, to turn the procession at least half an inch off course. Another way to put it is to say that because of the history I have outlined, because of the positions and concessions of earlier feminists, we are more numerous and more powerful today. I am optimistic that we will use that power ultimately and well.

Bibliography

Cole, A. C. *A Hundred Years of Mount Holyoke College*. New Haven: Yale University Press, 1940.

Conway, J. "Coeducation and Women's Studies: Two Approaches to the Question of Woman's Place in the Contemporary University." *Daedalus*, Fall, 1979.

Harter, A. H. *Wellesley: Part of the American Story*. Lexington, Mass.: Stone Wall Press, Inc., 1949.

Katz, M. B. "The New Departure in Quincy, 1873–81: The Nature of Nineteenth-Century Educational Reform." In M. B. Katz, ed., *Education in American History: Readings on the Social Issues*. New York: Praeger, 1973.

Riesman, D. Introduction. In J. Bernard, *Academic Women*. New York: American Library, 1964.

Sklar, K. K. *Catherine Beecher: A Study in American Domesticity*. New Haven: Yale University Press, 1973.

Thomas, M. C. "Education for Women and Men." In B. Cross, ed., *The Educated Woman in America*. New York: Teachers College Press, 1965.

Woolf, V. *Three Guineas*. London: The Hogarth Press, 1952.

Feminism and the Study
of Literature

(1976)

*I used to refer to this essay as my $2,000 dollar lecture. By
some coincidence, four invitations arrived for the spring of 1976
calling for lectures on feminist criticism. Three came from departments of English and women's studies faculty at Brandeis
University, the University of Cincinnati, and the Ohio State University. One came from a project in faculty development funded
by the National Endowment for the Humanities at the University of Chicago.*

*In each institution, the lecture created a stir, because of
young faculty interested in debating the questions I raised. On
one occasion, a woman about my age rose in wrath to deny the
existence of a male-centered literary curriculum, and concluded
her remarks by hurling a book across the room in my direction,
then stamping across the room and slamming a door on the startled audience.*

The Radical Teacher *published the lecture in November
1976.*

IN 1969, FOR THE FIRST TIME, I gave a public lecture away from my own
campus. The invitation came from a small midwestern university's English department: I was asked to talk about fiction, perhaps Doris Lessing
about whom I had written, but if possible with a somewhat broader perspective. I chose to think about a question that had been on my mind for
several years, since 1964, in fact, when, after returning from a freedom
school in Jackson, Mississippi, I began to consider the relationship between the literature I was teaching and the lives of my students—all of
whom were women. So I chose for my question, topic, and title—"Should
Women read Fiction?" My answer in 1969 was very embarassing not only

for the English department which had invited me—and all their students—but for my own teacherly life. My answer was no, women should not read fiction, unless they were either resolute about their own vocations or they were content to follow the path prescribed for most fictional heroines: marriage or death, these were the choices. I regretted my conclusion as feelingly as I could before an English department faculty and its students, but I could offer only the solace of Doris Lessing, of whom most people in the room knew little.

My analysis in 1969 was, it seems to me now, notable for its clarity of thought and argument, since it was based on remarkable ignorance. It was also based on a belief—which I do still hold—that literature affects the lives of those who read it. Perhaps I had become an English major and then an English teacher because I had been infected with a belief shared by critics as diverse as Matthew Arnold, Margaret Fuller, and Mao Tse Tung in the "power" of literature. I cannot reconstruct that right now, but I was at least dimly aware through my whole life that literature was my invisible but open window out of the Jewish ghetto in which I was born and raised. High on my list of favorites were books like *Microbe Hunters,* a series of what were to me thrilling stories about the lives of male scientists. Literature was my door into other people's lives, values, beliefs, traditions. At the same time, it did not tell me that, as a woman, I had a scientific or political future. Indeed, and I have told this story before, the female character I felt closest to when I was in graduate school at Wisconsin was Dorothea Causabon, who, in my view, had not made the mistake of marrying, but only of choosing the wrong man to marry. Even then, I assumed that my ultimate purpose was marriage and child-bearing.

My 1969 analysis linked the idea of Elizabethan conduct books with the theory expressed in Ian Watt's *Rise of the Novel* that fiction became a significant literary form when significant numbers of middle-class women became both readers and writers. Watt makes the useful connection between the "domestic" subject matter of most fiction and the "domestic" lives of most middle-class women. My method in writing that paper was simplicity itself: I reviewed or reread all the "major" British fiction of the eighteenth, nineteenth, and twentieth centuries that I had been exposed to as a student in college and graduate school. I had also read a few "major" European and American novels (written by men) and included them in the "sample." In each case, I asked, "What happens to the women in the novel?" "How does the novel leave them at its conclusion?" And the answer was: either dead or married—or both.

But I have said also that this analysis was based on remarkable ignorance. In the main, this ignorance reflects the narrowness of the literary canon as I had studied it and as I was then teaching it. It is still, needless to say, the literary curriculum that prevails. But there were at least three other important aspects of that ignorance: first, ignorance of the hundreds of women writers who wrote, were published and read, at least in their own lifetimes, and even by other women writers of subsequent generations, but who never made it into the literary curriculum. Second, and as critical: ignorance of feminist polemical literature—from before the eighteenth century forward, and on both sides of the Atlantic. Third, and most massive of all: the ignorance of the lives of women, educated or not, writers, lovers, revolutionaries, mothers, workers, sisters, witches, saints, slaves. In short, the ignorance was massive, for it reflected the fact that the education of all people—male and female—ignored half the human population, at least from conscious thought and critical study.

In response to a feminist movement now in its second decade, most disciplines are in some intellectual ferment. For two reasons, literature has been one of the leaders of that ferment. Understood in its broadest possible meaning—as the written account of people's lives—literature is a primary source for studying lives of women; in addition, an extraordinary number of women were writers both in the professional sense and as diary or record keepers.

In this essay I am more interested in the practice of literary criticism in the classroom than I am in reviewing the printed essay or book. Partly, it is that I have spent twenty-five years as a practicing classroom critic, teaching students the art of reading, of learning from literature. Partly it is that there is no single book or essay of systematic theory. For the foreseeable future, I expect that it is in the classroom, rather than on the pages of professional journals, that the criticism we call "feminist" will perform its useful educational function.

Hence, I shall combine the pedagogical and the critical and, thus, ask of the new feminist literary criticism certain difficult questions. First, how does it, will it, affect the lives of students who read literature in schools and colleges? Second, what does its challenge to the traditional classroom signify for the future teaching of literature? Third, can feminist criticism gain power sufficient to alter significantly the literary canon? Fourth, how will feminist criticism and scholarship change our understanding of literary history? My method, like my questions, is not simple. I begin first by attempting to outline what I perceive as feminist criticism's central assertion: that the critic, the writer, and their audience—all are rooted in their biographies and historical circumstances. Art is neither anonymous nor universal; it springs from the particularities of gender as well as class, race, age, and cultural experience. Similarly, critical methods and concerns shift with time and circumstances, and of course these would be more diverse still were we open to hearing from a more diverse population of critics. Then I turn to the feminist practice of analyzing "images of women in literature," and finally, I consider women writers, and questions about the canon, literary value, and literary history.

The Central Assertion

What is even harder for students to understand than the common mortality of the writer is the more common mortality of the critic. Few students learn, even in colleges, about the shifting of critical views from age to age, much less about the relationship between those views and the lives of the people who espoused them or the societies in which these people lived. Students I have taught tend to believe that criticism is something handed down from above by "those who know," the ultimate judges sitting in state on every book. A student's tendency to assume that critics are those best able to apply transcendent, universally agreed upon standards to art reflects our own assumptions, as well as the rather narrow range of critical writers whom we have studied. We—I speak of the teachers of my generation now—also resist the idea that a critic's class, race, age, and gender have very much to do with the "literary" judgements he or she makes.

Naturally, students come to view their own roots and experiences as interfering with the development of true literary standards. I remember a freshman paper in defense of Mr. Morel in *Sons and Lovers.* He reminded her of her own father, the student wrote, who drank and who was, therefore, according to her mother, "unreliable," and she described also the way in which her mother had managed to pit her children against her husband. The student wove her own experiences into a convincing reading of Lawrence's opening chapters, presenting in detail those complexities Lawrence clearly savored about the battle between his parents. Yet, she concluded her paper with a strong paragraph of denial. "Probably I am all wrong," she wrote, "because my experience is too much like the experience in the novel." "Probably I am all wrong." For this student and for many others, "the shock of recognition" belongs only to the *real* critics.

I deliberately chose a pre-feminist or non-feminist example out of my classroom experience, for I first want to make the point that one's experience must be seen as *enabling,* not crippling or disqualifying. It is not that without an experience immediately relevant to the events in a book you need necessarily be lost: witness the generations of women who voluntarily forswore their experiences and entered the literary classroom as though they were anthropologists studying a foreign, male world. Many of us now understand the value of a particular experience in relation to *writers* of black literature or of Jewish and other ethnic literatures. We have always understood it in relation to writers of national literatures. Applied to the critic, the idea is less acceptable. Applied to women and to men as writers or critics, it is still a very explosive idea.

When I first said in public that James Joyce and D. H. Lawrence were *male* writers whose views of women were limited by that perspective,

I was attacked by outraged women and men, insisting that great literature was "universal." Even as late as 1972, when at the Midwest Modern Language Association meetings, I read from a preface to a new feminist anthology of poems, *No More Masks!*, describing W. B. Yeats' "Leda and the Swan" as a man's view of the woman and god, and comparing it with Mona Van Duyn's views of the same episode, I was villified for daring to besmirch the "greatness" of Yeats as poet by calling attention to his maleness.

Similarly, Ellen Moers' book, *Literary Women: The Great Writers,* has been attacked both by male and female reviewers who cannot fathom the assumptions that have produced her book. Let me quote two sentences from Moers' preface that speaks to these assumptions:

> Once I thought that segregating major writers from the general course of literary history simply because of their sex was insulting, but several things have changed my mind.

> If ever there was a time which teaches that one must know the history of women to understand the history of literature, it is now.

Moers does not begin her book by describing, as Kate Millett did, the patriarchal society we live in. For better or worse (and worse, if the popular critics' response is considered), she assumes that in 1976, it is not necessary, that the consciousness of readers will have kept pace with her own. Instead, she opens the book with three brilliantly rendered portraits of women writers: the domestic Mrs. Harriet Beecher Stowe, one year before beginning *Uncle Toms' Cabin,* writing to her sister-in-law about her troubles with a plumber, and describing also the dozen interruptions—children, neighbors, servants, domestic chores—in the course of writing her letter; the imprisoned Miss Elizabeth Barrett, who is, however, so totally free of domesticity that she may learn foreign languages and read and write without interruption; and the indefatigable George Sand, freed by her male clothing to be, at once, mother, mistress, and prolific writer. But all the while, Moers is making one fact plain: the lives of women are utterly distinct from the lives of men.

It is hardly a novel discovery—that men's and women's lives are distinct each from each. The biblical chauvinist would insist that god meant it to be that way. And feminists, both female and male, have for centuries challenged the logic, justice, and legitimacy of such distinctions when they limit the lives of women. As feminists have looked back into history and around them at the lives of women in their own time, they have noted first and perhaps in greatest detail thus far the victimization of women of all classes. But that view has been generally tempered—at least when the feminist was female—by the fact of her enabling vision, of her own survival in patriarchal floods. It is possible, today, to construct the history of women survivors—not only the singular figures of Mary Wollstonecraft and Margaret Fuller, of Stowe, Barrett Browning, and Sand, but, as I shall suggest when I turn to literary history, of others whose names we do not yet recognize. That notion—that women have been not only victims but survivors with special talents resulting from their experiences— emerges in contemporary feminism in a song like Helen Reddy's "I am victorious. I am Woman." Or in a delighted acceptance by young poets of the charge of "witchery":

> I want my black dress.
> I want my hair
> curling wild around me.
> I want my broomstick
> from the closet where I hid it.
> Tonight I meet my sisters
> in the graveyard.
> Around midnight
> if you stop at a red light
> in the wet city traffic,
> watch for us against the moon.
> We are screaming,
> we are flying,
> laughing, and won't stop.
>
> —Jean Tepperman (1969)

All feminist criticism—indeed, all the ferment in every intellectual discipline—is based on conclusions about the distinctions between the lives of men and women. The feminist critic (who is usually but not necessarily female) begins with an acute consciousness of her own life, of what it has allowed her to see well and of what it has denied her. Such consciousness has not sent her and other feminists into isolation. Rather, it has led to a growing body of research into the lives of women and men, into written documents—autobiographies, letters, poems, novels, as well as children's books; and into other cultural artifacts—pots and quilts, as well as paintings and the TV screen. In addition, feminist consciousness both derives from and leads back to a social movement that is principally a teaching movement, gathering into its wave the transformed consciousness of millions, not only here but around the world. In the classroom, therefore, the feminist critic is not a quirky individualist, "doing her thing," or grinding a dull axe. Rather, she or he speaks from the force of scholarship, history, and a growing social movement.

The feminist teacher speaks to students who have also been touched by the contemporary women's movement. Not only are women students more confident in the classroom; they may have also grown conscious of and articulate about the reality of their lives. Such consciousness often helps them to read literature with an insight that male students must be taught.

After an enjoyable classroom performance of key sections of Albee's *The American Dream*—a play members of the class had chosen to read—I asked the students who played the roles what feelings they had had as the characters, not only during this performance, but through several prior rehearsals. Both males reported that they had had "no feelings," that the characters they played were "alienated" from society; indeed, that was what the play itself was really about, they offered. When queried, they were vague about the sources of that alienation. The three females reported "some feelings," especially Mommy's for Grandma, and Grandma's for "The American Dream." The play, from their point of view, was not about alienation, but represented Albee's attack on females for controlling male sexuality and robbing them of manhood—and hence of feelings. The males in the class listened attentively, but they were essentially bewildered by the interpretation. They had not seen the portraits of the women in the play as unflattering or unusually critical, much less unjust or incorrect; possibly, they shared Albee's view of women. I say possibly, since it is, compared with Mailer's, for example, a relatively mild chauvinism. When we turned next to Mailer's *An American Dream,* the men in the class were the first to attack the viciousness of that book, or, as they put it also, its "lack of reality."

Through the medium of literary discussion, consciousness generates consciousness. We know that as teachers. These days, in many classrooms, women's actual social experience becomes the driving force behind a review of literary perceptions and values.

"Images of Women in Literature"

Both the study of the images of women in literature and the study of women writers are part of much broader intellectual movements, and I think it is important to see them in that light, for they make connections between literature, other disciplines, and our changing society. The study of the images of women in literature began as part of an examination of the cultural perpetuation of stereotypes about males and females, even in the face of very different reality. At a time when women were one-third of the work force, for example, why was it that one could find few or no portraits of salaried working women in literature of any sort, at any classroom level? Had no literature of that sort been written? Such studies began by focusing on literature because, unlike history, women were not absent from its pages. If women were present in stories, poems, children's books, feminists asked, what did they look like? What "images" of women were projected? What "messages" did those images convey?

We are all familiar by now with at least some study of children's literature. Scholarship in print and in film has compiled detailed views of girls training to be mothers. Domestic duties done, they patiently wait behind windows for something to happen, or they virtuously clean up a brother's indoor messes, while brother scampers about the outside world, learning to be Dad's helper and an energetic, inventive, competitive working person. None of the responsibility—the travail or joy—associated with motherhood, moreover, appears in the literature offered to elementary or secondary students, nor is there a sign of the possibility of combining marriage, motherhood, and salaried work—as half the mothers in the United States do. Two visual images are particularly memorable in children's books: the apron; worn by females of all ages, whether human, rabbit, or great ape; the armless little girl, whose hands are joined behind her back. I have been present when the accumulation of such images, presented in the form of slides, has made women weep publicly for their motherly irresponsibility: they had bought such prize-winning books for their daughters.

In its essence, a study of the images of women in literature involves a methodology for examining the patterns of sex prejudice, either in the work of a particular writer, or a genre that involves several or many writers, or, in its most sociological manifestation, through thousands of children's textbooks or readers. The method extends also into an analysis of popular magazines, films, television, etc. Sociological and literary techniques for investigating female characterization have been used not only by scholars but also by feminist parents challenging the bias of their children's schoolbooks, and by feminist teachers challenging the consciousness of students in the classroom. The approach is responsible for such publications as *Dick and Jane as Victims,* for Millett's *Sexual Politics,* for Carolyn Heilbrun's *Towards a Recognition of Androgyny,* as well as for a spate of critical essays, doctoral dissertations, and published books on women in the works of male writers. Feminists in philosophy, in religion, in art history, and in other fields, are also engaged in similar work.

Hundreds of women's studies courses in English and foreign language departments, in high schools as well as colleges, are currently being given under the rubric of "Images of Women in Literature." Their presence, like other courses in women writers, indicates how immediately the classroom may be affected by social movements and scholarly energies. *Images of Women in Literature,* a text prepared by Mary Anne Ferguson during 1972 and published first in 1973, with such courses in mind, groups short fiction and poems into the following "images" of women: the "submissive wife," the "mother—angel or 'mom'," "the dominating wife—the bitch," "the seductress—goddess," "man's prey: the sex object," and "the old maid." Thus, Ferguson concludes that women in literature are portrayed chiefly in terms of their sexuality, not in terms of their capacities for work, thought, or social action. Ferguson's final section, "the liberated woman: what price freedom?" concludes with a question that underscores the relationship between literature and life, and renders—through the fiction of several women writers—the tensions, conflicts, and frustrations in the lives of women who have working lives—or who wish they had.

The authors in Ferguson's anthology are divided evenly—half male, half female. They contain the traditional Chekhov, Sherwood Anderson, and Mailer—and the nontraditional Ernest J. Gaines and Jean Toomer, Mary Wilkins Freeman, Susan Glaspell, and Mary Elizabeth Vroman. Similarly, although courses in "Images" began by reviewing the traditional canon—from Sophocles, Chaucer and Shakespeare, in some cases, through Hawthorne and James, to Hemingway and other moderns, mostly male—the fare needed leavening.

Images in the traditional canon, enriched even by extensive use of the few well-known women writers, still left unfulfilled at least two needs: for greater variety, especially in terms of race, class, and ethnicity; and for more positive images generally. The images, for example, of white working-class and black women who are feisty mothers as well as wage-earners sustaining their families break all kinds of stereotypes, even shallow feminist ones. When students first read Tillie Olsen's "I Stand Here Ironing," they blame the mother in the story for having spoiled her daughter's young life because, in order to support them both, the mother makes less than ideal arrangements for her young baby's care. Women and men in my classes, many of them parents and not well-to-do, have at first judged this woman harshly and have found the portrait of a devoted, working-class mother a negative one. When they turn next to "Tell Me A Riddle," the story of a dying woman who has devoted the whole of her life to mothering, and who in great agony queries that choice and the meaning of life, the same students have judged her wanting: why, one woman asked, did she waste her whole life, especially since she was so talented as a young girl?

In a discussion of Alice Walker's stories of black women, *In Love and Trouble,* students named as favorite "Everyday Use," because as one man said, it was the only story that was "hopeful," the only one in which a woman said "no to her would-be colonizer." The woman who tells the story describes herself:

> In real life I am a large, big-boned woman with rough, man-working hands. In the winter I wear flannel nightgowns to bed and overalls during the day. I can kill and clean a hog as mercilessly as a man. My fat keeps me hot in zero weather. I can work outside all day, breaking ice to get water for washing; I can eat pork liver cooked over the open fire minutes after it comes steaming from the hog. One winter I knocked a bull calf straight in the brain between the eyes with a sledge hammer and had the meat hung up to chill before nightfall.

The woman is also the mother of two daughters, one still at home, lamed in childhood by a devastating fire, the other, with special beauty and "a style of her own," who returns in the course of the story, her name changed from "Dee" to "Wangero Leewanika Kemanjo." The story turns on quilts—found in a chest and promised by the mother to the lame daughter who is about to be married. They were made by two generations of women in the family, including the mother of the "man-working hands," who has to decide whether to allow her visiting daughter to take the quilts for her urban walls. The mother almost does decide to give in, but the acquiescence of her lame daughter, who says, "I can 'member Grandma Dee without the quilts," and who mutely accepts her less than equal share of life, makes her change her mind. The mother snatches the quilt from Dee who departs shortly thereafter, following a final barb to her sister and mother about their misunderstanding their "heritage." The story portrays not only conflicting images of black women, but conflicting views of their relationship to each other and to cultural artifacts, "heritage," even art.

The classroom discussion of such stories—setting aside for a moment the subject of mothering—would not have seemed strange to Arnold or Emerson, for whom criticism meant instruction about values and the living of life. In our contemporary literature classrooms, such discussions come as something of a shock to those who expect only the dissection of a story's formal structure or its "symbolism," who have given up attempting to understand students' lives, much less the effort it would take to influence those lives.

The feminist classroom that works on "images" becomes a place in which what is read helps students to examine systematically what they have experienced and what others have; a place in which what one has experienced becomes directly relevant to understanding and evaluating what one reads. One of the women in that class on Alice Walker said that the story had been a shattering one for her, since she, too, had gone searching her mother's house for objects with which to *decorate* hers, without any regard for her mother's life or feelings. The experience of such insights makes readers more, not less, demanding of literature. Such an approach to literature is novel only if one forgets about the traditional function of criticism—and of literature—to entertain and to instruct.

Studying the images of women in literature has at least two consequences: first, it raises teachers' and students' consciousness either as women themselves, or, if they are males, of women as human beings; second, and at least as important for those interested in the value of literature, the literary work assumes a new position as part of the patriarchal problem. Those who still prefer the idea of "pure" literature will not relish the value I am describing. I do not think literature is, was, or ever can be "pure," that is, disengaged from its place in history. What is especially compelling about the study of "images" is that students are learning that literature assigned commonly in schools and colleges is part of an entire culture that has defined women as the second sex. Thus, literature is not more or less culpable than any other aspect of culture; at the same time, it is not to be ignored or despised as trivial.

Women Writers and the Literary Canon

It is hardly surprising that courses devoted to women writers followed soon after the establishment of courses on "images of women." It should be noted, at least parenthetically, that these have been more difficult to establish as "valid," since they constitute a break with the traditional (male) canon. They have also evoked a good deal of soul-searching (among feminists) and some hostile encounters (with antifeminists) about the act of "segregating" a group of writers on the basis of gender. Nevertheless, the value of feminists who continue to pursue such courses cannot be overestimated. For they, in concert with those pursuing "images," are providing the basis for revising the canon.

Before I get to the dimensions of the task before us, or even to a small assessment of the progress thus far, one general issue about the literary canon needs to be raised. The first issue—and the starting place for all the rest—is the passive acceptance of the canon, with and without the addition of Melville, Dickinson, and Donne during the twenties. I spent the year before this one on a fellowship, searching the catalogues of nineteenth century colleges and universities, looking for evidence that during the first women's movement, there was some effort in departments of literature and history to offer courses in feminist polemical literature or in the sources and history of the women's movement. I found little but George Eliot, whose *Silas Marner* got into the high school curriculum as a "modern" novel. I certainly never queried the curriculum, not while it was being taught to me, nor when I attempted to teach it to other students. Nor had I any sense of its sameness through the short near-century of its life. I remember feeling some sense of curiosity when I learned that T. S. Eliot had "discovered" Donne, and that, therefore, Donne had become required reading in seventeenth-century poetry courses; but I never bothered to ask how that had occurred, much less why.

Why is it, for example, that Rebecca Harding Davis's "Life in the Iron Mills," a story that Emerson in 1861 called a "work of genius"—and that *is*—never got into the canon? Or *The Awakening,* from the time of its publication in 1899 until 1964? Or, for that matter, black writers like Charles Chesnutt, W. E. B. DuBois, Zora Neale Hurston? Feminist criticism raises three sets of questions about this reality.

One: What has been left out of the canon? More than two years ago, Deborah Rosenfelt and I began work on a Goldentree bibliography of women writers in Britain and the United States from the renaissance to the present. Despite our "feminism" we were thoroughly unprepared for the "hoards of female scribblers"—to use Hawthorne's term of opprobrium—we would find. And we can begin now to understand Hawthorne's competitive concern about the number of women writers, for there probably were more women than men writing and being published in the nineteenth-century United States. It was, after all, one of the few occupations open to women.

By the time we had begun this project, Goldentree had already published thirteen other literary bibliographies, containing some 977 male writers and 84 female writers, more than half of whom (43) came from two of the volumes, (*African American Writers* (22) by Darwin Turner and *Nineteenth-Century British Fiction* (21) by Ian Watt). Using bibliographies available in most research libraries, Rosenfelt and I found some 1,000 women writers who merited inclusion. Since we were confined to one volume, and at first to 2,000 entries, we were forced to choose no more that 150 of those writers. Even so, we accumulated some 10,000 entries for those women, perhaps 80 percent of which were primary sources, not secondary. And we had eliminated already such alleged ephemera as children's books, juvenilia, single publications of poems or stories, journalism, and speeches. It is important to underscore that the sources of these thousand women writers were not the untapped manuscript collections just beginning to be catalogued, nor lost "gems" among popular fiction.

For each of the periods before the present, the lists of women writers are substantial, most of their work is out of print, little of it has been commented on critically, and very little of it recently. A few examples: Elizabeth Stuart Phelps (1844–1911), who renamed herself after her literary mother, wrote fifty-seven books and hundreds of shorter pieces. Mary Austin (1868–1934), a little more than a generation younger than Phelps, published thirty-two volumes and several hundred essays and stories. Had I had Phelp's *The Story of Avis* (1877) or *The Silent Partner* (1871) and Austin's *A Woman of Genius* (1912) in hand at the time I asked about whether women should read fiction, I might have come to another conclusion. For *Avis* concerns itself with the attempt of a talented young woman to set aside her painting for marriage to a seminary teacher, and for the two babies that quickly follow that marriage. Unlike most nineteenth-century novels that I had been brought up on, the pages recount not the courtship but the marriage itself, and the growing consciousness of Avis that she should not have abandoned her painting. Mary Austin's young woman also chooses marriage, expecting it to fulfill her needs, but leaves it for a career in the theatre—the novel's evocation of stifling small town life anticipates *Main Street* by eight years. And two young women in *The Silent Partner* both reject marriage for vocation.

Apart from what has been left out of the canon—and I have not begun to touch on all the significant aspects of that question—the second question is in what ways do the works we are rediscovering force upon us a revised sense of literary value? And, as T. S. Eliot asked, how do these new discoveries alter our sense of works we knew? For example, if we place alongside of Henry James' *The Bostonians* Elizabeth Cady Stanton's *Eighty Years and More,* what happens to our perception of James' view of the nineteenth-century women's movement and our evaluation of that novel? It is not unlike placing side by side *The Blithedale Romance* and Fuller's *Woman in the Nineteenth Century.* Reading Stanton's life and Fuller's long essay brings into sharp relief the narrow understanding of feminism that, at the heart of each of Hawthorne's and James' books, ends by corrupting their artistry. To write about people, a writer must know them well, in their political and social lives as well as in their personal relations. James and Hawthorne are ignorant or fearful of feminism, and in their novels, therefore, the characterizations become thin, the motivations arch, obscure, or absurd.

As I have already suggested, one significant effect of the addition of women writers to the canon has been a changed classroom. All through the sixties, at a women's college, I taught *Sons and Lovers* as the opening work in a freshman writing course, longing all the while for Miriam's side of the story, or some comparable piece of literature to set beside it. Of all the characters in the novel, my students could identify only with Miriam, but, they said, she was unsatisfactory as portrayed by Lawrence: why *was* she so sulky? *what* was that intensity about? what did she *really* want? why didn't she fight back? and most of all, what happens to her in the end, when Paul Morel leaves her with his view that, for a woman, work is not enough?

Two years after I had left Goucher and had stopped teaching *Sons and Lovers,* I found Agnes Smedley's *Daughter of Earth,* thanks to Tillie Olsen, and The Feminist Press printed it—in 1973. Since then I have taught the two books together, and I recommend the experience. Smedley's novel was written in 1928, a little more than a decade after Lawrence's, and it is also autobiographical, about the early life of a working-class woman, whose father, partly Native American, was a coal miner in the southwest, and whose childhood was both as harsh and as occasionally beautiful as Lawrence's. Marie Rogers, like Paul Morel, wants to escape poverty, and like him, she has a mother who will help, a father who is a drunkard, a sister and two brothers. As in Lawrence's book, the key is education, the goal to become a writer, rather than a painter.

But the differences are as striking as the similarities, and of course, provide some of the excitement of study and discussion. In both novels, adolescent sexuality is important, and both young people are slow to develop, although Marie never loses the sense that, for women, sexuality is sinful. Paul survives two protracted love affairs that apparently enrich and enlighten him without touching his vital center. He is whole and free as he moves off at the end of the novel toward the bright humming city. Marie, too, survives two sexual relationships, but they cost her dear: the first includes two abortions and their accompanying physical danger and humiliation; the second, an attempt to combine marriage and political work, ends by denying her the possibility of both. At the novel's conclusion, she is destitute, without love or work. Indeed, writing the novel is her salvation: that is all we know from the book. From Smedley's life, we know that, unlike Lawrence, she did not then walk into a deep and satisfying relationship with a male Frieda. She—perhaps Miriam after all—spent her life working.

In the classroom, the novels are evenly matched—which is what makes criticism through discussion interesting. The stories are both compelling narratives, endlessly comparable with regard to characterization, style, imagery, as well as theme. There is even, in both, the contemporary Freudian mystique: Lawrence, influenced by Frieda; Smedley, in the analytic hands of one of Freud's own students in Germany, just before writing the novel. What is most fascinating, then, is that both male and female students find Paul Morel a "sniveling brat," a weakling, placed beside Marie Rogers. They are struck by the differences between the responsibilities each has to assume even in similar class-bound societies. Marie, for example, whose mother's death occurs when her brothers are too young to fend for themselves, has to decide whether to give her life to them or to herself. Out in the world of the factory, the young Paul is looked after by women who mother his as well as love him sexually, for him an enriching experience; out in the world—at a variety of jobs ranging from cigar-maker to travelling salesperson—the young Marie finds a couple of (unexpected) male "fathers," but age is no deterrent for men who find young women engaging, and they prove ultimately dangerous for her.

I have not yet mentioned the single most compelling difference between the novels: the political perspective from which each is written. In some ways, Lawrence's can be viewed as a feminist work, at least in terms of his understanding of the limitations of his mother's life, and even, somewhat, of Miriam's and Clara's. But the novel's main attention goes to Paul Morel, his individual singularity, his future; and the experiences he undergoes with the three women are offered as preparations necessary for the life he is to lead as artist. The focus is on the working-class man who will, we know at the novel's end, leave that working-class life behind him, or who, at best, will be able to use it as subject for his fictional creations.

Smedley's novel is, even as the autobiographical narrative of an individual woman, something else throughout. She, too, is the supreme individualist, escaping from the grimy unfulfilled life of her mother. But at her core is a remarkable intensity about injustice, not only the injustice inflicted on her mother by her father, or on her, and not only the injustice inflicted on women. Fully one half of the novel is devoted to Marie Rogers' experience inside the political movement to liberate India. Marie's essential impulse, once free of acute poverty, is to put her life at the service of others who are enslaved. One of the novel's ironies hinges on the political rejection of Marie, not because she is American, but because she is female.

The third and last question about the canon leads directly into literary history. We know least about this question: what social, cultural, and political forces shaped the literary canon as it appears in traditional curricula and anthologies? Why for example, do we require students to read Ben Franklin, and not Frederick Douglass or Elizabeth Cady Stanton, whose autobiographies were both in print by the time the American literary canon became established; and whose autobiographies are at least of equal merit and interest? Who makes such decisions? And on what basis? Is Franklin's merit the style he uses or the life he portrays? If the life, what are its major values? I have often been told that the major point is to demonstrate Franklin's industry. Well, no one is more industrious than Douglass, not only at the jobs he is required to do, but at learning to read, at a time it was a dangerous ambition for a slave to hold. I know of no better book to offer to students who doubt the value of reading or learning in general. As for Elizabeth Cady, one would think that several women had to have been lodged in her one body—to account for the work she did in *Eighty Years and More,* in addition to bearing and rearing seven children. I do not want to belabor the value of Douglass' *Narrative* or Stanton's autobiography, but only to illustrate that the canon did not fall from the sky: rather, some people made decisions about books they would teach or foster; limited, sometimes racist and sexist decisions, rooted in cultural and social experience which we do not yet sufficiently grasp.

While no question about the canon is easy to answer, some of the answers will be based on new forays into literary history. One of the most helpful studies in this regard is an essay by historian Carroll Smith-Rosenberg called "The Female World of Love and Ritual: Relations between Women in Nineteenth-Century America." Smith-Rosenberg traces the female friendships among "women and men in thirty-five families between the 1760's and the 1880's" representative of "a broad range of the American middle class, from hard-pressed pioneer families and orphaned girls to daughters of the intellectual and social elite." The range is geographically and religiously broad; the study is of "many thousands of letters written to women friends, kin, husbands, brothers, and children at every period of life from adolescence to old age." These letters are not what people in literature ordinarily regard as "literary," but rather they are documents for the historian. Smith-Rosenberg contends that they are especially valuable for the historian, since they are indeed "private," written only for the eyes of a particular correspondent. But her findings are of some consequence to the questions we have been asking, too.

Generously quoting from letters often painfully intimate, Smith-Rosenberg traces relationships between mothers and daughters, "the supportive love of sisters . . . the enthusiasms of adolescent girls . . . sensual avowals of love by mature women." "It was a world," she concludes, "in which men made but a shadowy appearance." She describes, in fact, a female sub-culture, in which female "supportive networks were institutionalized in social conventions or rituals which accompanied virtually every important event in a woman's life, from birth to death." She continues:

> Such female relationships were frequently supported and paralleled by severe social restrictions on intimacy between young men and women. Within such a world of emotional richness and complexity devotion to and love of other women became a plausible and socially accepted form of human interaction.

If she is correct, and the evidence is persuasive, then we can begin to see the outlines of some of the work before us in reconstructing the literary history of women writers and in understanding their omission from the canon. In the long run, seen from Smith-Rosenberg's view, the very idea of a canon of literature may emerge as one tactic, a kind of literary credentialing process, for limiting the potential strength of the female subculture. Similarly, it may become evident that the divisions between what is generally considered "art" and what is generally considered "handicraft" are themselves ideologies, serving key roles in the sexual politics of culture.

In a significant way, Ellen Moers has begun to reconstruct women's literary history, for example, by tracing for us the reading women writers did—mainly in the works of other women—and their own "networks": the extensive letter-writing across continents and oceans in the nineteenth century that substituted for the male literary world to which few of them had personal access. Several examples will suffice.

"The real hidden scandal of Emily Dickinson's life," Moers writes, "is not the romances upon which biographers try vainly to speculate, but her embarrassing ignorance of American literature"—by males, that is. Besides Emerson and a bit of Thoreau and Hawthorne, Dickinson "read and reread every Anglo-American woman writer of her time: Helen Hunt Jackson and Lydia Maria Child and Harriet Beecher Stowe and Lady Georgina Fullerton and Dina Maria Craik, and Elizabeth Stuart Phelps and Rebecca Harding Davis and Francesca Alexander and Mathilde Mackarness and everything that George Eliot and Mrs. Browning and all the Brontës wrote."

"Mrs. Hunt's poems," Dickinson wrote in an astonishing letter of 1871, "are stronger than any written by Women since Mrs. Browning, with the exception of Mrs. Lewes. . . . "

"Who but Emily Dickinson cared so much for rating women poets?" Moers comments rhetorically. *But in fact it is important to know that Dickinson's models were women writers,* and it should not surprise us, therefore, that a long-ignored verse narrative by Elizabeth Barrett Browning, *Aurora Leigh,* the *Sexual Politics* of its day, provided Dickinson with suggestions for at least seventy different poems. Similarly, Moers compares Jane Austen's life and reading with the circle that Wordsworth was part of, partly because of friendships formed at Cambridge, but also because he sought the company of literary men. "Jane Austen," Moers writes, "almost the exact age [as Wordsworth] and from a similar social milieu [had she been a man, she would probably have gone to university], stayed at home with her mother at Steventon, Bath, and Chawton." It is not that Austen had not read the "major [male] English writers": "But scholarship" Moer says, "has averted its refined and weary eyes from the female fiction that Austen's letters inform us was her daily sustenance in the years that she became one of the greatest writers in the language." And that list is an endless one: Sara Harriet Burney, Mrs. Jane West, Anna Maria Porter, Mrs. Anne Grant, Elisabeth Hamilton, Laetitia Matilda Hawkins, Helen Maria Williams, and Mary Brunton, to name a few. It is obviously of some importance to feminist writers and critics to know that, at least in the case of two distinguished women writers, art did not spring full-blown from their heads and hearts, nor did it depend solely upon male writers, but it grew both from their own experiences of life and from the tradition of other women before them. "In the case of most women writers," Moers concludes, "women's traditions have been fringe benefits superadded upon the literary associations of period, nation, and class that they shared with their male contemporaries."

Most tantalizing of all is the list of themes Moers provides for us in the one chapter she attempts as literary history, "as sample of the way such a history might read." Women writers in their "epic age"—a period Moers designates as from *Jane Eyre* to Virginia Woolf—had one major characteristic: an involvement in social causes, including those of women like themselves, but also of the working classes, male and female, and of slaves. She finds close connections between feminism and radicalism and she finds a special sensitivity to the "theme of illiteracy," from which middle-class women themselves had only relatively escaped. She quotes George Eliot writing a letter to Harriet Beecher Stowe, "whom she honored as her predecessor in that great feminine enterprise of rousing the imagination 'to a vision of human claims' in races, sects and classes different from the established norm."

Moers does not move on to make a connection between the absence of women from the literary canon and literary history—and the social causes they espoused. It is clearly too early to make such a claim, but it would not be a surprising connection. It would not be surprising if it were at least one of the missing threads to account for the loss not only from the literary canon but from general view of such works as Davis's *Life in the Iron Mills,* Chopin's *The Awakening,* and Smedley's *Daughter of Earth.* For after all, literary values, like other values, are institutionalized in social and political forms—magazines, departments, associations, anthologies, curricula, a canon—which provide praise, money, legitimacy and power to those who control them. The powerless create their own forms—working people's reading circles, networks of correspondents—to assert their own values and definitions of what is important, beautiful, worthy of sustaining, and reproducing.

Further search will bring us many more Rebecca Harding Davises, Agnes Smedleys, Kate Chopins, as well as Nella Larsens, and Edith Kelleys. Historical search will also bring more clearly into view the "institutions" by which women have sustained and transmitted their values and ideas and their means of survival. We have hardly begun a task of reconstruction that, I am certain, will also engage our daughters and sons, and theirs.

Should women read fiction? Yes, of course—and polemic, autobiography, poetry, letters, diaries, published and unpublished until we know the answers to all our questions and more besides.

Myths of Coeducation

(1978)

This essay has a long and complex history as a lecture. It has never been published. I wrote it first for a formal convocation early in the fall of 1978 at Oberlin College. I was a visiting professor that fall, hired by the Great Lakes Colleges Association under a grant from the Fund for the Improvement of Post-Secondary Education (FIPSE). My assignment included teaching one undergraduate course and offering to faculty a seminar in women's studies. In addition, I was to give at least one public lecture on Oberlin's campus and on those of as many other members of the GLCA as possible in an academic year. In the spring, I was to be visiting professor at Denison University, another member college.

Because my assignment on the twelve campuses was connected to the education of women, and because I was also working on the history of women's education, I attempted an essay that would explain part of the logic—in history and in the present—for the development of women's studies. I focused on coeducation, since most of these campuses were coeducational. And of course, Oberlin College prided itself on being the first coeducational college in the nation.

During the academic year 1978–79, I wrote three versions of this essay, each of which included local campus history: for Oberlin's historic Finney Chapel, in September 1978; for the College of Wooster, in November 1978; and for Denison University, in March 1979. Other members of the GLCA requested that I deliver some form of this lecture on their campuses during the same period, although I did not attempt to rewrite sections in order to include local campus history. I gave the lecture in a form that included references to Oberlin and the College of Wooster

*at Antioch College, Kalamazoo College, DePauw University,
and Hope College. In addition, I was asked to give the same lecture on several other campuses in 1978 and 1979, including Pur-
due University, the University of West Virginia, Princeton Uni-
verstiy, and Hamilton College. In 1980, I agreed to read a
version of the lecture on the Capitol Campus of Pennsylvania
State University.*

*In February 1981 when I read this lecture at Yale, it pro-
voked discussion at least as lively as those on other campuses
four years earlier. Do I think that women's colleges serve a special function today—or are they irrelevant? What differences do
I perceive in the reactions of students, faculty members, and administrators to the development of women's studies today and
ten years ago? Why are so few men interested in women's studies? What is the future of women's studies, given the hegemony
of traditional disciplines over the curriculum, and the drive by
women's studies to be interdisciplinary? And even if the humanities were to become coeducational, what about science? Is science impervious to questions of gender, and is it implacably
male?*

*The Yale Women's Studies Faculty Seminar, minus its token
male member that evening, took me to an elegant dinner to debate these and other questions of coeducation at Yale. The lecture had begun at 4 P.M. We left the dining room at 10:15.*

*The version published here is the one I read at Yale, an
amalgam of the Oberlin, Denison, and Wooster lectures that
omits the detailed archival material used in each instance.*

> We must look for change in everything that
> has a vital principle.
> Frances Juliette Hosford, *Father Shipherd's
> Magna Charta*

> We live in years, swift flying, transient years.
> We hold the possible future in our hands but
> not by wish and will, only by thought, plan,
> knowledge, and organization.
> W. E. B. Dubois, *Essays on Education*

MYTHS ARE AND ARE NOT TRUE. The single most famous myths relevant to
the subject of coeducation concerns the creation of woman. Eve out of
Adam's rib or Athena springing full grown from the head of Zeus—we
who understand biology know these as mythic explanations of another reality; not the biological but the social, not the rude facts of life but the
complex systems of belief that code and codify the social world. Myths

provide meaning and structure to the flux of daily life, to the seemingly disordered behavior of men, women, and children.

Thus, Western myths about the creation of woman by man are representations of social order; of the patriarchy under which, at least in recorded time, we have been living. The mythic narratives establish the creative power of men and the position of woman as social extension of man's wisdom and justice, or as man's chattel, his wifely support, bone of his bone, flesh of his flesh.

Myths about coeducation spring from the same source, or at least the pattern is reminiscent of the creation myths. The prefix "co" allows women to join with men in an educational enterprise, sometimes a college. Coeducation. The education of women with men. Is that its meaning? Of course, coeds are not men. When a man goes to college, he gets an education; when a woman goes, she gets a coeducation. If a man says, "I go to a coeducational college," he means there are women in it. If a woman says, "I go to a coeducational college," she means she does not go to Wellesley or some other women's college. But what *is* coeducation? What emblem appears, what narrative captures its essence? First I will tell you what it is not—by drawing a fantastic essence.

Imagine a father and a mother who together create a son and a daughter, twins, who grow to maturity, together studying both the histories and achievements of women and men, preparing in the best of colleges for useful work in a world that will choose them for their merit, not their gender (and not their race or class). It is a simple enough fantasy. Yet it is fantasy, not myth.

Even before the words had formed on the page, I had thought of an acquaintance who came to see me nearly seven years ago. She had been brought to feminism, she told me, not by the consciousness of her own generation, but rather of her children's. Her twin son and daughter, at the age of eight, after two years in school, were no longer friends. The ideal parallel development that she and her husband had been so careful to nurture had been diverted into paths that were bewildering to them all. Her son, a capable student, had also become a star soccer player. He seemed to be thriving at school, but at home he alternated between bragging of his prowess and sulking because of his sister's snubs. She had become a whining or a dangerously silent child. Even her early love for books had faded, and her grades were poor. My friend had already decided on a course of action: for the next two years mother and daughter worked energetically to open soccer instruction to girls in elementary schools on Long Island.

The principal fact to be learned from my anecdote is the maleness of education. I cannot think of an instance in which boys or men want girl's or women's privileges. Can you imagine a boy asking to be allowed to sweep the floor in the doll-house corner, or to be allowed to rock the cradle? And yet we all know little girls who have wanted to play with the rocket toys or learn the rules of regular and not girls' softball.

Coeducation—in elementary schools or in colleges—functions within the patriarchal limits of the society in which it exists. In mythic terms, coeducation opened doors to women. And so it did. But those doors were—and to a significant extent still are—different from those open to men.

The principal myth is Oberlin itself: the first coeducational college in the nation. True and not true. True if we understand that coeducation meant the admission of women to a male-initiated, male-centered, male-controlled institution. For the brave experiment was just that. Its participants had no models: they came from male seminaries and colleges or from female seminaries. Their task through Oberlin's formative years was to chart, without detailed instructions from the founder, institutional and social arrangements under which the two sexes could be educated, although with clearly differentiated rights and duties for each. Oberlin was an effort to found not only a college, but a model society. Societies, of course, contain both women and men, grouped in families. It is not surprising that the one model available to Oberlin's pioneers was the family. And so the students sat opposite each other in the dining hall. And so women had their domestic chores, men their field work, and it was perfectly understandable in those terms that women were paid half or less than half the hourly wages of men. Indeed, when one considers that most housework is unpaid labor, Oberlin women were well-off.

But if we are looking for a coeducational institution that is a model of equality between the sexes, if we are looking for a coeducational curriculum, a coeducational faculty, coeducational assumptions about the rights of both sexes to work at the same jobs and for equal pay, even coeducational assumptions about the rights of men and women to a share in the drudgeries and the joys of family life: we will not find any of this in Oberlin's history. Nor will we find it anywhere, except perhaps in our dreams of a more perfect future society. And I do promise to get to those dreams before I conclude.

But before then I have two tasks. I want to talk further about the myths of coeducation in the nineteenth century and today. And I want to place these myths against the history of women's education, especially in the light of its two major patterns: education separate and different from men's; education modeled precisely on men's education. Both of these patterns flourish today. What we call women's studies is a new departure. Its patterns and purposes, as I shall indicate, bear heavily on the future of coeducation.

In 1821, Troy Seminary, in upstate New York, opened its doors to fourteen-year-old women interested in what we would now conceive of as the first part of a high-school education. Elizabeth Cady Stanton went to Troy Seminary, although she was not satisfied with her education there, but of course there were no colleges then open to women. During the next several decades many other seminaries were opened for women by pioneer women educators often denied the complimentary adjective "feminist." Emma Willard, Mary Lyon, Catharine Beecher, Zilpah Grant, and others, founded schools for women with the principle in mind that women needed to be educated separately and differently from their brothers. The curriculum, at least to begin with, did not include the standard Latin and Greek that prepared young men for college. Thus, even some seminary-taught young women had to enter the preparatory section of a college before they were able to take college courses in Latin or Greek. The women were taught, in addition to the ubiquitous training in moral character, enough reading, writing, and arithmetic, as well as some music and drawing, to enable them to become elementary school teachers, at least for the few years before their marriage. Since only spinsters could continue to teach, or married men—and this rule prevailed until the 1930s—most women's education would, finally, be put to use in the family, women's proper sphere.

The basic idea behind these early nineteenth-century visions of women's higher education was that women were biologically different from men and that this difference was closely related to women's child-bearing function. Thus, even the most militant of the women's leaders, who argued for the establishment of these early schools for women—in the 1820s and 1830s—and who raised money in nickels and dimes for them, believed that women's education had to be as different from men's as their biology was different.

These biological beliefs were a product of the understanding by the medical professional of physiological functions. Scientific belief held not only that the brains of women were smaller than those of men, but also that brain size was directly related to intelligence, and that hence women were less capable than men of academic learning. More important, however, was the medical assumption that only one bodily organ functioned optimally at any one time. Thus, if women used their brains during adolescence, their uterine development would be disturbed and their child-bearing abilities impaired, perhaps so severely as to cause the production of malformed or dead infants. Indeed, higher education might in and of itself sterilize women. Such medical theorizing was not confined to women, but when applied to male bodies, the effect was exactly opposite. Men, it was alleged, needed to avoid the company of women, since sexual activity during the years of intense study would drain the brain. "Spilling one's seed," to use the nineteenth-century euphemism, endangered the development and advancement of the male scholar. On the other hand, for the female scholar, intense study directly inhibited her ability to bear children, or to bear healthy normal ones, capable of surviving past infancy.

And so it is not difficult to appreciate the enormous step taken in the 1820s and 1830s to establish educational institutions for women. It is also understandable that the women interested in female education did not challenge the assumptions of their day. It is easy to dismiss them as reactionary, and even to see them as direct antecedents of today's ERA opponents. Certainly, as a group, they were opposed to most of the political reforms espoused by many of their students, Elizabeth Cady Stanton included. But these early reformers took the first necessary steps. They introduced into women's education what had always been essential for men's education: a vocational goal, teaching. They wanted to educate teachers, they said, not only because women needed a profession, especially if they did not or could not marry; they were also hopeful that women as a group would care more for the education of other women than men had. Hence, the education of teachers would in itself promote the education of women across the land. And this work would, because of the alleged nature of women, raise the quality of the nation's moral character. Women as a group, as Catharine Beecher put it, were closer to God than men. They were more sacrificing, less selfish, and hence, they had the requisite character necessary for molding children into Christians and citizens. The classroom was envisioned as the secular wing of the church; the woman teacher shared with the male minister the task of molding the character of a nation. Thus, this wave of feminism envisioned through education the elevation of women's status—although of course within her proper sphere.

The second wave of feminism is the one we usually associate with the term "feminism" itself. This idea is expressed most simply by the statement, "I can do anything that you can do," spoken by a woman with her eye on a man. It assumes the model of maleness, of maleness as normality, of women as coming up to that male level of normality. It eliminates theorizing about or ignores biological functions. It is also, of course, the mainstream view of the nineteenth-century women's movement. If one is looking for a date and an ideological statement, 1848 and the Seneca Falls Declaration of Sentiments are key. Elizabeth Cady Stanton, one of the first students to attend Emma Willard's Troy Seminary, was an organizer of the Seneca Falls meeting and one of the writers of that document. (It is important to mention, given what I have said about biology, that Stanton was already, at the time of the Seneca Falls Convention, the mother of three healthy normal children under the age of six.

Some of us who are teachers and administrators appreciate the fact that unpredictability is one of education's most telling lessons. But we may nevertheless be curious about the origins of this feminist vision—that women are not physically or intellectually inferior to their brothers; that biology is not destiny. How did it happen to spring out of soil that proclaimed quite another ideology? That is not an easy question to answer, although historians often forget that ideology and beliefs of various sorts often spring out of rather simple human experience.

Perhaps you already know the story of Elizabeth Cady Stanton's painful discovery that more than expert horseback-riding and the learning of Greek stood between her and a college education. She could not comfort her father for the loss of his one treasure, a son. All he said when presented with her evidence of manlike accomplishment was, "Oh, Elizabeth, if only you'd been born a boy." Not much consolation for the bright young eleven-year-old girl. Perhaps you also know Lucy Stone's story. Born nine years after Stanton, she could have come into one of Oberlin's earliest classes. She did not arrive until 1843, when she was 25 years old; her parents opposed education for women, and so she had to make her own way. In Lucy Stone's story, one senses the astonished indignation of the young girl, and the persistence. Her mother had told Lucy by way of consolation, that "all women were under the curse of Eve, and that they must submit." Small consolation for a rational mind! "Lucy could not believe," according to Frances Hosford, author of an early book on Oberlin, "that God had cursed all women, although the Bible seemed to say so, and nobody in her little world had ever breathed a question about the literal truth of every line in the Sacred Book. The child's logical mind found but one tolerable refuge—the translation of these terrible texts might be wrong! She would know for herself; she would go to college, study Greek and Hebrew, and find out exactly what the Bible said."

Obviously, Stone and Stanton alone did not make a movement, but thousands of women like them did. And it is not impossible to imagine these relatively privileged women asking why their rights to learning were different from their brothers' rights. The Seneca Falls Declaration lists nearly a score of injustices against women and makes recommendations for change. Suffrage was only one of these, and the least acceptable at the time, but the only one known to most Americans. The seventy-two-year history of the fight for suffrage parallels the movement for women's access to higher education equal to their brothers'.

In the 1870s major universities began to open their doors to women; in the same decade, women's colleges were opened that provided an education comparable to that offered men. More and more women wanted to attend colleges, especially if they were the daughters of the burgeoning middle class. And even some male colleges—Miami University in Ohio and Wesleyan University in Connecticut, for example—opened their doors to women in times of economic strain.

Coeducation had been tried earlier in the century by a few colleges in Ohio and elsewhere, but it was far from acceptable on such prestigious campuses as the universities of Wisconsin and Michigan. Not surprisingly, those few university campuses that already admitted women, did so through the doors to the Normal School or course: that is, through teacher education, which fast became the chief sex-segregated educational area for women.

What did institutions risk when they decided to admit women to the same degree programs offered to men? A great deal to begin with, as myths concerning the dire consequences of coeducation abounded. In 1869, at his inauguration, the new president of Harvard University,

Charles W. Eliot, took the time to explain why Harvard would not admit women. He protested that he was not casting aspersions on their possible merit, but he projected that, "Only after generations of civil freedom and social equality will it be possible to obtain the data necessary for an adequate discussion of woman's natural tendencies, tastes, and capabilities."

The risks of opening doors to women can be summarized quickly, since a vigorous debate about the merits of coeducation continued through the rest of the nineteenth century, indeed continues to this day, although some of the old myths have been replaced by new ones. First, there was the myth that coeducation would lower the intellectual standing of a college among other top colleges in the nation, since coeducation, critics argued, would lower the general standards of excellence: women as a group, it was said openly at first, and then in muted fashion later, were not as intelligent or capable as men.

I want to pause before going on to other myths, since this one is the most important, the one most easily defused by such decisive measures as admissions scores and grades in college: by all kinds of records. And such scores, actual records of achievement, exist to repudiate the myth that continues to flourish nevertheless. When one looks at another kind of measure—the achievement of male and female *graduates* of colleges, at least as measured by the proportion earning Ph.D.'s, one sees the two populations split—and without regard to ability. For example, a study by Elizabeth Tidball and Vera Kistiakowsky, published in *Science* in 1976, found that of those institutions that send students of both sexes on to Ph.D.s, relatively small, private, and coeducational colleges figure importantly for men and *not at all for women.* I will return to this theme later on.

A second myth about coeducation really concerned extracurricular life on campus. Opponents of coeducation alleged that it causes a "moral decline" among undergraduates. Not only do women keep men from concentrating on their studies, but the presence of women encourages immorality. President Eliot, in that same 1869 address, after praising the mature young men of Harvard as capable of exercising their rights to an elective curriculum, suggested, however, their incapacity, in the presence of women, to make equally coherent choices about their personal behavior. Eliot pointed to the "exceedingly burdensome" factor of "necessary police regulations," which he assumed would be "involved in a common residence of hundreds of young men and women of immature character and marriageable age." Unlike many of the institutions that opened their doors to women, Harvard, Yale, Princeton, and other institutions founded in the colonial period, were not interested in strengthening the nineteenth-century family, much less did they care about the issue of women's rights.

Two myths focused on the woman student herself: as already noted, the delicate health of women could be harmed by hard study. As if in preparation for the possibility that that myth might not be acceptable for long (although it actually was), there was a counter-myth: coeducation would cause "the decline of feminine charm." That is, women in the presence of men would become as "coarse" as they. On college campuses, one might see women drinking, cursing, smoking, asking questions, and speaking out in "promiscuous assemblies," that is, in groups of males and females. In short, women who studied on coeducational campuses might get ideas about independence, might attempt to imitate male models of achievement.

Still another myth focused on male students: the advocates of coeducation claimed that it would help tame the savage beasts. Male students would even eat in a more civilized fashion if women were present in the dining hall. And a pair of myths emerge from this one: coeducation would produce more manly men and more womanly women; finally, coeducation would prove "conducive to mating." Probably these last two myths are more "true" than any of the others. Certainly college students married each other, and perhaps they were more manly men and more womanly women. It is true enough that for coeducational colleges as a whole, such indices of achievement as the Ph.D. function for men only and not for co-eds.

When Wellesley College opened its doors in 1875, Henry Durant, who provided the money, also provided perspective: "Women can do it," he said, "and I will give them the chance." Wellesley began with an entirely female administration (and has continued in that form to this date). Durant insisted on a well-prepared faculty and administration. When properly trained faculty were not to be had, he found talented women and sent them abroad for a year or more, at the expense of the college, to prepare themselves. He is said to have visited Harvard's laboratory facilities regularly, to make certain that the laboratories at Wellesley would be equipped at least as properly. Moreover, he believed that the education of women was part of a larger and broader battle for women's rights, itself part of a still greater crusade for human justice. In the following extract from one of his sermons, given in 1875, he would make Lucy Stones of all the students at Wellesley:

> The Wellesley College plan of education may properly be made a lesson for the Sabbath day, because it is religious throughout. It asks the co-operation of teachers and students in the revolt which is the real meaning of the Higher Education of Women. We revolt against the slavery in which women are held by customs of society—the broken health, the aimless lives, the subordinate position, the helpless dependence, the dishonesties and shams of so-called education. The Higher Education of Women is one of the great world battle-cries for freedom; for right against might. It is the cry of the oppressed slave. It is the assertion of absolute equality. The war is sacred, because it is the war of Christ against the principalities and powers of sin, against spiritual wickedness in high places.

Wellesley College desires to take the foremost place in the mighty struggle. All our plans are in outspoken opposition to the customs and the prejudices of the public. Therefore, we expect every one of you to be, in the noblest sense, reformers. It is difficult in the midst of great revolutions, whether political or social, to read rightly the signs of the times. You mistake altogether the significance of the movement of which you are a part, if you think this is simply the question of a College education for girls. I believe that God's hand is in it; that it is one of the great ocean currents of Christian civilization; that he is calling to womanhood to come up higher, to prepare herself for great conflicts, for vast reforms in social life, for noblest usefulness. The higher education is but putting on God's armor for the contest.

In fact, the "armor" that women college students donned in such colleges as Wellesley or Oberlin was what M. Carey Thomas and others called "the men's curriculum." Strong arguments for admitting women to full curricular equality were made on women's college campuses, including such public ones as Hunter College. There, Thomas Henry Hunter, the first president, urged annually from 1870 to 1900, in his reports and budgetary requests to the mayor, that women in training to be public school teachers needed the same Latin and Greek as their brothers received at City College. Similarly, M. Carey Thomas, distinguished president of Bryn Mawr, argued for women's right to the "men's curriculum," and she pointed to the vocational purpose of education. Thomas, allegedly debating the question, "Should the Higher Education of Women Differ from That of Men," in reality pressed for the right of women to work in male professions. She is, by the way, alleged to have said about Bryn Mawr graduates, "only our failures only marry." The quotation that follows comes from the section on bridge-building in the 1902 debate.

Given two bridge-builders, a man and a woman, given a certain bridge to be built, and given as always the unchangeable laws of mechanics in accordance with which this special bridge and all other bridges must be built, it is simply inconceivable that the preliminary instruction given to the two bridge-builders should differ in quantity, quality, or method of presentation because while the bridge is building one will wear knickerbockers [trousers] and the other a rainy-day skirt. You may say you do not think that God intended a woman to be a bridge-builder. You have, of course, a right to this prejudice; but as you live in America . . . you will probably not be able to impose it on women who wish to build bridges. You may say that women's minds are such that they cannot build good bridges. If you are right in this opinion you need concern yourself no further—bridges built by women will, on the whole, tend to fall down, and the competition of men who can build good bridges will force women out of the profession. Both of these opinions of yours are side issues, and, however they may be decided hereafter, do not in the remotest degree affect the main question of a common curriculum for men and women in technical and professional schools.

Ultimately Thomas argued also that preliminary education, in particular the undergraduate curriculum, before a student reaches the school of engineering and architecture to learn to build bridges, should be identical for men and women. Here is her climactic argument:

> Even if we hold that women's minds differ from men's, this too is a side issue, for we must all recognize that for the purposes of successful competition it is desirable to minimize this difference by giving the *same* and not a different preparation. The greater the natural mental difference between the sexes the greater the need of a men's curriculum for professional women, if they are to hold their own in professional life after leaving the university.

But what was all the fuss about, you may well ask? Surely by 1902 men and women at Oberlin and at most of the major universities in the country were studying the same curriculum? Yes and no. The land-grant universities missed an extraordinary opportunity when they moved to extend the undergraduate curriculum to include such practical knowledge as agriculture and engineering. Kansas State University officials first did this in 1874, and at the same time they also announced a third curricular stream called "Women's," not an early precursor of women's studies, I am sorry to say, but rather the earliest version of home economics I know of. Moreover, the university did not admit women to courses on agriculture or engineering. Thus, the great coeducational universities of the land, responsible for the majority of graduate and professional degrees—and for the development of the natural resources of the nation—became institutions *that admitted both* women and men, but *encouraged their segregated study*: women to teaching, then later to home economics, library school, social work, and nursing; men to agriculture, engineering, forestry, marine science, law, medicine, business, and other specialized areas too numerous to mention.

On the other hand, that great fountainhead of assumptions and mythologies, the liberal arts curriculum, was indeed open to both sexes. Whether they sat side by side in classrooms at Oberlin or Kansas, or whether they separately attended Williams or Wellesley, they studied "the men's curriculum." Indeed, after the 1920s, even if they were black women and men in sex-segregated or coeducational colleges of the south, they studied the (white) "men's curriculum." I doubt that this is a novel idea today, but it was a novel idea to feminists only a little more than a decade ago. The discovery has been of some consequence, but it has also made its discoverers feel understandably foolish: for why had it taken so long to see what was utterly visible and obvious?

What is this men's curriculum that we have long since gained the right to study? Indeed, in 1981, eleven years after the term "women's studies" was first coined, some of us think that the men's curriculum is not fit for either men *or* women.

The men's curriculum educated me from the day I entered kindergarten in 1934 to the day I left graduate school in 1954. In kindergarten and through elementary school, the men's curriculum told me that when I grew up I would be a mommy, married to a daddy who would go to work each day while I cleaned the house, shopped, cooked, sent my two children—an older son, a younger daughter—to school, and waited for everyone to come home so that I could make life truly pleasant and comfortable for them. Because I was the daughter of working-class immigrant Jews, I was taught at home that I was also to become a teacher, an elementary school teacher. That lesson was not overtly part of the men's curriculum, for I never met a woman teacher in my text books, but of course there was an example for me to observe every day in the classroom.

All through my school days and at Hunter College High School and Hunter College and Smith College—all schools only for women—I studied the men's curriculum. That is, I learned the history of the fathers of this country, the laws they passed, the wars they fought, the land they pioneered. I accepted without a blink phrases like "the pioneer and his wife," and I never asked whether women had always been able to vote or whether any woman had ever run for president. I simply accepted that boys and men could do more interesting things than girls or women could. Of course, like many girls, I was a tomboy. I played baseball and followed the Brooklyn Dodgers avidly in person when I could get the money or on the radio when I could not. But of course I knew I could not be a baseball player, even in my wildest dreams: that was for boys only. One of my favorite books was *Microbe Hunters*, a series of dramatic, even thrillerlike, short biographies of the men who made important medical discoveries. In high school, I loved the study of biology, but I never dreamed of being a biologist or making a medical discovery. Rather, I thought I might become a biology teacher. That is what the curriculum—and the presence of a female biology teacher—had taught me.

In college and graduate school I studied literature and art history. I also studied sociology and anthropology. My teachers at Hunter taught me about race prejudice and the biological fallacies about race people still believed in; they taught me about the significance of environment and culture, and they also taught me respect for the varieties of human culture, the different peoples who inhabited the planet. But there was never a mention of gender, of men and women, of the fallacies people still believed about them. At the University of Wisconsin where I studied art history as well as literature, I saw no women painters, although of course men painted women, often nude, and certainly more often than they painted nude men. Similarly, although there were no British women poets before Elizabeth Barrett Browning (and we were told that she was really not very good) male poets seemed to write mainly about their love for women. I certainly got the idea early in my academic career that women could teach literature but they could not produce it.

When I began to teach in 1951, you know what I taught: the "men's curriculum." How could I teach anything else? It was all I knew. The best I could say about women was that, if one worked exceptionally hard to learn the "men's curriculum," she could become a *superior* woman—a special case—a woman who worked in a man's world.

Please understand: I was not conscious of teaching the "men's curriculum." I was not conscious at all. I was teaching what I thought was true. I had never heard of the women artists whose paintings appeared in a special show several years ago—*Women Artists 1550–1950*. I would probably have laughed if anyone had suggested to me that women artists had been painting in the sixteenth and seventeenth centuries, or earlier. I had heard of Virginia Woolf, but she was, I thought, obviously an exceptional woman, and probably inferior to most men, certainly to James Joyce and D. H. Lawrence. I had not heard, of course, of Mary Wollstonecraft or Margaret Fuller, and certainly knew nothing of Stanton or Stone or even Susan B. Anthony, nor even of Abigail Adams and her poignant plea to husband John to "remember the ladies." I had not heard of Sojourner Truth, Ida Wells Barnett, or Mary Church Terrell, let alone Phillis Wheatley or Zora Neale Hurston. Nor the hundreds of painters and thousands of writers and millions of others who were women and lived and breathed and created the life of this planet since the days that humans lived and breathed and created.

Never before our own time has a group of women questioned the "men's curriculum." If you are surprised, at least one logical explanation may help. It is difficult to criticize adversely an institution you want access to. It is difficult also to criticize an institution you have access to but want equality in. At least as the nineteenth century women's movement understood the issue of equality, it came to mean the ignoring of gender. One was not a *woman* in the university; one was some other species of being. It was an unreal position, and of course it had clearly begun to break down by the time our own feminist movement touched the campus about a decade ago.

For more than ten years across the land feminists, according to Elizabeth Janeway, have begun the exploration of social mythology. That is her way of describing women's studies, the contemporary feminist movement for change on university campuses. Slowly but firmly during the past decade, women's studies has inched its way into the educational establishment. As a program, women's studies exists on more than 450 campuses. As discrete courses, on more than 1,500, perhaps on all campuses—I have not surveyed the larger scene since 1974. There is now a national professional association, a number of consequential journals, and an annual convention each June that hosts between 1,500 and 2,000 participants.

But if women's studies is a response to the effort to gain for women the right to the men's curriculum, it may also be a reactionary move—back to the separate curriculum for women. Early in the seventies, women's studies began as a compensatory curriculum that would raise the consciousness of women to their place in this world. But knowledge moved hand-in-hand with consciousness, and the result is very different than our first few simple glimpses of the future. For it is impossible in most areas of knowledge to simply add women to the curriculum. Let me explain with an important illustration from the work of historian Joan Kelly-Gadol:

> If we apply Fourier's famous dictum that the emancipation of women is an index of the general emancipation of an age—our notions of so-called progressive developments, such as classical Athenian civilization, the Renaissance, and the French Revolution, undergo a startling re-evaluation. For women, "progress" in Athens meant concubinage and confinement of citizen wives. In renaissance Europe it meant domestication of the bourgeois wife and escalation of witchcraft persecution which crossed class lines. And the Revolution expressly excluded women from its liberty, equality, and "fraternity." Suddenly we see these ages with a new, double vision—and each eye sees a different picture.

"*Suddenly we see these ages with a new double vision—and each eye sees a different picture.*" Women in history; men in history. If you find this distressing—why can't we simply talk about *people*? We simply can't. That is not the way the world has ever been, nor are brothers and sisters, even if they are twins today, simply "people." But why is this so important? Why must you hear that sometimes unnerving sound of urgency in a feminist's voice? For two reasons. First, there is the matter of truth, of knowledge that is accurate and honest, which omits no essentials—like the history of half the human race in making a judgment about an age and civilization. Second, there is the purpose of truth and knowledge: to affect the lives we live, the opportunities we have. I am deadly serious about the fact that the liberal arts curriculum shapes our assumptions, forms the mythologies of women and men that allow them to live or die. What you learn in school is not a joking matter. It forms an invisible network of belief—interfaced by the networks of church and family and now the media—that may blind us or may free us to see.

I promised a concluding vision, and there are a few signs in sight to support my dreams: that within the next decades whole colleges will consider essential for the well-being of its students and for its allegiance to knowledge and truth the development of a new curriculum. I hesitate to call this curriculum coeducational, given my explorations of that word.

But it will be something beyond both the men's curriculum and women's studies as we know it today. This is not the end of the vision, but the beginning. For it is not simply for its own sake that we will, in this new curriculum, study the social mythology that has separated the sexes in unnatural ways. Rather, and I say this with the consciousness of the purposes of the original Oberlin Collegiate Institute: such study will move us to action, to plan for and organize a more equitable society. So I dream of a new form of coeducation in which the curriculum considers all the inhabitants of the planet. And I expect all of you, faculty, students, administrators to begin now the dynamic process . . . *to be, every one of you, reformers*, part of the process of change.

Breaking the Disciplines

In the Nineteenth Century and Today
(1978)

*I wrote this essay as a lecture for the Fourth Annual Confer-
ence of the Great Lakes Colleges Association held in November
1978. I was in residence on Oberlin's campus, and had already
delivered "Myths of Coeducation" as the Convocation lecture.
In one sense, this was a sequel to that lecture. I had just reread
Lawrence Veysey,* The Emergency of the Modern University, *and
I had been surprised to find in it no allusion to the education of
women. Still, Veysey's description of the breakup of the traditional nineteenth-century theistic curriculum into the science-
based elective system contained within its outlines and meta-
phors analogies to the major feminist shift we are witness to
today.*

*The essay owes much to Veysey's book, therefore, as a start-
ing place. It appeared in 1979 in a monograph of the* Proceedings *of the GLCA Conference.*

As a FEMINIST interested in the future of women's studies, I turned to the
history of higher education for women in search of what I assumed would
be analogies. I found none. Rather, I found an interesting and coherent
development that led, if not directly then logically, to women's studies in
our own time. Women in the nineteenth century achieved the right to
study what men did, the "men's curriculum." Fifty years after gaining
that right—I am using the date of suffrage for convenience and because it
has a certain educational logic as well—women in our time began to challenge the accuracy and value of that men's curriculum, not only for themselves but for men as well. Most of the disciplines have begun to respond
to the challenge of women's studies. Scholars are finding it essential and
interesting to open new books and to consider, perhaps for the first time in

221

their intellectual lives, the histories and present existence of half the human race. Women's studies, then, is a departure in the history of women's education.

Here I want to look at women's studies against another historical perspective: that of the development of the mainstream of higher education's curriculum, the "men's curriculum," those myriad disciplines and divisions of knowledge we call traditional. They are less than a century old.

Before the Civil War and for more than two hundred years, a college education was conceived of as "discipline" for religious and moral "piety." The college transmitted the values of the society to future ministers, lawyers, and members of what were called in the seventeenth century "the ruling class," obviously men. While the central vision of the college was religious, the main subjects of study were Greek, Latin, and mathematics, in addition to moral philosophy, the Bible, and rhetoric. Greek, Latin, and mathematics were the hard subjects, in fact, around which the concept of mental "discipline" was formed. "Discipline" was not used to describe a particular branch of learning in the nineteenth century, but rather the exercise of one's mental faculties. Discipline in that sense was alleged to be cumulative and contagious: that is, if one exercised one's mind on Greek irregular verbs or on solid geometric axioms, one's store of "discipline" would grow and would allow the "catching" of other knowledge. It is also clear that Latin and especially Greek were the "filters" (that mathematics still is today) for keeping certain people—including women—out of the mainstream college curriculum, or out of the colleges altogether.

So for nearly two hundred and fifty years colleges educated a thin stream of relatively privileged white males in the colonies and then the states through a stable curriculum that we would describe as "required," rather than "elective"; holistic rather than fragmented; religious rather than secular; and thoroughly traditional, in that its focus was the Greeks, the Romans, the Hebrews and early Christians, and more rarely Europe. By the mid-nineteenth century, such education produced the Christian *man*, not so much for a particular vocation, but for what Lawrence Veysey calls "manliness," a combination of culture and piety, a posture substituting for American aristocracy.

During the period immediately after the Civil War, almost to the end of the century, there was accomplished in higher education, according to Veysey, "the transformation of the curriculum," a phrase that women's studies advocates of course use commonly today to express their future goals. Argument raged, through much of the nineteenth century, about the "relevance" of college education to students' work lives. As Veysey has put it, "What the orthodox college president would not concede, in effect, was that a minister was simply one kind of careerist and an engineer another."

The nineteenth century's new curriculum, was, of course, science. In its broadest meaning, as "an organized body of information about a particular subject," it was not threatening. But its advocates saw science as "a philosophy which claimed to account for the entire universe." Such claims were, of course, mistrusted or seen as efforts to unseat the religious charge of the curriculum. "Science, paraded nakedly," Veysey tells us,

> seemed vulgar; it appeared to denigrate the position of man in the universe. Its subject matter was also believed too easy and undemanding to deserve a major place in the classroom. In theory, science might reluctantly be given a realm of its own, comparable to that of religion in providing an understanding of the universe. In practice, science was chastised for abandoning its humble subservience. "The spirit of science," said a New York professor in 1879, "while it is positive and affirmative in its appropriate sphere, becomes negative and contradictory, if not even blasphemous and scoffing, the moment it transcends the proper boundaries of that sphere to speak of things spiritual. . . ."

Of course by now you have heard the analogy: it is striking how much the battle over the transformation of the curriculum and the divisions of knowledge one hundred years ago mirrors our own battle today. To repeat—think now of women's studies: as "an organized body of information about a particular subject,"—I am adding "women"—it was not threatening. But as "a philosophy which claimed to account for the entire universe," it is both "mistrusted" and "seen as efforts to unseat the religious charge"—read "mainstream" today—of the curriculum.

It is also striking to those of us whom women's studies has sensitized to language and imagery to hear science described as female. Only a woman would be "paraded nakedly," and of course would, in such condition then be called "vulgar." Describing science as "reluctantly being given a realm of its own," or as being "chastised for abandoning its humble subservience" and as "transcending the proper boundaries of that sphere to speak of things spiritual"—reminds us of the male-centeredness of the universe of knowledge that can in one of its sectors denigrate the detestable newcomer—science—as female and at the same time, in the burgeoning research university, declare the new kingdom of science as off limits to women.

There are striking differences, as well as similarities, between our own battle and this one. Here's one similarity: science was seen then, as women's studies is today, as dangerously critical of the mainstream curriculum. A difference: the science curriculum was a fragmented one: its impact on the mainstream was to transform the curriculum into a galaxy of separate "disciplines," with departments and professional associations, and subspecializations, etc. This transformation was accomplished between the mid-seventies and the First World War. It is this galaxy of departments, all less than a century old, that is now the campus mainstream.

If we look at Oberlin's curriculum exactly one hundred years ago—in 1878—we can see the beginnings of the shift from the required transitional curriculum to the new electives in science. A freshman student in 1878 was required to study Latin (Livy, Horace, and prosody, as well as Latin composition); Greek (Xenophon, Greek historians, and prose composition in Greek); the history of Rome; mathematics (algebra and trigonometry); and rhetoric. During the following three years, students continued the study of Latin and Greek, mathematics, and rhetoric, as well as Evidences (advanced Bible study). They also studied French and German as well as English language and literature. In addition they were to select from the following group of science courses, one or two of which were offered each term: physics, botany, astronomy, chemistry, zoology, engineering, minerology, physiology, geology, psychology. In the seventies and eighties at Oberlin, two courses in psychology were offered: one focused on the "Nature of the Soul. Consciousness. Sense of Perception. Memory and Imagination." The other on "Powers and Processes of Thought." Finally, for seniors in their last semester, there was one course in economics, one in art, one in ethics.

More clearly even than the current women's studies curriculum, the new nineteenth-century curriculum was a smorgasbord, an introduction to as many of the sciences as possible, added to the staples I have already mentioned—Latin, Greek, the Bible, rhetoric, mathematics. The principle is accretion: more and more new offerings. There were no "departments" as we understand the term: what was then called "The Department of Philosophy and the Arts" administered the curriculum I have described—the "Classical" curriculum, as well as the one called at first the "Ladies," then the "Literary" curriculum. Its major distinction had been the substitution of the modern languages—French, German, and English—for the classical ones. In addition, beginning in the fall of 1891, Oberlin freshmen could enter a "Scientific Course" that was described (differently from the Literary one, I should note) as "upon an entire equality with the Classical Course." The battle, one could assume, had ended, and science had won. No Greek was required for admission or for graduation and somewhat less Latin for admission (only 2 books of Virgil!). Relatively few subjects were, in fact, required, and even some of them were in science: hence, students could enjoy an enormous intellectual smorgasbord in science. Only the following nonscience subjects were required: four courses in German, four courses in French, three in philosophy, three in English, and three in Bible. It is interesting to note that, during this lengthy transitional period, in colleges like Oberlin, the proliferation of various "subjects" continued: by 1909–10, courses were offered in Italian, Spanish, Gothic, sociology, economics, and political science, among others.

The fragmentation of the curriculum was followed, not surprisingly, by the organization of departments, and perhaps Oberlin was relatively slow in this development, since, of course, such new graduate institutions as Johns Hopkins University were leading the way by 1876. And professional associations, formed in order to support the faculty who were organizing undergraduate and graduate departments in various disciplines, were founded with astonishing regularity during the years between 1883 (Modern Language Association) and 1911 (College Art Association). Indeed, Veysey says that by 1910 the departmentalization of academe into "disciplines" was complete.

Writing in 1936, Robert Hutchins described *The Higher Learning in America*. "The modern university," he said, "may be compared with an encyclopedia. The encyclopedia contains many truths. It may consist of nothing else. But its unity can be found only in its alphabetical arrangement. The university is in much the same case. It has departments running from art to zoology; but neither the students nor the professors know what is the relation of one departmental truth to another. . . ." Looking back wistfully, Hutchins adds, "The medieval university had a principle of unity. It was theology. . . . It was an orderly progression from truth to truth. . .humanism was theocentric. . . ." Hutchins's view usefully summarizes that "tranformation" that created the departmentalized, professionalized curriculum: the disciplines have not only fragmented knowledge; the college has organized nothing that reassembles the fragments into a holistic vision. Indeed, if all courses of study are "equal" to all other courses of study, the university becomes an institution that accredits persons for particular kinds of work, including the development of knowledge in these specific areas.

But I want to suggest that there has been still another pattern of curricular development in American higher education. It is not the liberal arts college pattern, to begin with, for it is vocational, not disciplinary in the sense in which the separate sciences and social sciences develop. I am thinking of the courses of study labeled "agriculture" and "mechanics" in the late 1860s and 1870s in Kansas and elsewhere, which became agriculture and engineering, and similarly the "woman's" curriculum, which became home economics by the early twentieth century. There are still other examples of this kind of curricular development, and I think we need to remember that it is always present, although it represents a strand quite different from what we think of today as the divisions of knowledge within the humanities, the sciences, and the social sciences. Nursing, social work, medicine, and law, for example, are curricular streams, that, like theology and teacher training, provide interdisciplinary study, vocational in function.

If, however, as Veysey says, the fragmentation of the curriculum had gone as far as it could go by 1910, then there was still another pattern to be developed, that of area studies. The Linguistic Society of America was founded in 1924 for example, and there are still ongoing debates about the interdisciplinary fields of biochemistry and American studies, both products of the thirties. Since then, other area studies have been established, not only geographical—Far Eastern studies, for example—but temporal: medieval studies. And of course, during the sixties a particular form of area studies developed: black studies and other ethnic studies, and, finally, of course, women's studies.

Ten years into women's studies, what are its approaches to the curriculum? to knowledge? to the breaking of disciplines? What, from a feminist perspective, that is, from the perspective of women's studies, are the significant elements to keep in mind as we approach and develop the structure of knowledge? I will name five elements: the historical view, which I have already made use of; a critical view; an empirical practice; a holistic view; a problem-centered practice.

Although I have spent time on history already, I will make a few comments more. It is important strategically to keep remembering how new the "traditional" disciplines are. Some of those grouped under the rubric "humanities," about which I have said very little, are even newer than the sciences and social sciences. In one sense, modern English departments and the literary curriculum, especially in American literature, are hardly fifty years old. In general also, the basic characteristic of the curriculum these past hundred years has been its instability. Compared to the previous two hundred years, it has been in a continual state of development, mainly through accretion, although it has also continued both to splinter into subspecialties and to unite in interdisciplinary areas. It is also useful to remember that women's studies is not an isolated example of an interdisciplinary approach to knowledge.

These remarks suggest that for women's studies a historical approach is an essential tool. Indeed, it would not be an exaggeration to say that we have used history to locate ourselves, to emerge from invisibility, to rebuild our connections with the past and with each other all over the planet. For me at least, perspective on knowledge begins with history.

Second, there is the critical view. This is the perspective with which, to use a bit of more recent history, all of us approached our disciplines or our children's textbooks ten years ago, or, if we are just coming to women's studies, last week. It was the initial step: we asked at first either "where are the women," or what are the "images" offered of those women as imagined either as cats or flowers, sexy and dishonest or beautiful and also dishonest, since the flower's beauty is so evanescent. For students there is often an unpleasant shock implicit in the naming of these images—we have all had that experience. We have also looked with disbelief into indexes of significant books—including histories—to discover *nothing* at all on women. (I will set aside the still more difficult questions about why women should be an index entry at all).

When we approached the disciplines with questions about the presence or absence of women, we discovered the assumptions about women's lives and needs that a male-centered culture and curriculum had produced. We announced our findings: the curriculum, we regretted, was untrue; it taught lies either through omission or distortion; it was biased in favor of males, male history, male writers, even males as subjects of experimental work then reported as research findings in *human* behavior. Even *child* development, I remember one feminist critic announcing this with disgust in a classroom at Johns Hopkins in 1969 or 1970, even child development was about male children.

Element number three is an empirical practice. Indeed all of the foregoing—the critical and the historical perspectives—emerge and are palpable in an avalanche of information, an outpouring of scholarship, studies, and statistics. It is not only that we learned early that we can not be critical without being accurate and exhaustive in our gathering of data, and scrupulous in our analysis of that data—what we used to call "doing our homework." We also decided early to fill in the gaps and blank spaces: if women were not in the history texts, perhaps it was as much out of ignorance as malice. We would restore that history. The task of that restoration, its myriad details, will occupy scholars for a century. In some respects, we have only begun to explore the areas of women's experience still untouched by historians.

One other note about this empirical practice. One hundred years ago, in some areas, there was similar excitement about knowledge, and students studying the "higher criticism" or geology, for example, may have felt also that they were on—if you will forgive the cliche—the "frontiers of knowledge." One characteristic peculiar to our time, however, is the rapidity with which our "frontiers" are shared. On the whole, we do not need to wait for learned journals or meetings of annual professional associations. Manuscripts are circulated in typescript: xeroxes of new essays may be placed on reserve in college libraries for students years before they will be published. And findings are reported orally to groups who then report to other groups. Since we in women's studies are teaching a developing curriculum, we live close to the empirical bone. Those of you engaged in this practice know both its possibilities for error and its intense excitement.

The fourth and fifth elements need to be viewed together. From the perspective of the existing "traditional" disciplines, both appear profoundly antithetical to critical, empirical scholarship. It is one thing to say I am studying the function of women in a particular village society in India: that is acceptable, even in departments that regard studying women as a less important activity than studying men; it is still scholarship, although perhaps trivial. But when I say I am coming at this study from a feminist perspective that claims to make sense of women's lives and men's lives and the village society in a coherent, holistic sense, then I am treading dangerous waters. Furthermore, to get on to the fifth element—the problem-centered practice—if I say I am doing this study because I am interested in, indeed highly motivated to, improve the lives of women in that village and in many other villages of the world, I have probably just removed myself from consideration as an "objective" scholar or researcher.

The holistic perspective is not altogether new to higher education. After all, the battle I described earlier in this talk was won by the foes of educators whose central perspective was theist and whose central text was the Bible. Their fears that science would ascend to the control of the curriculum were justified, and yet, despite the flirtation with Social Darwinism, there has been no effort to replace the earlier orthodoxy. Indeed, one finds scientists and social scientists talking of "objectivity" and the "objective method," as though they were substitutes for a value-centered curriculum. Note that the campus has not been without values: in human terms, it valued men and not women; white folks and not folks of color; Protestants rather than Catholics or Jews; and Americans (I do not mean Native Americans) above all other peoples of the earth.

What do feminists have to say about values? Why is their perspective regarded as unobjective, unorthodox? Are feminists biased? What is the difference between a feminist perspective viewed as a "lens" and a feminist perspective viewed as a "normative" position?

First, when we say we value women, and are interested in their advancement, many men and some women assume that we mean to devalue men or deliberately block their advancement. It is not surprising that men expect women coming to power to be as nasty as men have been in power, and some women at least are not going to disappoint them. On the other hand, women may be smart enough to learn not to repeat the mistakes of centuries of male domination.

Second, when we describe ourselves as researchers or teachers with a feminist perspective, we do not mean that our research is flawed either by poor design or execution slanted to achieve certain results. Nor do we mean that we teach dogma to true believers. There is a great deal of confusion abroad about the issue of "objectivity" in research and teaching. Generally, "objectivity" is confused with what I would describe in the classroom as fairness or openness to many points of view; and in the area of research as rigorous, exact, and honest gathering and reporting of data. But, no human being, and few statements other than facts—and they are few—can be without perspective. Only the announcement of today's date, the geographical location of a meeting, and the number of people in the room might be classifiable as "objective" facts, without perspective. Were I to begin to talk about a particular day, group, meeting, I would have to assume a perspective, I would talk from my position as a conscious person, a woman, a feminist teacher, and a scholar.

As feminist teachers and scholars, most of us live in two worlds: in the disciplines that trained us, and in women's studies. We bring to courses in women's studies a complex body of interdisciplinary knowledge. It is this complex body of interdisciplinary knowledge informed by a feminist perspective that allows us to communicate across disciplines. We also bring something else: what I have called the problem-centered curriculum. From a feminist perspective, knowledge has a normative social purpose—not the continuation of the world as we know it, but the transformation of that world, in part by the knowledge we are producing and teaching. It is this part of feminism, for example, that urges students and faculty to turn their attention to research that is needed, that will make a difference: let us have no more dissertations on Henry James, I continue to urge, or on Melville or Hawthorne; let us remember the ladies, those hoards of female scribblers that Hawthorne feared. It is interesting to me that a number of women scientists I have met recently, trained in graduate schools to run rats or experiment on other animals, after a relatively brief association with women's studies have decided, even against the advice of male colleagues, to begin research on human subjects, in all cases on women, and in at least two, on questions relating to menopause.

A word about dangers: they are many for a new area of study. The most obvious is oversimplification—which may follow ignorance about history, or a failure to consider race, class, or religious or national practices, conditions, beliefs. There is also the danger attendant on all efforts to be holistic, idealistic, and visionary. However satisfying such efforts may be for students and scholars, we may, from the outside, seem to be ingenuous, naive about the complexities of a technological, multicorporate universe, in which, mainland China has just invited Panam to build hotels for tourists. How can knowledge be viewed whole cloth in so complex and technologically sophisticated a world as ours? How can we teach undergraduates without being simplistic? These are real difficulties and real problems that we must consider. There are others, of course, that one can add, among them the fact that these days it is impossible for a women's studies scholar to read in more than two disciplines, and often that is terribly difficult.

I want to conclude on a somewhat different note, not problems or dangers, but the problems we present to the world out there that has just begun to hear that women's studies lives. And I want to have a bit of fun with this one. You remember my quoting from Laurence Veysey's version of the impact of the new science curriculum on the old orthodoxy. Here is his analysis of the two decades during which that battle over the curriculum was fought one hundred years ago. I ask you to listen, keeping in mind our own current battle with the traditional, male-centered disciplines:

> When someone is convinced that he and his circle of associates know
> what is absolutely true, and at the same time that this truth is losing rather

than gaining power in the world at large, his responses are somewhat limited. At least several possibilities exist, however: intransigence, panic, or self-deceptive compromise in an effort to gain leverage. It is probable that during the twenty years of major resistance by pious educators, from 1865 to 1885, all these symptoms appeared. The predominating spirit, nonetheless, was one which combined stubbornness with partial resignation.

It has struck me from the first that "intransigence" has been our first problem, not so much with the administrators of colleges, but with certain strong senior elements in the faculty, and especially on graduate faculties. "Panic": what can be said about that? I see it especially in the graduate schools' closing of ranks behind disciplines, in opposition to interdisciplinary research and programs. And as for "self-deceptive compromise in an effort to gain leverage," that is what we may have to thank, along with our primary invisibility, for gaining such legitimacy on campuses as we have won thus far. Veysey's final picture—"The predominating spirit . . .which combined stubbornness with partial resignation"—I leave to you to envision the persons on your faculty or in your administration who come to mind. Ten years ago we should not have been able to enjoy the parallels in this portrait of an academic battle. Perhaps we can look forward, ten years from now, to still other portraits.

The Past Ten Years

A Critical Retrospective
(1979)

I am grateful to Jane Gould, former director of the Women's Center at Barnard College and to Elizabeth Minnich, former dean at Barnard, for the invitation to write the overview-lecture for a very unusual conference they organized. Barnard invited administrators and other key personnel associated with women-centered institutions in the northeast region of the country to consider the accomplishments of a decade of working for women in higher education. Because I came to the task—in the spring of 1979—from the perspective of my year in the midwest, the lecture probably contains a harsher portrait of that work than I might otherwise have written.

One of a series of resolutions proposed during a concluding session of the conference called on the "National Women's Studies Association to undertake . . . publication of a women's guide to higher education . . . which evaluates the adequacy of support for women on campus. . . ." The resolution, prepared by Elizabeth Minnich and others, was introduced by Joan Kelly, while Elaine Reuben, then national coordinator of NWSA, and I reacted with pleasure to the expression of an idea we had already talked about. In 1980, the Fund for the Improvement of Post-Secondary Education awarded a two-year grant to the Feminist Press for the development of Everywoman's Guide to Colleges and Universities, *published in 1982.*

This essay appeared in the conference proceedings published by the Women's Center of Barnard College.

RECENTLY, AT A CONFERENCE in the Midwest, a man who was welcoming the mostly female group at the start of the meeting, and introducing me in

231

the process, chose to focus his remarks on what he considered a sensitive matter: the allegedly "political" nature of the feminist movement, which, he was glad to note, had all but vanished from academic meetings. This was a weekend meeting of librarians gathered from twelve colleges to consider women's studies resources. I was jarred by the man's opening remarks. I thanked him both rhetorically and sincerely for reminding me of our present and ultimate political purposes, which are, indeed, often easy or comfortable to forget. And since this was a gathering of librarians, I talked about the immediate educational and political purpose of women's studies scholarship on campuses today—to change the male-centered curriculum—and of the ultimate responsibility of those we are teaching for the women around the globe still denied the right to literacy. I was glad of that man's presence, just as I have found it useful to be working in the "great valley of the West" this year—in Ohio, Michigan, and Indiana, with side trips to West Virginia and Kentucky—mainly on campuses that have not been affected by the women's movement as so many of ours were ten years ago. It is a sobering experience as well as an energizing one. I will use some of that experience to define how far we have come and how far we still have to go.

To state it simply, on more than half the campuses where I have been this academic year, there is no women's studies program, there is no women's center, there is no continuing education for women. Indeed, on all of the college campuses, there are no older or returning women students. Perhaps *Signs* has been ordered for the library; often *Women's Studies Quarterly* is not to be found, nor are most of the other journals central to women's studies. There may be a course or two offered on women, and even good enrollment in them. But as often there is nothing more, not even a committee. And where there has been some further development, it dates from 1973 at the earliest and is still without institutional budget or legitimacy. Indeed, most of the small groups of feminist faculty I have on occasion met with since this past fall would be dazzled by the company in this room, would think it was nirvana to be on any *one* of our campuses, let alone in the presence of as many resources as are represented here.

In one respect, I am commenting on the phenomenon of uneven development: the farther away from the coasts, the farther away from metropolitan centers, the farther one gets from the impact of the women's movement on campuses. But since we are talking about women's higher education from the vantage point of the Northeastern section of the country, I am saying something else as well. Here women's colleges have been a strong force for a hundred years. Hence, at least at the undergraduate level, the idea exists that an institution may be woman-focused *and* excellent. That idea is not a reality, even so far west as Ohio. I have routinely met two perceptions of women's colleges, whether elite or not. Male faculty hostile to women still view the women's college as a "retreat" from the competitive reality of the first-class coeducational college: in a women's college, it is assumed, students find a comforting and easy home-away-from-home, support for their fears, and an easier, noncompetitive (with males, who are, it is assumed, the only possible competition) environment in which to study, and to study for what is still assumed to be a degree worth less than one from a male college or a coeducational one.

There is a second stereotype that I have just begun to hear, and one that also has roots in the nineteenth century: the eastern women's college is a feminist stronghold and the place where students will become lesbians, if they are not attracted to those institutions in the first place because they already are lesbians. Indeed, on one small college campus where I recently spent two days, the faculty seminar I conducted opened with a question that included a definition of feminism as "dirty, frightening, and ugly." One need add only the old age and the broom to begin a new witch hunt. Feminist students interested in transferring, and searching for women's studies and an excellent writing program, have said that their parents would not want them attending a women's college because they might become lesbians. (I will return to this theme later.)

Residence on the campuses of old and distinguished coeducational or formerly male colleges has convinced me anew of the maleness of higher education; of what I can only call at best the continued *toleration* of women, as faculty or administrators or students. I am not talking of the exceptional male administrator or the male faculty member already teaching women's studies, or even of those willing to participate in faculty seminars on women's studies. I am talking of the general tenor of campus life in which football, fraternity wet T-shirt contests, and drunken brawls command the scene and coeds conform, whatever the record of their academic achievement in courses. For that is also a fact of life on coeducational campuses: the women are better students, although they still do not use their degrees in the ways that men continue to do. I am also talking of faculty meetings in which the handful of women present are silent; and of the constitution of faculties in which a majority of the men are my age and a majority of the women are young enough to be my daughters. And, needless to say, none of these faculties contains more than 20 percent of women; most, of course, are untenured. The administrations are almost all 100 percent male.

I begin with that bleak picture for two reasons: it will help us to be not less critical but more appreciative of what we have built; it will also reinforce a responsibility we have to illuminate the path we travel for those who follow. For the current institutions I have been working in are not standing still; they will have our current problems before the eighties are out. I hope we have solved them by then.

What are those problems? Why do we have them now? Why do *we* have them now? Who are we? Whom do we serve?

Geographically, the people in this room represent the richest concentration of feminist resources in the country, of women-centered education: research centers, women's centers, libraries, counseling centers, centers for returning students, centers for continuing education, journals, professional associations, women's studies, and women's colleges. All of these exist elsewhere in the country, and in abundance, but the distances between them are greater the farther south and west one goes. We are a relatively small and compact region of the country, even if one extends our boundaries to Washington, D.C. We ought to have a functional series of networks that allow for information to flow and for tasks to be accomplished with ease and pleasure, and without competitive nastiness, the waste of duplication, or the exhaustion of human resources. In New York State and New England alone, one can find women's colleges in numbers disproportionate to the rest of the country. Similarly, there are women's centers for younger and older students; special institutions for women like The Radcliffe Institute (now the Mary Ingraham Bunting Institute); or newer ones like Higher Education Resource Services (HERS). One-third of the 450 women's studies programs in the nation are located in New York and New England. If one slips geographically down to Washington, D.C., one-third of the newly-forming research centers on women can also be found in this area of the country.

We are also an extraordinarily diverse region. I have perhaps overemphasized the presence of women's colleges, especially the elite ones; and for various historical reasons, they do provide a certain tone for the region absent from all other parts of the country. But the region is dominated by such public systems as the State University of New York (SUNY) and the City University of New York (CUNY), the largest in the nation, and especially in the New York City area, serving the most diverse student populations to be found anywhere. We will need to remind ourselves, as we begin discussions, that we serve campus populations diverse in race, national origin, religion, sexual preference, social class, and age. Those diversities are not as apparent in many areas of the country as they are here.

And, of course, in our own region we also find uneven development. Some institutions have barely begun to consider the presence of women. A number are former men's colleges, now coeducational, and not unlike those I have been working in this year. Dartmouth has a new Women's Studies Program; Yale and Princeton have Committees; and now that Kirkland has disappeared, Hamilton is also about to have a Committee.

What did it take to get us to this point? And where are we? With the exception of the women's colleges, we are "add-ons," novel additions to the institutions that pay our salaries or support our services. As "add-ons," some of us are additions to women's colleges themselves. Add-ons have two possible futures: they may be eliminated as appendages that have outlived their function; they may be incorporated within the institution as separate units. Continuing education programs have had the latter kind of history: they are now, moreover, especially valuable and integral parts of higher education since they pay their own way. But women's centers, women's studies programs? Do we envision them as moving in the direction of continuing education programs? Or do we see them being eliminated in a period of tight budgeting, for example? Before I try to answer those questions, I want to talk about the past ten years, not in an effort to describe its history chronologically—it would take too long, I am afraid—but rather ideologically, assessing its purpose; and institutionally, suggesting the patterns responsible for its development.

Why do we have these appendages "for women" on women's campuses and coeducational campuses? From a male perspective, and I have heard this said in an effort to be allegedly helpful, "Women *need* supportive services beyond those provided for men." The implication is that women are not tough enough for the real world of college. It is rare to find a dean like Louis Brakeman at Denison University who said at a recent ribbon-cutting ceremony for the new Women's Center that the Center would be needed so long as the institution continued to serve women and men unequally, and that he hoped it would not take another century to right the imbalance on Denison's campus. It is that perception that educational institutions are not organized to serve women students that gives us our charge and our dual responsibility, and most of our problems: for we immediately have two jobs, not one. We must serve women students to compensate for the institution; we must also, and this is much harder, work to change the male-bias of the institution in which we exist. And, needless to say, we have both of these jobs before us in a time of fewer and fewer financial resources.

My hunch is that we are doing the first job well: and that we are doing the second job only rarely. It is the second job, of course that might bring us into direct collision with our host institution, but I doubt that we have begun to do that work yet. If we are feeling backlash, and indeed we are, it is, I think, mainly because we are doing our first job very well, which means that we have an increased flow of students through our doors, which means that we need more staff and services, more budget, in effect; and, of course, money in institutions is not only tight, it means power. A women's center, you might argue, should serve all the women in a coeducational institution: could it on the budget provided? Of course not: obviously, then, it is intended to serve only a few. What might happen if it should begin to move toward serving most or all?

I talked earlier of a meeting with librarians. In the course of that meeting, we discussed indexing systems—the card catalogue. And I asked what was happening to the subject index "Women." Wasn't that expanding beyond all bounds? If librarians were filing under "Women" all the materials currently being published, wouldn't one begin to find under "Women" all the other subject index headings in the catalogue? Wouldn't one eventually have two indexes: one for everything up to 1970; and then, after 1970, one for "Women" that included, as subtopics, even "Men's Liberation" and "Gender," as well as "Sex Roles" and "Sex Stereotypes"? Do you see what I'm getting at? It's not unlike the question of the Women's Center or the Women's Studies Program that might grow enough to serve generously its potential clientele of students in the coeducational institution, or even in the women's college. What if half of all the women students on campus wanted counseling from the Women's Center? What if even a third of the courses in each department were women's studies courses? Would we at some point "tip" the balance? Would we at any point become the institution we are trying to change?

I have gotten far ahead of myself here, and I want to back up and repeat, in another fashion, some of my questions—coming at them from a different angle.

Many of us a decade ago were studying the status of women on our campus, and mostly the status of faculty and administrators. Some of us studied the status of women in professional associations, and there we often took a broader view and included students. Especially in those disciplines that attracted women at the undergraduate level—like English and sociology, for example—we noticed the attrition of women as they progressed through the university and into the work world. Most of us in this room took what I call the long view and set to work to change the institutions in some fundamental respect—because we saw that attrition as institutionally-caused, as a result of sex-role stereotyping in textbooks and curriculum, of sex-biased counseling, of the sex-differentiated behavior of teachers and administrators, and so forth. The list is hardly exhaustive, and would include all the aspects of the social world that impinge on a human life, beyond the campus and school. In short, we set about to change the world: not only to free it of short-term discriminatory practices, but to revise its consciousness, beliefs, attitudes, and behavior—all of which might and should affect institutions.

Our major tool—in addition to hard work and courage, the skills learned from other movements, and the concept of sisterly cooperation—our major tool was and is knowledge. Thousands of studies of the status of women, of images of women in texts and on TV that most of us may have forgotten, are still the basis both for women's studies research and curricular development and for the existence of women's programming and new consciousness. In the past ten years, we have helped to build a body of knowledge about women and gender significant enough to suggest an epistemological shift qualitatively and quantitatively comparable to the nineteenth century's shift from theology to science. Like our nineteenth-century forefathers, we are also shifting the object of study, even as we are making the lenses of study a new issue. Some of the traditional disciplines have already been so affected that they will never again be the same; some are beginning significant revisions; others, like my own, have barely begun. We are also part of a general shift away from the separate disciplines toward an understanding of their intersections and an effort to use knowledge to solve major human problems. Those among us who consider women's studies a new "discipline" are usually focusing on solving problems related to women's status, role, and autonomy.

Needless to say, such intellectual work, such new visions of the lives and communities of women, have not also been responsible for changing the status of academic women. And how could they? We are not simply joining that "procession of academic men" that Virginia Woolf described and judged harshly four decades ago. Rather, we are revising its precepts, its patterns, and its destination. Some of us have been rewarded; some of us have not. We can all tell anecdotes here; we also all know that the statistics, especially in the upper ranks, have not shifted significantly. We also know that women's studies scholars do not have an easy time getting tenure, that often the battle takes the form of debate about the value of scholarship on women; or about their having allegedly divided their time between the legitimate discipline, say, of economics, and teaching a course or doing research on women in the labor force. It may seem terribly simple: indeed, people away from academe often are incredulous about such matters: but it is still not widely established that teaching or research directed at women is indeed a legitimate part of the discipline of economics, or, for that matter, literature or history. Or, if such research is grudgingly granted legitimacy, it is then labeled of "limited" significance.

But my impression of the job market is that the job seeker prepared both in the traditional fields of study *and* in women's studies has a definite advantage over those women or men prepared only in traditional ways. Especially because of tight budgets, department heads may search for people who are versatile. On campuses where there are strong women's studies programs, moreover, there may also be some informal pressure or, indeed, some of that precious impact we seek—that makes the department alert to the new knowledge.

In short, to conclude this section of my talk, if the possibilities of our growth are at least as enormous as those of the card catalogue entry called "Women," such possibilities are tempered by the controls of host institutions—not only the tenure process, but the general value placed on women-centered work, and thus the resources allocated to such work. Few of our friends—or enemies, for that matter—would deny that we have done an enormous amount of that work on limited resources; that, had we begun in 1959, rather than 1969, we would have grown with the decade that doubled enrollments and faculties in higher education, rather than the decade that cut back or stood still. Finally, I turn to consider the really hard questions of this paper: what have we learned? what have we still to learn? what serious problems confront us—both old and new? The question of resources is an important place to begin.

While we will never have enough—that is clear, of course—we have had some support during the past several years that, many of us fear, will not continue. We have seen this pattern before: while there are resources enough to go around, however sparingly, the unity of a political group is possible; and also a relatively calm relationship between the group in question and the source of resources. That, at least, is my reading not only of the rising competition among women's groups even on the same campuses, but also of the recent conflict between Bella Abzug and President Carter. Bella was speaking for a committee that challenged national priorities, that said that the military budget was an issue to be decided not only by the men in the Pentagon and the White House, but the women in the nation. It was a statement about shrinking resources, although it was turned into an alleged personality clash. I have seen similar clashes between directors of women's studies programs, for example, and deans. We will probably see more of this.

Just as serious is the competition among women's projects and groups for the same small slice of budget. In the early seventies, on a number of campuses where continuing education for women and/or women's centers may already have been in existence, women's studies programs grew out of the collaboration of these two groups with mainly younger feminists, graduate students and faculty. By 1973, for example, on the campus of the University of Minnesota, three separate budgets served women: continuing education, student affairs, and the academic budget of arts and sciences. The three women-centered programs sat on interlocking boards and committees, shared their budgets and information, and avoided duplication of services, including library holdings and academic offerings.

On campuses where none of these programs exist at all, or where they are without budget lines, efforts at implementation in 1979 are likely to be seen as necessarily competitive. In general, there are as many tensions among women-centered units on campuses as there is cooperation. If some of the problem has been the allocation of resources, that problem can only worsen. But of course only some of the problem has been money.

One central problem is the view of women by other women. I am talking of both the general question of status and the question of self-esteem. I am deliberately placing together two or three questions that might be discussed separately: academic women vs. nonacademic women on campus or in the community—that is, the question of hierarchy and elitism; and what I shall call, in shorthand, self-esteem, although I am thinking not of individuals here but of the way in which individual women have identified, or have not, with women as a group. I will very quickly also move from the latter topic into homophobia. For these topics are at the ideological heart of our present condition, our uneven development, and our future problems and possibilities. It is also a sign of the growth of the women's movement that those of us who used to discuss these questions by and large no longer do. We take for granted that those we meet or are assigned to teach or talk with understand what we may have taken more than a decade to learn. And, in fact, most women have not yet begun to think about these matters. And here, therefore, I am suggesting that we must go back to basics—I mean feminist theory—as we approach each other as well as those who are hostile to us.

Let me take first the question of academic women vs. community feminists. In West Germany, the university is so male-identified that the feminist community would rather have no women's studies research institute at all than one located inside the university. When one says that the university is male-identified, one is not so far from saying that knowledge is male-identified, or from claiming that proper feminist activity is organizing welfare mothers rather than documenting research about their lives. But, some of those suspicions advanced by feminists off-campus come from the not unreasonable assumptions that a feminist scholar on a university campus will, like other scholars, function for her own individual advancement, and/or for the advancement of knowledge—abstractly, I mean. I am not going to paper over the potential gulf by claiming that perhaps the feminist scholar is truly interested in the welfare of all women, and has chosen her field of research because the information is vitally needed, etc. Rather, let us leave the gulf at least for this discussion: would it be better to have or to deny the research?

In Berlin, I found myself powerless to convince community-identified, woman-identified feminists, some of whom were teachers or students at the university, of the need to institutionalize women's studies research and curricular development. Nor could I convince them in Berlin or on another, provincial campus in West Germany, that men needed to be involved, and that male students also needed to be instructed. Their ideology, in fact, could not comprehend mine: they were totally woman-identified, whatever their sexual preference. Their view was of a sex-segregated world: the battle they wanted to wage was a sex-segregated one.

Since my return, I have had a series of very different experiences. On more than a dozen U.S. campuses, I have been challenged with the following kinds of questions, and only by women: I. (from faculty): Isn't women's studies creating a ghetto?—for women only? And isn't that bad? 2. (from faculty): Isn't it better to teach men and women than only women in your classes—and won't you have only women if you give women's studies courses? 3. (from students assigned to all-women discussion groups): Why can't we have a man in our group? why should those groups have four or five and we have none? 4. (finally from faculty and students alike): Why can't we find another word for "women"—either to label "women's studies" or to label a research institution like a Center for Research on Women? Don't you think that, if we found another word, we'd have fewer problems in, say, getting resources or tenure?

I am not going to answer these questions. You know what I am getting at: none of them is very far away from that lack of self-esteem, or downright self-hatred, with which some of us found ourselves ten or fifteen or more years ago—and perhaps when we were on women's college campuses. All these questions, of course, can be applied to women's colleges. And it should not surprise us that such views are still part of the poison of our culture. They are also, I am coming to believe, one side of a continuum that stretches to include the fears of heterosexual women about lesbianism. And it is also clear to me that, from the outside at least—from a male perspective, that is—woman-identified women look alike, whether they are heterosexual or lesbian. They are not male-identified, and that causes at least some disruption of expectations.

From the inside, homophobia is a problem United States feminists have not yet dealt with as well as some Europeans have. It is part of our ambivalence toward ourselves, that, I would add, lesbian women also share; it is also part of our ideology that would, in the manner of nineteenth-century feminism, blur differences between the sexes so as to include men. My hunch is that male allies will follow us even if we are woman-identified, perhaps especially if we are.

If this seems abstract, let me turn the question back again to status—and to what we are teaching, perhaps unwittingly, to our women students. I am using my own teaching here as an example. This week I read a student paper with the following sentence: "I am guilty of using my mother and my elementary school teacher as my role model." That was bad enough, but the paper continued. The student then apologized for being a Spanish major, rather than the law student her sister had become, and she added, "I don't ever remember looking at a man and dreaming of being like him. It never occurred to me to be adventurous, to be challenging, to have a male-oriented career goal." She hoped that, given women's studies, younger students in the future would "dream and work toward a higher goal," and she defined her terms, "by higher I mean in the male-oriented business world." Are we teaching students even accidentally—to value men *rather than* women?

I am going to stop here—although with regret—and go on to two other areas that are also very much on my mind, and that I want to talk about briefly. The first of these is the women's studies curriculum. Women's studies has developed mainly an undergraduate curriculum, and mainly a complementary one. Where programs are large, their offerings may look like a mini-college, a parallel curriculum; where they are very complex, programs may have the capacity to focus streams of courses into concentrations for majors. In the main, however, the curriculum resembles an undergraduate smorgasbord: perhaps twenty-five courses in nearly as many departments, mainly the social sciences and the humanities.

Recently, I have suggested to the faculties of small Midwestern colleges and large Midwestern universities that, as they search for a general education curriculum, they examine the one created by the women's studies research of this decade: a curriculum focused on women and the issue of gender. I suggest that this is an appropriate curriculum—as well as an essential one—for *all* students, at least for one full year of college, possibly two. The response, as you can imagine, has been "mixed."

My justifications would surprise none of you. Among them I note that, if one is in the business of truth and knowledge, one can hardly proceed as though half the population had never existed. I must admit that I enjoy giving this particular talk, and I enjoy as much the notion that the decade of work in undergraduate women's studies has prepared us for the issue of general education. I see that as an urgent agenda item for the next year or two.

On the other hand, we have never carefully considered women's studies at the graduate level. Indeed, in some institutions one simply has not been free to do that. For graduate students are the sources of the university department's power, and they are also the profession's method of controlling knowledge—whatever some interdisciplinary units in the colleges may be doing. I think we need a conference and some research on this issue of graduate education and women's studies. Among other things, we need to look at the relationship between graduate assistantships, including teaching assistantships, and the teaching of women's studies. We need also to look at the correlation between the presence or absence of an undergraduate women's studies program and the possibility of dissertations focused on the study of women. If we allow drift to take us through the eighties on this issue, we may be surprised to find that the new generation of faculty coming into our colleges in the nineties will themselves need training in women's studies.

Inside the women's studies world, there are new internal problems. There is the pull, mainly of research, in the direction of the disciplines: the network-form of women's studies programs also tends to push the curriculum, expecially at the advanced levels, back to the disciplines. Those programs are rare that attempt to distinguish between interdisciplinary courses and disciplinary ones, and that spend time on teaching and research methodologies appropriate in each case.

One additional problem has been born, it might be said, of academic success. That is the separation of teaching from research. In the beginning, the women's studies teacher was the researcher—either a graduate student like Lenore Weitzman at Yale, or a professor like Gerda Lerner. Now, increasingly, the research scholar in women's studies is on leave, writing books, or away from teaching students altogether, or, if we are lucky, teaching a handful of graduate students (which, of course, is very helpful). I am not complaining about the fact that we are also producing the necessary books and monographs. The addition of new research centers on women—twenty-one such centers were represented at a recent meeting at the Ford Foundation may accelerate the trend. Without some attention to the articulation of teaching and research, however, the field may lose one of its most precious assets.

And now I want to turn to my sense of another agenda that has already begun, an agenda for the eighties that will, inevitably, fragment our resources further. I said earlier in this talk that we have spent most of our energies providing compensatory education and services for women students, rather than changing the male-centered institutions we are part of. I said that we have functioned mainly as "add-ons," and I said that in the colleges I have been working in, mainly we don't exist. In most places, committees don't even exist. Where committees have existed—at Oberlin College, for example, and at Denison University—I have worked with them and with department heads this year to organize an ongoing faculty seminar in women's studies. (At Oberlin, the faculty has continued this semester without me.) The aim of the faculty seminar is threefold: to provide interdisciplinary support for those faculty attempting (with the assistance, often, of release time) to prepare women's studies courses: to provide the very beginnings of awareness about the field of women's studies to those who are just beginning to consider the possibility of teaching a course or organizing a unit of a course: to provide at least minimum consciousness to those who will never teach in this area, but who are curious about what others are doing. In fact, one of the "nonpurposes" may prove as useful as all the others: the faculty seminar, which had a regular attendance of twenty at Oberlin, and is now having a regular attendance of thirty-five at Denison, provides both visibility and legitimacy for women's studies on campuses that are thoroughly male-centered. (It is interesting to note also how careful the students in each institution have been about those seminars. Considerate but caring, they understand the faculty's need to study, and they cheer them on.)

As we move into the eighties, I expect that we will begin to take on this task in more and more institutions, although I admit that I am not certain about just who that "we" may be. It is clear right now that such foundations as Mellon have provided some funds at least to private colleges for faculty development of the sort I have described. Here, the differences between private and public institutions may become significant—and the cost of such re-education, if it is to be done on foundation or on public funding, boggles the imagination. And yet, we need such programming, if we are to create a shift in the climate on campuses keen enough to allow women's programs not simply to continue but to grow. We need such programming, moreover, if we are interested in changing the institution itself.

To what end do we see that change? What is our vision of an education—I will confine myself to women here—different from the one that women currently receive on most, if not all, campuses? When women's studies was in its beginning stages, Alice Smith invited me to address the concluding session of a Radcliffe conference. She was concerned, she said, about the possibility that women's studies repeat the history of home economics. I assured her that this was not possible for two reasons: women's studies took as its responsibility more than household and hearth: also, women's studies was developing in a nondepartmental institutional form—as a network/program.

Similarly, when we think about gender, we are unwilling to accept either the early view of women as biologically different and hence inferior: or the mainstream feminist view of the nineteenth century that we are equal to men and need to "come up" to male status through the provision of education and certain legal rights. No, neither view satisfies: we are not men, we are women; we are not inferior, nor, I would add, superior; yes, we are different, but it is not clear to me yet exactly what forces are responsible for these differences, nor, I would add, whether I want to maintain or change these differences. Perhaps it is men who need to be changed, not women—at least with respect to some qualities, attitudes, and values.

There is no simple way out of the institution or the epistemological quandaries. I do not want to see women's studies programs become departments prematurely, nor do I want to see them phased out after having sanctioned twenty-five departmental-based courses. The debate on "difference"—in France, at Barnard, and elsewhere—will need to continue. But in the meantime, what else are we doing about the education of women?

We are, I trust, no longer confining that education to a limited sphere, nor a reproduction of the men's curriculum. Both of these educational processes split women, albeit in different ways. Let us talk about an "integrated" education for women. What would it be like? The education of men has always integrated curricular and extracurricular life, although not everyone participates fully. But the male-dominated colleges do provide men with the opportunities to learn about power and domination, as well as teamwork; to establish processes and products of male bonding; to learn how to "use" if not especially to respect intellect; to learn just how far it is productive to be "crude." All these matters are keyed to the world of business, and they are integrated into college life—which is why personality and sports are still important to admissions decisions.

One might, of course, debate whether or not that model is good for men. Or one might attempt to construct a parallel model for women. Perhaps one is already in progress.

On the other hand, we might ask another question: do we have the institutional support to transform education for women? Can our women-centered programs suggest another approach to an integrated education? There is the women's center: one might think of women's friendships and support groups; of learning how to plan programs, how to be an educational center. There are extension programs, some of which also may include internships and fieldwork, practical community experience in learning to organize other groups of women and in learning about the processes of change. Some of our institutions already have good sports programs for bodily health, physical security, pleasure, and games. And of course there are the curricular elements in women's studies. What kind of students might this mix produce, were we to work at it consciously and plan to integrate our resources to implement such an educational program?

Our students talk about and write of the way in which women's studies—usually the whole experience, the mix of information about their histories, their lives, and the process of good teaching strategies we have developed—the way in which women's studies *changes their lives*, transforms their apprehension of the social reality and the mythology that supports it. The transformation often is metaphorically, as Adrienne Rich put it in 1972, *re*-vision. It is a particularly memorable form of learning—we have all had it—since it keeps before us the old mythology as we struggle to disentangle its errors and reconstruct a new reality. Such learning has special transforming power; it does, to put it in one variety of language, turn women (and some men) into "feminists."

This is our major task, still, and I return to where I began, with the idea that we have difficult political and educational work before us: feminist work. A long agenda at this meeting, and a longer agenda still in the decades to come.

It may be helpful for future decades to consider becoming a clearly-identified, politically-conscious, regional coalition of women-centered programs and institutions, indeed, to invite all the others in the region to join us. We need the consciousness and the power of a coalition willing to identify one with the other: elite and public and non-elite private institutions; research centers and women's colleges with women's studies and women's centers; academic with nonacademic programs. What would it take to find the resources to support what we may need to survive? What would we want from a regional network? How would such a coalition duplicate or support and strengthen such other networks and organizations as the Coalition of Women's Colleges or the National Women's Studies Association?

As I have said, we have a long agenda for the next days and the decades to come. I'd like to read Marge Piercy's "To Be of Use," which Nancy Hoffman and I chose to conclude our anthology, *Women Working*. It describes, I think, the best aspects of the feminist work we have done in this first decade on campuses. It is a poem that also prepares us in metaphorical terms for what Juliet Mitchell called, in the early sixties, "the longest revolution."

To Be of Use

The people I love the best
jump into work head first
without dallying in the shallows
and swim off with sure strokes almost out of sight.
They seem to become natives of that element,
the black sleek heads of seals
bouncing like half-submerged balls.

I love people who harness themselves, an ox to a heavy cart,
who pull like water buffalo, with massive patience,
who strain in the mud and the muck to move things forward,
who do what has to be done, again and again.

I want to be with people who submerge
in the task, who go into the fields to harvest
and work in a row and pass the bags along,
who stand in the line and haul in their places,
who are not parlor generals and field deserters
but move in a common rhythm
when the food must come in or the fire be put out.

The work of the world is common as mud.
Botched, it smears the hands, crumbles to dust.
But the thing worth doing well done
    has a shape that satisfies, clean and evident.
Greek amphoras for wine or oil.
Hopi vases that held corn, are put in museums
but you know they were made to be used.
The pitcher cries for water to carry
and a person for work that is real.

The Power of Education

Change in the Eighties
(1980)

The Fund for the Improvement of Post-Secondary Education (FIPSE), a federal agency responsible for funding The Feminist Press project called Everywoman's Guide to Colleges and Universities, *invited me to give one of the two keynote talks at its annual conference of project directors to be held in November 1980, in French Lick, Indiana. My assigned subject was autobiography: I was to explain how and why I became part of a movement for educational change, and from that perspective, I was to describe directions for the eighties.*

The essay was completed, except for a final paragraph, the day before the national elections in 1980. I read it to a full audience of activist-educators the day after the elections, when, since Ronald Reagan had won, it seemed prescient. In the spring of 1981, Russell Edgerton decided to publish the lecture in the Bulletin *of the American Association for Higher Education. Before then, I read the lecture on several campuses, including the University of South Florida and the Claremont Colleges in California. In March, I read it also at the Conference on Scholars and Women of the Sixteen Women's College Coalition, meeting at the University of Maryland. The Coalition will publish the essay in 1983 in its Proceedings.*

In the essay, when I say that education has "power," I am not thinking only of the jobs it is a route to, or the status it may (or may not) confer. Rather, I am interested in the power of education to enable, to empower people with the political vision to see through and around status and money. Most important today, because we live in a world in which the slogan "knowledge is power" is becoming a reality, the education that empowers allows us to challenge the sources and priorities of knowledge, the

*choice of research subjects, methodologies, even, of course, of
perspectives.*

I WILL BEGIN WITH a haunting passage from the *Narrative* of Frederick
Douglass. Douglass heard his master telling his wife that "it was unlaw-
ful, as well as unsafe, to teach a slave to read." Douglass overheard him
say, "If you teach that nigger . . . how to read, there would be no keeping
him. It would forever unfit him to be a slave. He would at once become
unmanageable, and of no value to his master. As to himself, it could do
him no good, but a great deal of harm. It would make him discontented
and unhappy." Douglass was but eight years old, and, as he recalled the
event more than forty years later, he wrote:

> These words sank deep into my heart, stirred up sentiments within that lay
> slumbering, and called into existence an entirely new train of thought. It
> was a new and special revelation, explaining dark and mysterious things,
> with which my youthful understanding had struggled, but struggled in
> vain. I now understood what had been to me a most perplexing difficul-
> ty—to wit, the white man's power to enslave the black man. It was a grand
> achievement, and I prized it highly. From that moment, I understood the
> pathway from slavery to freedom.

The pathway was, of course, education, the first step literacy. But Douglass did not leave us there; he had more to say to us as people thoughtful
about the power of education. He continued to analyze how he learned
this special lesson—he described both the master's views, and his own:

> What he most dreaded, that I most desired. What he most loved, that I
> most hated. That which to him was a great evil, to be carefully shunned,
> was to me a great good, to be diligently sought; and the argument which he
> so warmly urged, against my learning to read, only served to inspire me
> with a desire and determination to learn. In learning to read, I owe almost
> as much to the bitter opposition of my master as to the kindly aid of my
> mistress. I acknowledge the benefit of both.

The ideas expressed here by Douglass about learning as "revelation" and
his acknowledgement that "learning to read" was fostered both by political opposition and by what we would call "teaching"—these are the em-
blems of my talk. Once Douglass could comprehend his social position,
education became a power with which to change it.

Educators often say that the public expects too much from education. I too have said that "schools reflect the society they serve," meaning
that one should not expect too much from them. We have all heard people
say that the family has to change first, or the society as a whole, before
schools and colleges can change. At best, such statements are half-truths.

Those of us who have taught women's studies through the seventies have grown accustomed to hearing from students that such courses have "changed their lives." A law like Title IX, moreover, assumes that schools and colleges should make independent, even vanguard contributions to the well-being of future or actual citizens by treating girls and women as equals to boys and men. It is irrelevant to Title IX that the family and the society in general do not yet accord girls and women such treatment, have not yet accepted beliefs about the equality of women and men. Title IX directs educational institutions to act as agents of reform for a society that has only recently, and partly, begun to consider such reform essential. It may be that one reason we have Title IX and that we do not have the Equal Rights Amendment is that many people do not understand educational change as a powerful instrument of social change.

From as far back as I can remember, I modeled my life on the teacher in the classroom: first, the elementary school teacher, then the high school biology teacher, and then the college professor of English. I was unswervingly school-centered, classroom-centered. It is no mystery to explain why: that was where women were, and to my immigrant family, teaching was a woman's route out of poverty, and into middle-class American society. I had learned one significant lesson of my childhood exceedingly well. Girls and boys were different, my mother had explained on countless occasions: boys could throw their clothes on the floor and leave their beds unmade; girls were supposed to pick up their own clothes and those of their brothers, and they were supposed to make all the beds. That was the way it was, she would continue. Hadn't I seen what she did—didn't she pick up Daddy's clothes?

And as if that instruction were not enough, there was the orthodox synagogue, where, though I was more learned at nine than boys my age, I had to sit upstairs with old women behind a curtain. My mother, who had not been instructed in Hebrew or Yiddish, had too much work at home to go to synogogue, and so I went with my grandmother, who could not read or write in any language. She sat there because she was the wife of a rabbi and had always sat upstairs with the other women. Sitting with my grandmother was not a religious experience. I remember slipping out, running down the narrow dark stairs into the bright sunlight to toss hazel nuts with other children in a formal holiday game along the synogogue wall.

My first religious experience was reading William Wordsworth's "Tintern Abbey" and "Intimations of Immortality" in a freshman English class, and the religious instructor, a woman, was my English professor. I have only just begun to understand what it was that Wordsworth touched in the sixteen year-old girl, totally without consciousness of class, race, gender, or even national origin or religion. Pride of national origin was not part of my family's gift to me, nor was Jewishness a gift as such, since it was mixed with the hatred of non-Jews, and since it was confused with the question of gender. That is, boys who were Jewish had to study to be Jews, and they could participate; but Jewish girls whose grandfathers died when they were ten, as mine did, were then free to forget being Jews. And even before age ten, I was a Jew only when my Zaida was teaching me—ten hours a week.

But Wordsworth, here was someone who understood what it was to feel free or confined; what it was to have to do what you did not want to. Also, here was someone who loved what this city kid did—the beach and the ocean, flowers and the countryside. Here was someone for whom a tree was important, and yet who cared deeply about people who were burdened, confined, closed in.

Somewhere in my college years at Hunter, I studied sociology with a black woman named Mary Diggs, the first black teacher I had known. From her I learned about racism, though I do not think that precise word was ever used in her classroom. But she gave us a little pamphlet called "The Races of Mankind," from which I can date my second religious experience, the experience of knowledge, of knowing that I had science on my side in debates with my parents about new friends I had made at college who were neither Jewish nor white.

I do not want to make too much of these youthful experiences, my feelings that the division of labor between my brother and me was "unfair," that the religious and race-bound views of my family were "unfair," that, as a female, I was not really part of the Jewishness of the household. I do not even want to make too much of the power of my college education to change some of those feelings, and to give me quite a different perspective on race than my family had provided. But I will note that I entered college aiming to become a high school biology teacher; I left college bound for graduate school and a profession in academe. My parents' feelings were at best mixed. Of course they were proud of me, but as my uneducated father said prophetically, I was giving up the opportunity for what he called a "normal life."

In the years between 1950 and 1964, I worked hard to become that member of academe and I tried twice to find that "normal life." I had no analysis of my professional success and my personal failure except to blame myself.

In 1964, I wrote my first essay on educational change, "Mississippi's Freedom Schools: The Politics of Education." It opened with the sentence, "All education is political." I did not know it then, for I had not read Douglass, but it was another way of saying what he had said. I wrote that sentence and that essay to explain to friends and colleagues in Maryland—and to myself—why I felt suddenly "changed," why I longed to be back in Mississippi where I had spent part of that long, hot summer of 1964. Part of a summer in Mississippi, teaching black students in the basement of a church: and it had "changed my life." What were the ingredients of change?

First, the palpable experience of skin color. My skin color had not changed, but I had volunteered myself, and had been accepted into, the black community in Jackson. Such an act made me vulnerable to a share of the savagery of official and unofficial racism. I not only felt the hatred of the white community; I was a target of its attempts to do bodily harm to civil rights workers, white or black. More important, I had the opportunity living inside the black community, to feel the self-esteem and the spirit with which that community survived. In the freedom school classroom, I had further opportunities to see the effect of such spirit and energy on young people ready for education. In short, there was no room for cynicism, defeatism, or whatever sense of doom often afflicts intellectuals. In this brief glowing hour, I became part of a church of freedom. I felt the power of people who, while they would give their lives to the struggle, understood that a different process was needed. It was no accident that at the center of that summer was the freedom school that included not only a new curriculum but a new pedagogy.

The second ingredient of change for me was that new curriculum and pedagogy, a coherent educational program for those coming south to work in the freedom schools. Seven hundred came south, mainly college students. I was one of the "older" ones. At 35, I had been a teacher for thirteen years. Wherever I had taught, I had been praised for classroom performance. I was colorful in the classroom: I walked around the room while I lectured in an entertaining fashion. I was good about answering questions, but I had no idea how to ask them, or that they were of any importance. After all, I had not been a question-asker in my days as a student; I had been a listener and a careful note-taker. That was what I expected of my students. As for curriculum, I taught what I had been taught in the manner of all college teachers. No rebel I: when I had a choice, I chose those authors I had learned were the best; Shakespeare, Milton, Swift, Wordsworth, Shaw, Yeats, Eliot—these were my favorites. Virginia Woolf, whom I had not studied, became material for my dissertation in the early sixties, but not for my classroom.

As a teacher in Mississippi, *I* went to school. The first lesson I learned was that, seated in the circle prescribed by the freedom school pedagogy, I was effectively silenced. Apparently, I could lecture only when standing or walking. I learned something else as well: that students might know something valuable that teachers did not; and that such knowledge shared in a classroom might spark a discussion, might provide one of those magical moments in which learning is "revelation," the kind of learning Douglass experienced, the kind that sticks to the marrow of minds.

The freedom school curriculum was, of course, as nontraditional as the pedagogy. It began with plumbing—descriptions of bathrooms in the black community and in the white community. Obviously, as teacher, I was the least informed person in the circle. But I had been provided with a mimeographed sheet of statistics about indoor and outdoor plumbing in the state of Mississippi, and in other states in the nation, and with regard to race, so that once experiences had been shared and compared for patterns, I could take that pattern and try it against what we call the information of social science. You may be familiar with this procedure if you teach women's studies or other courses experientially: you begin with the experiences of your students (or, if the class is too large, or the subject too intimate, with the experience of a character in a fiction or an autobiography); you share experiences; then you leaven them with information, facts, data, what social science knows and does not know; and you proceed to analysis, the hard questions. Why were most black Mississippians without indoor plumbing? How could that be changed? What did voting have to do with change? What were the advantages and disadvantages of seeking indoor plumbing in New York City, rather than in Jackson, Mississippi—if you were a black youngster thinking about the future?

I spent the rest of the sixties trying to apply my Mississippi experience to my teaching at a woman's college. I followed my hunch and began to experiment with the writing classroom, and because my students were white and female, I followed another hunch, and began to insist that they consider the question I had avoided for more than thirty years—gender. They and I learned a great deal during the next five years, so that when the women's movement touched the campus in 1969, I was ready.

My conversion to feminism, despite all I have said of my early sense that life was "unfair" to girls, was slow and late in coming. I fought against it for reasons similar to those of nineteenth-century women and men who saw women's rights as a divisive issue in a time critical for the freeing of slaves. I saw the women's movement in the sixties as dividing attention from the civil rights and antiwar movements. Wait, I urged: one thing at a time. First racism and war—then women. Without a knowledge of history, one could only repeat it.

What changed all that? A process, the elements of which by now should be clear: the personal experience, important but by itself insufficient; the sharing of that experience, and the intellectual analysis, the knowledge that helps make sense of the experience—deep and lasting sense, revelation. The experiences were different from the shock of Mississippi; they were brief pepperings over many years, not one great explosion in a summer. These are samples of shot, some personal, some public.

First, an election to a high office in an organization I once cared about, and, as token woman, had helped to build. The other women running for the seven slots allotted to women were all ten years younger and innocent of the organization. When the votes were counted, I was the only experienced "founder" of the group not elected. The seven men elected were all my age; the seven women all younger; and I was out. This particularly virulent brand of sexism had been perpetrated by women and men together.

Second, I decided that I would not be responsible for my husband's laundry, nor even for the sheets and towels that had gone with his laundry. For more than a year I fought my own backward consciousness in this effort not to think about laundry. (I also bought more sheets and towels that year than I had ever owned.) Third, in 1970, Paul Lauter and I published a book called *The Conspiracy of the Young* that we had been researching and writing since 1967. For reasons I still do not understand, the publishers did not put our names in alphabetical order on the jacket: his name went first—Lauter and Howe, not Howe and Lauter. And in those days I was innocent about publishing. Even our friends, however, assumed that it was really Paul's book, that I had smoothed the language, that I was the stylish writer, and of course that I had typed the manuscript. And so it was Paul who got invited to talk at M.I.T., for example, about the book's themes.

Such experiences would not have been the "awakenings" they were, except that they were preceded and accompanied by years of reading and conversation in classrooms and in other groups. Since 1964, I had been trying to teach my writing class about the connection between "identity and expression." With those students, some fifteen a quarter three times a year ultimately for six years, I read or reread *A Room of One's Own* and *The Second Sex*, John Stuart Mill, Mary Wollstonecraft, Henrik Ibsen, Doris Lessing, Mary McCarthy, Anne Moody, Kate Chopin, Lillian Hellman, Maya Angelou, and others.

My political commitment to feminism finally emerged from an academic assignment. In 1969, I was asked to become the first chairperson of the Modern Language Association's Commission on the Status of Women, and to attend a meeting of the Executive Council of the MLA. The room was filled with men, and at first I did not see the middle-aged woman in the middle of one long row of tall male-filled chairs. In a corner against the wall, then, I noticed two secretaries taking notes, though there were spaces around the long table they might have filled.

During my report, one man interrupted me several times, wanting to add his own statistics. He was eager, he said, to make sure I did not overlook the "good news," in what he assumed was my effort to demonstrate the pattern of discrimination against women in the profession. I tried to assure him that I was not interested in hiding any information, that I was delighted to report, for example, that women Ph.D.'s in English and the modern languages had been about a third of the total since early in the century. On the other hand, I added, although graduate schools had not discriminated against these women as students, what had become of them afterwards? "Aha," he said, "That's what I was getting at. You haven't said anything about the two-year colleges." And indeed I had not, in part out of inexperience, in part out of some latent element of politeness, for there was not a man in the room out of any but the most elite institutions in the country. But the young man was persistent, and finally, I said, "All right, present your 'good news,' " knowing what he would say. His good news was that although women were statistically insignificant at elite institutions in departments of English and modern languages, and although they made up approximately 22 percent of the faculty in such departments of ordinary four-year institutions, they made up 44 percent of the faculty in such departments at two-year colleges. That was true, I said: and many of these women teaching in community colleges held Ph.D.'s similar to those of the men in this room—from Yale, Indiana, Northwestern, Harvard, and the Hopkins. Why were these women teaching at community colleges while their male peers taught at Yale, Indiana, Northwestern, Harvard, and the Hopkins? How had that "happened"?

That was the first of a series of critical experiences in which the personal was combined with what Carolyn Elliott has called the "galvanizing statistic." In the late sixties and early seventies, academic women in all disciplines embraced numbers. We talked privately about the need—this was our expression—"to do our homework" before going into a meeting of male administrators either in professional associations or on campuses. I spent 1969 and the first two years of this last decade immersed in sociology and other social sciences, so that I could become expert at numbers and so that I could deepen my social and political analysis of what we had come to call patriarchy. Counting was our most important activity in those years. We counted the women at each rank in each institution and profession; we counted undergraduate majors and graduate and professional school admissions and attrition rates; we counted the pictures of women in first grade readers; we counted the numbers of women authors in college literary anthologies. We also noted absences: no women artists in art history texts (although endless nude female bodies were present of course); no women in history except an occasional wife or object of laughter; no black women or other female members of minority groups at all in history books or art history books, or almost any books given to school and college students. And we invented women's studies to begin to turn around the portrait of women in academe and in all schools and other educational institutions.

We were accused, of course, of being a fad and a fashion, of being "thin" or "narrow," of being "too broad and general," of being too "specialized," of being a distraction from the human and the humanist. Finally, we were accused of being "political," the worst charge of all in academe.

Of course we were and are political, as were the schools and colleges we wanted to change. Patriarchy is political, we said, and a patriarchal institution does not serve women as it serves men.

This has been more than an ordinary decade of change, following the truly extraordinary sixties. I believe that the seventies will be seen as the decade that shifted not simply the status of women, but the lens through which we perceive that status. This has been an experience for women of all races and classes and sexual preference comparable to Douglass's experience of blackness in his youth. For the first time we could see: not only what there was to learn, but *the opposition to that learning*. That opposition has not disappeared or diminished. In certain areas of the society in general and in academe, it has stiffened. Even before the national elections, we had already felt the backlash against women of all races and against men who are members of minority groups. We are aware that those efforts of the sixties and the seventies to broaden the formerly narrow Western, white, male, elite curriculum—the history of laws and wars and the men who made and fought them, the Horatio Algers and the Napoleon Bonapartes—have more than cracked the mirror. The traditional curriculum has been splintered so mightily that some of its advocates have already reinvented "general education" to shore up the fragments. And in many instances, the white male elite curriculum has been restored only with the addition of patriarchal Asian religions to its generally Western patriarchal orientation.

What are the major tasks that lie ahead, and how can we use what we know of the power of educational change to get on with them? Knowing all the time that that power is dual: it is the power to teach effectively in the classroom; it is also the power to reveal and be jogged by the political reality of the opposition. The opposition, indeed, may help us more than they would wish.

I am going to single out one of these tasks, the most important one and the most difficult, and the one most central to a society and world depending more and more on knowledge. That is, the task of instruction: of the curriculum and the pedagogy. In 1980, we have approximately three hundred and fifty women's studies programs and on such elite campuses as Yale, Harvard, M.I.T., and Princeton, new ones in formation. Large programs offer on their own and many shared departmental budgets as many as one hundred courses a year. Smaller programs offer at least twenty-five courses, sometimes from as many different disciplines or departments. Perhaps another six or seven hundred institutions offer as many women's studies courses, but without the possibilities for undergraduates of integrating these into what we call a "minor" or a "major" or a "certificate program." Although no one has counted courses since 1973, when that statistic was in the area of five thousand, today an estimate has to exceed twenty thousand. Indeed, twenty thousand becomes the most conservative estimate one can come up with in 1980. While I do not want to burden or bore you with numbers, it is important to gauge the size of this movement if we are to consider its potential use in the eighties.

I see the task of the eighties to broaden that curriculum to match the broadening population of students entering higher education: I am thinking of the multiracial, multiethnic, multireligious, and multiclass society we live in; I am thinking of older students as well as those entering directly from high school; and I am thinking of women as well as men. All of these people at the end of the twentieth century need to understand not the melting pot but the specific cultural traditions out of which this multicultural society has been woven. It is not that other groups in academe could not become the chief reformers of the curriculum; it is that they have not. It has taken the combined efforts of black studies and other ethnic studies programs and women's studies to attempt a curriculum that contains the complexities and realities of history and the present, from perspectives that are outside those of the mainstream and with the additional assumption that change is possible.

From the first, there were two conscious goals in women's studies: to develop a body of scholarship and a new curriculum about women and the issue of gender; second, to use this knowledge to transform the traditional curriculum, turning it into what it has never been, a coeducational one. Until now, we have concentrated on the first goal. We have tended our own gardens, we have fought for our own tiny budgets, we have written grant proposals for two dozen research institutes in women's studies that have the new decade before them. Both in curricular design and in research development, women's studies is on the edge of significant new breakthroughs: in women's history and in the ways in which we will begin to teach women's history with and without men's history; in economic theory and in the understanding of women's role in the economies of capitalist, socialist, industrial, and developing countries; in theories of women's moral and intellectual development; in sex differences and in the socialization of boys and girls—I am thinking here of the longitudinal study at Stanford now in its seventh year; in the restoration of women writers and artists and other intellectuals that will see their works back into print or on the walls of museums and accompanying reevaluations of their achievement. And this is a very small sampling of important work that needs support. Women's studies is the other half of that intellectual ferment that began in academe about a century ago when the professional associations and the graduate schools first thought to amass what we now call scholarship. The scholarship of patriarchy will remain in question until it is corrected by this new surge of research. And we must not rush the reports we need; we must not slight the importance of findings about humans, who are of two genders, several sexual preferences, and many races and ethnicities and social classes.

Whether or not you are in women's studies, its scholarship will affect your discipline. That is one vision of the eighties.

The second vision of the eighties is of transforming that so-called mainstream, the male-centered curriculum. The process has already begun, and in a form not unlike the development of women's studies itself. For example, in 1979 the National Endowment for the Humanities held a six-week Summer Institute on the campus of the University of Alabama, in which twenty-five faculty members studied nontraditional women's literature, not with the aim of producing a women's studies course per se, but a course to be added to the curriculum of traditional English departments. The course in Women's Autobiography and Journal-Writing might also be cross-listed in women's studies, if there were such a program on that particular campus, but the MLA effort followed years of a FIPSE-funded project aimed at integrating courses on women writers into an English curriculum that is still, of course, male-centered.

Beyond the efforts to "mainstream" women's studies by adding on new courses to departmental offerings, there is *transformation*, that ultimate vision of reforming the curriculum with which women's studies began more than a decade ago. Courses on "Women in Colonial America" and "Colonial American History" would both disappear into a "transformed" "Women and Men in Colonial American History." In small, individual ways, that process has already begun by faculty who, for example, teach, in addition to a course called "Women Writers," one called "American Fiction of the Twenties and Thirties" that includes not only the traditional Hemingway and Fitzgerald, but Richard Wright, Zora Neale Hurston, Agnes Smedley, Tillie Olsen, and Meridel Le Sueur, among others.

To leap into the transformation of introductory courses in all the disciplines, one needs two ingredients at least: a willing faculty and an informed strategy for unifying knowledge about women and men into a single course. Let me take the easier question first: the informed curricular strategy. We do not have that, I am the first to admit, in literature, and according to several feminist historians—Kathryn Kish Sklar, Carolyn Lougee, Amy Swerdlow, Gerda Lerner—we are groping toward such a strategy in history. And as for other disciplines, I cannot at this moment say. But from thirty years of teaching, I can say that an interesting curricular problem in itself is a useful strategy for teaching. It is energy-producing for the faculty member and for students: here is a real problem to wrestle with—how do you read the Renaissance for women and for men? what are the factors that controlled women's lives and men's lives and made for those differences? Although one does not have the detailed teacher's guide, one has as much as the Mississippi freedom school teacher had: the key questions; the key strategy of comparison and contrast; and an approach that combines experience and information.

But there is still the difficult question: what I have called "the willing faculty." Where are they to come from? We know that most departments are chaired by men; that most faculties are entirely male-controlled. The statistics we so painfully gathered at the beginning of this decade have not been changed by any of the processes I have described in this lecture. There are two questions here, and I am going to leave them as questions. Will these men be "willing"? And, if they are, can they teach students in what we have come to call "a feminist manner"? Can they, to put it in other words, teach about women and men so that both groups of students will be offered their history, their dignity, and their identity?

I do not know the answers to those questions, but I do know something else: I do believe that many of us in academe—feminist women mainly, but a few feminist men as well—who have taught women's studies and have produced scholarship on women during this decade are ready for the new challenge. We are ready because we understand our own history, because we have moved past anger to a new perspective not only on women, but on the "other half of the human race." Those last words were by Virginia Woolf, as she tried to consider the question of the woman writer's attitude toward the men who controlled (or had controlled) her life. She described her "new attitude" once she had five hundred pounds a year (and I would say now that we have women's studies):

> I need not hate any man; he cannot hurt me. I need not flatter any man; he has nothing to give me. So imperceptibly [Woolf continues] I found myself adopting a new attitude toward the other half of the human race. It was absurd to blame any class or any sex, as a whole. Great bodies of people are never responsible for what they do. They are driven by instincts which are not within their control. They too, the patriarchs, the professors, had endless difficulties, terrible drawbacks to contend with. Their education had been in some ways as faulty as my own.

Of course we have begun to hear the sarcasm in the exaggerated "endless difficulties, terrible drawbacks," and to feel the steel rapier in the final thrust, "Their education had been in some ways as faulty as my own." She broadened the irony into a portrait of educated men:

> Their education had been in some ways as faulty as my own. It had bred in them defects as great. True, they had money and power, but only at the cost of harbouring in their breasts an eagle, a vulture, for ever tearing the liver out and plucking at the lungs—the instinct for possession, the rage for acquisition which drives them to desire other people's fields and goods perpetually; to make frontiers and flags; battleships and poison gas; to offer up their own lives and their children's lives.

The portrait is one that men who want to work with feminists to transform the curriculum will have to begin to see, if not to accept, dislike, and reject. I do not know whether Woolf would have offered such men the experience of feminist "freedom schools," but in fact her 1928 essay from which I quoted, *A Room of One's Own*, is one such offering of strength, wisdom, humor, warmth, and intellect. We will need all those attributes, and more, as we continue to plan, raise funds for, and work in those faculty development programs, summer institutes, and other inventions for the reeducation of generations of male-centered faculties.

And although the political elections may seem (or actually be) discouraging, if one knows history, they are not exactly surprising. Feminists in the nineteenth century worked for seventy-two years before the Congress of these United States passed the suffrage amendment. You and I have been at work in a mass movement for less than fifteen years. In the seventy-two years between 1848 and 1920, another massive effort moved forward: it took that long for colleges to open doors wide to women, and to allow them to study what was called the "men's curriculum" by our nineteenth-century foremothers. We have been at work only a little more than ten years reviewing that "men's curriculum," correcting its errors, and providing another perspective and body of knowledge about women. When I say it is not surprising to feel the opposition to our efforts, I am also returning to my opening theme: it is essential to revelatory learning to see the opposition clearly. That is, if we are still learning *about being human,* if we are still needing to teach each other that humans are precious whatever their skin color or gender, then our educational politics and vision must correct the bias of narrow and prejudiced views that infect other parts of our society. As educators, we work in a society in which education is mandatory and the schools and colleges are institutions that most people attend on route to their adult lives, or on route to changing those adult lives. As educators, therefore, we have enormous responsibility and power, and these will not diminish in the eighties. In a period when the opposition will be most visible, we may be able to do our best work.

Why Educate Women?

The Responses of Wellesley and Stanford (1981)

In 1974, under a Ford Fellowship for the Study of Women in Society, I began a study of higher education for women. I was interested particularly in the curriculum as a formal institutional response to the question: Why educate women? The archives of such institutions as Wellesley, Spelman, Hunter, and the Universities of Utah, Washington and Kansas State revealed patterns that allowed me to describe an overview of this history. But until a Mellon Fellowship at Wellesley College in the fall of 1979 gave me a semester's leave, I had no opportunity to use this archival material. I am grateful to Carolyn Elliot, former director of Wellesley's Center for Research on Women, for this opportunity, as well as to archivists at Wellesley and at Stanford for their generous assistance.

This essay, then, is a first attempt to explore major themes in the history of women's education through pairing institutional histories. The pairing in this instance provides two sharply contrasting portraits of influential, private institutions, the lives of whose founders contain remarkable similarities. That the institutions were from the first and still are coeducational and single-sex ones adds a special dimension to the contrast.

For the Berkshire Conference on Women's History held at Vassar College in the spring of 1981 I wrote a version of this essay, later revised early in 1982 for the opening session of the first celebration of Mount Holyoke College's sesquicentennial. Subsequently, I have used parts of this essay on other occasions, including a lecture at Northern Illinois University in the fall of 1982. A brief portion of that lecture was published in Comment *in 1983.*

WHY EDUCATE WOMEN? At Wellesley, education was conceived of as ending the possibility or probability of women's leading useless lives. Women were to become teachers, and to work either before marriage, or during widowhood, or in the event that women did not choose to marry. Teaching was conceived of as activity vital to communities and essential to the building of a nation. Eventually, teaching was also a "higher" profession for women, since those especially gifted could teach in colleges and universities like Wellesley itself. And of course the almost wholly female faculty illustrated the axiom.

At Stanford, education was conceived of as leading to useful work, especially in the sciences and in business, and especially for men. Education for women was to lead to the cultivation of the home and the intelligent rearing of children. For the few women who might not choose that path, education might lead to professional work, as it did for the three women graduates of Stanford who by the early decades of the twentieth century held positions on the Stanford faculty. Three out of several hundred men.

Both Wellesley and Stanford were founded by a husband and wife who had lost their only and much beloved son. Despite the fact that the lost child was male, in Wellesley's case, the focus was placed wholly on women's education; in Stanford's, women's education was valued enough to make that institution coeducational from the start. In both instances, these were traditional nineteenth-century husband and wife teams: the men had made fortunes; the women had been morally and religiously and psychologically supportive of their husbands. Henry Durant, one of the founders of Wellesley, envisioned the education of women teachers as essential to the creation of a nation of strong men. Leland Stanford, one of the founders of Stanford, had, during his days as a senator in Washington, signalled his support of Stanton and Anthony and the suffrage movement.

In both cases, the male founder of each institution died shortly after the founding: Henry Durant six years later; Leland Stanford, two. In both cases, the female founder of each institution survived their husbands' deaths to function significantly or as essential to the institutions' survival. Although there was never any question but that Wellesley would continue after the male founder's death, since the estate had long been settled, Pauline Durant, the female founder, continued to work with the board of trustees as a living reminder of the ideology of the founder.

After Leland Stanford's death, on the other hand, Jane Stanford was under strong pressure to close the institution and conclude the strange experiment that many of her financial advisors thought would lead her and the Stanford wealth directly to ruin. In addition, the entire estate was tied up in several complex suits, along with the sorting out of the terms of the will. After two weeks in meditation, Jane Stanford decided that the memorial to her son, and now to her husband as well, must not be abandoned, and set herself the task of managing the financial affairs of the new institution personally, her first act to cut her own domestic budget by two-thirds, giving that amount to Stanford's president, to help pay faculty salaries.

All these historical similarities aside, the most essential aspects of these institutions are their differences. Wellesley, founded as a college for women, was woman-centered from the start, at least in ideology. Henry Durant found women to staff the administration and the faculty, and sent other women off for further education, promising them a job on their return. But as witnesses to the college's early years reported consistently, "Mr. Durant rules the college, from the amount of Latin we shall read to the kind of meat we shall have for dinner"—this from Elizabeth Stilwell, first president of the first class of 1879. What might have happened had he lived, we do not know, but after his death, the control of the institution continued to be placed in the hands of women. Henry died in 1881. By 1895, certain of his treasured ideals for the college were abandoned by the trustees, notwithstanding the disapproval of Pauline Durant and her "impassioned plea to remain loyal" to Henry's abandoned ideals. These ideals included refusing to increase student fees to help cover costs; or to abandon the domestic work by students, the required twenty minutes of "silent time" morning and evening, the edict against students attending the theatre and opera, and the closing of the library on Sundays. But in 1899, when Mrs. Alice Freeman Palmer proposed a man to succeed President Irvine (Mrs. Palmer was then a member of the board of trustees), "an earnest Christian man . . . with a very fine wife," Pauline Durant responded: "If we get a man now we will never again have the place for a woman in all probability." Whether or not Pauline Durant's words were responsible, a woman was appointed, and future debates about the virtues of male or female presidents of Wellesley concluded similarly. In 1911, the ideology was stated frankly by the committee then searching for a replacement for President Caroline Hazard:

> It ought to be frankly stated that there is a decided difference of opinion among educators over the question whether it is better to have a man or a woman at the head of a college as large as a university. There are not only the great educational problems which have to do with a college of over 1,200 members, but there are great physical problems, especially with an institution situated as Wellesley is, away from a great city, and having to provide its own water supply, drainage, electric lighting, etc. The college community is double the size of many of the towns. The argument in favor of having a man preside over such a trust has been presented to us with great force and ability by those who hold that position.
>
> Everything that could be said upon that side we believe was brought before us. Your sub-committee, however, at a meeting held several weeks

ago decided that it would adhere to the traditional policy of the College to nominate a woman for the presidency. We found that to change that policy would be considered a severe blow to those who are in favor of the higher education of women. If Wellesley had started, as did Smith and Vassar, with a man for President it would be very different. But for us after all these years now to change our policy *would be saying to the world that no woman could be found* to carry on the succession of women Presidents.

Until the most recent appointment of President Nan Keohane this year, Wellesley's nine presidents have been spinsters or widows, and only one of the widows, the previous president, Barbara Newell, a mother. Two of the spinster presidents married while in office, and promptly resigned. Thus, to conclude this bit about Wellesley, Mrs. Durant, and the succession of women presidents: "Women can do it," but, until recently, this meant only women who give up marriage and motherhood. College administration was, not surprisingly, in a world defined by separate spheres for women and men, considered "men's work." Those who argued for the rights of women to do this and other work are, in Henry Durant's language, part of "the great revolt that is the higher education of women." The great purpose, in Christian terms, is to put the other half of the human race to work in the service of Christ, to make this a better world. Even as late as 1910, thirty-five years after its founding, in the President's Report, we find a reminder of this purpose: "one of the prime objects of the college, as Mrs. Durant has told us, is the training of Christian teachers." Although these teachers may have been assumed to be mainly elementary and secondary school teachers, Wellesley, like the other eastern women's colleges, also produced its share of college and university faculty, again mainly with the understanding that, in doing what was allegedly "men's" work, such women could not be married women or mothers.

At Stanford, the function of coeducation was proclaimed as the production of educated wives and mothers. The institution's founding grant announced its intention "To afford equal facilities and give equal advantages in the University to both the sexes," and Leland Stanford's following address elaborated:

> We deem it of the first importance that the education of both sexes shall be equally full and complete, *varied only as nature dictates*. The rights of one sex, politically and otherwise, are the same as those of the other sex, and this equality of rights ought to be fully recognized. (Italics mine.)

"Varied only as nature dictates" is the caveat, and the Articles of Endowment further define the terms of nature:

> We have provided that the education of the sexes shall be equal, deeming it of special importance that those who are to be mothers of the future generations shall be fitted to mold and direct the infantile mind at its most critical period.

It is not, as some writers on the subject have said, a question of whether or not any of the parties to the founding of Stanford were *opposed* to coeducation. It is, rather, that coeducation did not ever mean what the higher education of women meant at least to begin with at Wellesley.

Defending coeducation as preferable to women's colleges or coordinate colleges for women, in an essay called "How Shall We Educate Our Girls?" published in *The Sequoia*, a campus magazine in September 1895, David Jordan, Stanford's first president writes: "In coeducational institutions of high standards frivolous conduct or scandals of any form are unknown. The responsibility for decorum is thrown from the school to the woman, and the woman rises to the responsibility." Women at Stanford were conceived of by Jordan as maintaining a certain level not only of "decorum," but of refinement and culture. Their main purpose, to prepare to be cultured and refined wives and mothers. In a later version of the same essay, this one appearing in *Harper's Bazaar*, May 5, 1900, Jordan emphasizes that women should *not* be "encouraged" to work for higher degrees, as men should, for they were not in general fit for such work. Jordan's view of women was as a group distinct from men, and disadvantaged intellectually as students:

> Women have often greater sympathy, greater readiness of memory or apprehension. In the languages and literature, often in mathematics and history, women are found to excel. They lack, on the whole, originality. They are not attracted by unsolved problems, and, in the inductive or "inexact" sciences, they seldom take the lead. In the traditional courses of study, traditional for men, they are often very successful; not that these courses have a special fitness for women, but that women are more docile and less critical as to the purposes of education.

These generalizations are softened for students reading them by Jordan's admission of "many exceptions" but he is defining the limitations of coeducation. Yes, women shall receive a college education, but no, even seated beside men, that college education is bound to be as different as their "natures" are and are meant to be different. To the question, is the coeducational institution the best place for women, Jordan urges the affirmative, and writes a critique of the women's college that is interesting in light of our view of Wellesley:

> A woman's college is more or less distinctly a technical school. In most cases its purpose is distinctly stated to be such. It is a school of training for the profession of womanhood. It encourages womanliness of thought as something more or less different from the plain thinking, which is often called manly.
>
> The brightest work in women's colleges is often accompanied by a nervous strain, as though the students or teachers were fearful of falling short of some expected standard. They are often working toward ideals set by others. The best work of men is natural and unconscious—the normal

product of the contact of the mind with the problem in question. On the whole, calmness and strength in woman's work are best reached through coeducation.

In short, the main advantage to women of coeducation is the presence of men, not only as administrators and faculty, but as members of the student body. As a male feminist, if that term is appropriate, Jordan may remind you of Jonathan Swift who thought women ought to be educated so that they might be good companions for their husbands once their beauty had faded, and who assumed that only men could educate women, since women as a class were unable to educate one another. This is, of course, exactly antithetical to Wellesley's position: that the presence of women as administrators and faculty members will greatly encourage women to do likewise.

But we may need another bit of evidence to make clear that the coeducational institution sees one mission of the institution with regard to women, another with regard to men. Here is David Jordan in 1904, reminiscing about Stanford's opening years:

> It was Mr. Stanford's thought that the new institution should be highly specialized. It should have the noble provision for technical education characteristic of Cornell, and the encouragement to advanced study and research characteristic of Johns Hopkins. Its aim should be to fit men for usefulness in life, and for this an unspecialized general training would not suffice. He had no sympathy with the use of the college as a group of social clubs, nor did he wish to train gentlemen of leisure. A Stanford man should be one who knows something thoroughly and can carry his knowledge into action.

In this same essay, Jordan brags about the original Stanford faculty—all male, of course, and adds, "The alumni roll in the faculty has arisen until of the 115 in all, thirty-two are Stanford men." He continues to brag about Stanford alumni, "scattered the world over": "The Stanford man is a type of his own; fearless, democratic, self-confident. He believes in truth, he believes in himself, and everywhere and always, *ubique, omnes, semper*, he is loyal to Stanford."

Where, one needs to ask, *are* the women? This is 1904, and five years earlier, in an edict that surprised President Jordan and others, Jane Stanford had written that "Whereas the University was founded in memory of our dear son Leland, and bears his name, I direct, under the power given me in the original Grant, that the number of women attending the university as students shall at no time ever exceed five hundred." The percentage of women students at the university had, in the eight years of its existence, grown from approximately 20 to approximately 40 percent, and Jane Stanford was afraid of what we would call "tipping." The problem was financial. Like Wellesley, Stanford had been founded on private wealth that was meant to serve those who could not ordinarily afford college. Thus, its student body was drawn from a large pool across the nation. Yet, for the first decade, its funds were tied up in litigation, and thus its dream of laboratories and agricultural facilities, of premedical and preengineering training had to be put off. Thus, male students transferred at mid-college to Berkeley or to Cornell or the Hopkins. And yet the female students continued to flock to Stanford. By 1899, there were 463 women and 690 male students. That high of 40 percent was not to be reached again until recent times, and, between 1899 and 1933 the proportion of women dropped to about 17 percent.

The edict about "the five hundred," as women at Stanford were called for three decades, was removed in 1933 for financial reasons: the depression was having its effect on the institution, even with its originally beneficient endowment. The enrollment of qualified men had been dropping steadily, and of course, the limitation on the 500 had prevented hundreds of qualified women from entering.

Student reaction to the opening of admission beyond the 500 women was mainly negative—from women and men both. From the *Stanford Daily*, May 15, 1933, comes one man's point of view: "At present Stanford is a man's school with five hundred women in attendance—in a mild sort of way, of course. With 1500 women it will be a woman's school with the men hanging around. At best it will be coeducational. That is serious indictment enough." The women were also not pleased, according to other news articles of the times. But as enrollments increased during the thirties, questions began to be raised about the education of women, questions heard earlier but not acted upon. These focused on changing the "scholastic curriculum to develop feminine intellectual capabilities"—in the words of two *Stanford Daily* (male) writers. They ask of what use can the Stanford (male) curriculum be to "women (except those desiring careers, of course) . . . in the drawing room or nursery or kitchen?" And they ask for courses in which women can have the "opportunity to learn a few of these necessary feminine attributes." Eventually, through the thirties, courses were begun called "Women in Modern Society," "Women in the Home," and the like, and some male students petitioned for entrance to "courses in personal problems and marriage relationships." Eventually also, certain professional curricula designated as of interest to women appeared—Nutrition, for example, and Physical Therapy, Physical Education, Institutional Management, Pre-Social Service, and others. The characteristic response of the institution to women's presence in consequential numbers was thus to establish curricula in several sex-segregated areas of specialization for women.

Interestingly, Wellesley resisted almost all of these areas, with the exception of teaching. Its curricular model from the first was the elite men's college, and its faculty were directed by Durant and subsequent presidents to equip themselves to teach in the most modern methods, using laboratories for science, art, and music, offering archeology and astronomy, as well as the other sciences. Interestingly, like Stanford women, Wellesley students before the thirties majored mainly in the humanities; after the thirties, mainly in the social sciences. In neither instance, were science majors the majority, and yet, for science the proportion was higher for Wellesley than for Stanford women.

Finally, what did the students at Wellesley and the women at Stanford see as they entered their classrooms? The faculty at Wellesley, predominantly women, occupied the laboratory and the lecture hall, ran the observatory, organized archeological expeditions, and wrote poetry, philosophy, and history. The faculty were also feminists, socialists, pacifists, social reformers, and activists. Their reform work drew students into action, on the picket line and in the settlement house, as well as in the suffrage parade. Not all Wellesley students participated; many were engaged in genteel social activities; others in intellectual pursuits alone. But these opportunities were present, and those who pursued such activities added to the college's elan and purpose.

Questions of feminism, suffrage, the "work" of women were debated in the dining hall, on special occasions by outside speakers, as well as in at least a few of the unique courses on women taught by Emily Greene Balch at Wellesley in the decade before the First World War. The ideological underpinning of the institution, described by Durant in terms of providing work for heretofore wasted female lives, was extended, at least in some of Wellesley's classrooms, to women less privileged than the students. My sense of Wellesley's history, and especially of the environment provided for its students, is that they saw a rich array of achieving women, albeit mainly unmarried, in significant action. Thus, the institution provided female students with live possibilities for their futures, both in the faculty and administration, and, further, in the alumnae who continued to be a force in the college's daily life.

At Stanford, there was Clelia Mosher, a physician, scholar, and faculty member, whose presence looms large because she was a single feminist magnet for women students, rather than the large cluster one finds at Wellesley. She is a larger than life-sized figure also because she spent the last decade of her life putting her papers into startlingly clear order so that researchers today may see her more whole than many other similar academic women of the past. Dr. Mosher taught a class in hygiene for women students, a ubiquitous phenomenon for women students everywhere, but at Stanford a very different experience. The premise of the course was an assumption that women students needed models of achievement, if they were to aspire. Her course—outlined and with all its materials clearly provided in hundreds of pages of typescript—presages women's studies courses half a century later. That she was conscious of the connections between her research on as well as her teaching about women there can be no doubt. Mosher did research on women's diaphrams as their breathing mechanisms, on women's muscle tissue to see whether it was, as believed, different from men's, and on the definition of menstrual blood. In one of her journal entries she remarks on the completion of an experiment that erased the alleged gulf existing between women's and men's physiology, by noting "Another blow struck for women's freedom." She is an example *par excellance* of the singularly committed, uniquely gifted "token" woman—usually a feminist—one can find on each university campus during the early years of this century.

At Stanford, one gets a sense of what life was like for undergraduate women by reading the complaints of male undergraduates about women who spend all their time studying and hence gain more places among the Phi Beta Kappas than should be theirs proportionately; or who spend so much time studying that they give none to extracurricular activities, as though the male students would wish to give up their control of campus institutions to women. One also hears occasionally a lone female voice raised in the campus publications, and, alas, anonymously: The article is called "The Higher Education of Woman: Some Observations by One of Them" and the date is April 1909 in the *Sequoia*. The writer opposes the idea that the university should introduce courses "as might conduce to the effectiveness of the girl in the service of her husband and her family"— viz., courses in "household economics, cooking, physiology, child-culture, and others." The writer declares that she is opposed to such courses: Marriage includes "more than that she should be able to feed him. It is of importance that woman should be the friend, companion, equal-citizen of man, especially if she be married, and that servitude is the death of the spirit in marriage as in everything else." "The first pre-requisite for successful wifehood," the female student continues, "is freedom. The second is liberty, and the third is independence. . . ." and she adds, "And as these are semi-synonymous words their juxtaposition should convey some adequate sense of their importance. The truly successful wife is the friend and comrade of her husband and her children, and is never for an hour his "hired help."

> Thus it becomes necessary for every woman to have an interest, a profession, a craft, an art, a life, all her own. She is then a human being; and that she is also at the same time the wife of a free and independent citizen should only add to her self-containment and not in any degree detract from it. . . . The girl must go to school and college as though there were no marriage, as though she were going to grapple with a life-work from the start, and more than that—to the finish. Then she will be a fit comrade for the strongest man, for strength comes from doing and purpose, and not from lying around awaiting commands.

In the following month, another anonymous woman student responds, urging the sanity of preparing for domesticity, and she reminds students that "Our divorce courts are filled with the clamor of men and women seeking freedom, liberty and independence from the responsibilities that come with the making of the home." She quotes David Jordan without naming him as "one who speaks with rightful authority" on the importance of the "character and influence of . . . mothers and . . . wives: 'The higher education of women means more for the future than all conceivable legislation reform. It means higher standards of manhood, greater thoroughness of training, and the coming of better men.'"

We have come a full circle to Durant's view that to found a college for women would be a commendable memorial to his son, since the education of women is important to the education and development of male character. And of course the Stanfords saw women as needing education if they were to be fine wives and mothers.

Perhaps the differences ideologically are not astonishing, and yet in action they proved enormous: in the one case, the institution developed as a female-centered one, offering students an environment in which to observe women filling every kind of position, and offering faculty and administrators, and alumnae, the continued sense of a shared mission—the education of women. This mission continued to be connected to the more general mission with which the institution began, which, as Henry Durant called it, was the more general one of "the revolt of women" against the enslavement which had been their lot for centuries. Although the years from 1875 to the present offered shifts in the vision and in the actions that supported the vision, the ideological mission—that connected education and women's rights—does not disappear and makes for the distinctive quality of the institution.

At Stanford, where the major mission of the university was male-centered, women as a group might be described as invisible, ignored, deferred to as future wives and mothers, or restored eventually to places in a sex-segregated curriculum as "coeds." They are campus leaders only as exceptions; they are described in texts about Stanford's achievements only on occasion and as exceptions. They are, in short, the second sex on Stanford's campus, and barely that in Stanford's history. One has to search for them, as one has to search for "women" in the archival catalog.

And yet, after one has said all that, there is still one more turn of the screw. For we have been looking at the institutions internally, from the perspective only of persons within it. We were considering the health of women students, their need for role models, for example; and for the pleasures of women-centered institutions and relationships, such a view might be sufficient. But institutions of higher education reside in a universe in which maleness and femaleness are ranked and in which women's colleges continue to be seen as somewhat special, unique, not quite "mainstream," and certainly without the power to affect change, to lead the way. Or to put the question another way: the Stanford woman student who achieves may be valued more than the Wellesley student, for she has come through the halls of the Jordans and Eliots, rather than those of the Calkins and Colmans. It is not surprising that, in the hierarchy of institutions, Harvard and Yale should have remained the models both for the coeducational Stanford *and* the female Wellesley. In the contemporary hierarchy of institutions, little has changed, except that the dominant male institutions have now adopted coeducation, their ideology untouched, unchanged, but in the modern manner, with women expected to conform to the maleness of the institution and to be superwomen: that is, to be women and men both, while the men continue their "normal" lives.

It will be interesting to see, in the decades to come, whether the women's colleges, the women's studies programs, the women's centers, the centers for research on women, and other female-centered institutions, will have the courage sufficient to their ideology; whether they will be able to articulate with the clarity of that Stanford undergraduate I quoted earlier in this paper—that women need to study because they are intelligent persons who can learn; that they are persons first, then possibly lovers, wives, or mothers; that work is as important to women's lives as love and friendship; and that education for women is as important and for similar reasons as education for men.

Feminist Scholarship

The Extent of the Revolution
(1981–1982)

When I held the Mellon Fellowship at Wellesley's Center for Research on Women, Peggy MacIntosh encouraged me to compose a "laundry list" that might describe the women's studies interdisciplinary curriculum. The first version of this list of "understandings" appeared as part of the introduction to the special double issue by the Harvard Educational Review *on Women and Education in early 1981. In September 1981, Diane Fowlkes of Georgia State University invited me to participate in a session at the American Political Science Association on feminist scholarship. For that session, I wrote a brief version of this essay, in which I used an abbreviated form of the list of "understandings." That lecture has been published by the American Political Science Association.*

The essay that follows is an expanded version of the APSA talk, prepared for a special issue of Change: The Magazine of Higher Learning *called "Women's Studies at the University," which appeared in April 1982. A portion of the essay, and the list, appeared in the* Women's Studies Quarterly *in 1982. The essay has also appeared in 1983 in a book edited by Charlotte Bunch and Sandra Pollack called* Learning Our Way: Essays in Feminist Education.

WHEN I WENT TO COLLEGE in the forties, I could not have imagined questioning the teacher, the syllabus, or the texts I was given to read. I was at Hunter College, in those days still a women's college, with a high percentage of women faculty, even a few women administrators. None of these persons, however, seemed concerned about the fact that the entire curriculum taught women that their education would carry them into domesticity. If they were to work, it would be because they had to and only in the few fields open to them: school teaching, social work, the library, or, if they were exceptional, teaching on a women's college campus. The message of the curriculum was, in brief: men achieve and work; women love and marry. The twin message of love and marriage, I should add, was present in sociology and literature; elsewhere, women were almost entirely absent, except for the traditional nudes painted by scores of male artists one viewed in art history.

In the forties, I thought nothing was wrong with this portrait of the world. And in the fifties, when I proved one of the exceptions and went on to graduate school, the curricular portrait extended itself without any changes, although I went from Hunter to Smith and then to the University of Wisconsin, where I taught and studied for the first time in an obviously male world. The garment of my studies, their cloth and design, never varied. When I began to teach in 1960—as expected, at a women's college—I taught what I had been taught: the male-centered curriculum, male writers, male perspectives, about mainly male worlds—bear hunting and whales and priest-ridden young men, for example, not birthing, mothering, not even school-teaching. When I was asked to design the required sophomore survey in British literature, I chose not a single work by a woman writer, nor did I include a work by a male writer that contained a strong and sympathetic female character. I was not only without consciousness of gender; I had accepted that male-centered world as "universal." The question of where I was located in that world—had anyone asked it of me—would have been puzzling or irrelevant.

At Goucher College, where I began teaching in 1960, I was not only not interested in gender; I was, from the first, regretful that *it was* a woman's college, and I supported those who wanted to see that campus a coeducational one, arguing that it was not "healthy" for women to be isolated from men. If the "real" world, the "public" world was male, women could only gain access to it through being at least in the presence of those who could enter it. I did not know it then, but those arguments also reflected the homophobic, male-centered curriculum I had been studying and teaching without consciousness, and of course without understanding and knowledge thereof.

At Goucher, my friends were male faculty members: how could I feel anything but concern that my students did not have the opportunity to form friendships with young men? At Goucher, especially in the composition classes I taught three times a year, something else began to puzzle, then concern me. These students were bright, they came in with high scores and good skills, and yet their writing was bland, empty of conviction, opinion, idea. In conference, they were directionless, without ambition. They were without vocation; even those who had arrived with a vocational goal had lost it within the first quarter of college life. They were at Goucher because their parents wanted them in a safe place between the years of high school and the years of marriage, and in a safe place that would allow them to marry well—they could choose from Annapolis or the Hopkins. And in the students' own words, they saw the usefulness of their liberal arts education as preparation for entertaining their husbands' friends, clients, or business associates. Those who know Swift's eighteenth-century prescription for women's education—that it was necessary for women who wished to keep their husbands' interest beyond the years of youthful beauty—understand that these Goucher students had leaped to a new depth: they were going to prove useful to their husbands' achievement in a postindustrial world, by serving cultured conversation about the arts and politics along with the salad and *hors d'oeuvres*.

By the fall of 1964, and for reasons that had nothing to do with the women's movement, I was teaching composition through the use of literature by and about women, although to keep the peace, I always included Lawrence's *Sons and Lovers*. At the conclusion of that novel Paul Morel is talking with Miriam—they had been young lovers together—about her current life. He asks whether she is in love, and she says she is teaching. He voices Lawrence's view that for a man work is sufficient; for a woman, not so. A woman to be complete must have love; work for women is insufficient. Following this segment of the course, my students talked one day about their views of work, and an intrepid freshman who had been tutoring in Baltimore's black ghetto offered the view that she *enjoyed* such work, and that she planned to enjoy work the rest of her days. I was as surprised as the rest of the class to hear this view expressed, and asked others in the small group of fifteen how they felt about the expressed view. Some students thought the young woman could not have been doing her job if she had "enjoyed" herself, since work was not supposed to be enjoyable. Others thought it was morally wrong to "enjoy" such work, since the point of it was altruistic—you were supposed to be thinking only of helping others. Unmentioned in the discussion that followed were two elements important even to my gender-unconscious life: the need to earn money through working and so to be self-supporting, which was also essential for Miriam in Lawrence's novel; and the ambition to achieve, to become "somebody" through one's work. These fifteen students, and generations of others I taught in the following seven years, maintained the ideology that separated middle-class white women from the male work world and ethic. Such women students expected to marry and to be cared for economically. Their privilege cost them their history and of course their future.

The single most important difference in 1982 is that, regardless of social class, young women today know that they are likely to spend most if not all of their lives working outside the home. Older women are returning to the campus in large enough numbers to help academe over rough times—and their urge is also vocational. Many circumstances have contributed to this new social milieu: the economic belt-tightening amid rising expectations and a rising inflation around the globe; concern about the population explosion, about food shortages, and an awareness of the relationship between birth rates and the access of women to job markets; in some countries, the need for a new underclass of women workers; as well as the energy of a women's movement in several countries of the West, and the broad-based consciousness-raising experience of the late sixties that led to the women's studies movement. Whatever the combination of circumstances, young women and young men see a different vision from the one that my generation viewed. Indeed, privileged women students on ivy-league campuses may be somewhat blinded by the rhetoric of "you can be anything you want to be." Such students do not want to hear about wage differentials between women and men, or about discriminatory hiring and promotion policies. They want to believe they can attain their vocational goals as easily as the young man in the chair next to them.

The last decade, moreover, has been one of vocationalism on campus. Indeed, in a manner I find touchingly ironic, Goucher College, for example, insisting on its educational mission as a women's college, has turned its back on some traditional aspects of liberal arts to initiate career training programs in dance therapy and museum technology. Whether this is better or worse for students at Goucher is not my point. I am interested in the shift in the social milieu in which young women as well as men are going to college. The expectation of both groups of students is that they will work outside the home most of their days; further, students believe that the function of a college education is to get one a job.

I want to emphasize this point, for this function of higher education has been present from the founding of Harvard and other sectarian institutions in the seventeenth century for the training of ministers, through the founding of women's colleges for the training of teachers. The vocational mission of higher education is one rich and important stream that sometimes rises above ground where it visibly carries all varieties of vessels, even trash, in its wake; at other times, the vocational mission sinks far below the surface, hidden by the gardens, the shrubbery, the forests we call the liberal arts curriculum. While the vocational curriculum has segregated female and male students openly—to continue the metaphor, we see the ships of engineers sailing separately from the social welfare vessels— the liberal arts curriculum, similarly assigned to women and men, thrives upon and supports the assumptions beneath sex segregation.

It is the liberal arts curriculum that defines the possibilities for boys and girls, tells them how they will become masculine and feminine beings; offers them a reading of history in which they do *not* all appear; offers to boys, images of hundreds of vocations; to girls, still only a few—despite all the energies of the seventies. The liberal arts curriculum still tells college students about their fathers, not their mothers; teaches students not only how to think, but that men have been the only thinkers. The point may be obvious, and painful still that the sex segregation of the workplace has, for the most part, not changed, and will not continue at least the small changes begun in the seventies unless educators continue to press still more urgently for curricular reform.

But it is also obvious that the liberal arts curriculum is currently in trouble, and for many reasons. Attacked as irrelevant by the vocationalists, it had begun to lose students, especially in the humanities, long before the women's studies movement had gained its current position on campuses. By the mid-seventies, such courses as Women's History in the U.S. were compensating for low enrollments in other history courses. By the mid-seventies also, campuses were gearing up for the next round in the battle to save the liberal arts: through faculty development and the new push for a general education curriculum, the liberal arts were to reemerge as sovereign. This last development, of course, has occurred with little or no communication with or acknowledgement of the concurrently developing area of women's studies. In general, the reforms proposed return the campus to basic books in the white, elite Western male tradition, or add several Eastern male texts.

These texts won't do, for many reasons, including the obvious fact that a male-centered curriculum that continues to forward a misogynist view of achieving men and domestic or invisible women will clash with or confuse the vision and aspirations of half, or a bit more than half, the student body now attending college. Perhaps more important even than that humane reason is another: a return to the old masters does not forward the search for truth which has traditionally been at least part of the liberal arts mission. St. Augustine, Aristotle, Erasmus—these men return us to the monstrous misogyny of the past, which we must of course understand, but which, as the mainstay of the curriculum is hardly sufficient. In short, then, if the traditional liberal arts curriculum won't do, what will? Nothing short of transformation, the major source for which is women's studies.

When women's studies began in 1968 and 1969, it had hardly a name. But faculty on less than two dozen campuses began to meet to consider what, in addition to teaching single courses, they were attempting to do. If one reads the early manifestos—and that is what they sound like—of early women's studies *programs,* one finds five goals listed:

1. to raise the consciousness of students—and faculty alike—about the need to study women, about their absence from texts and from the concerns of scholarship, about the subordinate status of women today as well as in the past

2. to begin to compensate for the absence of women, or for the unsatisfactory manner in which they were present in some disciplines, through designing new courses in which to focus on women, thus to provide for women in colleges and universities the compensatory education they needed and deserved
3. to build a body of research about women
4. with that body of research, to reenvision the lost culture and history of women
5. using all four goals, to change the education of women and men through changing what we have come to call the "mainstream" curriculum, though we know even more clearly than we did a dozen years ago that it represents far less than half of human history, and only a small portion of human achievement.

Because this body of knowledge and this curriculum are as revolutionary for our century as the original body of scholarship that changed the theistic patterns of education in the United States a century ago, I want to take the time to list their major components. The list is both disciplinary and thematic. It is also meant to be interdisciplinary: that is, whatever the discipline, if one is to teach about women, one will need at least a slight acquaintance with almost all the other elements on the list. This list also describes the basic curriculum in mature women's studies programs, and serves as a design for developing an interdisciplinary program of courses for those who would transform the liberal arts. And perhaps I should say, in anticipation, that this list, and all the scholarship it represents, is both our major resource for the future and—because it is formidable—one of the major barriers to the goals we seek. Someone I was reading recently wrote that, to begin in the 1980s to gain an understanding of the new scholarship on women—whatever one's discipline—is comparable to beginning to earn a new doctorate. I do not think that is an exaggeration; understanding the dimensions of our task may help us to move forward.

The list:

1. an understanding of patriarchy in historical perspective, philosophically and sociologically, its relationship to the religions of the world, and to ideas of knowledge and power—hence, an understanding of what it means to be born "permanently" into a subordinate or dominant status; a knowledge of feminist theory
2. an understanding of the complex, confusing, and still chaotic area of biological psychological sex differences; the importance of null findings
3. an understanding of socialization and sex roles, as well as of sex-role stereotyping; the relationships among gender, race, and class—all from a cross-cultural perspective

4. an understanding of women in history, not only in the United States, but throughout the world, recognizing that such study includes legal as well as medical history—the history of birth control, for example, which is essential to the study of women, even to the study of fiction about women

5. an understanding of women as represented in the arts they have produced, some of which have been buried or ignored as arts—quilt-making, for example, or the pottery of North American Indian women; and as represented in the significant literature by women of all races and nationalities that never was included in the literary curriculum; as well as an awareness that the images of women portrayed by the male-created arts have helped to control the dominant conceptions of women—hence, the importance of studying images of women on TV, in film and the theatre, and in advertising

6. an understanding of the ways in which post-Freudian psychology has attempted to control women's destiny; an awareness that other male-centered psychological constructs like those of Erikson and Kohlberg are potentially damaging to women; an understanding of new women-centered theories of female development

7. an understanding of female sexuality, including perspectives on both heterosexuality and lesbianism; special issues involved in birth control and reproduction

8. an understanding of the history and function of education as support and codifier of sex segregation and of limited opportunities for women; some perspectives on education as an agent for change in the past and present

9. an understanding of the history and function of the family in the United States and cross-culturally; of the current variety of family structures, and of the conflict between beliefs and research findings with reference especially to issues surrounding children

10. an understanding of women in the workforce through history, in the present, and cross culturally; the economy in relation to women; the relationship between money and power in personal interactions, in the family, and in society

11. an understanding of the relationship between laws affecting women and social change; the history of women and social movements

All the items noted above are meant to include women of all social classes, races, nationalities, and ethnic, religious, and sexual identities. This approach distinguishes women's studies from the traditional male-centered curriculum.

Two methodological issues need also to be noted. The first is the *comparative approach*. Since most if not all learning occurs through comparisons, it would be strange indeed if the study of women did not also illuminate the study of men. On the other hand, it is possible to study cohorts of half the human race in their own contexts and on their own terms, without reference to the other half—which is, of course, what male-centered social science has done for almost a century. Obviously, we need both the comparative data and the data for each sex separately, but it may take a couple of generations before we have sufficient data about women to move on to some of the comparative questions. In the meantime, of course, there are also scholars attempting to look at the male data anew, and from a feminist perspective.

Second is the *documentary base.* Though we could see the outlines only dimly in 1969, more than a decade later we have many full portraits of the lives of women both famous and obscure, public and private, singly and in groups, and we understand that we have only touched the surface of the material still to be collected, studied, sifted, made available. For several hundred years, women have been recorders, letter-writers, diary-keepers, secretaries of clubs and other women's groups, as well as professional writers. There are also many more women painters and composers than we had even been able to dream of. Beyond those documents still coming to light in attics, county museums, and private libraries, women speak mutely in statistics of births, marriages, employment, deaths. In addition, there are the millions who await the social scientist: subjects of research for the next century at least, to compensate for their absence, and to improve by their presence the body of knowledge on which public policy is based.

During the first five or six years of its existence, on many campuses women's studies programs carried on their work in a form Gayle Graham Yates of Minnesota has called "creative anarchy." Courses were described on flyers turned out on mimeograph machines and circulated "underground" on campuses. Faculty risked when they taught a women's studies course, and many of them, especially in the early seventies when there was still some elasticity, especially in the heavily endowed private colleges or richly funded public universities, played musical chairs: they left one institution's English department where they had taught women's studies and had, therefore, been considered "not serious" to go to another where they tried similar courses.

By 1976, when the National Advisory Council on Women's Educational Programs asked me to review the status of women's studies programs, mature ones were well on their way to being institutionalized: they had modest budgets; a paid coordinator, often in a line administrative position; and a formal procedure for regularizing the curriculum that was, increasingly, leading to minors, and B.A.s, if not to M.A.s, graduate minors, and Ph.D.s. But what was also clear was that the format of women's studies programs was not that of academic *departments.* The model, even in all its variant forms, was that of an interdisciplinary program, more like the initial form of American studies than like the newer form of black studies.

Women's studies programs function as networks on campuses, not departments, and certainly not as what are commonly understood as "ghettos." That means that most faculty members who teach in a women's studies program do so from a location in a traditional department. That is the way in which 90 percent of all women's studies courses are taught. Whether the campus is one of the three hundred and fifty with formal programs, or whether, like Smith College, it is not (but offers more "courses on women" than some programs), the same fact holds: the courses are listed in departments as well as by the women's studies program. Faculty in those departments have one foot, sometimes only a toe, in the women's studies program. Only very few programs—fewer than the fingers on one hand—have tenured faculty or directors in women's studies itself. Almost all have to depend on departments that are willing to tenure faculty who teach one or two women's studies courses each year.

What distinguishes a women's studies course from a course on women taught in a department? In general, the major distinction may be no more than the existence or absence of a women's studies program. And what, therefore, is the virtue of having a women's studies program? Programs offer introductory, interdisciplinary courses, and sometimes a few additional core courses as well, and sometimes all of these under their own label, as well as senior integrative seminars. They also advise majors and minors, and prepare a logically organized curriculum within an interdisciplinary framework for those students wishing either to be majors and perhaps to become scholars in the area, or to enlarge their educational perspectives to include the other half of the human race. We need women's studies programs because we need to prepare another generation of scholars able to contribute to the new scholarship on women.

During the last four or five years, some of the oldest women's studies programs have attempted to think strategically about their second mission: the transformation of the traditional curriculum. In addition, on more than a dozen campuses without women's studies programs, and in several cases funded generously under the Women's Educational Equity Act, projects were begun under the rubric of "mainstreaming" or "integrating" women into the curriculum.

Perhaps this is the place to pause for a few paragraphs on terminology. A women's studies course that I teach, for example, on women writers includes material on patriarchy, on socialization, on the social, medical and legal history of women, as well as the literary tradition of which they are a part. The course is literary, yet interdisciplinary, more interdisciplinary than the course I used to teach called Twentieth Century American Fiction that consisted entirely of male writers and focused entirely on the texts. What does it mean to "mainstream" or to "integrate" women into the curriculum? Leaving to one side the unsatisfactory psychology of the idea of women as necessarily out of the mainstream, the term has been used to signify a process: that women's studies courses, are *ipso facto,* ghetto courses; that a course on women in a department, thus, is "mainstreaming." That is one use of the term, and, if you understand that most women's studies courses are, in fact, *in* departments, this idea adds little to what we already have in progress. In fact, it reminds me of the dean I interviewed during my year of work on *Seven Years Later* who felt that women's studies at his institution had completed its job and should, in fact, be congratulated and dismantled. Women's studies at this dean's institution had developed fifteen different courses in some twelve departments. The rest of the curriculum had not been altered one jot, but this large urban university now offered its students fifteen different courses on women. The revolution had arrived; indeed, was over. Could I tell him that, in my view, the work had not yet begun—that these courses were, in one sense, preliminary to the real job?

"Integrating" women into the curriculum, or "integrating women's studies" has still a different meaning, or series of meanings. It is coming to signify, at its worst, what Charlotte Bunch has called the "add women and stir" method of curricular revision. In practice, it may mean a single lecture in a course of forty lectures; or the ubiquitous week on suffrage in the American history course; or the addition of a woman writer or two to the traditional literature course.

All of this—"mainstreaming" or "integrating," adding tokens even—may be better than nothing (at least one can argue that case); but it is not what I mean when I describe the task ahead as "transformational." I am talking about "changing the form of"—that is what transformation means—"changing the form of" the teaching of the curriculum so as to include all the human race, and not just a small segment of it. I am assuming, and there is much now on which to base that assumption, that research on women is changing the shape of the disciplines, and that therefore the shape of courses based on such research will similarly be transformed. If we are serious about including the literature that women have written in courses *with* the literature that men have written, we will have to think anew about the bases on which we organize these courses; we may revise the genres we emphasize, as well as the significant themes, not to mention the historical backgrounds and biographical information we need to offer to students. The study of literature, *qua* literature, may be very different twenty years from now. Similarly, art history, if one begins to include the art produced by women, and of course history itself will, of necessity, have to be organized rather differently if it is to include both sexes: even basic matters—dividing courses into what are called historical periods—will probably be different, as will the chief themes, the strategic data bases, and so forth.

One more word about "mainstreaming," "integrating," and "transforming." The first two—mainstreaming and integrating—represent reforms that all faculty can begin on; like women's studies in its initial stages, mainstreaming projects and projects that call for the integration of women into the curriculum can be included, perhaps, in a single summer institute with a few months of study. The more depth here, of course, the more time to read, the more adequate the provision for some other means of learning, the better. Whether one organizes seminars, or a lecture series for faculty just beginning to study about women; or whether one devises a coherent process of team-teaching, faculty need more organized support for these efforts today than they needed a dozen years ago, when the field was new and when a handful of intrepid persons, who saw each other during national professional association meetings, developed the scholarly base on which much of their own teaching about women moved forward. But now the scholarship accumulated through the past decade is itself formidable, in some sense a barrier as well as an aide, for those who wish to begin to add women to the curriculum in some form. It is simply hard for many faculty to know where to begin—at least without a guide.

On the other hand, it is clear enough that the place to begin is to read and then to teach *about women*. It is, in my view, impossible to move directly from the male-centered curriculum to what I have described as "transformation" of that curriculum into a changed and coeducational one—without passing through some form of women's studies. One might begin with the "unit" on women, or even the single lecture; one might get on to a week or two, or a month, but one will have to teach a whole course on women, and will have to understand the interdisciplinary base generally before one can begin to work at that transformed curriculum.

In short, there is no way around women's studies, if by that term we mean a deep and rich immersion in the scholarship on women. I am not being, in the manner of academics, territorial about my claims. There is no need to be—the goal is quite the opposite. But without a clear view of the dimensions of the task, we may never get to it. How do we, in the 1980s, face this problem in ways that are both realistic and productive, not discouraging, but not falsely optimistic?

I will try to list the resources and the barriers we have as we try to move forward—the barriers first, so that I can end, at least, on an optimistic note, and I should add at once that I do feel optimistic. I know that, despite retrenchment, the reactionary backlash, despite the state of academe in the country and the world, there is still a great deal of energy for this work. I believe strongly in the relationship of this work to the daily fabric of lives of millions of women and men around the globe. I believe that this educational work will make a difference to people for a century to come.

First, that the body of knowledge now is formidable may be seen as a barrier. A second is what Wheaton College President Alice Emerson called recently the "devaluation" of women by women and men alike, the trivialization of the work and lives of women, the assumption that women's history is less important than men's history. This leads directly to what two colleagues described to me as the greatest barrier on their urban campus—the "indifference" of the mainly male tenured faculty. Jessie Bernard combines these barriers in an interesting formulation and links them to still another: the rewards in academe are not, thus far at least, for scholarship on women. As she points out in *Prism of Sex,* men find female scholarship dealing with women boring, dull, unimportant. It is not about them and hence not interesting. If it is critical of them, they find it painful. In any event, they look to one another for professional recognition, and mastery of the products of female scholarship will not win that recognition for them.

At least one other internal barrier should be mentioned—the possible resistance of vocationally bound students who may unthinkingly judge that learning about women will not get them a job. (Parenthetically, I should note that women's studies programs often claim to be equipping students for the real world of work, and many do make good on their claims.)

External barriers these days are deepening. There is the "Moralistic Minority," a force in some areas of the country and on some campuses. There is also the elimination of some federal programs that had just begun to serve this area of curriculum reform, and the cutting of others. There is also the new strain on the private foundations who have, in fact, led the way in this area, and who may not be able to do all that they would wish.

But what of the resources? First of all, on every campus, we have some core of persons with whom to begin working. We have our organizing committee; we need only to recognize them and call them by that name. Where there is no women's studies program, there are at least a handful of courses, the faculty of which might be a core, perhaps along with some faculty development folk. These people need to devise an appropriate strategy on campus for the year ahead and for the decade. Such work needs both time and space, and the vision of change as an ongoing process.

In addition to the body of knowledge, which I am, of course, listing here as a very real resource, we also have a coherent conceptual frame. The frame has two parts: What is a feminist perspective? Do we need it to teach about women? Is this feminist perspective political?

A woman in Montreal asked me, "How can you teach faculty—male or female—to teach about women, if they are not sensitive to women's perspective, to feminism? How can you teach them to be sensitive?" I had been lecturing about how I came to feminism and women's studies, and for me the two terms are interchangeable. The process involved experience, sharing that experience with others, and then making sense of it through reading, thinking, analysis, often with the tools of social science, history, literature, philosophy. In other words, it was a complex process, and, of course, I had the advantage of a life as a woman. I even had the advantage of my previous lack of consciousness. And it is that lack of consciousness that can be viewed both as barrier and as an aide, at least if one can pierce it.

Coming to a feminist consciousness meant, for me, coming to the painful understanding that the world was divided into male and female, and that those categories, like those of race, were not to be changed or exchanged. Unlike students who might become teachers, or children who often become parents, males and females do not in a sexist society change places any more than blacks and whites. Can men come to this understanding? Of course. Though they may not be able to replicate female experience, men can understand and study its existence. Provided they are alert to the differences between their experiences and those of women, men can develop a feminist perspective. And perhaps I should not assume, but should mention, that being alert to women's experience, listening for it, also includes valuing it for its own sake. This is perhaps the most difficult element. As Dorothy Smith, a Canadian sociologist has said, "It has not been easy for women (any more than for men) to take what women have to say as authoritative nor is it easy to find our own voice convincing. It is hard for us to listen to ourselves." And so it is not surprising that it is harder for men to learn to listen to women. But if we are to succeed at this task, we need both the patience for it and the belief that it is possible.

As complex is the associated question: is a feminist perspective, "political"? Is research about women politically biased research rather than objective truth? Again, it is easier today to answer this question, not only because some esteemed male scholars have been writing about the ways in which a variety of perspectives help to shape the information we call "knowledge." It is, indeed, impossible to avoid a perspective from whence we teach or organize our scholarly projects. For me, it is more dangerous either to ignore or to support openly the patriarchal assumptions that govern our society than to challenge them openly through the feminist lens, and to ask that questions be reopened, that female experience be viewed alongside male.

In the broadest context of that word, teaching is a political act: some person is choosing, for whatever reasons, to teach a set of values, ideas, assumptions, and pieces of information, and in so doing, to omit other values, ideas, assumptions, and pieces of information. If all those choices form a pattern excluding half the human race, that is a political act one can hardly help noticing. To omit women entirely makes one kind of political statement; to include women as a target for humor makes another. To include women with seriousness and vision, and with some attention to the perspective of women as a hitherto subordinate group is simply another kind of political act. Education is the kind of political act that controls destinies, gives some persons hope for a particular kind of future, and deprives others even of ordinary expectations for work and achievement.

In a university whose goal is that abstraction called truth, no political act ought ideally to be excluded, if it might shed light on the ultimate goal. And the study of half the human race—the political act we call women's studies—cannot be excluded without obvious consequences to the search for truth.

One last word: Though we may sit in a room in the middle of the United States, concerned about U.S. higher education, women's studies is a worldwide movement. And perhaps, if I try to conclude in that context, my final point will be clearer. For we are not only searching for truth when we design educational programs. We know that these programs send people out to the world they must live in, and guide them to think about themselves and others in human or inhuman ways. Everywhere in the world, education for women is a new frontier. In some European countries, very few women go to college at all. In Italy, women's studies courses are part of trade union activity for women who are learning that they have a right to read, and a right to the pleasures of a cultural heritage as well as to the eight-hour day. In most of the so-called developing countries, women are the majority of illiterates, and some in charge of their education are learning that access to education is not enough, if what women gain are, first, instruction in maintaining their subordinate status, and second, access only to the worst-paying jobs.

In developing countries, the need for accurate information on which to base decisions that affect millions of persons, half of whom are inevitably women, makes women's studies—meaning, at least, research on women—hardly a luxury. Thus, a pan-African women's research organization claims research on women as an essential activity for survival of the nation's economy and heritage, as well as the lives of women. In India, research on women at the beginning of the seventies turned up a singular demographic pattern: a declining percentage of women in the adult population, despite the higher rate of female births. This is a singular phenomenon worldwide, the changing of which—through education, among other means—might mean life rather than death to millions of women and female children over a single decade.

Thus, to conclude, the study of women in the curriculum and in research institutes is not only an academic question; it is not only a question of the right of women to a place in the curriculum that will allow them images of achievement and aspiration comparable to those the curriculum has generally afforded at least to white middle class males. It is also essential if the university is to continue to be able to stake its claim to truth; and because of the increasingly significant way in which knowledge is used in our shrinking world, it is also of ultimate importance to the present and future lives of women all over the world.

American Literature and
Women's Lives

(1983)

When the University of Wisconsin planned its centennial celebration of the teaching of American literature, I was invited to give the opening lecture, not on "literature," but on its "effect" on women's lives. Even in 1983, I was to be "token woman," a reminder that there was still much to be done in this century and the next. Thanks to advice from Gerda Lerner, I ignored the circumstances of the invitation and concentrated on the contribution made in the last decade to the rediscovery of women's voices in American literature. I wrote the lecture in April 1983, and rewrote it once for a public lecture at the University of Tennessee in May, and finally, in October, for this book. I am pleased to be able to conclude this volume with a literary essay that uses the history and sociology of the new scholarship on women.

IN ANY DISCUSSION ABOUT WOMEN and American literature three questions need to be raised. First, which women are we talking about? Second, which American literature? And third, how does one measure a relationship between literature and life?

The question, which women? raises the central issue for all of American life, past, present, and future: the nature of our polyglot society. Women of which color, of which social class, and which ethnic identity? In my student days, the melting pot was still a governing metaphor, and ethnicity was at best a joke, at worst a slur. Certainly, to wear one's ethnic origins as a badge was unknown. The ghetto protected me until I was twenty; outside its benevolence, I learned quickly that, from a WASP's perspective, Jews and "Coloreds"—this was 1950—were a single category of nonpersons. Even in Madison, Wisconsin, in the very early fifties, I was so rare a specimen that friendly but curious persons would tell me that they had never met a Jew before. What was it like, being Jewish? I was asked. And, in the company of one or two other Jews among the teaching assistants and the junior English department faculty, I gave potato pancake and blintze parties for the ethnically-curious.

But I never admitted to my working class origins, nor was I conscious of a Jewish literary heritage, either European or American. Indeed, I shunned American literature as such, preferring British literature in general. It never occurred to me to work on a dissertation topic close to my own background and experience, and when I moved my area of concentration from the eighteenth century and Jonathan Swift to the twentieth century, I first began to work on Rudyard Kipling and E. M. Forster and on Anglo-Indian literature: twice or thrice removed, you might say, from my own origins. In the disputes between the British and the Indians, in the racial conflicts portrayed by Kipling, and in the ethnic quarrels depicted by Forster, I suspect that I searched for something I could not even have enunciated: my own quarrels with a culture I could not feel at home in, that I could only continue to study, much as a foreigner learning a language she could never feel totally comfortable using.

And was I a woman? Yes, of course, and conventionally, for I never imagined being more than that teaching assistant. I had no fantasies about publishing and professorships. I expected my graduate-school husband to have the professorship and I the part-time job, between children. I loved teaching for its own sake. I did not think of myself as a "professional" woman in those days, but rather as an "exceptional" one who had worked hard enough to be admitted to the teaching assistants' society, but I was not confused about my loyalties. I left Wisconsin after taking my preliminary examinations only because my former husband had said he would divorce me had I stayed. I envisioned my woman's life as centered on husband and children first, not, certainly, on my life's work. I did not know I had a life's work beyond teaching, the traditional occupation of second-generation immigrant Jewish working-class women. In short, I had none of what we would now call "consciousness."

The second question—which American literature?—raises similar problems. Are we interested in what has been written by Americans? Or in what was published by Americans and saw its way into print? Or do we include as American literature only what has remained in print, kept there mainly through its incorporation into the classroom curriculum, especially the collegiate one? But even if we defined American literature as the literature of the classroom, we would have to note the usual caveats: that Herman Melville remained unknown until the twenties, as did Emily Dickinson; that some white women writers, particularly novelists, were important in the early part of this century, but by the forties, when American literature really became established as such, they had disappeared from texts, anthologies, and critical notice; that black male writers were not read in the classroom until the sixties, black women writers not until the seventies, and writers of other minority groups not until very recently, if at all.

If, on the other hand, American literature is to be defined as what has been written by Americans, we must look at women as the major writers of their time. Especially from the nineteenth century forward, women wrote far more than men, if we are willing to countenance as literature the writing of diaries and letters, of journals, memoirs, and autobiographies. The quantity continues to amaze those finding these buried materials, and they have not all been found. Not only did women maintain lifelong friendships through correspondence, for example; but they kept the long letters they wrote to each other, leaving them to their families as a gift that, perhaps like quilts, both created and recorded history in the manner of art. Several decades from now, we will have a different portrait of American history, chiefly because we will have sifted through these records of daily lives. As for literature, perhaps we will read these "fragmentary genres" with a fresh aesthetic apprehension, and will even study them formally as we now study novels, poems, and plays. As I will indicate, many are worthy of such study, and the aesthetic questions are not altogether obvious, nor have they been exhaustively catalogued.

Given the quantity of unpublished writing we are finding, it is not surprising that an enormous quantity of literature was published by women from the nineteenth century forward—in some genres—poetry, for example—more than was published by men. After all, relatively few occupations were open to women. If one believes that talent and genius are not gender-bound, and if one also understands the barriers that kept women from other satisfying work, even in the arts, one can see why so many chose a working life that demanded little more than a table, a pen, and some sheets of paper, and no formal training as such. But the autobiographies, the novels, poems, and plays published by women did not stay in print past their own time, did not become standards as classroom texts or as parts of anthologies, in the manner of books by Hawthorne, Emerson, or even Ernest Hemingway and F. Scott Fitzgerald. Despite the aesthetic merit of their work and others', even those women writers we can all now name disappeared. In my school years we read Henry James, not Edith Wharton, as we read D.H. Lawrence, not Virginia Woolf. And we read many male writers of lesser stature than Sara Orne Jewett, Willa Cather, Ellen Glasgow, and Zora Neale Hurston.

Hence, when we talk about *American literature,* we will need to define clearly what we are talking of. It may be the white male literary canon as codified in the forties, excluding all minority writers and all white women but Emily Dickinson. It may be that plus Richard Wright and Ralph Ellison beginning in the sixties, and perhaps Sylvia Plath and Kate Chopin in the seventies. My emphasis will fall on the literature written by women and published or not in their own time, but not yet acknowledged beyond then as important enough to be a continuing source of pleasure or information.

And that statement allows me to approach the third of my questions: what is the relationship between literature and life? One student at Goucher in the sixties answered the question most succinctly: "I read," she said, "in order to figure out what to do with my life." She read also, she said, for pleasure. It is the classical formula: literature both instructs and entertains. It teaches pleasingly. The mixture is important. If there is pain, we want to feel it move us, at least to reflect on its source. "I read," the student said, "to figure out what to do with my life." If she read the American literary canon, the traditional white male one, she would be hard-pressed to come up with a program for living as a woman; even if she extended her scope to the traditional British canon, and added a few European novels, she would still come to the conclusion supplied by the endings of most of these: women in this fictional world either marry or die, and sometimes, they manage to do both, almost at once. The *bildungsroman* available in the traditional canon are, with few exceptions, about male persons who, in the end, can anticipate "great expectations," or, can put off being "sons and lovers" and walk toward the bright city, confident of finding artistic success and personal happiness in its arms. But the exception, *The Mill on the Floss,* for example, ends tragically for the heroine, as does even the newly-admitted *The Awakening.* What are young women—or men—to make of the pattern of novels that predict life for men—along with success as artists or businessmen—and death for women, however bright or talented, perhaps especially bright and talented. I thought I had found the one exception and returned *Sister Carrie* to my classroom canon, but of course she is punished by Theodore Dreiser as Lawrence does not punish Paul Morel: although successful, Carrie is to be a lonely woman. The price a working woman has to pay for success is personal unhappiness.

What *is* the relationship between literature and life? Is Dreiser reflecting reality? What is reality? And does it matter unless we hypothesize that this literature being written and published and read affects the readers' views of themselves and others? And can we ever know the answer to that last question, even if we cannot answer the others? In general this is an area still largely unexplored, and difficult to explore, for our conceptions of reality have a great deal to do with our own positions as persons in history at a particular time, our own social class and gender, our own racial and ethnic identities, and what we have experienced and read. And so I am hedging on this question.

But I will also venture three large hypotheses on the relationship between literature and reality, and then explore them. My basic assumption is, of course, that literature does have some effect on those who read it, especially if they read a great deal of it, as I did, by the way. Thus, one has a way of explaining how it is that all hypotheses may work equally well, since not all have been readers, and in this television society few still read as those in my generation did.

Hypothesis one: that the vast bulk of published and unpublished American literature by women in the nineteenth century nourished, and sustained the movement for women's rights especially through the period following the close of the Civil War. That fifty-year period, roughly from 1870 to 1920, represents not only the final phase of the suffrage movement; but also the period that opened up collegiate education for women in separate colleges modeled on the elite men's colleges founded two hundred and fifty years earlier. That same period also opened up coeducation to women, at such institutions as Cornell, Stanford, and the University of Chicago. In both kinds of collegiate institutions, the goal was similar. As M. Carey Thomas, distinguished president of Bryn Mawr, put it succinctly, women had a right to the "men's curriculum." This "men's curriculum" in American literature and American history was, as you might expect, entirely male-centered, since it had been designed understandably for a male student body. And quite understandably too, it was not designed to support or even to provide information about the claims of women to equality of opportunity in American society. That is not the case even today. Those who insist on the importance of women's history and literature by and about women, for both women and men, are still doing just that: insisting, and accepting what space they can manage to acquire in which to continue the insisting. But despite the fact that there are over four hundred and fifty women's studies programs, forty centers for research on women, more than fifty women's studies curriculum projects aiming to transform the "mainstream" curriculum, and more than thirty thousand separate women's studies courses, probably three thousand of them in literature, the general literary curriculum of most classrooms is no different from what it was thirty years ago, when I was still a student.

So here is my *second hypothesis:* that the white male literary canon sustains and encourages no women; rather, it confirms the oppression of women through offering portraits of women's lives that are limited, stereotypic, and without hope even of change in the future. These portraits also, needless to say, bear little resemblance to historical reality. Indeed, such portraits may be very confusing for those who think they are gaining a sense of historical reality. I assume that the best literature is imaginatively faithful to the complexity of history, and that by history I mean the faithful representation of the complexities of life. Among those traditional complexities of time and circumstance, a fresh layer of cultural life has only recently become visible through the reading of this lost or buried, published or unpublished literature by American women writers: the world as seen through their eyes. The "female subculture," a phrase ten years ago that feminist historians argued about and other historians ignored, is now an undeniable historical and literary fact. Not only did women live and work in worlds separated from their men folks, but they were conscious of that fact—as the men were not. Like other groups of oppressed peoples, women—whatever their class or color—had to know enough about men's lives in order to continue to live peaceably with them. Within the traditional politics and psychology of subjection, superiors need not know much about the culture of those they control; what they want is obedience and comfort. But those in thrall may—indeed, they probably must—create a way of surviving, especially if they are responsible for the comfort of their menfolks and their children. And if at the same time, these women see as their responsibility the freeing of all women from the yoke of subjection, then the cultural configuration becomes more complex still: it is not only survival, it is freedom. And the process of change as a political strategy becomes not a private process only, but a communal one.

Which brings me to my *third* and final *hypothesis:* today, and I am considering the last fifteen years as part of that word today, the recovery of this lost literature and history of and by women is also having a remarkable effect on women's lives. Not only do we understand where, for example, this "men's curriculum" came from, and why it is damaging especially to women; but we also see that it is more than damaging: it is ahistorical or nonhistorical. If we include the accuracy of psychological portraiture as part of literature's claim to excellence, much of the men's curriculum as literature is also shallow and stereotypic, untrue to what we now understand about the lives of women. But that is the negative part of the hypothesis. The positive part is more important: for women, reading the buried literature of the past—written by women—is encouraging, sustaining, nourishing, inspiring, energizing, perhaps even more to us today who have been starved for so long. Or so it seemed to me when I began to read these old new texts.

I do not speak for myself only when I say that reading this buried literature has changed my life, and my life's purpose.

As I turn to this literature, and to a few other examples as well, I will offer still another question: what do we *know* of women's lives? If we are women of my generation, for example, of my class and ethnicity, we never studied even our own lives: our whole *informal* education focused on how to live with a man, not how to live with ourselves, and certainly not on how to live with another woman. Our formal education supported the informal: the proper subject of study was Man and there was no generic understanding in Pope's use of the term, or in the literary classroom. Women were not regarded as worthy of study either in the present, or in the past. Not surprisingly, the ignorance about women in history and as history is particularly massive.

I want to consider the ignorance about birth control and sexuality before moving on to marriage, work, and the psychology of women's resistance to oppression. First, then, two anecdotes from the teaching of *Sister Carrie* and *The Awakening* in a single course called "Life or Death in American Fiction." I was teaching very bright students at Oberlin who were interested in reading books; most but not all of the students were women. No one asked why Carrie never became pregnant, however, because, although they had all had several courses in American history in high school and at Oberlin, birth control was certainly not part of American history. When pressed to consider the question, they read the work ahistorically. They were not interested in Dreiser's avoidance of the issue of pregnancy. When they read *The Awakening,* the reaction was different. Although I had been teaching that novel for a decade, I had never been satisfied with the analysis commonly offered to explain Edna's suicide at the conclusion of the novel. You remember, perhaps, that she removes all her clothes and walks into the Gulf to swim out until she drowns. This time I had a new theory, developed from reading outside the traditional curriculum. Edna was not cutting off her life because she could not bear the *consciousness* of her sexuality; in a world without birth control, she could not bear the *consequences* of sexuality—at least not without paying the female cost, childbirth.

I will never forget the outrage of one student, one of those especially well trained by the Oberlin English department, and a senior: "Do you mean to tell me" she fairly shrieked, "that this novel's magnificent ending depends on the absence of The Pill?" Her final tone was withering—"The Pill"—and disbelieving. She was not accustomed to having the real world of women's lives present in the classroom, on the table and with some historical perspective. And of course her privileged sexual life *with* the Pill could not imagine a world in which it was unknown and substitutes were undependable. In the novel, set in 1899, Edna spends an exhausting evening watching her friend give birth; babies and birthing are as strong a thematic presence in the novel as sexuality and the warm Gulf-fed ocean. She returns from this experience to find her lover has abandoned her again, and she thinks about her own abandoned children present and future and decides to go to the sea. Several students stayed after class to express fears that they could not read these new or old books well until they understood what life was like for women at the turn of the century. How were they to judge a woman's character, or even to make sense of the author's decision to have her live or die, without understanding what choices were open to her then? They were taking the first step to becoming able as readers and critics.

What I should have given my students to read along with those two novels was another work of literature in the form of a correspondence, only I was too much the slave of genre five years ago to have been bold enough for such an act.

But this book, *The Maimie Papers,* offers another glimpse into women's sexuality, their limited choices early in the twentieth century, and the consequences of such choices. This is not a novel, not an autobiography as such, not even a diary or journal, although as a volume, it has the effect of all three, as well as the immediacy and intimacy of correspondence written to one person. These were private letters, written by a young—she is 25 at the start, 38 at the close—second-generation Jewish ex-prostitute, alone, destitute, and newly reclaimed from syphilis that had resulted in the loss of an eye, from addiction that had followed the use of morphine in that operation, and from an attempted suicide that had followed the morphine addiction. Maimie wrote these letters to Fanny Quincy Howe, who not only saved them, but left them in her will to Helen Howe, the daughter she often writes of to Maimie; and Helen Howe gave them to the Schlesinger Library; later The Feminist Press and the Schlesinger Library published these letters.

The author of these long letters—many of them over five thousand words long—used writing for the same purposes many professional writers do. First, as therapy: we know how many writers (Edith Wharton among them) used writing, as Maimie did, to save their lives. Second, the letters are vehicles through which she learns how to turn her daily life into interesting stories. It is as though she were having a correspondence course in writing stories. And the success is astonishing. These letters have a *literary quality* one does not often find in self-conscious "art." The narrative thread is sustained effectively through two means. Maimie does not, in some cases, especially early in the correspondence, know what is going to happen daily, as she tries to reconstruct a life, without money, friend, or skills, in 1910 at age 25, in Philadelphia, where her hostile family resides. She does not know what will happen until she has lived through the next day and written the next letter. In this part of the correspondence, she is as breathless as the reader. Alternatively, and especially as she gets more sophisticated both about narrative style and about how to manage her increasingly complex and productive life, she does not write daily: she is forced by circumstance to write less frequently, and then she tells what has happened in a manner that preserves suspense by altering chronology, even as a writer of fiction would.

A quotation cannot offer a sense of this narrative style, but it can provide two other qualities: the sound of the narrative voice, and the sense of Maimie's stance with regard to the world she does battle in, her "persona," to use the literary term, her self, her identity.

This extract is from the middle of the correspondence and was written on November 27, 1913. Maimie uses a conventional literary device in a sophisticated manner: she tells Mrs. Howe the story of her early fall—at age thirteen—and her subsequent imprisonment. The villains in this interpolated story are Maimie's mother and an uncle, her mother's brother. In 1913, Mamie was twenty-eight years old.

I do not recall whether I wrote you that I had, among my many experiences, spent some time in the Phila. prison. Perhaps I told you, but I know I've told no one else but Mr. Welsh. And of course my immediate family know it—for it was they who were the cause of my being sent there. I don't think I did tell you; and since I feel in the mood tonight, I will tell you what I remember of it. It was such a terrible experience, and I was only past thirteen years old! It was the regular prison, and not the place of detention that they use now to send juvenile offenders to. I think of it but seldom. Tonight I thought of it due to re-reading *The Ballad of Reading Gaol* and talking about prisons to Miss Brown.

I had left school directly after my father's death, and was put to work in the house, doing the sort of work I despised, because I had never been taught how—and, too, because I loved school and books and the things that school meant. I was thirteen in July, and in September—my second term at the Phila. high school—I was not permitted to go back to school. Prior to my father's death, we had a general servant in the house, and a laundress and scrubwoman who came, each two days in the week. After his death, I was given it all to do but the laundress's work—and I did it very poorly, and always only after receiving severe whippings. In October, or perhaps November, I told a young girl who was librarian in a city library close to my home, of the reason that I did not come for books any more—which was, that my mother wouldn't permit me to read them, and a book for which the librarian wanted to collect 80 cents had been thrown into the fire when I had been found reading it. Of course, I had no 80 cents to pay her, and I was very much ashamed of it. I think this was my original reason for getting work in a neighborhood store, to work at night for a small weekly sum, as a "saleslady." After this—and after a violent scene with my mother, who told me if I didn't like my life at home, that I should get out—I went to the city, and there got a regular job in a department store, at $5.00 a week, though I was only past thirteen years old. I was a "saleslady"—and this store, to this day, is quite the place for men to come during the afternoon hours to make "dates" for the eve. I found I could stay away from dinner, and go along with some boys, and come home and tell some sort of story—and that it was accepted, due to the $5.00 I was bringing home! Once, there was some kind of a fuss again—and when I threatened to leave home, my mother said she hoped it was soon.

Of course, the inevitable thing happened. Some young chap took me to his room; and I stayed three or four days before I put in an appearance in the neighborhood of my home. As I neared our house, a man spoke to me by name, and told me he was a "special officer" and that he had a warrant for my arrest. He took me to the Central Station, which is in the City Hall—the large building which is in the center of the city of Phila. Of course I was terribly frightened—but imagine my horror when I was placed in a cell! It was a horribly filthy, vile-smelling hole. I cried and begged they should send for my mother—and though they did, after awhile, she refused to come. It was nighttime, and there was no light; and I could hear the rats, which I feared more than death. I was terrified, and pleaded to be taken out of there. It was only after I permitted one of the men, who seemed to be in charge at the time, to take all sorts of liberties with me, that I was permitted to come out of the cell; and I sat up for the rest of the night in the room where he, too, sat all night. The man was perhaps fifty, or even older.

In the morning, there was a hearing. My mother was present; and I recall my uncle was with her—and he was acting with her to persuade the "Commonwealth" that I should be sent to some house of refuge as being incorrigible. This uncle is the same one who did me the first wrong, when I was a tiny girl, and any number of times since then. It seemed that in order to prove me immoral, so that I should become a public charge (without excuse to my mother), it would have to be proven that I had committed a crime, and the man produced. A further hearing was demanded for this—as, in my terror, I had told the name and address of the chap, and of course they were going to arrest him. I was led away to the same cell, pleading to my mother, in shrieks, to take me home. It was morning, and not so bad as at night; but as I had nothing to read, and the terrible fear of spending another night there seemed imminent, the hours seemed years. There was only a bench and an exposed toilet in the cell, and it was, as I thought, terrible.

At noon, there were footsteps and the jangling of keys, and the cell was opened. I thought for sure my mother had relented, and I was so grateful. I put on my hat and coat, and came out to the large room—and though I did not see anyone I knew, I was laboring under the delusion that I was being taken home. I saw some men in line, and I was told to get behind the last one. Still, I had no suspicion of what was coming. The line moved, as did I. And oh! what a lot they were! There were perhaps eight men (three Negroes), and they were the dregs and scum of the earth. I looked on them with alarm, and was dismayed that I had to walk with them, though I did not even guess at my destination. We filed down the stairs, and the line in front got outside; and as I was last, I saw them filing into a prison van—the kind called "Black Maria." They are usually painted quite dark, and resemble a closed box with air or peep-holes on top. It was just at noon; and there were thousands going thru the courtyard, enroute to their lunches. Quite a crowd had gathered to watch the prisoners; and as I saw that, I became so mortified that I could not move—though, due to the imprecations of the guard behind me, I really wanted to. Of course, little ceremony was wasted on me. I was fairly dragged to the van, and thrown in. When I recovered my senses, I found the wagon was moving. The men were each in a compartment. Though there was no door between, there were sheets of iron that made semi-walls, permitting only one person between each wall. Yet they all seemed to disregard this, and sat out on their seats, talking and laughing. The ride lasted perhaps an hour. Time can never efface my impressions thru that ride. Their humor was shocking—such obscenity and scurrility! One of them told me to cheer up, and said he would look out for me after he got out—for he would only get thirty days, whereas no doubt I'd be sent away for a number of years, until I was of age. I then knew for sure I was going to prison—and oh! how I feared it! The ride was probably the worst of the whole harrowing experience.

In the prison, which was the Moyamensing Prison, I was led away by a woman to a room where a man sat before a large book—no doubt to enter the names, etc., of the prisoners. It was to this same prison that my father had given a library of two-hundred books, printed in the Yiddish language, for the benefit of the few Jewish prisoners who were kept there and who could not read English. I recalled, as I stood there, hearing my father speak of the place, and the pity of sending Hebrews there—who generally committed an offense only because they were not familiar with the laws. I was overcome with the thought of what my father would think of my being there; and I don't remember what happened, exactly, only that later, I found myself in a little bed, in what seemed to be another cell. As there was a woman sitting beside me, I did not seem to mind it so much, for I only cried quietly. Presently, the man who had sat by the books came in with a notebook in hand, and asked me many questions, which I recall I answered freely. I know now, that he knew from my name—which was not a common one—that it was my father who had given books and money to help Jewish lawbreakers, and that he communicated with my uncle; but no step was taken by him to have me released from there. I recall hearing him and the woman who sat by me, comment on the fact that I was sent there; and they both didn't seem to understand it. After the man left, the woman brought me some very coarse, rough-looking clothes and took away my own, though I cried dreadfully to not have to put them on. Then they took me to another room, and before I knew what they were going to do, they had combed my hair out—it was cut off to the ears. I was taken back to the cell, which was similar to the one I had occupied in the Central Station, only larger, and had a pallet of straw on a black iron frame bed. Besides, there was a chair and a lamp and a stone floor, and one tiny window, with bars, that faced a courtyard; and on the other side—perhaps three or four yards away—was another wall with the same window, at which I could see faces that were pressed against the bars and fingers clutching them. The woman left me after awhile, and brought me a Bible—for which I was grateful enough. She said the books were all taken that day, but tomorrow she might get me a real book. I entreated her to remain with me—for she was indeed kind, and had much commiseration for me. She assured me she would return as soon as she could. When she left, I went to the window. And immediately I was seen, the persons began to call to me, asking what I was put there for.

Maimie entered Magdalen Home for wayward girls in 1898 and was released a year later; two years after writing the entry in 1913 describing the experience of her early youth, Maimie planned to reclaim girls on the street in Montreal who also suffered from syphilis, as well as other ills, including tuberculosis.

Here is one other excerpt, this one dated August 24, 1912, which describes the conditions of employment for a clerical worker. Maimie earned $12.00 a week, not only because of her skills at stenography and typing, but also because of her ability to write. Nevertheless, her skills were suspect, since even with a patch over one eye, she was still an attractive woman.

. . . When I got ready to go, he asked to look at what I had been writing while I was talking—a matter of ten minutes—and he seemed to marvel because I made no errors, and all the punctuation complete. He seemed to like the writing, which was like this:

But all through the conversation, not one word was said as to my ability as a letter-writer, or was any reference to anything made that might give a hint as to my writing the letters our manager is supposed to write. On our return to White Plains, not a word did he say to me—though he also said nothing to anyone.

The next day, after two hours work in our own office, we went again to New York. On the train, I was told that if I valued my job, I'd reject the "private office" this time. And I answered that, as now I felt more acquainted, I didn't think I'd feel at all uncomfortable with the rest. When we came in, I took the place originally assigned to me, and I worked until luncheon time. . . . About two o'clock I saw the N.Y. man coming my way; and pretty soon I heard him say, "I want you to do a few letters for me." As I was his employee for the day, I could not but obey. As I got up, collecting some loose sheets, something made me look up, and I saw our man glaring at me; and I grew cold, for I saw I was going to get into trouble. I walked directly over to him and told him. And he shrugged his shoulders as though it was one to him, no matter what I did. In the private office, I took three letters for reply, and one to quote some prices to a prospective customer. Of course, the three letters were form letters—but the other one had to be personal; and I said, "Hadn't you better dictate this, as I am not acquainted with this exact style of work." He said, "Quit stalling, now. I knew all the time that 'Beef' "—as he calls our man—"was working someone to death out there—and when I saw the collapse, I knew it was you." I was not able to speak, for I knew he knew; and to lie would be silly. And yet I saw trouble ahead. I went to work there—and frankly, I wrote the letter in question in my best style. Will you be sure to tell me this: Should I have pretended, and written it poorly? I don't feel I should, but perhaps I don't see it in the proper light. On the return, not a word was spoken to me; and I slept little that night. Two days more elapsed before any reference to it was made; and during that time conditions were about the same in the office, only that I was not spoken to except directly in reference to my work.

Then today came the climax. I worked hard—harder than usual, having had a new idea as to filing references for new business, and was trying it out. Just as we were finishing up the day's work, the last mail came; and as usual, I opened the letters, expecting to answer any that required immediate answer. Of the eleven letters and three postals, two needed answering, as I thought; and it is always left to my judgment. I only answered two. Everyone but the manager had gone when I got up to go. He asked me if I had answered necessary letters, and I said yes. He said, "Wait until I look them over." As he did, I saw him making two piles, and I knew he was going to say I had to answer one of them. I felt myself getting hot and then cold—because it was not just. I was very tired and hungry, and it was 6:30. And I felt I was going to cry, so I walked to the door. And he sprang up, and said, "You'll finish this work or you needn't come back." Surely I could not afford to lose my position—but oh you can't understand how terrible it is to feel you just have to take such treatment. He grabbed me by the arm and jerked me back. And I just couldn't control myself—and I picked up a heavy letter file and went after him. I believe I could have killed him, I became so furious and strong. Of course, it was all over in a minute. He took hold of me, and instantaneously I lost my temper and dropped the file. But I could see he was pretty well scared. I then cried—and sat on a chair, while he went over to the washbasin, preparing to go. When I began to think calmly, I saw what I had done was going to cost me my position. And the terror of being in the position I was in last spring frightened me so. I began to explain to him how tired I was, and how the extra work was wearing on my nerves. And as I talked, he said nothing. Finally I became quiet. And then he started in to say how I had tried to impress the New York office and finally "worked my way into the manager's attention"—and then he said he supposed I'd kept a few "dates" with him, and that I only made an ass of myself, etc., etc. He heaped abuse on me; and when I could stand it no longer, I told him that he had no right to accuse me of being friendly with the N.Y. manager, as I gave him no reason to believe I was the sort. And he laughed insinuatingly and said he could have made a "hit" with me too, had he cared to, but he didn't go in for "one-eyed women"—And I didn't wait to hear any more, but came home.

I have written it all out as I know it, and if I seem to spare myself, it is not because I am lying. I worked hard and faithfully, and I don't know what to do. I am so tired mentally as well as physically, and I am so hurt, that I don't feel I ever could possibly go back to that office again. Of course, it may appear that he would not let me work there further, but I know better. As long as I want to, I can work there—provided, of course, I can stand for his tricky, dastardly character. Probably when morning comes, I will see light, and act accordingly. I told no one in the house; and as I couldn't eat any supper, I have a frightful headache. I wish I could ask you right now what to do. You see, by the time you could possibly answer, I will have to go back to work, or make up my mind to quit there; and yet as I see winter approaching I get frightened. For under no conditions will I ever go to my brother's to live; and I have no other place.

I am going to close, and before I go back to bed I am going to ask God to show me what to do in the morning. I am all shaken up; and probably when I get calm, I will know what to do.

Why is a story like Maimie's not part of our literary heritage? What would it mean to include it, even now, to place it side by side with *The*

Scarlet Woman, with *Sister Carrie?* Would those works look different afterwards?

The Silent Partner by Elizabeth Stuart Phelps, a novel first published in 1871 also deserves inclusion in the literary curriculum. Like Maimie, Phelps understood that most women had to work in order to eat, and she understood also that most humans needed work. In a magazine piece that she wrote for *Harper's* in 1867, Phelps said, "Whether for self-support, or for the pure employment's sake, the search for work—for successful work, for congenial work—is at the bottom of half the feminine miseries of the world." In her autobiography, written nearly thirty years later, Phelps describes herself as "proud . . . that I have always been a working woman and always had to be." She did not in fact "have to be," if one considers who her father and mother were. For she was born into a privileged family and could have married an academic theologian, as her own mother did, and lived happily or unhappily ever after. But Phelp's mother died in childbirth when her first daughter was eight, and somehow, that little girl decided that she would not follow in her mother's exact footsteps. Her mother had published three books before her death, all bestselling sentimental religious novels. The younger Phelps discarded her own name, Mary, and took her mother's—Elizabeth—and apparently decided even then, as she wrote later, "It was impossible to be her daughter and not to write." Her first published piece appeared in *Harper's* when she was still in her teens. Her first novel, *The Gates Ajar,* written in her early twenties in an unheated room in which she wore her mother's fur cape across her shoulders, was published to immediate acclaim when she was twenty-four. (*The Gates Ajar* was quickly translated into fourteen languages, and of all books published in the nineteenth century, only *Uncle Tom's Cabin* sold more copies.)

In the forty-two years between the publication of *The Gates Ajar* in 1869 and her death in 1911, Phelps published fifty-six volumes of fiction, poetry, reminiscences, advice, theology, and drama, as well as some two hundred uncollected shorter pieces. Her life and her writing span almost the whole of the period now known as the "century of struggle." She was four years old when Elizabeth Cady Stanton and others met in a little church in Seneca Falls, New York, to ratify the Declaration of Sentiments that established the agenda for the nineteenth-century women's movement. That agenda, although she might not have described it as such, reflected the major concerns of Phelp's fiction: the right of women to equal educational opportunity, to satisfying and decent-paying work, and to political equality in the ballot box. She is one of the best examples of a writer who illuminates my hypothesis that the literature published by American women a hundred and more years ago sustained and encouraged their contemporaries engaged in the Women's Rights movement. And of course she is as powerful for us today.

Phelps writes about women who manage to see through and past the institution of marriage, and about women who understand their need for work. Not all her heroes say no to marriage: Avis, the painter, succumbs finally on page 200 and lives to regret her choice, although, at this novel's conclusion, more than 200 pages on, the husband is dead, and Avis, surrounded by two young children, has picked up her neglected paintbrush. At the end of another novel "Doctor Zay" agrees to marry the young man whose smashed bones she has restored, but only with the understanding that her work will continue.

The Silent Partner adds another dimension to our understanding of women's lives and our pleasure in fiction, for here women in search of work attempt to cross not only the forbidden boundaries of gender, but the still more rigid boundaries of social class. The novel is about two women from opposite ends of the social scale who, under ordinary conditions, could not have been friends. The novel is also about silences, between these women and between women and men, and about silences breaking into speech.

For many readers, the most important silence broken by the novel will be the silence between the two women, Perley, the factory owner, and Sip, the factory worker. Their encounters are unsentimentally portrayed, for they are not afraid to say what they think. In their first encounter on the issue of class differences, Sip points out that she usually "hates" Perley's "kind of folks," that indeed all working people do hate Perley's kind of folks, not "because they don't care, but because they don't *know;* or they don't care enough to *know.*" As the friendship between the two women grows, so does their strength to redirect their lives. Sip gains the confidence to become a public figure, an evangelist serving the mill workers. Through her life Christianity serves not social control, but social justice, the truth of social solidarity that will ultimately free people. Perley, who has learned that she needs to act on her sense of social responsibility, finds new purpose in the practical work of helping to organize a cooperative, self-help society among the female mill operatives.

For many students today, the most interesting facet of the novel is the refusal of both heroines to marry. Sip says no to a good man who loves her and whom she feels affection for, insisting that she will not bring into this world children for the factory to destroy. Perley refuses two men, one "bad" and one "good." To the good man, she says,

> The fact is that I have no time to think of love and marriage, Mr. Garrick. That is a business, a trade, by itself to women. I have too much else to do. As nearly as I can understand myself, that is the state of the case. I cannot spend time for it.

And a little later on in the conversation, she adds:

> I do not need you now. Women talk of loneliness. I am not lonely. They are
> sick and homeless. I am neither. They are miserable. I am happy. They
> grow old. They have nothing to do. If I had ten lives, I could fill them. . . .
> Besides, I believe that I have been a silent partner long enough. If I mar-
> ried you, sir, I should invest in life, and you would conduct it. I suspect
> that I have a preference for a business of my own.

Students today find this ringing affirmation of a woman's energy for work
inspirational enough to applaud. It is not, they explain, that they hear it as
a condemnation of marriage; rather, that marriage alone is not a woman's
goal.

For black women in this country, marriage has not been a single goal,
of course. And in the literature written by black women in this century, we
often hear that longing for fulfilling work and satisfying love. In a short
story by Paule Marshall called "Reena," published first in the early sixties, and to a large feminist audience again in Toni Cade's 1970 anthology,
The Black Woman, and now in a volume called *Reena and Other Stories,*
the focus is on satisfying work. Also, as in *The Silent Partner,* this piece of
fiction offers the intimacy of two women talking, their voices almost in-
distinguishable from each other. They are meeting at a wake for a spinster
aunt who spent her life cleaning houses and never slept in her own bed except on alternate Thursdays. They are on this bed, on the pink satin
spread, sharing the past 15 years of their lives—since they were last together—and recalling the years of their youth before that.

> I asked her after a long wait what she had done after graduating.
> "How do you mean, what I did. Looked for a job. Tell me, have you
> ever looked for work in this man's city?"
> "I know," I said, holding up my hand. "Don't tell me."
> We both looked at my raised hand which sought to waive the discus-
> sion, then at each other and suddenly we laughed, a laugh so loud and vio-
> lent with pain and outrage it brought tears.
> "Girl," Reena said, the tears silver against her blackness. "You could
> put me blindfolded right now at the Times Building on 42nd Street and I
> would be able to find my way to every newspaper office in town. But tell
> me, how come white folks is so hard?"
> "Just bo'n hard."
> We were laughing again and this time I nearly slid off the trunk and
> Reena fell back among the satin roses.
> "I didn't know there were so many ways of saying 'no' without ever
> once using the word," she said, the laughter lodged in her throat, but her
> eyes had gone hard. "Sometimes I'd find myself in the elevator, on my
> way out, and smiling all over myself because I thought I had gotten the
> job, before it would hit me that they had really said no, not yes. Some of
> those people in personnel had so perfected their smiles they looked almost
> genuine. The ones who used to get me, though, were those who tried to
> make the interview into an intimate chat between friends. They'd put you

in a comfortable chair, offer you a cigarette, and order coffee. How I hated that coffee. They didn't know it—or maybe they did—but it was like offering me hemlock. . . .

"You think Christ had it tough?" Her laughter rushed against the air which resisted it. "I was crucified five days a week and half-day on Saturday. I became almost paranoid. I began to think there might be something other than color wrong with me which everybody but me could see, some rare disease that had turned me into a monster.

"My parents suffered. And that bothered me most, because I felt I had failed them. My father didn't say anything but I knew because he avoided me more than usual. He was ashamed, I think, that he hadn't been able, as a man and as my father, to prevent this. My mother—well, you know her. In one breath she would try to comfort me by cursing them: 'But Gor blind them' "—and Reena's voice captured her mother's aggressive accent— "if you had come looking for a job mopping down their floors they would o' hire you, the brutes. But mark my words, their time goin' come, 'cause God don't love ugly and he ain't stuck on pretty . . . ' And in the next breath she would curse me, 'Journalism! Journalism! Whoever heard of colored people taking up journalism. You must feel you's white or something so. The people is right to chuck you out their office. . . . ' Poor thing, to make up for saying all that she would wash my white gloves every night and cook cereal for me in the morning as if I were a little girl again. Once she went out and bought me a suit she couldn't afford from Lord and Taylor's. I looked like a Smith girl in blackface in it. . . . So guess where I ended up?"

"As a social investigator for the Welfare Department. Where else?" We were helpless with laughter again.

"You too?"

"No," I said, "I taught, but that was just as bad."

Such reclaimed works of literature as *Maimie* and *The Silent Partner* and such newer works as "Reena" are still single images in a blurred and distorted literary world of women's lives. I want to make this point by describing as briefly as I can two works that I happen to have seen recently on the stage and in film by notable American male authors—*Our Town* by Thornton Wilder and *Sophie's Choice* by William Styron—that reminded me of all the work still to be done, if we are to have better literature even by male writers in the future, and if teachers are to make better choices of what they offer to their students. Although they seem, and in some ways are, nearly a century apart, their ideology is identical; their portraiture from the same patriarchal brain.

I recently attended a production of *Our Town* in which my goddaughter played one of the leading roles. This play is Wilder's effort to portray middle-class white America in New England after the turn of the century, and in a so-called timeless manner that tries to catch pre-urban, pre-industrial small town life. The two families portrayed include husbands who are, respectively, the editor of the town paper and the town physician, although the two men are otherwise interchangeable; and two wives who are also interchangeable, except that one dies before the end of the play. These women are shown preparing meals, calling their children to these meals, cleaning the kitchen, gardening, and singing in the church choir. Each family includes both a male and a female child, a pair of whom conveniently fall in love with each other and, in act 2, marry. The male child chooses marriage and farming, rather than college and then marriage and farming, on the principle that what he has at home—this lovely young girl—is good enough for him. And the female child, without such options, tells him she is willing to wait for him or to accept him at once. She dies in childbirth less than a decade later. The final act takes place in the graveyard, with some of the characters on stage in the place of their tombstones speaking to the audience in mournful tones. In one of those tones, one of the women says that life was really terrible—especially, I should add, for women. And finally, through the desultory conversation that follows, we are given to understand that it is better to be dead and apparently still interested in the changing weather and the comings and goings of the stars than alive and so busy cooking and cleaning and getting the children off to school on time that one is unobservant of the things that really matter, which are not the weather and the stars, but loving one another.

To prepare for her role as one of the mothers, my goddaughter spent weeks reading about the lives of women in new feminist histories and in the newly-recovered fiction by women of the period. She also chopped wood, practiced wearing a period corset and costume, cooked three meals a day for a family of four, and scrubbed an apartment. In the play, the two mothers perform some of these motherly tasks in mime. In the one intimate moment between them, Mrs. Gibbs, the mother played by my goddaughter, reveals her one dream, to use the $350 she can get for selling a piece of furniture on a trip to Paris with her hard-working physician husband. She is afraid that the hard work will kill him. Ironically, but hardly unexpectedly, she is the one dead before the play's end, and the $350, her daughter-in-law tells her when she joins her in the graveyard, has been spent on a feeding trough for farm animals.

The play seems to have been given to the women characters. They have the last word; it is to them life happens (or rather death), or life disappoints. We have a portrait of the stoic good mother, to the end unconscious even of her goodness, the strong person dead at an early age—no cause is indicated. And we have a portrait of the beautiful young wife and mother, dead in childbirth. Both are portrayed as without many, in some cases, any, choices. They live and they die, and even speak after death, without consciousness of themselves as women.

Like Wilder, Styron places the female character at the center; unlike Wilder, he seems to give her a choice, for that word appears in the title *Sophie's Choice*. But although there are two choices, they are both empty ones. First, choose whether your daughter or son is to die; second, choose whether you are to be consort to a tall and handsome schizophrenic American male or a shorter, younger, male writer who is also a voyeur with respect to the first consortial relationship. So first Sophie is depicted in the hands of the mad world of Hitler's holocaust, in which life has no value (even her own father is inhuman), and pain and sadism are the rule. Second, Sophie, having escaped with her own life, but with neither of her children, is depicted in the sane world of post–World War II United States. But this world is also peopled by men who control her life; she cannot escape to a world without them, apparently. She is in their grip: physically and psychologically as a way of compensating for having chosen her daughter's death, she must die also, but not before she takes the time to initiate her substitute son sexually. That younger male person, the voyeur, the writer, wants her to marry him and begin a new family of children. This is the only place in the work in which Styron authentically portrays the blindness of young men to women's—especially older women's—lives. But Sophie, trapped still, as mother, gives her body to her son, and then returns to accept her death at the hands of her schizophrenic lover, a Jew who at least some of the time regards her as the major enemy of the Jews, responsible for the deaths of others in order to save her own life.

In both cases, Wilder and Styron present the world women live in as one closed to their control, as a prison in which they have no options but to survive mindlessly or in mental private pain for as long as they can and then to die. And even in the living, there is no joy except in the serving of others, especially male persons without consciousness of women's needs or lives. More than that: there is terribly little consciousness about the possibility of anything else. There are no other visions for women in the heads of these women characters or the male writers who conceive them.

I do not think that these works are unique: they may be especially visible examples, not only because they are theatre and film, respectively, but because they are written by men who probably imagine they are portraying women sympathetically. And perhaps compared with the nonexistence of ordinary women in the work of Hawthorne, Melville, Emerson, Twain, and the kinds of women present in the work of Hemingway, Fitzgerald, or Faulkner, these by Wilder and Styron are relatively sympathetic portraits. But they are portraits of women imprisoned in the minds of these male writers, who do not know either the minds of women or the real world in which women have been living since life began. I mean that these men, however sympathetic, cannot imagine being a woman, not because that is a biological matter, but because they have not been able to imagine themselves out of their male, white skin privilege sufficiently to understand how it is to be a woman.

I do not want to leave you with these images. As I was walking around Washington, D.C., recently, an image I have not thought of in more than a decade floated into view. Remember "The Love Song of J.

Alfred Prufrock" and his view of himself as a "patient etherized upon a table"? Between the image and the poem for me have come more than a decade of feminism. And the lines that floated to the surface of my mind were these:

> If one, setting a pillow by her head, should say:
> That is not what I meant at all,
> That is not it, at all

And later, the lines appear again, amplified a bit.

> If one, setting a pillow or throwing off a shawl, and
>   turning toward the window, should say:
> That is not it, at all
> That is not what I meant, at all.

It's a marvelous poem, and a perfect insight—it turned the tables etherized or not on Prufrock, and it suggests that even T.S. Eliot had some sense that women might see things differently from men.

How differently women saw things in history, and how differently they still see we are only just coming to realize. It is still hard for men and for women both to accept the voices of other women as authentic or authoritative. I want to conclude with two voices from the past that we are only now able to hear, since some of what they wrote now appears in a volume edited by Ellen DuBois. The correspondence between Elizabeth Cady Stanton and Susan B. Anthony gives us courage and heart for the future. It contains a vision we all need to sustain us. Here is one small interchange between them, written in 1856. Susan complains about the "crime" that Elizabeth and Lucy Stone and Antoinette Brown are engaged in: "baby-making," leaving "poor brainless me to do battle alone." Elizabeth responds:

Seneca Falls, June 10, 1856

Dear Susan,

Your servant is not dead but liveth. Imagine me, day in and day out, watching, bathing, dressing, nursing, and promenading the precious contents of a little crib in the corner of the room. I pace up and down these two chambers of mine like a caged lioness, longing to bring to a close nursing and housekeeping cares. I have other work on hand too. . . . Is your speech to be exclusively on the point of educating the sexes together, or as to the best manner of educating women? I will do what I can to help you with your lecture. Let Lucy and Antoinette rest awhile in peace and quietness and think great thoughts for the future. It is not well to be in the excitement of public life all the time; do not keep stirring them up or mourning over their repose. You need rest too, Susan. Let the world alone awhile. We cannot bring about a moral revolution in a day or year. Now that I have two daughters, I feel fresh strength to work. It is not in vain that in myself I have experienced all the wearisome cares to which woman in her best estate is subject. Good night.

When Denise Levertov wrote the poem called "Stepping Westward," she undoubtedly did not think of the lives of Stanton and Anthony and of the paths reformers walk today. Her vision of women's lives, nevertheless, follows in that tradition. The image of "eating as we go," of consuming the energy in order to reproduce it, of accepting ourselves as eternal parts of the earth, active, feeling, thinking parts—is an appropriate one on which to conclude.

STEPPING WESTWARD

What is green in me
darkens, muscadine.

If woman is inconstant,
good, I am faithful to

ebb and flow, I fall
in season and now

is a time of ripening.
If her part

is to be true,
a north star,

good, I hold steady
in the black sky

and vanish by day,
yet burn there

in blue or above
quilts of cloud.

There is no savor
more sweet, more salt

than to be glad to be
what, woman,

and who, myself,
I am, a shadow

that grows longer as the sun
moves, drawn out

on a thread of wonder.
If I bear burdens

they begin to be remembered
as gifts, goods, a basket

of bread that hurts
my shoulders but closes me

in fragrance. I can
eat as I go.